# Student Study Guide

to accompany

# BASIC MICROBIOLOGY

Student Study Guide to accompany

Volk

# BASIC MICROBIOLOGY

Seventh Edition

R. Wilson Gorham
Northern Virginia Community College

HarperCollinsPublishers

Study Guide to accompany BASIC MICROBIOLOGY, Seventh Edition



**ISBN: 0-06-501012-4**
92 93 94 95 9 8 7 6 5 4 3 2 1

## CONTENTS


| | | |
|---|---|---|
| CHAPTER 1 | WHAT IS MICROBIOLOGY? | 1 |
| CHAPTER 2 | LABORATORY EQUIPMENT AND PROCEDURES | 10 |
| CHAPTER 3 | BACTERIAL MORPHOLOGY | 23 |
| CHAPTER 4 | PROPERTIES OF BIOLOGICAL MOLECULES | 33 |
| CHAPTER 5 | BACTERIAL NUTRITION | 42 |
| CHAPTER 6 | BACTERIAL METABOLISM | 51 |
| CHAPTER 7 | BACTERIAL GENETICS: GENE FUNCTION AND MUTATION | 61 |
| CHAPTER 8 | BACTERIAL GENETICS: THE NATURE AND TRANSFER OF GENETIC MATERIAL | 71 |
| CHAPTER 9 | METHODS FOR THE CONTROL OF MICROORGANISMS | 81 |
| CHAPTER 10 | SURGICAL AND MEDICAL ASEPSIS | 93 |
| CHAPTER 11 | ANTIMICROBIAL AGENTS IN THERAPY | 101 |
| CHAPTER 12 | CLASSIFICATION SCHEMES FOR COMMON PROCARYOTES | 114 |
| CHAPTER 13 | UNUSUAL PROCARYOTIC CELLS | 124 |
| CHAPTER 14 | VIRUSES | 133 |
| CHAPTER 15 | EUCARYOTIC MICROORGANISMS | 144 |
| CHAPTER 16 | INFECTION AND BACTERIAL INVASIVENESS | 155 |
| CHAPTER 17 | NONSPECIFIC HOST RESISTANCE | 164 |
| CHAPTER 18 | ANTIGENS AND ANTIBODIES | 173 |
| CHAPTER 19 | MEASUREMENT OF ANTIBODIES AND THEIR ROLE IN IMMUNITY AND HYPERSENSITIVITY | 183 |
| CHAPTER 20 | CELLULAR IMMUNITY | 194 |
| CHAPTER 21 | ANTISERA AND VACCINES | 202 |
| CHAPTER 22 | INTRODUCTION TO THE PATHOGENS | 211 |

| | | |
|---|---|---|
| CHAPTER 23 | THE NORMAL FLORA OF THE HUMAN BODY | 219 |
| CHAPTER 24 | BACTERIA AND FUNGI THAT ENTER THE BODY VIA THE RESPIRATORY ROUTE | 227 |
| CHAPTER 25 | VIRUSES THAT ENTER THE BODY VIA THE RESPIRATORY TRACT | 242 |
| CHAPTER 26 | PATHOGENS THAT ENTER THE BODY VIA THE DIGESTIVE TRACT | 252 |
| CHAPTER 27 | PATHOGENS THAT ENTER THE BODY VIA THE GENITOURINARY TRACT | 268 |
| CHAPTER 28 | PATHOGENS THAT ENTER THE BODY VIA THE SKIN OR BY ANIMAL BITES | 278 |
| CHAPTER 29 | PATHOGENS THAT ENTER THE BODY VIA ARTHROPOD BITES | 290 |
| CHAPTER 30 | MICROBIOLOGY OF WATER AND SEWAGE | 303 |
| CHAPTER 31 | MICROBIOLOGY OF FOOD AND MILK | 312 |
| CHAPTER 32 | AGRICULTURAL AND INDUSTRIAL MICROBIOLOGY | 321 |

# PREFACE

Microbiology, the course you are beginning now, has a "tough" reputation. It is true that there is an enormous amount of information to learn in the field. Much of it is complex material. There are difficult concepts to master as well as a whole new lexicon of terms. The good news is that microbiology is exciting! The field is on the cutting edge of new knowledge, new technologies, and revolutionary theories. What you learn in this course will be of benefit in any curriculum in which you are engaged. If you are a biology major, you will be learning about organisms given short shrift in zoology and botany courses. If you are in a pre-med or allied health curriculum, you will learn much about diseases, immunity, and microbial control. If you are in a liberal arts curriculum you will learn much that will make your own health care comprehensible and prepare you to make intelligent decisions about major issues that may arise in the next century.

The purpose of this study guide is not to replace your textbook or your lectures, but rather to assist you in organizing the information being covered. Each chapter in the study guide covers the same material, in the same order, as is covered in the corresponding chapter in the textbook. You should read the chapter in the text **before** you make use of this guide. Each chapter in this study guide begins with a chapter summary. The chapter summary is **NOT** complete enough to enable you to skip reading the chapter in the book! It does, however, try to present the high points of the chapter in a streamlined fashion. Where I have felt it appropriate, I have attempted to explain some concepts in slightly different ways from the text in order to heighten your comprehension.

Each chapter follows the summary with a set of "learning activities". A highlight of this section is the vocabulary list. I have attempted to include here all bold-faced terms from the text as well as other critical terms which experience teaches me are worth studying. If you have studied the chapter thoroughly, and have phenomenal comprehension, you should be able to define or cite the significance of the terms immediately. If you need to look some of them up in the chapter (they are presented in the order they will be encountered in the book) that's nothing to be ashamed of! To give you an idea of how thorough your definitions should be, I have included a completed list in the first two chapters.

Next in order in each chapter is a series of fill-in-the-blank questions which may or may not be accompanied by other learning activities (tables, names of important scientists, etc.). Answers to these questions, or filled-in tables, are found at the end of each chapter. If you feel the need to practice some essay-type questions, I suggest you utilize the "questions for review" at the end of each chapter in the textbook.

Last in order in each chapter is a mastery test. These typically consist of multiple choice, matching, and occasional true-false sections. Again, answers are provided at the end of the chapter.

How valuable do I think these various aids are? Well, I have been teaching biology for over twenty years, so I have a fair idea how instructors think and what they are likely to feel is important material in a textbook. I was also a student in biology for almost a decade, and learned on that side of the lectern many study tricks that served me well. I have tried, in these pages, to give you the benefit of my experiences. I hope you find microbiology as fascinating and, yes, as much fun to learn about as I do! Good luck!

I would at this point like to thank my brother, Ken Gorham, for his encouragement and advice, and my wife, Jo, for her patience.

R. Wilson Gorham
Professor of Biology
Northern Virginia Community College
(Annandale Campus)

# Student Study Guide

to accompany

# BASIC MICROBIOLOGY

# CHAPTER 1

## WHAT IS MICROBIOLOGY?

### CHAPTER SUMMARY

Microbiology is the study of tiny living things (micro- means small, -biology is the science of life). Generally, microorganisms (or microbes) are too small to see with the naked eye. Among the most important kinds are: bacteria (studied by **bacteriologists**), viruses (studied by **virologists**), yeasts and molds (studied by **mycologists**), and protozoa (studied by **protozoologists**).

Barely a century ago microorganisms were so poorly understood that many scientists believed they could arise from nonliving material by **spontaneous generation**! The work of Redi, Spallanzani, Pasteur and Tyndall eventually overcame this popular perception and established that microorganisms were derived from pre-existing individuals like all other living things.

In a little over a century we have progressed to an appreciation of the importance of microorganisms as agents of disease, as model systems for the study of basic biochemistry, molecular genetics, and recombinant DNA technology. Much disease can now be prevented by proper sewage disposal, water sanitation, immunizations, and through the use of antibiotics. Major new therapies may be in the offing through the practice of recombinant DNA technology, using microorganisms as biochemical factories.

One must appreciate that microorganisms are much more than threats. Most species are not even **parasitic** (living off of the tissues of a host), much less **pathogenic** (capable of causing an infection). Many are actually utilized in the food industry, aiding in the production of such items as yogurt, cheese, sauerkraut, wine and beer.

Nevertheless, major attention has always been focused upon microbes as the agents of disease, dating back at least to the work of Bassi who attributed a silkworm disease to infestation by fungi. **"Koch's Postulates"** (Robert Koch, 1843-1910) played a major role in the blossoming of medical microbiology by making it possible to establish a cause-and-effect relationship between microorganisms and diseases.

## KOCH'S POSTULATES

1. The same organism must be found in all cases of a given disease.
2. The organism must be isolated and grown in pure culture.
3. The organisms from the pure culture must reproduce the disease when inoculated into a susceptible animal.
4. The organism must then again be isolated from the experimentally infected animal.

Microorganisms come in two major varieties, based upon their cell structure. **Procaryotes** have no true, membrane-bound nuclei (pro- means primitive, -caryon refers to the nucleus). Bacteria and cyanobacteria ("blue-green" bacteria) are the most common types of procaryotes. They have extremely simple cell structures when compared to the **eucaryotes**. Eucaryotes have true, membrane-bound nuclei (in fact, the name **means** true nucleus; eu- means true, -caryon means nucleus). Eucaryotes have extensive internal organelles such as **endoplasmic reticulum** (smooth and rough), **Golgi apparatus**, **mitochondria**, **chloroplasts** and **microtubules**. Many eucaryotes are capable of phagocytosis (engulfing foreign materials) and cytoplasmic streaming - neither of which can be performed by procaryotes.

The difference between the two cell types continues down to the gene level. Procaryotes have almost all of their genes in one circular chromosome composed entirely of DNA (not complexed with histone proteins). Eucaryotes, on the other hand, have 2 to hundreds of long, linear chromosomes in which the DNA is heavily complexed with proteins such as histones. The numerous chromosomes require an elaborate process to prepare the cell for cell division - **mitosis**. In mitosis the chromosomes align at the center of the cell, split into two equal halves (chromatids), and migrate to opposite sides of the cell. Cell division is completed by splitting of the cytoplasm (**cytokinesis**). With their much smaller, more compact genetic systems, procaryotic cells divide in a quick, simple process called **binary fission**.

Even though we laud the efforts of Redi, Spallanzani, Pasteur and Tyndall for exorcising the concept of spontaneous generation from microbiology, it is ironic that this same concept is at the basis of modern ideas about the origin of life. Spontaneous generation does not occur today, but it must have occurred at least once in the distant past! Approximately 3.5 billion years ago procaryotes arose from some precellular antecedent. The earliest procaryotes must have been **anaerobic** (the word means "without air"), since oxygen was not present in the early Earth's atmosphere. Only after the development of cyanobacteria, with their oxygen-generating photosynthesis, could **aerobic** organisms develop (aerobic means "with air").

Modern forms of life have been divided into five large aggregations called **Kingdoms**. Microorganisms are found in four of the five Kingdoms.

Bacteria, cyanobacteria and mycoplasmas are all found in the **Kingdom Monera** (all are procaryotic). Yeasts and molds are placed in the **Kingdom Fungi**. All are eucaryotic, unicellular or filamentous. **Helminths** are multicellular eucaryotic worms found in the **Kingdom Animalia**. They are considered "microbes" despite their relatively large size because of their medical importance (tapeworms, pinworms, etc.).

Protozoans are members of the **Kingdom Protista**. They are eucaryotic unicellular organisms of considerable medical importance for their involvement in causing such devastating diseases as malaria, trypanosomiasis, and dysentery.

**Viruses** are a special case. Since they are not cellular organisms they do not belong in any of the five kingdoms. They are unable to reproduce unless they have penetrated into a living procaryotic or eucaryotic cell. Those that parasitize bacteria are called "**bacteriophages**" to distinguish them from those that attack eucaryotic cells.

All organisms, regardless of their affiliation, are named according to the rules laid down in 1735 by **Carolus Linnaeus**. Each kind is given two names; a genus name (always capitalized) and a species name (always lower case). Such scientific names should be either italicized or underlined (e.g. *Streptococcus mutans* vs. Streptococcus mutans).

In addition to dividing the field of microbiology into sections concerning the type of organism studied, it is also possible to divide the field according to the general emphasis. This process results in such subdivisions as: medical microbiology, immunology, industrial microbiology, agricultural microbiology, etc.

OBJECTIVES After reading this chapter, you should be able to:

1. Define bacteriology, mycology, protozoology, and virology.

2. Discuss the theory of spontaneous generation and the types of experiments that disproved the generation of microorganisms from inert matter.

3. List several benefits to society that have resulted from a knowledge of microorganisms.

4. Explain the purpose of Koch's postulates.

5. Differentiate between the structure and gene organization occurring in procaryotic and eucaryotic cells.

6. Describe some proposed events that resulted in the origin of the first primitive procaryotic cell.

7. Outline the principal divisions of microbiology and the major interests of scientists in each discipline.

## LEARNING ACTIVITIES

### Vocabulary

Having read the chapter, you should be able to define or cite the significance of the following terms. If you cannot, look them up in the text. Terms are presented in the order you will encounter them in the book.

microbiology
bacteriology
virology
mycology
protozoology
pathogenic
parasitic
endospore
aerobic
anaerobic
chemoautotrophs
eucaryotic
smooth endoplasmic reticulum
rough endoplasmic reticulum
Golgi apparatus
lysosomes
mitochondria
chloroplast
microtubules
Protista
Fungi
bacteriophages

### Names

Having read the chapter you should be able to cite the discovery or principle for which the following individuals are primarily known. If you can't, look them up!

Pasteur
Leeuwenhoek
Redi
Needham
Spallanzani
Tyndall
Winogradsky
Bassi
Lister
Koch
Hesse
Semmelweis
Gaffky
Loeffler
Kitasato
Ricketts
Miller
Urey

Complete each of the following statements by supplying the missing word or words.

1. mycology ____________ is the name used to describe the division of microbiology involving fungi.

2. viruses ____________ are the subject of study of people called virologists.

3. meat ____________ in covered and uncovered jars was the subject of an experiment conducted by Francesco Redi disproving spontaneous generation of flies.

4. Louis Pasteur ____________ achieved the disproof of spontaneous generation of microorganisms by means of "swan-necked" flasks.

5. eucaryotic cells are complex and contain many internal organelles.

6. John Tyndall observed that light beams cannot be seen if dust particles are not present in the air in a sealed box. He used this information to finally disprove spontaneous generation of microbes.

7. Agostino Bassi is credited with an early connection between microbes and disease involving a fungal infection of silkworms.

8. Robert Koch put the investigation of microbial causes of diseases on a firm footing with his "four postulates".

9. Joseph Lister is generally credited with the first use of phenol as an antiseptic during surgical operations.

10. procaryotes have a chromosome which is a closed circular DNA molecule.

11. Eucaryotes always have sterols (including cholesterol) in their cell membranes.

12. mitosis is the process involved in division of the nucleus of eucaryotic cells.

13. cytokinesis is the name of the process which completes cell division in eucaryotes.

14. 3.5 billion years ago the first procaryotic cells appeared on the Earth.

15. RNA, according to some, was the first self-reproducing molecule on the planet.

16. archaebacteria are the group of procaryotes which most closely resemble the eucaryotes.

17. cyanobacteria are probably responsible for the presence of oxygen in the atmosphere of the early Earth, making possible the development of aerobes.

18. medical microbiologist are primarily interested in the disease-causing aspects of microorganisms.

19. Immunologists are most interested in host reactions to foreign substances in the body.

20. Food microbiologist would be primarily interested in the contamination of processed foods by microorganisms and ways to prevent such contamination.

## MASTERY TEST

1-8: Match the principle, discovery, etc. with the individual (use no answer twice)

ANSWERS

| | | |
|---|---|---|
| A. Bassi | G. Lister | M. Ricketts |
| B. Gaffky | H. Loeffler | N. Semmelweis |
| C. Hesse | I. Miller | O. Spallanzani |
| D. Kitasato | J. Needham | P. Tyndall |
| E. Koch | K. Pasteur | Q. Urey |
| F. Leeuwenhoek | L. Redi | R. Winogradsky |

Redi 1. L First to disprove theory of spontaneous generation of flies using covered and uncovered jars containing meat.

Leeuwenhoek 2. F First to publish descriptions of bacteria based upon observations made on lenses of his own design and manufacture.

Miller 3. I Performed experiments (with his professor Urey) on the origin of life using containers of gases similar to those in the atmosphere of the primitive Earth.

Winogradsky 4. R Discovered chemoautotrophs.

Koch 5. E Formulated the "four postulates" to be followed in trying to identify the causative agent of a disease.

Pasteur 6. K Used "swan-necked" flasks to disprove spontaneous generation of microorganisms.

Lister 7. G Introduced antiseptic use in surgical operations (phenol).

Needham 8. J Supported concept of spontaneous generation by performing experiments with infusions that always grew microbes no matter what precautions were used.

9-15: Circle the choice that best answers the questions.

9. Term used to describe metabolism which uses oxygen.
   a. aerobic
   b. anabolic
   c. anaerobic
   d. catabolic
   e. parasitic

10. Which of the following is NOT considered to be one of "Koch's Postulates"?
   a. The same organism must be found in all cases of a given disease.
   b. The organism must be isolated and grown in pure culture.
   c. The organism grown in this way will show specific susceptibility to antibodies isolated from blood of infected animals.
   d. The organisms from the pure culture must reproduce the disease when inoculated into a susceptible animal.

11. Which of the following is a field of study concentrating its attention on viruses?
   a. bacteriology
   b. mycology
   c. virology
   d. immunology
   e. protozoology

12. All of the following are eucaryotes EXCEPT:
   a. animals
   b. cyanobacteria
   c. fungi
   d. protozoa
   e. plants

13. Life on Earth is thought to be ____________ years old.
   a. 6,400
   b. 75,000
   c. 100,000,000
   d. 3,500,000,000

14. Which of the following is the correct format for the name of a common mouth-dwelling bacterium?
   a. *Streptococcus mutans*
   b. *Streptococcus Mutans*
   c. *streptococcus Mutans*
   d. Streptococcus mutans
   e. <u>streptococcus mutans</u>

15. A diverse group of multicellular worms which many feel belong under the study of microbiologists are:
   a. Protozoans
   b. Helminths
   c. Molds
   d. Slime Molds
   e. Worms

---

16-20: TRUE-FALSE: (T for true, F for false)

_____ 16. All evolutionary biologists are in agreement that RNA was the first self-duplicating molecule.

_____ 17. Water sanitation and sewage disposal techniques owe nothing to microbiology for their success.

T 18. Most protozoa are free-living organisms, but some cause disease.

T 19. Procaryotic cells can reproduce much more rapidly than eucaryotic cells.

T 20. Spontaneous generation does not occur now and has never occurred in the history of the planet Earth.

---

21-25: Match the characteristics with the cellular type exhibiting them (may use answers twice)

ANSWERS: A. Procaryotes only B. Eucaryotes only

A 21. The chromosome consists of circular DNA with no histone proteins.

B 22. Cell division proceeds by mitosis plus cytokinesis.

B 23. They have numerous internal membrane-bound organelles.

A 24. Kingdom Monera.

B 25. Membranes always contain sterols.

## ANSWERS TO LEARNING ACTIVITIES

### Names

**Pasteur** - provided proof that spontaneous generation of microbes does not occur; identified anaerobic fermentation; **Leeuwenhoek** - made lenses, microscopes; discovered bacteria; **Redi** - provided proof that spontaneous generation of "macro" life does not occur (maggots from flies); **Needham** - proponent of spontaneous generation of microbes; **Spallanzani** - provided early proof that spontaneous generation of microbes does not occur; **Tyndall** - provided final proof that microbes develop from other microbes, not spontaneously; discovered endospores; **Winogradsky** - discovered chemoautotrophs (organisms able to survive with no organic nutrients at all); **Bassi** - early demonstration of disease; silkworm fungus; **Lister** - introduced antiseptic use (phenol); **Koch** - Koch's Postulates; identified disease causes; **Hesse** - suggested use of agar to solidify microbiological media; **Semmelweis** - suggested that childbed fever was transmitted by physicians themselves *via* unclean hands; **Gaffky** - isolated the typhoid bacillus; **Loeffler** - first to identify the diphtheria bacillus; **Kitasato** - first to culture the plague bacillus; **Ricketts** - along with Prowazek, died of typhus as consequence of research into its cause; **Miller** - performed experiments (with Urey) concerning origin of life; **Urey** - along with his student Miller performed experiments concerning origin of life.

Vocabulary

**microbiology** - subdivision of biology dealing with very small living things; **bacteriology** - division of microbiology dealing with bacteria; **virology** - division of microbiology dealing with viruses; **mycology** - division of microbiology dealing with fungi; **protozoology** -division of microbiology dealing with protozoans; **pathogenic** - organism capable of causing an infection; **parasitic** - way of life in which one organism (the parasite) feeds upon another living organism (the host); **endospores** - resistant forms of life discovered by Tyndall; cannot be killed by boiling; **aerobic** - "with air"; organism use oxygen in metabolism; **anaerobic** - "without air"; organism does not use oxygen in metabolism; **chemoautotrophs** - organisms that can grow without any organic "food"; generate energy by inorganic reactions; **eucaryotic** - cells with true nuclei; **smooth endoplasmic reticulum** - organelle in eucaryotes which is responsible for protein storage, transport; steroid synthesis; **rough endoplasmic reticulum** - organelle in eucaryotes which is responsible for much of the protein synthesis in the cell; **Golgi apparatus** - organelle in eucaryotes which synthesizes polysaccharides, packages proteins; **lysosomes** - organelle in eucaryotes which contains hydrolytic (digestive) enzymes; **mitochondria** - organelle in eucaryotes which produces ATP (adenosine triphosphate); **chloroplast** - organelle in some eucaryotic cells that performs photosynthesis; **microtubules** - organelle in eucaryotes responsible for producing the spindle apparatus during mitosis; **Protista** - Kingdom of eucaryotic organisms which contains the protozoa and the eucaryotic algae; **Fungi** - Kingdom of eucaryotic organisms which contains the yeasts and the molds; **bacteriophages** - viruses that attack bacteria;

Fill-In-The-Blank Questions

1. Mycology; 2. Viruses; 3. Meat; 4. Pasteur; 5. Eucaryotic; 6. Tyndall; 7. Bassi; 8. Koch; 9. Lister; 10. Procaryotes; 11. Eucaryotes; 12. Mitosis; 13. Cytokinesis; 14. 3.5 billion; 15. RNA; 16. Archaebacteria; 17. Cyanobacteria; 18. Medical microbiologists; 19. Immunologists; 20. Food microbiologists.

**MASTERY TEST ANSWERS**

| | | | | | | | | | | | | |
|---|---|---|---|---|---|---|---|---|---|---|---|---|
| 1 L | 2 F | 3 I | 4 R | 5 E | 6 K | | 7 G | 8 J | 9 a | 10 c | 11 c | 12 b |
| 13 d | 14 a | 15 b | 16 F | 17 F | 18 T | 19 T | 20 F | 21 A | 22 B | 23 B | 24 A | 25 B |

# CHAPTER 2

## LABORATORY EQUIPMENT AND PROCEDURES

### CHAPTER SUMMARY

Microbes are so small that it is impossible to handle or study individual organisms as you might dogs, rats, tomato plants or clams. Techniques to visualize, cultivate and care for microorganisms have been developed over the past century or so and continue to be improved today. Leeuwenhoek used a **simple microscope** consisting of a single lens. The light microscopes used today are **compound microscopes** which have optical systems consisting of two separate lenses: an **objective lens** (located near the object being viewed) and an **ocular lens** (located near the observer's eye). Modern light microscopes can magnify images approximately 1000 times (1000X).

The **resolving power** of a light microscope is not set by its type of lens but rather by the nature of light itself. The absolute limit of resolving power is roughly one half of the wavelength of the illuminating source. For visible light this limits resolution to about 0.2 μm (μm=micrometers, $10^{-6}$ meters). This means that you cannot distinguish between two points separated by less than 0.2 μm **and** that you cannot see anything smaller than 0.2 μm. The ultraviolet light microscope uses an illumination source with a shorter wavelength and can resolve down to 0.1 μm. By contrast, the transmission electron microscope (TEM - discussed later) can resolve down to 0.5 nm (nm=nanometers, $10^{-9}$ meters) - that's 0.0005 μm!

Modifications of the basic light microscope for special purposes include the **fluorescence microscope**, the **darkfield microscope**, and the **phase-contrast microscope**. The fluorescence microscope depends upon the use of special dyes which "fluoresce" (emit light of longer wavelength) when illuminated with ultraviolet light. In the darkfield microscope, the only lighted objects in the field are obstacles in the light path such as living cells (cells show up bright against a black background). Another modification is the **phase-contrast microscope** which takes advantage of the **phase difference** that results from light passing through objects of differing composition in the cell. Objects of the same color but different density will appear in varying brightness levels in this type of microscope.

The electron microscope uses a beam of electrons rather than light to "illuminate" the object. The TEM (transmission electron microscope) has an extremely good resolution (approximately 0.5 nm) and a high magnification (up to 1,000,000X). Unfortunately, since objects must be observed under vacuum conditions, the TEM can only be used on dead material which has been sliced into extremely thin sections (0.1 $\mu$m in thickness). No dyes useful in light microscopy can be used; heavy metals which are "electron dense" are used instead. Often the metals are "sprayed" over the object at a sharp angle to produce **shadow casting**. **Freeze etching** is another technique useful in electron microscopy. In this technique tissues are frozen, fractured, stained and then observed. **Ion bombardment** allows a similar view of internal details of tissues and cells by eroding surface layers from the preparation prior to staining.

The SEM (scanning electron microscope) uses a beam of electrons in a different way which produces spectacular three-dimensional images of objects. The resolution and magnification potential of the SEM is, however, lower than that of the TEM (resolution of 0.02 $\mu$m, magnification of 10,000X).

Observing bacteria in an ordinary compound microscope is extremely difficult unless one does something to enhance the image. One of the most important enhancements of practical use is the chemical stain. About the only time you will look at unstained bacteria is if you are attempting to determine if they are motile. This requires that the cells be alive and functional, and is an observation inimical with staining. Motility is usually determined using the **hanging drop** preparation. In this technique one places a drop of a live bacterial suspension on a coverslip and suspends the drop over the hollow in a depression slide. Any cells that are clearly moving "from point A to point B" are considered to be motile. Cells which haplessly jiggle about point A (or point B) are merely demonstrating "brownian movement" (not true motility).

Stained bacteria, on the other hand, are killed bacteria. No "vital" activities can be observed in them, but morphology of the cells, size, any repetitive cell arrangements, as well as the presence or absence of some internal structures such as granules or spores can be observed in stained preparations. Some techniques even allow one to distinguish between classes of bacteria (these are called **differential stains**).

Bacteria which are to be stained are first spread over the surface of a slide (this is called a **smear**). Once a smear has air-dried it must be **fixed**. Fixation is usually achieved *via* heat (passing the slide over a flame, smear upwards) but may also be done using methyl alcohol as a fixative. Heat fixation is faster but may distort cell morphology.

Bacterial stains are usually of the "basic dye" type. In basic dyes the **chromophore** is positively charged and binds to the negatively charged DNA in the cell. Common basic dyes include crystal violet, safranin, basic fuchsin and methylene blue. Acid dyes are actually repelled by the bacterial cell (allowing their use in **negative staining**).

A **simple stain** is a technique in which a single dye is used (almost always a basic dye). Such techniques are often all that is needed to determine cell size, shape or arrangement. In **differential stains** at least two dyes are used (a primary stain and a counterstain). The most important differential stain was developed in 1884 by Christian Gram. It is called the Gram stain in his honor. The Gram stain is so important because it distinguishes between two taxonomically important classes of bacteria: the gram-positive and the gram-negative bacteria. The gram-positive bacteria retain the primary dye (crystal violet), while the gram-negatives lose the primary dye in the decolorization step (washing with 95% ethyl alcohol) but retain the counterstain (safranin). As a result, the gram-positives stain purple or blue, the gram-negatives stain pink to red.

The Gram reaction (positive or negative staining) is of taxonomic importance because it relates to a basic difference in the cell structure and physiology of the organisms. This has important consequences in terms of antibiotic sensitivity, tolerance to basic dyes, etc. One example is the sensitivity of gram-positive organisms to **penicillin** and **gramicidin** vs. the sensitivity of most gram-negatives to streptomycin. Other differential stains have been developed which determine if an organism is acid-fast, a endospore-former, has flagella, etc. When bacteria or other microbes are being studied in the laboratory they are usually being grown as **pure cultures**. A culture is a medium containing living organisms; a pure culture is a medium containing one **kind** of living organisms. Pure cultures are derived from single **colonies** of microbes which develop in one of two common culture conditions: the **streak-plate** and the **pour-plate**. In the streak-plate an initial **inoculum** is spread in a progressive fashion over the surface of an agar petri plate. The spreading effectively dilutes the organism so that in its final sectors colonies develop from single cells. In the pour-plate technique the organisms are diluted volumetrically by inoculating them into liquified media which is then poured into a petri dish and allowed to harden. Again, colonies develop from single cells or very small groups of genetically identical cells.

Most common bacteriological media are **infusions** - media in which a diverse group of organic molecules are provided in dissolved form. Such media can be in liquid form (**broths**) or may be solidified with agar. Agar-solidified media may be in the form of plates (in petri dishes) or as **slants** or **deeps** in tubes. Slants have a large surface area and are streaked with microbes on their surface. Deeps are usually stabbed, with microbes being introduced throughout the depth of the medium.

**Artificial** or **complex** media contain at least one complex, heterogeneous ingredient such as beef extract, yeast extract, tryptones, etc. Such media are of general utility because they are easy to make and support the growth of many types of microbes. **Synthetic** or **defined** media contain only known ingredients in measured, precise quantities. Their main use is in nutritional studies.

Carbohydrate media are supplemented with specific carbohydrates and are commonly used to determine the form of metabolism being expressed by the microbes growing on them. Some bacteria will use a given sugar aerobically, reducing it to carbon dioxide and water, while others will ferment the sugar with the production of acids and gases. Such behavior is often of taxonomic importance.

**Selective media** contain materials added to inhibit the growth of certain bacteria. The additives may be basic dyes (which inhibit gram-positive organisms), antibiotics, acids, or salts. Only the "desired" varieties of microbes can grow on these media. **Differential media** don't inhibit any bacteria, but rather make some types grow in a distinctive fashion. Acid indicators, for example, may detect the presence of fermentative species while aerobic species may grow in an undistinguished fashion. Still other media serve as **enrichment cultures** by providing particularly luxuriant growth conditions to desired species. Organisms represented poorly in a mixed culture may be enhanced by such media.

Microbiological media must be carefully monitored for proper pH. Bacteria typically prefer to grow in media of a pH near 7.0 (**neutral** pH). Very few species prefer to grow in media which have a pH much above 7 (**alkaline**) or much below 7 (**acidic**). Similarly, most bacteria do not adapt well to extreme temperatures; growth at temperatures below 10°C or above 45°C are rare.

The oxygen requirements of bacteria must also be considered when they are being grown in culture. Some bacteria, the **strict aerobes,** require oxygen in high concentrations. **Microaerophiles** require oxygen but can't tolerate high concentration of free oxygen. **Facultative aerobes** (or **facultative anaerobes**) can grow aerobically in the presence of oxygen, anaerobically in its absence. The **strict (obligate) anaerobes** not only do not require oxygen for growth, they may be killed by it. **Aerotolerant** species are anaerobic (do not use oxygen) but can tolerate exposure to oxygen.

Media used for the growth of microorganisms are always sterilized before use. Most commonly the media are **autoclaved** unless they contain delicate materials that would be degraded by heat. **Membrane filter** sterilization is a substitute method which preserves fragile organic materials. **Hot air ovens** can conveniently sterilize glassware and other dry goods.

Once bacteria have been established in pure culture it is possible to attempt to identify them. Minimal information required for this process includes the size, shape and arrangement of the organism; its gram-staining reaction; whether it is motile; and the overall size and appearance of the bacterial colony. Further information of a biochemical and immunological nature will then be required for full identification of the species.

OBJECTIVES — A study of this chapter should result in a clear understanding of:

1. The different types of microscopes used to study microorganisms and the resolving power of each type.
2. Techniques for studying live bacteria.
3. Types of stains used to visualize bacteria and the details of the Gram stain.
4. Techniques for the isolation of a pure culture and several types of media used to grow bacteria.
5. Terms such as pH, aerobic, anaerobic, facultative, and sterile.

## LEARNING ACTIVITIES

### Vocabulary

Having read the chapter, you should be able to define or cite the significance of the following terms. If you cannot, look them up in the text. Terms are presented in the order you will encounter them in the book.

simple microscope
compound microscope
resolving power
ultraviolet light microscope
fluorescence microscope
darkfield microscope
phase-contrast microscope
phase difference
electron microscope
TEM
SEM
shadow casting
freeze etching
ion bombardment
hanging-drop preparation
brownian movement
motility
simple stain
differential stain
smear
fixation
chromophore
basic dye
acid dye
negative staining
Gram stain
counterstain
decolorization
gram-negative organism
gram-positive organism
acid-fast organism

culture
pure culture
streak-plate
colony
pour-plate
infusion
slant
deep
artificial medium
complex medium
synthetic medium
defined medium
selective medium
differential medium
enrichment cultures
pH
neutral
acidic
alkaline
strict aerobes
strict anaerobes
microaerophile
facultative aerobes
aerotolerant
autoclave
membrane filter
hot-air oven
agglutinate
antiserum
antibody
immunofluorescence

Complete each of the following statements by supplying the missing word or words.

1. ___compound___ microscopes consist of two separate magnifying stages, rather than one.

2. ___Resolving power___ of the light microscope is determined by the wavelength of light, not by the quality or power of its lenses.

3. ___Darkfield___ microscopes exhibit very bright objects against a dark background.

4. ___ultraviolet___ microscopes can resolve down to 0.1 $\mu$m because of the short wavelength of the illumination source.

5. ___Transmittion___ electron microscopes have a resolution of 0.5 nm and magnification up to 1,000,000X.

6. ___Freeze___ etching is a technique used in electron microscopy which demonstrates internal details otherwise not obtainable.

7. ___Hanging drop___ preparations are used to determine if a given species of bacterium is motile.

8. ___smears___ are thin layers of bacteria spread over the surface of a glass slide.

9. ___Heat___ is the most common fixation technique used for bacteria, although some labs use methyl alcohol.

10. ___Acid___ dyes are the most useful class for bacteria, as they bind to the DNA inside the cell.

11. ___differential___ stains use at least two dyes (a primary stain and a counterstain).

12. ___Gram___ invented the most important example of the stain technique described in question #11.

13. ___Gram +___ bacteria remain purple in the staining technique discussed in question #12.

14. ___Pure___ cultures are media containing living organisms of one type only.

15. ____streak____-plate techniques produce isolated colonies by progressively diluting organisms over the agar surface in the petri dish.

16. ____slant____ are tubes of solid media which have a large surface produced by cooling them at an angle.

17. ____artificial____ or complex media contain heterogeneous ingredients such as tryptone, peptone, beef extract or yeast extract.

18. ____selective____ media contain materials added to inhibit the growth of certain bacteria.

19. ____differential____ media contain materials added to make some types of bacteria grow in a distinctive fashion while others grow in an undistinguished fashion.

20. ____autoclaves____ are giant pressure cookers used to sterilize microbiological media at high temperatures and pressures.

Fill in the blank regions in the table below by converting micrometers to nanometers (or the reverse) and by indicating with a YES or NO answer whether the items are within the resolving power of the instruments mentioned.

| STRUCTURE | MICRO-METERS | NANO-METERS | LIGHT MICROSCOPE | ELECTRON MICROSCOPE |
|---|---|---|---|---|
| CELL MEMBRANE | | 7.5 nm | | |
| NUCLEUS | 10 μm | 10,000 nm | | |
| BACTERIUM | 2.0 μm | | | |
| VIRUS | | 100 nm | | |

MASTERY TEST

1-9: Circle the choice that best answers the questions.

1. The microscopes used by Leeuwenhoek were of the ____simple____ type.
   a. simple
   b. SEM
   c. compound
   d. darkfield
   e. TEM

2. Compound microscopes have two sets of magnifying lenses, the objectives and the ___oculars___.

a. inobjectives
b. subjectives
c. oculars
d. oraculars
e. anulars

3. In a technique called immunofluorescence fluorescent dyes are bound to ___antibodies___ which then specifically bind to certain bacteria or even internal cell parts.

a. antigens
b. antibodies
c. chromophores
d. ligands
e. flagella

4. The reason that electron microscopes have a much greater resolving power than light microscopes is:

a. electron beams have a longer wavelength than light does
b. light is more easily refracted and this degrades the image
c. electron beams have a shorter wavelength than light does
d. electron beams are more easily refracted and this improves the image
e. all of these

5. Ion bombardment is a technique used to exhibit internal detail of cells when used with specimens observed by the:

a. SEM
b. TEM
c. phase-contrast microscope
d. darkfield microscope
e. all of these

6. The most important advantage of the SEM (scanning electron microscope) over the TEM is the:

a. higher resolution of the SEM
b. 3 dimensional nature of the SEM images
c. higher magnification possible with the SEM
d. lack of a vacuum requirement for the SEM

7. Cells that do not exhibit a directional movement in a hanging drop slide, but rather jiggle about a point in space are demonstrating:

a. true motility
b. gliding motility
c. phase difference
d. brownian movement
e. fixation

8. Stained bacteria can demonstrate all of the following EXCEPT:

a. cell morphology
b. cell arrangements
c. presence of endospores
d. motility
e. size of cells

9. Bacterial smears must be allowed to air-dry, after which they must undergo:
   a. fixation
   b. oven drying
   c. direct staining
   d. autoclaving
   e. decolorization

10-16: Match the term with the technique, bacterial type, etc. (use no answer twice)

ANSWERS

| | | |
|---|---|---|
| A. Complex Media | D. Gram-Negative | H. Pour-Plate |
| B. Defined Media | E. Gram-Positive | I. Pure Culture |
| C. Differential Stain | F. *Mycobacterium* | J. Simple Stain |
| | G. *Myxobacterium* | K. Streak-Plate |

_J_ 10. Staining technique in which a single dye is used. Simple stain

_D_ 11. Bacterial type which stains pink to red in the Gram stain. G−

_F_ 12. Bacterial type which stains acid-fast. Mycobacterium

_B_ 13. Type of medium characterized by a makeup of measured and precisely known ingredients.

_K_ 14. Technique in which bacteria are spread over the surface of an agar plate with the intent of producing isolated colonies.

_E_ 15. Class of bacterium which is sensitive to penicillin and gramicidin.

_C_ 16. Staining technique in which at least two dyes are used, a primary stain and a counterstain.

---

17-25: Circle the choice that best answers the questions.

17. A medium which has a pH of 3.5 is said to be:
   a. alkaline
   b. acidic
   c. hyperbolic
   d. octahedral
   e. basic

18. When attempting to culture bacteria which are found in few numbers in the initial inoculum one often uses:
   a. differential media
   b. selective media
   c. enrichment media
   d. infusion media

19. Organisms which require oxygen in high concentrations for proper growth are called:
a. aerotolerant anaerobes
b. facultative anaerobes
c. microaerophiles
d. strict aerobes
e. strict anaerobes

20. Organisms which have an anaerobic metabolism but which can grow in the presence of oxygen are called:
a. aerotolerant anaerobes
b. facultative anaerobes
c. microaerophiles
d. strict aerobes
e. strict anaerobes

21. Organisms which can grow aerobically in the presence of oxygen or fermentatively in its absence are called:
a. aerotolerant anaerobes
b. facultative anaerobes
c. microaerophiles
d. strict aerobes
e. strict anaerobes

22. Organisms which require oxygen, but prefer it in very low concentrations, are called:
a. aerotolerant anaerobes
b. facultative anaerobes
c. microaerophiles
d. strict aerobes
e. strict anaerobes

23. The most common method of sterilizing microbiological media is:
a. boiling
b. heating in a hot-air oven
c. autoclaving
d. membrane filtration
e. acidification

24. If the media contain very fragile organic constituents it is often necessary to sterilize the media by means of:
a. boiling
b. heating in a hot-air oven
c. autoclaving
d. membrane filtration
e. acidification

25. Which of the following is NOT one of the basic pieces of information used in identification of bacteria?
a. size and shape of cells
b. number of cells per typical colony
c. gram-staining reaction
d. motility
e. arrangement of the cells

## ANSWERS TO LEARNING ACTIVITIES

### Vocabulary

**simple microscope** - microscope with a single lens; **compound microscope** - microscope with two sets of magnifying lenses; **resolving power** - ability to distinguish between two points or the ability to resolve very small objects; **ultraviolet light microscope** - microscope with high resolution (down to 0.1 $\mu$m) due to use of short-wavelength light; **fluorescence microscope** - microscope that uses ultraviolet light to cause special dyes to fluoresce; **darkfield microscope** - microscope that uses special illumination techniques to present cells as bright objects against a dark background; **phase-contrast microscope** - microscope which uses the phase difference of light passing through different densities of objects to create images of varying brightness; **phase difference** - the shift in light phase as it passes through objects of differing density; **electron microscope** - microscope which uses a beam of electrons instead of light to "illuminate" an object; **TEM** - variety of electron microscope which depends upon transmission of electrons through an object for viewing; **SEM** - variety of electron microscope which depends upon scattering of electrons from surfaces to obtain an image; **shadow casting** - electron microscope staining technique in which metals are sprayed over objects at an angle; **freeze etching** - another EM technique in which tissues are frozen, fractured, then stained and observed; **ion bombardment** - using a beam of charged particles to erode surfaces to expose internal detail; **hanging-drop preparation** - light microscope technique which is used to determine motility; **brownian movement** - "false motility" of small objects due to their being hit by moving water molecules; **motility** - true movement of microbes in which cells move in a particular direction; **simple stain** - stain technique using a single dye; **differential stain** - stain technique using at least two dyes and a decolorizing step; **smear** - thin layer of bacteria spread over the surface of a slide; **fixation** - technique to attach cells to a slide and prevent their further deterioration; **chromophore** - colored part of a dye salt; **basic dye** - dye molecule in which the chromophore has a positive charge; **acid dye** - dye molecule in which the chromophore has a negative charge; **negative staining** - staining technique in which the cells are bright and the background is dark; **Gram stain** - differential stain which can distinguish between the two main classes of bacteria; **counterstain** - the second (or last) dye used in differential staining techniques; **decolorization** - step in differential staining which removes the primary dye from some types of bacteria and allows the counterstain to color them; **gram-negative organism** - species which stain pink to red in the Gram stain; **gram-positive organism** - species which stain purple in the Gram stain; **acid-fast organism** - species which stain red or magenta in the Acid-Fast staining technique; **culture** - medium containing living microorganisms; **pure culture** - culture which contains a single species of organism; **streak-plate** - one method of obtaining a pure culture by spreading inoculum over the surface of an agar plate; **colony** - visible clump of bacterial cells on solid medium; **pour-plate** - another technique to obtain a pure culture by mixing live bacteria with liquified agar media which is poured into a petri dish and allowed to harden; **infusion** - medium which contains organic materials derived from soaking or boiling solid material such as meat in water; **slant** - solid medium in tubes which are allowed to cool at an angle; **deep** - tubes of solid medium which are stabbed rather than streaked; **artificial medium** - same as complex medium; **complex medium** - medium which contains a heterogeneous organic ingredient; **synthetic medium** - same as defined medium; **defined medium** - medium which is composed of known, measured materials only; **selective medium** - medium which contains an additive which inhibits the growth of undesired species; **differential medium** - medium which permits some species to grow in a distinctive fashion for easy identification; **enrichment cultures** - medium is specially designed to favor the growth of an organism poorly represented in the initial inoculum; **pH** - the system used to quantify the acidity or alkalinity of a solution; **neutral** - pH of 7; **acidic** - pH below 7; **alkaline** - pH above 7; **strict aerobes** - organisms that require oxygen in large amounts for growth; **strict anaerobes** -organisms that do not use oxygen and may be killed by it; **microaerophile** - organisms which use oxygen but require it in very low concentrations; **facultative aerobes** - organisms which can use oxygen when it is available or grow fermentatively in its absence; **aerotolerant** - anaerobe which can tolerate the presence of oxygen; **autoclave** - giant pressure cooker used for sterilizing microbiological media; **membrane filter** - alternate method to sterilize media without the use of high temperatures; **hot-air oven** - method of sterilizing glassware and other dry goods which avoids the dampness caused by other methods; **agglutinate** - characteristic clumping of bacteria when exposed to antibodies against their surface antigens; **antiserum** - solution containing antibodies against specific antigens; **antibody** - protein produced by an animal's immune system against specific chemical structures called antigens; **immunofluorescence** - microscopic technique utilizing a fluorescent microscope and fluorescent antibodies.

| STRUCTURE | MICRO-METERS | NANO-METERS | LIGHT MICROSCOPE | ELECTRON MICROSCOPE |
|---|---|---|---|---|
| CELL MEMBRANE | 0.0075 μm | 7.5 nm | NO | YES |
| NUCLEUS | 10 μm | 10000 nm | YES | YES |
| BACTERIUM | 2.0 μm | 2000 nm | YES | YES |
| VIRUS | 0.1 μm | 100 nm | NO | YES |

Fill-in-the-blank questions

1. Compound; 2. Resolving power; 3. Darkfield; 4. Ultraviolet light;
5. Transmission; 6. Freeze; 7. Hanging-drop; 8. Smears; 9. Heat;

10. Acid; 11. Differential; 12. Christian Gram; 13. Gram-positive; 14. Pure; 15. Streak; 16. Slants; 17. Artificial; 18. Selective; 19. Differential; 20. Autoclaves.

| MASTERY TEST ANSWERS | | | | | | | | | | | | |
|---|---|---|---|---|---|---|---|---|---|---|---|---|
| 1<br>a | 2<br>c | 3<br>b | 4<br>c | 5<br>b | 6<br>b | | 7<br>d | 8<br>d | 9<br>a | 10<br>J | 11<br>D | 12<br>F |
| 13<br>B | 14<br>K | 15<br>E | 16<br>C | 17<br>b | 18<br>c | 19<br>d | 20<br>a | 21<br>b | 22<br>c | 23<br>c | 24<br>d | 25<br>b |

# CHAPTER 3

## BACTERIAL MORPHOLOGY

### CHAPTER SUMMARY

The study of bacterial morphology includes the external shape of the cells, cell arrangements, and the internal anatomy of the cells. Most bacteria fit into one of three cell shape classes: **cocci**, **bacilli**, and **spiral forms**. Cocci are spherical (round in two dimensions) and come in some important characteristic arrangements: **diplococci** (pairs of cells), **tetrads** (groups of 4 cells in one plane), **streptococci** (chains of cells), and **staphylococci** (grape-like clusters of cells). **Bacilli** are cylindrical or rod-shaped and may come in pairs or short chains. If the cells are very short they may look much like cocci and are called **coccobacilli**. Curved bacilli are called **vibrios**. The spiral bacteria are divided into two groups according to the rigidity of the cells. Rigid spiral cells are called **spirilla**, while flexible spiral cells are called **spirochetes**. No matter what their shape, reproduction in bacteria is exclusively asexual by means of a cell division method called **binary fission**.

Many bacteria have surface structures called **flagella** which enable them to move (exhibit **motility**). Flagella are found on almost all spiral bacteria, on about half of all bacilli, but on virtually no cocci. They are only 12 to 30 nm in diameter, so are invisible in the light microscope. Patterns of flagellation (see Figure 3.4 in the textbook) include **monotrichous** (one flagellum per cell), **amphitrichous** (flagella on both ends of the cell), **lophotrichous** (tuft of flagella on one end of the cell) and the **peritrichous** condition in which flagella are found all over the cell.

The **flagellum** actually originates at the cytoplasmic membrane and projects out through the cell wall. They are composed of protein subunits called **flagellin**. Flagella rotate (they do not wave about like the eucaryotic flagellum) and their direction can be reversed. Rotating in one direction it propels the cell straight through the water, in the other direction it causes the cell to tumble. This change in direction is related to the ability of bacteria to respond to **chemoeffectors** and to demonstrate **chemotaxis**. They tumble more in the presence of nutrients and other attractants.

Motility in some bacteria is accomplished without flagella. Such forms exhibit "gliding motility" and can crawl over surfaces. Spirochetes exhibit still another form of motility which is made possible by their **axial filament**.

**Fimbriae** are short, straight, very thin structures found on many gram-negative bacteria. Their primary function seems to be adhesion, as they allow cells that possess them to stick to one another as well as to the cells of their hosts. Many parasitic forms of bacteria lose the ability to cause disease if they suffer a mutation that prevents them from producing fimbriae. **Pili** are structurally similar to fimbriae but are much longer and found in fewer numbers per cell. They function in a pseudosexual process in some bacteria called **conjugation**.

Many bacteria secrete a polysaccharide-based material across their surface called a **glycocalyx**. If the layer is very organized and discrete it is called a **capsule**, if it is unorganized and loosely attached it is called a **slime layer**. Capsules have several possible functions: they probably help prevent the cells from drying out, they aid the cell in resisting ingestion by phagocytic cells, and they permit adhesion to smooth surfaces such as tooth enamel (allowing the formation of dental plaque).

All bacteria (except mycoplasmas) have **cell walls.** The primary function of the cell wall is to prevent the cell from swelling up with water and bursting when placed in an environment less concentrated than the cell is. The material upon which the strength of the cell wall of bacteria depends is called **peptidoglycan.** This giant molecule is based upon chains of two amino sugars, N-acetylglucosamine (NAGA) and N-acetylmuramic acid (NAMA), along with short chains of amino acids (tetrapeptides) attached to the NAMAs. The tetrapeptide chains may be linked together with cross-links called **bridges** (or cross-bridges). These links are much more common in gram-positive cell walls than in gram-negative walls. See Figure 3-9 in the text for a schematic diagram of peptidoglycan.

Peptidoglycan accounts for 60-80% of the mass of a gram-positive bacterial cell wall. The peptidoglycan is extensively cross-linked to produce an immensely strong three-dimensional mesh. **Teichoic acids** are another material found in gram-positive cell walls. They are attached to the NAMA units and are based upon 3- or 5-carbon alcohols (glycerol or ribitol). The long teichoic acid molecules project out beyond the peptidoglycan where they serve as intense antigens and stimulate profound immune responses in animals.

Peptidoglycan accounts for only 10-20% of the mass of gram-negative cell walls. The peptidoglycan constitutes one thin layer (sparsely cross-linked) just outside the cytoplasmic membrane. Exterior to the peptidoglycan layer is a second "membrane" structure composed of proteins, **lipoproteins**, **phospholipids** and **lipopolysaccharides** (LPS). This latter material is highly toxic to animals and is called an **endotoxin**. The lipopolysaccharide is found only in the outer leaflet of the outer membrane and serves to make it more rigid than a typical membrane, as well as less permeable to hydrophobic (water fearing, water insoluble) materials. This, in turn, may help protect gram-negative cells from some harsh chemicals. Lipoproteins in the gram-negative wall extend from the outer membrane down to the peptidoglycan layer; they anchor the outer membrane to the cell.

The basic differences between gram-positive and gram-negative cell walls are clearly illustrated by seeing what happens to the cells if their peptidoglycan layer is damaged. The enzyme lysozyme dissolves the bonds between NAMA and NAGA, thus destroying the peptidoglycan. Gram-positive cells turn into **protoplasts**, surrounded by a naked cytoplasmic membrane. Such structures are extremely fragile. Gram-negative cells retain their "outer membrane" even if their peptidoglycan layer is destroyed. The become **spheroplasts** - a much less fragile structure than a protoplast.

The results of the Gram stain itself are dependent upon the structural differences between the cell walls of the two classes of organisms. When the alcohol decolorization step is performed it strips away the lipids in the gram-negative cell wall, allowing the crystal-violet-iodine complex to escape from the cells. The dense mesh of the peptidoglycan layer of the gram-positive wall retains the dye.

The **cytoplasmic membrane**, which separates the living portion of the cell from its environment, is composed of phospholipids and proteins. Phospholipids (glycerol, fatty acids and phosphate) have two ends, one **hydrophilic** (water-loving), the other **hydrophobic** (water fearing). The hydrophilic parts form the outer and inner surfaces of the membrane, with the hydrophobic parts making up the middle. Embedded in this matrix are the proteins (see Figure 3.15 in the textbook).

In many gram-positive bacteria the cytoplasmic membrane is invaginated (infolded) to produce the **mesosomes**. They undoubtedly increase the surface area of the membrane, which may have important consequences on respiration or transport. Other functions have been suggested.

The volume of the cell is filled with **cytoplasm** (cell sap). This complex mixture is 80% water and holds in suspension nucleic acids, proteins and other large molecules as well as various inclusions such as ribosomes. It also contains many dissolved materials, both organic and inorganic.

The bacterial **chromosome** is one of the materials suspended in the cytoplasm of the cell. It is not surrounded by a membrane as it would be in eucaryotes, nor is it heavily complexed with proteins. Instead it is a single, circular molecule of DNA. Some bacteria have other circular DNA molecules in their cytoplasm called **plasmids**. These small molecules do not usually contain genes necessary for bacterial growth. They are capable of being transferred to other bacteria via **conjugation** or even by artificial means as in **recombinant DNA technology**.

**Ribosomes** are another cytoplasmic inclusion. These structures are made of RNA and protein and comprise the workbenches on which protein synthesis occurs. The bacterial ribosome is of the **70S** type (S for Svedburg unit, a measure of sedimentation rate in centrifuges).

**Metachromatic granules** (**volutin granules**) are another cytoplasmic inclusion. They are composed of polyphosphate and represent a reserve supply of the essential nutrient, phosphate. Other inclusion granules may consist of glycogen, polyhydroxybutyric acid (PHB) droplets, etc. Generally they represent nutrients being stored for a "rainy day". Photosynthetic bacteria and cyanobacteria contain special cytoplasmic inclusions called **chromatophores**. These membrane systems impregnated with the pigments of photosynthesis are sometimes found as flattened sheets just beneath the cell membrane in which case they are called photosynthetic **lamellae**.

**Endospores** are highly unusual cytoplasmic inclusions produced by only two medically-important genera of bacteria, *Bacillus* and *Clostridium*. the endospore is a minute, highly durable body formed within the cell and capable of developing into a new vegetative organism. It is not a reproductive structure, since one cell makes one endospore, which can produce one new cell if it "germinates". Endospores are extremely hard to kill, as they can withstand high temperatures, radiation and chemical treatments. They are also difficult to stain.

OBJECTIVES  A study of this chapter should provide an understanding of:

1. Major groupings and shapes of bacteria.
2. Flagella, axial filaments, fimbriae and pili, capsules, the cytoplasmic membrane, and cytoplasmic inclusions such as storage granules, chromatophores, and endospores.
3. The differences between the cell wall structure for gram-positive and gram-negative cells.

## LEARNING ACTIVITIES

### Vocabulary

Having read the chapter, you should be able to define or cite the significance of the following terms. If you cannot, look them up in the text. Terms are presented in the order you will encounter them in the book.

morphology
coccus
diplococci
streptococci
staphylococci
bacillus
vibrio
spirillum
spirochete
tetrads
coccobacilli
binary fission
axial filament
fimbriae
pili
glycocalyx
capsule
slime layer
dental plaque
peptidoglycan
N-acetylglucosamine
N-acetylmuramic acid
tetrapeptide
lipoprotein
lysozyme
cytoplasmic membrane
protoplast
spheroplast
mesosome
cytoplasm
bacterial chromosome
plasmid
conjugation

stum. NB IR.
G+ intense antigens

flagellum
monotrichous
amphitrichous
lophotrichous
peritrichous
chemotaxis
chemoattractants
teichoic acids
antigenic
phospholipid
lipopolysaccharide
endotoxin
hydrophobic
hydrophilic
70S ribosome
metachromatic granules
volutin
chromatophores
endospore
sporulation

Complete each of the following statements by supplying the missing word or words.

1. MORPHOLOGY__________ is a term which includes the external shape of cells, cell arrangements, and the internal anatomy of cells.

2. coccus__________ are bacteria which are spherical in shape (round in cross section).

3. streptococci__________ is an arrangement of spherical bacterial cells in which the cells are in long chains.

4. spirochetes__________ are flexible spiral bacteria.

5. Flagella__________ are thin, protein-based structures which are responsible for movement in most motile bacteria.

6. CHEMOTAXIS__________ is a term used to describe the movement of bacteria toward attractants or away from irritants.

7. Fimbriae__________ are short, straight, very thin structures found on many gram-negative bacteria.

8. pili__________ are longer than fimbriae and are used exclusively during conjugation.

9. Peritrichous__________ bacteria have flagella scattered over their entire surface.

10. Capsule__________ is the term used for a glycocalyx if it is very organized and discrete.

11. Peptidoglycan__________ is the name of the material most responsible for the strength of bacterial cell walls.

12. N-acetylglusosamine__________ and N-acetylmuramic acid are the two main sugars found in peptidoglycan.

13. ___60% to 80%___ of the mass of a gram-positive cell wall is composed of peptidoglycan. Only 10-20% of a gram-negative wall is peptidoglycan.

14. ___Teichoic acids___ are found in the walls of gram-positive bacteria. They are based upon chains of glycerol or ribitol.

15. ___Lipopolysacchride___ is found only in gram-negative cell walls and is often called endotoxin.

16. ___mesosomes___ are invaginated areas of cytoplasmic membrane found in many gram-positive bacteria.

17. ___plasmids___ are small, circular DNA molecules found in some bacterial cells.

18. ___ribosomes___, composed of RNA and protein, are the workbenches on which protein synthesis occurs.

19. ___metachromatic granules___, also called volutin granules, are cytoplasmic inclusions which are composed of polyphosphate.

20. ___Endospores___ are extremely durable bodies formed within the cells of *Bacillus* and *Clostridium*. They are incredibly hard to kill.

Fill in the following chart with a "+" if the structure is found in the cells, a "-" if it is not.

| STRUCTURE'S NAME | PRESENT IN THE CELLS OF | |
|---|---|---|
| | GRAM-POSITIVE | GRAM-NEGATIVE |
| TEICHOIC ACIDS | ✓ | |
| LIPOPOLYSACCHARIDES | | |
| MESOSOMES | ✓ | |
| LIPOPROTEIN | | |
| PILI | | |
| FIMBRIAE | | |
| THICK PEPTIDOGLYCAN LAYER | ✓ | |
| ENDOTOXIN | | |

MASTERY TEST

1-9: Circle the choice that best answers the questions.

1. All of the following are components of peptidoglycan EXCEPT:
   a. N-acetylmuramic acid
   b. tetrapeptides
   c. N-acetyldipicolinic acid
   d. N-acetylglucosamine

2. All of the following are bacterial shapes EXCEPT:
   a. cocci
   b. bacilli
   c. vibrios
   d. coccobacilli
   e. tetrads

3. Spirochetes are unique in that they always possess a(n):
   a. flagellum
   b. axial filament
   c. mesosome
   d. pilus
   e. nucleus

4. The results of the gram stain are directly related to differences in the ________________ of gram-positive and gram-negative bacteria.
   a. cell walls
   b. cytoplasmic membranes
   c. flagella
   d. mesosomes
   e. capsule

5. Gliding motility occurs in bacteria and cyanobacteria which are:
   a. entirely lacking flagella
   b. lophotrichous
   c. covered with fimbriae
   d. amphitrichous
   e. spheroplasts

6. Pili allow the transfer of DNA from one cell to another during a process called:
   a. fermentation
   b. sporulation
   c. respiration
   d. conjugation
   e. ovulation

7. Treatment of gram-positive cells with lysozyme produces the protoplast; treatment of gram-negative cells with lysozyme produces the:
   a. xeroplast
   b. spheroplast
   c. tonoplast
   d. protoplast
   e. cytoplast

8. The main components of the cytoplasmic membrane are phospholipids and:
   a. N-acetylglucosamine
   b. protein
   c. N-acetylmuramic acid
   d. lipoprotein
   e. lipopolysaccharide

9. The capsule (glycocalyx) is thought to be useful for all of the following EXCEPT:
   a. prevents microbes from drying out
   b. provides extracellular nutrient storage
   c. protects the microbes from phagocytosis
   d. protects the microbe from virus attack

---

10-16: Match the anatomical description with its name (use no answer twice)

ANSWERS

A. amphitrichous
B. bacilli
C. cocci
D. coccobacilli
E. diplococci
F. lophotrichous
G. monotrichous
H. peritrichous
I. spheroplast
J. spirilla
K. spirochetes
L. staphylococci
M. streptococci
N. tetrads
O. vibrios

vibrios O 10. Type of bacterial cell which could be described as a curved rod.

staphylococci L 11. Arrangement in which cells are found in irregular clusters (resembling bunches of grapes).

D 12. Bacilli which are so short they might be confused with cocci are called: coccobacilli

G 13. Cells which contain ONE flagellum (usually in a polar position) are said to be: monotrichous

F 14. A similar arrangement to the above is one in which a tuft of several flagella are found on one end of the cell. This type of flagellation is called: Lophotrichous

J 15. Rigid cells of spiral form are called: spirilla

K 16. Flexible cells of spiral form are called: spirochetes

---

17-20: Circle the choice that best answers the questions.

17. Fimbriae are thought to perform all of the following functions EXCEPT:
   a. provide limited cell motility
   b. permit cells to attach to one another
   c. permit cells to attach to host cells
   d. permit attachment to polysaccharides
   e. all of these are functions of fimbriae

18. All of the following are true of the bacterial flagellum EXCEPT:
   a. flagella rotate like a ship's propeller
   b. flagella are driven by electrons entering the cell
   c. flagella are not formed from microtubules
   d. flagella originate from the cytoplasmic membrane

19. The term "hydrophobic" means:
   a. water loving; water soluble
   b. water seeking chemotaxis
   c. water fearing; insoluble in water
   d. water absorbing; hydroscopic

20. Teichoic acids are referred to as "antigenic", which means that they:
   a. confer camouflage on the cell, hiding it from the immune system
   b. protect the cell from phagocytosis
   c. stimulate a profound immune response
   d. permit transfer of DNA from cell to cell
   e. all of these are true of antigenic materials

---

21-25: TRUE-FALSE: (T for true, F for false)

F ____ 21. Metachromatic granules are commonly found in cells growing in phosphate-poor environments.

F ____ 22. Chromatophores are structures found in all aerobic bacteria, but never in anaerobes.

T ____ 23. The main purpose of complex sterilization procedures used in the canning industry and in medicine is to be sure that endospores are killed.

F ____ 24. Endospore production (sporulation) is a true example of bacterial reproduction.

T ____ 25. The results of the gram stain are totally due to the differences between the gram-positive and gram-negative cell walls.

ANSWERS TO LEARNING ACTIVITIES

Fill-in-the-blank questions:
1. Morphology; 2. Cocci; 3. Streptococci; 4. Spirochetes; 5. Flagella; 6. Chemotaxis; 7. Fimbriae; 8. Pili; 9. Peritrichous; 10. Capsule; 11. Peptidoglycan; 12. N-Acetylglucosamine; 13. 60-80%; 14. Teichoic acids; 15. Lipopolysaccharides; 16. Mesosomes; 17. Plasmids; 18. Ribosomes; 19. Metachromatic granules; 20. Endospores.

| STRUCTURE'S NAME | PRESENT IN THE CELLS OF | |
|---|---|---|
| | GRAM POSITIVE | GRAM NEGATIVE |
| TEICHOIC ACIDS | + | - |
| LIPOPOLYSACCHARIDES | - | + |
| MESOSOMES | + | - |
| LIPOPROTEIN | - | + |
| PILI | - | + |
| FIMBRIAE | - | + |
| THICK PEPTIDOGLYCAN LAYER | + | - |
| ENDOTOXIN | - | + |

**MASTERY TEST ANSWERS**

| | | | | | | | | | | | | |
|---|---|---|---|---|---|---|---|---|---|---|---|---|
| 1 c | 2 e | 3 b | 4 a | 5 a | 6 d | | 7 b | 8 b | 9 d | 10 O | 11 L | 12 D |
| 13 G | 14 F | 15 J | 16 K | 17 a | 18 b | 19 c | 20 c | 21 F | 22 F | 23 T | 24 F | 25 T |

# CHAPTER 4

# <u>PROPERTIES OF BIOLOGICAL MOLECULES</u>

## <u>CHAPTER SUMMARY</u>

Pasteur predicted it, Hans Buchner proved it; cell-free extracts of yeast cells can change sugar to alcohol. We now know the change is effected by **enzymes**, a member of one of the four main classes of organic macromolecules (macro- means large). The four classes are the **proteins** (which includes enzymes), **polysaccharides**, **lipids**, and **nucleic acids**.

Macromolecules, like all chemical compounds, are held together by **chemical bonds**. Some chemical bonds involve the sharing of electrons between two atoms, others involve electrostatic attractions between oppositely charged atoms. **Covalent bonds** involve shared electrons. They are very strong and are the basic type holding together organic molecules. **Ionic bonds** are much weaker. They form between atoms that have lost electrons (positive charge) and atoms that have gained electrons (negative charge). **Hydrogen bonds** are the weakest of all. They form between atoms with slight positive charges (usually hydrogen atoms in organic molecules or water) and atoms with slight negative charges (often oxygen or nitrogen).

Some molecules, such as proteins, have all three types of bonds. Proteins are composed of subunits called amino acids (so called because each molecule contains an amino group and a carboxyl group). There are 20 different kinds of amino acids. Individual amino acids are bonded together by strong covalent bonds called **peptide bonds**. Different proteins (they are either **structural proteins** or **enzymes**) differ in the sequence of amino acids that make up their chains. The reaction that results in bonding two amino acids together is an important and universal one called **dehydration synthesis** (water is released during its formation). The reverse reaction, called **hydrolysis**, uses water molecules to break the bonds between amino acids in proteins.

The long chains of amino acids that make up the protein fold and twist in a complicated fashion to produce a three-dimensional **tertiary structure**. This structure is largely stabilized by weak ionic and hydrogen bonds (although some strong **disulfide** covalent bonds help). If the tertiary structure of a protein is changed by external forces (like heat) the protein won't work properly any more. Such proteins are said to be **denatured**.

Polysaccharides are long chains of simple sugars (**monosaccharides**) held together by strong covalent bonds called **glycosidic bonds**. These bonds are produced by dehydration synthesis reactions, just like the peptide bonds in proteins. The most common monosaccharides used are **pentoses** (five carbons) and **hexoses** (six carbons). If polysaccharides are complexed with protein they are called **glycoproteins**; if complexed with lipids they are called **lipopolysaccharides**. Polysaccharides may have a **structural** function (cell walls), or they may be used for **energy storage** (e.g. glycogen and starch).

Lipids are molecules composed mostly of carbon and hydrogen atoms. **Fatty acids** are lipids with carboxyl groups at one end. They can be combined with glycerol to form **glycerides** (glycerol + 3 fatty acids = **triglyceride**; glycerol + 2 fatty acids + phosphate = **phosphodiglyceride** or **phospholipid**). The strong covalent bonds that hold together the glycerol and the fatty acid are called **ester bonds**. Phospholipids are especially important because they are a basic component of cell membranes. Their structure includes a portion which is **hydrophilic** (water loving) and another portion which is **hydrophobic** (water fearing). The hydrophilic portion tries to be in contact with water while the hydrophobic portion tries to stay away from water. Thus phospholipids automatically self-assemble into double-layered structures with two hydrophilic surfaces and a hydrophobic core (see Figure 4.8 in the Text).

None of these molecules make themselves; they are all produced in reactions which require a **catalyst** in order to proceed at reasonable speed. Catalysts speed up chemical reactions without being used up in the reaction. Organic catalysts are called **enzymes**. Enzymes serve two main functions in cells: they break down or oxidize food material to provide energy and they use this energy for the synthesis of new cell material. Enzymes are moderately specific because their natural **substrate** (the compound upon which an enzyme exerts its catalytic effect) must fit into its **active site**. Molecules that are too big or too small or of the wrong shape will not fit into the active site and will not be acted upon by the enzyme.

Catalysts like enzymes work by lowering the **energy of activation** requirement for a reaction. Even reactions which are very favorable do not occur spontaneously; they need a spark to touch them off. The strength of the spark required is reduced in the presence of a catalyst - that's what catalysts are for.

Enzymes are typically named by adding the suffix **-ase** to the end of the substrate's or the product's name. Enzymes are divided into six major classes after the type of reaction which the catalyze. **Oxidoreductases** carry out oxidation and/or reduction types of reactions. **Transferases** move chemical groups (such as amines, carboxyls, phosphates, etc.) from one substrate to another. **Hydrolases** break down (**hydrolyze**) macromolecules into their constituent building blocks, using water as a coreactant. Many bacteria secrete such enzymes into the external environment as **exoenzymes**. **Lyases** are enzymes which remove chemical groups from molecules, leaving a double bond (or they add groups to double bonds). **Isomerases** change one isomer to another (isomers are molecules with the same number and kind of atoms but in different arrangements). **Ligases** (synthetases) catalyze the linking together of two molecules (e.g. two amino acids into a peptide).

Some enzymes need help. If the helper is a small, organic molecule often working as a carrier of a group being transferred from one molecule to another the helper is called a **coenzyme**. The B vitamins are used by our bodies as precursors to form coenzymes.

The three-dimensional tertiary structure of proteins is easily damaged, and any environmental factor that disturbs it will reduce the enzymes's performance. Temperature and pH are two important environmental factors that effect enzymes. In both cases there is an **optimum** (pH or temperature) above or below which the enzyme functions poorly. The activity of enzymes is also related to available substrate concentration. Enzyme activity increases with increasing substrate concentration **up to a point**. In all cases there is a substrate concentration which produces maximal activity and beyond which no further increase occurs. This point is called **saturation**.

Many of the reactions occurring in cells release energy; such reactions are often used to produce **ATP** (**a**denosine **trip**hosphate). The hydrolysis of ATP is an important energy-yielding reaction in cells, since the two terminal phosphates in ATP release approximately 8000 calories when hydrolyzed. There are two main ways in which ATP can be produced: by substrate phosphorylation or by oxidative phosphorylation. Anaerobic breakdown of sugar depends upon substrate phosphorylation and produces only 2 ATP per glucose; aerobic breakdown, using oxidative phosphorylation, produces 36 to 38 ATP per glucose.

OBJECTIVES After studying this chapter, you should:

1. Know the basic components of proteins, polysaccharides, and lipids.
2. Understand how phospholipids interact to form a cell membrane.
3. Be sure to describe what is meant by the tertiary structure of proteins.
4. Know what enzymes do and be able to list the general types of enzymes.
5. Understand how energy is liberated and stored.

## LEARNING ACTIVITIES

### Vocabulary

Having read the chapter, you should be able to define or cite the significance of the following terms. If you cannot, look them up in the text. Terms are presented in the order you will encounter them in the book.

proteins
polysaccharides
lipids
nucleic acids
electrons
covalent bonds
ionic bonds
hydrogen bonds
peptide bond
dehydration synthesis
hydrolysis
tertiary structure
disulfide bonds
denatured
catalysts
enzymes
glycosidic bonds
simple sugars
monosaccharides
pentoses
hexoses
glycoproteins
ester bond
triglyceride
phospholipid
substrate
active site
energy of activation
-ase
oxidoreductases
dehydrogenases
oxidation
transferases
kinases
hydrolases
exoenzymes
cellulases
amylases
proteases
lipases
nucleases
lyases
isomerases
recemases
epimerases
ligases
synthetases
coenzymes
optimum pH
optimum temperature
saturated
affinity
ATP
adenosine triphosphate
high-energy phosphate
substrate phosphorylation
oxidative phosphorylation

Complete each of the following statements by supplying the missing word or words.

1. ____________________ was the first individual to carry out the conversion of sugar to alcohol using yeast cell extracts.

2. ____________________, ____________________, are two of the four classes of organic macromolecules.

3. ____________________ bonds form when two atoms share one or more electrons.

4. ____________________ bonds form between atoms which have gained or lost electrons and therefore have an electrical charge.

5. ____________________ bonds are the specific type of bond involved in protein formation.

6. ____________________ is the number of different kinds of amino acids found in proteins.

7. ____________________ is the full name of the reaction type involved in making proteins out of amino acids, polysaccharides out of sugars, and glycerides out of glycerol and fatty acids.

8. ____________________ is the name for the opposite process to that discussed in #7, in which water is used to break the bonds in proteins, polysaccharides, etc.

9. ____________________ is the technical name for simple sugars. They are linked together to make polysaccharides.

10. ____________________ are polysaccharides that are bonded to proteins.

11. ____________________ are molecules formed from glycerol plus three fatty acids.

12. ____________________ are molecules formed from glycerol, two fatty acids, phosphate, and choline or ethanolamine. They are important constituents of cell membranes.

13. ____________________ are materials which speed up chemical reactions without being used up in the reaction.

14. ____________________ is the compound upon which an enzyme exerts its catalytic effect.

15. ____________________ is the region of an enzyme into which the substrate must fit. The fit must be precise.

16. ____________________ is the class of enzymes which carry out energy-releasing reactions for the cell.

17. ____________________ are an important class of enzymes which break down macromolecules into their constituent parts by hydrolysis reactions.

18. ____________________ are small organic molecules needed by some enzymes as a carrier of an organic group or hydrogen atoms.

19. ____________________ and temperature are two environmental factors that can effect enzyme activity.

20. ____________________ breakdown of sugar only produces 2 ATP per glucose as opposed to 36 ATP per glucose for aerobic breakdown.

## MASTERY TEST

1-9: Circle the choice that best answers the questions.

1. Which of the following groups would be called an aldehyde?

```
         O                                          H
         ‖                                         /
a.   R-C-OH                          c.     R-N
                                                  \
                                                   H

         O
         ‖
b.   R-C-H                           d.     R-OH
```

2. Which of the following is NOT one of the four major groups of biologically important macromolecules?
   a. Proteins
   b. Monosaccharides
   c. Polysaccharides
   d. Lipids
   e. Nucleic Acids

3. In hydrogen bonds, the atom which most frequently has the slight positive charge is:
   a. hydrogen
   b. carbon
   c. oxygen
   d. nitrogen
   e. chlorine

4. Which of the following bonds is the strongest?
   a. covalent
   b. hydrogen
   c. ionic

5. Amino acids are fairly complex for small molecules. In addition to an amino group, they also always possess a:
   a. hydroxyl group
   b. methyl group
   c. keto group
   d. carboxyl group
   e. sulfhydryl group

6. Amino acids to proteins, sugars to polysaccharides, fatty acids and glycerol to glycerides; all are made possible by which of the following reaction types?
   a. oxidation
   b. reduction
   c. dehydrogenation
   d. hydrolysis
   e. dehydration synthesis

7. If a protein is exposed to conditions which cause its structure to be so altered that its function is destroyed it is said to have been:
   a. dehydrogenated
   b. denatured
   c. acidified
   d. oxidized
   e. reduced

8. A simple sugar (monosaccharide) which contains five carbon atoms is called a(n):
   a. aldehyde
   b. pentagon
   c. hexagon
   d. pentose
   e. hexose

9. A complex molecule containing lipid and polysaccharide portions is called a(n):
   a. lipoprotein
   b. phospholipid
   c. lipopolysaccharide
   d. glycoprotein
   e. none of these

---

10-15: In the following table, fill in the appropriate term for the specific bond type found linking together molecules in the macromolecule and the name of the building block (small molecule) used to make the macromolecule.

| MACROMOLECULE | LINKING BOND TYPE | BUILDING BLOCK |
|---|---|---|
| **Protein** | 10. | 13. |
| **Polysaccharide** | 11. | 14. |
| **Glyceride** | 12. | 15. |

16-25: Circle the choice that best answers the questions.

16. Phospholipids self-assemble to produce a double-layered structure in water in such a way that the hydrophilic "head groups" are facing outward toward the aqueous environment, while their ______________ groups face inward.
   a. hydrophobic
   b. parabolic
   c. hydroxyl
   d. denatured
   e. esterified

17. An example of an inorganic catalyst (it is used in the catalytic converter on your car) is:
   a. plutonium
   b. iodine
   c. platinum
   d. potassium
   e. sodium

18. The molecule upon which an enzyme exerts its catalytic effect is the:
a. inhibitor
b. active site
c. catalyst
d. kinase
e. substrate

19. Which of the following classes of enzymes is capable of linking together two molecules (acting as a synthetase)?
a. oxidoreductases
b. transferases
c. hydrolases
d. isomerases
e. ligases

20. Which of the following classes of enzymes is capable of performing the opposite function to that described in the previous question, i.e. breaking down a macromolecule into its constituent parts?
a. oxidoreductases
b. transferases
c. hydrolases
d. isomerases
e. ligases

21. Exoenzymes secreted by bacteria are sometimes capable of acting as:
a. toxins
b. ligases
c. recemases
d. antibodies
e. hydrophobics

22. The B vitamins are converted into ________________ by human cells and by bacterial cells.
a. enzymes
b. glycoproteins
c. coenzymes
d. antigens
e. amino acids

23. The temperature at which an enzyme operates best is called the:
a. optimum temperature
b. best temperature
c. high temperature
d. maximum temperature
e. peak temperature

24. _____-affinity enzymes reach saturation at very low substrate concentrations.
a. high b. low c. medium

25. The ________________ phosphate bonds on ATP are high-energy phosphate bonds.
a. first, second, and third
b. first and third
c. second and third
d. third only

## ANSWERS TO LEARNING ACTIVITIES

Fill-in-the-blank questions:
1. Hans Buchner; 2. Proteins, Polysaccharides, Lipids, and/or Nucleic Acids; 3. Covalent bonds; 4. Ionic bonds; 5. Peptide; 6. 20; 7. Dehydration synthesis; 8. Hydrolysis; 9. Monosaccharides; 10. Glycoproteins; 11. Triglycerides; 12. Phospholipids; 13. Catalysts; 14. Substrate; 15. Active site; 16. Oxidoreductases; 17. Hydrolases; 18. Coenzymes; 19. pH; 20. Anaerobic.

## ANSWERS TO MASTERY TEST

1. b; 2. b; 3. a; 4. a; 5. d; 6. e; 7. b; 8. d; 9. c;

| MACROMOLECULE | LINKING BOND TYPE | BUILDING BLOCK |
|---|---|---|
| **Protein** | 10. Peptide | 13. Amino Acids |
| **Polysaccharide** | 11. Glycosidic | 14. Simple Sugars (Monosaccharides) |
| **Glyceride** | 12. Ester | 15. Glycerol and Fatty Acids |

16. a; 17. c; 18. e; 19. e; 20. c; 21. a; 22. c; 23. a; 24. b; 25. c.

# CHAPTER 5

## BACTERIAL NUTRITION

### CHAPTER SUMMARY

Organisms need **nutrients** to synthesize new body mass and to supply energy for life processes. The exact materials they need and the means by which it is assimilated is called **nutrition**. For most organisms nutrients come from food, but the food must first be digested. Bacteria and fungi, being unable to ingest solid matter, must **digest** their food externally using exoenzymes. Much of their food is oxidized for energy.

All organisms need water and nutrients of the following types: a carbon source, a nitrogen source, inorganic ions, and essential metabolites (vitamins, etc.). Bacteria are fortunate in that they can assimilate carbon from virtually any organic material. Some bacteria get their **nitrogen** directly from atmospheric nitrogen gas *via* a process called **nitrogen fixation**. Other bacteria can utilize inorganic sources such as ammonium salts, while still others must have organic **bound nitrogen**.

Inorganic nutrients required by most organisms include **phosphate**, **sulfur**, and various **ions**. Phosphate is needed for structural purposes and as part of ATP and other high energy compounds. Sulfur is found in two of the twenty amino acids. Many of the ions are needed as **cofactors** of enzymes (similar to coenzymes, only inorganic). Iron may be a particularly difficult ion to assimilate. Most bacteria secrete **siderophores** which capture the iron and allow it to be brought into the cell. Successfully pathogenic bacteria must make siderophores that can "steal" iron from their host's iron-binding proteins (**transferrin** or **lactoferrin**).

**Essential metabolites** are organic molecules needed by an organism but which it cannot make for itself. Some bacteria are so biochemically adept that they need none of these materials, others are so biochemically incompetent that they need a drugstore full of them. Many bacteria require at least some of the B vitamins, some amino acids, or a pyrimidine or two. Pathogens, in particular, tend to have complex nutritional needs. Table 5.1 in your textbook lists some of the important B vitamins and some of their functions.

Eucaryotic cells, particularly those of animals, are harder to culture than are bacteria. Complex media supplemented with **protein growth factors** which stimulate cell division are required for such cell cultures.

Good growth of microbes requires more than supplying the cells with nutrients. Their environment must also have the proper pH (for most bacteria between pH 4 and pH 7.4). **Buffers** must also be incorporated to overcome the acidic or basic products of microbial metabolism. Typical buffers like potassium phosphate function as acids at high pH (donating $H^+$ ions) and as bases at low pH (absorbing excess $H^+$ ions).

Bacteria will also grow best if their environmental temperature is to their liking. Most bacteria, called **mesophiles**, are happiest at temperatures between 20 and 40°C. **Psychrophiles** like cold temperatures (between 0 and +20°C) - some can even grow in your refrigerator! **Thermophiles** are heat-loving bacteria; they are happiest at temperatures above 45 to 50°C.

Oxygen must be supplied to aerobes; facultative anaerobes can take it or leave it. Many obligate anaerobes, however, must be protected from oxygen, since it can kill them. The main reason for this toxicity seems to relate to the fact that anaerobes do not make two enzymes, superoxide dismutase and catalase, that are necessary for survival in contact with molecular oxygen. Anaerobes die, then, from the toxic effects of the superoxide ion or hydrogen peroxide.

If everything is set up properly, **growth** should occur. A bacterium divides by **binary fission**, each daughter cell then divides also and growth in numbers proceeds in an exponential (logarithmic) fashion. Growth can be quantified in a variety of ways. One of the commonest and most important is performed on pour-plates which contain diluted samples of the material being quantified. One merely **counts the colonies** on the plate that has 30 to 300 colonies on it and multiplies the colony number by the **dilution factor** to obtain the original population density [$B_o$ = (D)(C); initial number = dilution factor times colony count]. This method is direct, quite accurate, and counts only **viable bacteria** (bacteria which were alive and capable of forming colonies). Similar results can be achieved by the **membrane filter** method (filter a diluted sample through a membrane filter, place the filter on growth media, count the resultant colonies). Again, only viable bacteria are counted.

Other techniques for quantifying bacteria numbers have a major drawback in that they count both dead and living cells. Measurements of dry weight, total nitrogen content, turbidity, and direct counts (using stained smears, *Petroff-Hauser Counting Chamber*, or **Coulter counters**) all will overestimate the viable cell numbers obtained by colony counting.

When careful studies on microbial growth are carried out a repetitive pattern emerges (see Figure 5.4 in the textbook). The pattern includes four phases of growth, the first of which is called the **lag phase**. No cell divisions occur during the lag phase, so cell number is constant. Cells do grow in size, however, as they build up cell mass and synthesize new enzymes needed for the period of growth to come. Next comes the **log phase** (logarithmic growth phase) during which the cells divide at their maximal rate. The population doubles every few minutes or hours (depending upon the organism's **generation time**). This produces a straight line if the log of cell numbers is being plotted. Food is plentiful in the log phase, wastes have not built up yet, and plenty of oxygen should be available for aerobes.

The log phase continues until the supply of food begins to be depleted, toxic waste products build up, or population density exceeds the oxygen supply. At this point the **stationary phase** begins. During the stationary phase there is either no cell division or cells dividing are balanced by cells dying. In either case the population is constant. Endospore forming bacteria undergo sporulation in this phase.

Eventually food runs out completely (or toxic wastes reach lethal levels). At this point cells begin to die off faster then they are replaced. Total die-off may be rapid (1 day or less) or may be prolonged for weeks. Cells in this phase often look highly abnormal (**involution forms**).

## OBJECTIVES

After studying this chapter, you should know and understand:

1. The basic nutrients required for bacterial growth.
2. The external conditions necessary for bacterial growth, and how bacteria can be categorized according to their optimal growth temperature.
3. How a buffer works to stabilize the pH.
4. Why oxygen is toxic to anaerobic organisms.
5. How to enumerate bacteria.
6. A bacterial growth curve and what occurs during each phase of growth.

## LEARNING ACTIVITIES

### Vocabulary

Having read the chapter, you should be able to define or cite the significance of the following terms. If you cannot, look them up in the text. Terms are presented in the order you will encounter them in the book.

nutrition
nutrients
digestion
carbon source
nitrogen source
nitrogen fixation
bound nitrogen
protein growth factors
buffer
transmembrane signal
mesophiles
psychrophiles
thermophiles
logarithmic
colony counting
dilution factor
membrane filter
viable bacteria
turbidity
Coulter counter

cofactors
siderophores
transferrin
lactoferrin
essential
metabolites
B Vitamins

superoxide
superoxide
dismutase
catalase → Hydrogen peroxide ($H_2O_2$)
growth
exponential

generation time
lag phase
log phase
synchronous growth
chemostat
stationary phase
death phase

Complete each of the following statements by supplying the missing word or words.

1. __nutrition__ is the process which concerns the kind of food used by an organism and the methods by which it is assimilated and utilized.

2. __digestion__ is necessary to convert food to useable nutrients; it must be performed outside of the cell in bacteria and fungi.

3. __Carbon__ is available to bacteria by the breakdown of virtually any organic material (with the possible exception of synthetic plastics and a few pesticides).

4. __nitrogen fixation__ is a process whereby bacteria can use atmospheric nitrogen to satisfy their needs for this nutrient.

5. __siderophores__ are compounds secreted by bacteria which solubilize and bind to iron so the cell can absorb it. Successful pathogens make especially good ones.

6. __Essential metabolites__ are organic molecules needed by bacteria because they cannot make their own due to biochemical deficiencies. Vitamins are a common example.

7. __Pyridoxine ($B_6$)__ is one of the B vitamins which functions as a coenzyme in deamination, transamination, and decarboxylation reactions of amino acids.

Mycobacterium leprae (leprosy)

8. __T. Pallidum (syphilis)__ is an example of a pathogenic bacterium that has such complex nutritional requirements it has never been grown in artificial culture.

9. __Buffers__ are needed in growth media to maintain a stable pH even if the microbe is releasing acids or bases as part of its metabolism.

10. psychrophiles are capable of growing in refrigerators and could not, in fact, grow successfully in the human body. All human pathogens are mesophiles.

11. Superoxide is an extremely reactive free radical of oxygen which is deadly to anaerobes (which lack an enzyme to destroy the substance).

12. growth is defined as a process resulting in an increase in number of constituent cells. In microbes it is an exponential (logarithmic) process.

13. Colony counting is an accurate way to determine the number of viable cells in a sample. It can be done in a pour-plate or using a membrane filter method.

14. Dead and living cells are counted in most techniques that measure dry weight, total nitrogen, or in direct cell counts.

15. Turbidity is a term which describes the cloudiness of a liquid culture of bacteria which is just detectable when populations of 10 million bacteria per milliliter are reached.

On the following graph, draw a typical bacterial growth curve and label it appropriately. Explain what is happening in each phase of growth and cite the reasons for that activity.

A: LAG phase: cells begin to synthesize inducible enzymes & use stored food reserves.
B: Log phase: the rate of multiplication is constant.
C: Stationary phase: death rate is equal to rate of increase
D: Death phase: cells begin to die at a more rapid rate than that of reproduction

Log
#
Cells

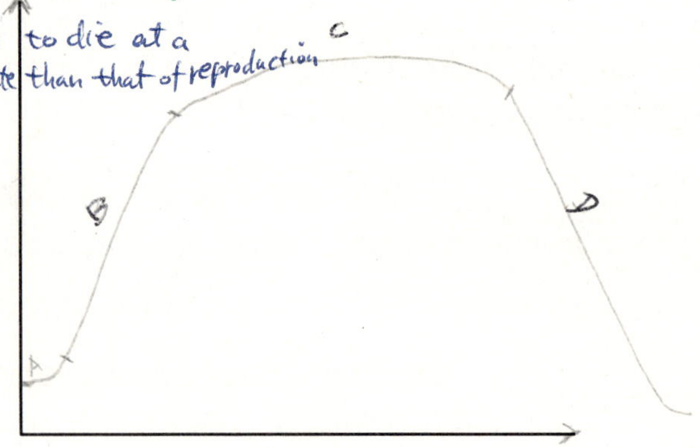


Time

## MASTERY TEST

1-16: Circle the choice that best answers the questions.

1. All of the following are nutrients needed by all organisms EXCEPT:
   a. a carbon source
   b. an oxygen source
   c. a nitrogen source
   d. inorganic ions
   e. essential metabolites

2. Bacteria and fungi must obtain their nutrients in dissolved form because, unlike animal cells, they cannot __________ solid food.
   a. digest
   b. encounter
   c. ingest
   d. oxidize
   e. reduce

3. All of the following are known to be acceptable sources of carbon to bacteria EXCEPT:
   a. wood
   b. asphalt
   c. gasoline
   d. carbon dioxide
   e. synthetic plastics

4. Which of the following is an example of bound (organic) nitrogen?
   a. nitrogen gas
   b. ammonium salts
   c. peptide digests
   d. nitrates, nitrites
   e. sulfites

5. Many of the inorganic ions required by bacteria serve as enzyme helpers. Such ions are called:
   a. coenzymes
   b. cofactors
   c. coeds
   d. coreactants
   e. carboxyls

6. Siderophores in bacteria and the proteins transferrin and lactoferrin in humans all have the ability to bind:
   a. calcium
   b. iodine
   c. platinum
   d. iron
   e. energy

7. All of the following are common essential metabolites except:
   a. nicotinic acid
   b. thiamine
   c. riboflavin
   d. pantothenic acid
   e. superoxide

8. Most vitamins are converted to _______ in cells.
a. cofactors
b. energy
c. peroxides
d. coenzymes
e. hydrophilics

9. Many eucaryotic cells require more than nutrients to be successfully cultured. They also require _____________ which bind to specific receptors on the cell membrane and initiate a transmembrane signal which triggers cell division.
a. essential metabolites
b. protein growth factors
c. antigen-antibody pairs
d. protein kinase
e. hydrogen peroxide

10. Which of the following prefers temperatures in excess of 45-50°C?
a. anglophiles
b. hydrophiles
c. mesophiles
d. psychrophiles
e. thermophiles

11. Which of the following includes all pathogens of humans and other warm-blooded animals?
a. anglophiles
b. hydrophiles
c. mesophiles
d. psychrophiles
e. thermophiles

12. Aerobic organisms contain an enzyme called superoxide dismutase which can convert the superoxide radical to the slightly less dangerous:
a. ozone molecule
b. hydrogen peroxide
c. supraoxide radical
d. singlet oxygen
e. hydroxide

13. If a bacterium has a generation time of 20 minutes and starts with a population of 400 cells per milliliter, how many cells will be present in 2 hours (assuming log growth throughout)?
a. 12,800/ml
b. 25,600/ml
c. 409,600/ml
d. 3,276,800/ml
e. 13,107,200/ml

14. When counting colonies, one should always try to count plates with:
a. between 30 and 300 colonies
b. between 10 and 100 colonies
c. between 256 and 512 colonies
d. between 2,000 and 3,000 colonies

15. Both colony counting and membrane filter techniques count only ____________ cells
a. live
b. dead
c. viable
d. labile
e. vigorous

16. If you count 226 colonies on a plate which represents a 1:100,000 dilution, the original solution contained how many cells per milliliter?
a. 226,000
b. 2,260
c. 2,260,000
d. 226
e. 22,600,000

17-25: MATCHING: Match the description, characteristic, utility with the phase in bacterial growth cycle. You MAY use answers more than once.

ANSWERS

A. Lag Phase
B. Log Growth Phase
C. Stationary Phase
D. Death Phase

_____ 17. Cells in this phase reach their maximum size.

_____ 18. Cells in this phase are often highly abnormal "involution forms".

_____ 19. Cells can be maintained in this phase easily using a chemostat.

_____ 20. Cells in this phase are most easily killed by antibiotic treatment.

_____ 21. Cell divisions are exactly balanced by cell deaths in this phase.

_____ 22. The main cause of this phase is the total exhaustion of food and/or the buildup of wastes to toxic levels.

_____ 23. Endospore production occurs principally in this phase.

_____ 24. This phase may last anywhere from a day to weeks or even months for some species.

_____ 25. The typical characteristics of active cells should generally be observed in this phase.

---

## ANSWERS TO LEARNING ACTIVITIES

Fill-in-the-blank questions:
1. Nutrition; 2. Digestion; 3. Carbon; 4. Nitrogen fixation;
5. Siderophores; 6. Essential metabolites; 7. $B_6$ (pyridoxine);

8. *T. pallidum* or *Mycobacterium leprae*; 9. Buffers; 10. Psychrophiles; 11. Superoxide; 12. Growth; 13. Colony counting; 14. Dead; 15. Turbidity; 16-20: Check against Figure 5-4 in your Textbook.

| MASTERY TEST ANSWERS | | | | | | | | | | | | |
|---|---|---|---|---|---|---|---|---|---|---|---|---|
| 1<br>b | 2<br>c | 3<br>e | 4<br>c | 5<br>b | 6<br>d | | 7<br>e | 8<br>d | 9<br>b | 10<br>e | 11<br>c | 12<br>b |
| 13<br>b | 14<br>a | 15<br>e | 16<br>e | 17<br>A | 18<br>D | 19<br>B | 20<br>B | 21<br>C | 22<br>D | 23<br>C | 24<br>D | 25<br>B |

# CHAPTER 6

# BACTERIAL METABOLISM

## CHAPTER SUMMARY

The sum of all chemical reactions in a cell is called **metabolism**. It can be divided into two mirror-image processes called **anabolism** and **catabolism**. Anabolism involves the synthesis of macromolecules and uses energy. Catabolism involves the oxidation and breakdown of macromolecules and releases usable energy. Many of the reactions that occur during catabolism are **oxidation** reactions. Oxidations result in a loss of electrons and a release of energy. Many of the reactions that occur in anabolism are **reduction** reactions. Reductions result in a gain of electrons and require an input of energy.

**Dehydrogenases** are a class of enzymes that perform biological oxidations. In biology, oxidation results in a loss of **hydrogen atoms** (hydrogen ions plus their electrons) rather than just electrons. These are transferred by dehydrogenase enzymes from the oxidized molecule to a coenzyme electron acceptor such as **$NAD^+$** (**N**icotinamide **A**denine **D**inucleotide) or **$NADP^+$** (**N**icotinamide **A**denine **D**inucleotide **P**hosphate). The reduced coenzymes (e.g. NADH) are eventually processed through the **electron-transport**, **oxidative phosphorylation** (ET-OP) system to produce energy and reduce oxygen or some other inorganic oxidant.

Mitchell's **chemiosmotic** model is the best current explanation of ET-OP and how it works. According to this model, the electron transport chain passes high-energy electrons from **carrier** to carrier within the cytoplasmic membrane while at the same time pumping **protons** (hydrogen ions or $H^+$) across the membrane from the inside to the outside. This quickly results in a **pH gradient** across the membrane which, along with the membrane potential, produces the electrochemical potential called the **protonmotive force**. Some cellular systems can tap the energy of the protonmotive force directly - the bacterial flagellum is one of them.

The protonmotive force can also be used to create ATP energy by means of oxidative phosphorylation. If protons reenter the cell through **proton channels** containing an **ATPase** enzyme, ADP and inorganic phosphate are combined to produce ATP.

Energy is also used in two of the four mechanisms by which materials are brought into the cell. **Active transport** systems use membrane proteins called **permeases** to bring nutrients into the cell. The process requires energy, either in the form of ATP or through the direct use of the protonmotive force. Active transport can accumulate materials to much higher internal concentrations than exist outside the cell. **Group translocation** also uses energy to bring nutrients into the cell. The PTS (**p**hosphoenolpyruvate-sugar **t**ransferase **s**ystem), for example, uses a high-energy phosphate from phosphoenolpyruvate (PEP) to drive the accumulation of sugar. **Passive** and **Facilitated diffusion** do not use energy to carry materials into the cell, but they don't accumulate them to high concentrations, either. Both allow materials to move until they reach equilibrium; passive diffusion unaided, facilitated diffusion aided by carrier molecules in the membrane.

No matter how energy is used, there are two ultimate sources of energy: sunlight and chemical oxidations. Organisms that can use sunlight are called **photosynthetic** or **phototrophic** (photo- refers to light, -trophic means to feed); organisms that use chemical oxidations are called **chemosynthetic** or **chemotrophic** (chemo- refers to chemicals). Photosynthetic organisms come in two main groups, the green plants and cyanobacteria and the noncyanobacteria. Both groups use solar energy to power the reduction of carbon dioxide to sugar but differ in their pigments, and their sources of hydrogen atoms.

**Photosystem I**, which is shared by both groups of organisms, is capable of producing ATP from sunlight by a process called **cyclic phosphorylation**. The process is called cyclic because the electrons ejected from chlorophyll by light energy return to the same chlorophyll molecules. The high-energy electrons created in this process are passed through a series of electron carriers and, as was true in ET-OP, result in the pumping of protons across a membrane. Again, the protons reenter the cell and release enough energy to add a phosphate to ADP, producing ATP.

Green plants and cyanobacteria do not always practice cyclic phosphorylation, however. Some of the high-energy electrons created in Photosystem I are used to help reduce $NADP^+$ to **NADPH** (a critical reductant needed to convert $CO_2$ to sugar). The hydrogen ions needed for this process come from water molecules via **Photosystem II**. Photosystem II splits water (**photolysis**), producing oxygen gas, hydrogen ions and electrons. The electrons are returned to Photosystem I to replace those it has lost, but in the process they are used to generate still more ATP by means of a process called **noncyclic phosphorylation**.

**Noncyanobacteria photosynthesis** lacks Photosystem II, and never uses water as a source of protons needed to reduce $NADP^+$, nor does it include noncyclic phosphorylation. The **Chlorobiaceae** (green-sulfur bacteria) use sulfur-containing compounds or hydrogen gas as sources of hydrogen ions. The **Chromaticeae** (purple-sulfur bacteria) carry out similar reactions. Quite different are the **Rhodospirillaceae** (nonsulfur purple bacteria) which do not use sulfur compounds but rather use hydrogen gas or certain organic compounds as a source of protons. All of these organisms perform their photosynthetic reactions under anaerobic conditions only; they not only do not produce oxygen, their metabolism is not compatible with it.

All truly photosynthetic organisms are **autotrophs** (self-feeders; auto- means self, -troph means to feed). The reference here is to their ability to survive with no organic food. Some autotrophs, however, do not use light energy to drive the conversion of $CO_2$ to sugar; they use inorganic oxidation reactions instead. These organisms are called **chemolithotrophs** (sometimes called **chemoautotrophs**). Some oxidize sulfur, some oxidize nitrogen compounds, some even oxidize hydrogen gas. The energy released by these inorganic oxidation reactions is used to pump protons across membranes and the energy so created is captured when the protons reenter the cell through proton channels (sound familiar?).

Organisms that must consume organic materials for food are called **heterotrophs** (nourished by others; hetero- other, -troph to feed). If they get their energy and their carbon from organic compounds they are called **chemoheterotrophs**, but if their energy comes from light and only their carbon from organic compounds they are called **photoheterotrophs**. There are three main groups within the chemoheterotroph class, distinguished by the nature of the **final electron acceptor** of their metabolic pathways. **Obligate aerobes** always use molecular oxygen as a final electron acceptor. **Facultative anaerobes** use either oxygen (**aerobic respiration**) or an organic compound (**fermentation**) as the final electron acceptor. **Obligate anaerobes** use either an organic compound (fermentation) or an inorganic compound other than oxygen (**anaerobic respiration**).

Aerobic and anaerobic respiration generate most of their energy in the manner already discussed (electron transport and oxidative phosphorylation). Fermentative pathways generate all of their energy by **substrate phosphorylation**. All three groups may start by breaking glucose down to pyruvic acid *via* the **Embden-Meyerhof** pathway. During this pathway two net molecules of ATP are produced by substrate phosphorylation (four produced, two invested, net of two produced). Two molecules of **NADH** are also generated during the Embden-Meyerhof pathway. Respiratory organisms will run the NADH through the electron transport system and produce ATP from it. Fermentative organisms have to regenerate $NAD^+$ from the NADH by using it to reduce an organic molecule. Thus the final electron acceptor in fermentation is a **stable fermentation product** (an organic molecule).

Different bacteria practice a variety of fermentation pathways. Homolactic acid fermentation produces one product only - lactic acid. Mixed acid fermentation, by contrast, produces nine or more distinct products. In all cases, however, there is only one function of fermentation - to regenerate $NAD^+$.

Aerobes, however, have better use for their NADH. Each is worth three ATPs when passed through the electron transport, oxidative phosphorylation pathway. Including the NADH produced in the Embden-Meyerhof pathway with those produced in the **tricarboxylic acid cycle** (along with two $FADH_2$), and adding in the two ATP produced in the tricarboxylic acid cycle (TCA) cycle by substrate phosphorylation, a grand total of 38 ATP (36 in some organisms) are produced per glucose. This is 19 times as much as is made by fermentative organisms! Similar results can even be achieved anaerobically by organisms capable of **anaerobic respiration**. Most of these organisms are anaerobes, but some are facultative anaerobes. They use an inorganic final electron acceptor other than oxygen, such as sulfate, nitrate, or carbon dioxide.

OBJECTIVES After studying this chapter, you should understand:

1. The difference between respiration and fermentation.
2. How energy is captured during oxidative phosphorylation.
3. The function of each photosystem used in green plant and cyanobacterial photosynthesis.
4. How noncyanobacterial photosynthetic organisms form a reductant in the absence of photosystem II.
5. The difference between autotrophs and heterotrophs and how each obtains its energy from chemical oxidations.
6. How stable fermentation products are formed and what some of these products are.

## LEARNING ACTIVITIES

### Vocabulary

Having read the chapter, you should be able to define or cite the significance of the following terms. If you cannot, look them up in the text. Terms are presented in the order you will encounter them in the book.

metabolism
endoenzymes
anabolism
catabolism
oxidation
reduction
dehydrogenases
$NAD^+$
$NADP^+$
chemiosmotic
electron carriers
electron transport
flavoprotein
quinone

reductant
NADPH
photolysis of water
noncyclic phosphorylation
cyanobacteria
photosynthetic bacteria
noncyanobacteria photosynthesis
Chlorobiaceae
Chromaticeae
Rhodospirillaceae
chemoautotrophic

substrate phosphorylation
homolactic acid fermentation
alcoholic fermentation
mixed acid fermentation
butylene glycerol fermentation
propionic acid fermentation
butyric acid, butanol, acetone

| | | |
|---|---|---|
| cytochromes | autotrophs | fermentation |
| protonmotive force | chemolithotrophs | aerobic respiration |
| proton channels | heterotrophic | tricarboxylic acid cycle |
| ATPase | heterotrophs | Krebs cycle |
| active transport | chemoheterotrophs | oxaloacetate |
| permease | chemoautotrophs | FAD |
| group translocation | photoheterotrophs | anaplerotic reactions |
| PTS | photoautotrophs | glyoxylate cycle |
| facilitated diffusion | final electron acceptors | anaerobic respiration |
| photosynthetic | obligate aerobes | sulfate reducers |
| phototrophic | obligate anaerobes | nitrate reducers |
| chemosynthetic | facultative | methane bacteria |
| chemotrophic | fermentation | denitrification |
| photosystem I | oxidative phosphorylation | proteases |
| chlorophyil | stable fermentation products | lipases |
| cyclic phosphorylation | Embden-Meyerhof | citric acid cycle |
| photosystem II | | |

Complete each of the following statements by supplying the missing word or words.

1. ____________________ and catabolism are the two parts of metabolism.

2. ____________________ is defined as a loss of electrons (or hydrogen atoms).

3. ____________________ is the full name of the compound often called $NAD^+$.

4. ____________________ reactions involve a gain of electrons (or hydrogen atoms); the conversion of $NAD^+$ to NADH is an example.

5. ____________________ (also called hydrogen ions) are pumped across membranes during electron transport, according to the chemiosmotic model of Mitchell.

6. ____________________ is the term applied to the pH gradient plus the membrane potential. It represents a direct energy source for many cellular activities.

7. ____________________ carry only electrons; flavins and quinones carry electrons and hydrogen ions.

8. ____________________ enzymes, in proton channels, use the energy released by incoming protons to add an inorganic phosphate to ADP.

9. ____________________ are the specific carriers used by active transport systems.

10. ____________________ occurs when a solute is modified during its transport in such a way that it cannot be transported out of the cell at any appreciable rate.

11. ____________________ is the main mechanism of entering cells used by water, oxygen, nitrogen, fatty acids and other lipid-soluble materials.

12. ____________________ or phototrophic organisms are those that obtain the energy for living from sunlight.

13. ____________________ are the direct acceptors of light energy absorbed by chlorophyll. They are passed from carrier to carrier with the consequent pumping of protons across the membrane.

14. ____________________ and green plants have virtually the same photosynthetic mechanisms; they have both Photosystem I and Photosystem II.

15. ____________________ is the main reductant used in photosynthesis; it is cooperatively manufactured by Photosystem I and Photosystem II in green plant and cyanobacterial photosynthesis.

16. ____________________ are organisms that get their carbon from carbon dioxide, their energy from inorganic oxidations.

17. ____________________ are organisms that get their energy and their carbon from organic compounds.

18. ____________________ is the final electron acceptor of aerobic organisms.

19. ____________________ are the final electron acceptors of fermentative organisms; they are called stable fermentation products.

20. ____________________ are used to replenish metabolites lost from the Krebs cycle to biosynthesis; the Glyoxylate Cycle is an example.

## MASTERY TEST

1-5: Circle the choice that best answers the questions.

1. Aspect of metabolism which consists of the synthesis of body mass and the use of energy.
   a. metabolism
   b. catabolism
   c. dehydrogenation
   d. cannibalism
   e. anabolism

2. Which of the following is a class of enzymes that transfers electrons and hydrogen ions from organic compounds to the coenzyme $NAD^+$?
   a. peptidases
   b. dehydrogenases
   c. isomerases
   d. epimerases
   e. oxidases

3. Peter Mitchell won the Nobel Prize in 1978 for his ________________ model of how electron transport and oxidative phosphorylation work.
   a. chemiosmotic
   b. anaplerotic
   c. recombinant
   d. fermentative
   e. respiratory

4. Most of the carriers in the electron transport chain can carry electrons and ________________. Cytochromes can only carry electrons.
   a. photons
   b. positrons
   c. hydrogen ions
   d. oxygen
   e. NADPH

5. ADP + Inorganic P ------> ?
   a. phosphoenolpyruvic acid
   b. NADPH
   c. Glycerol Phosphate
   d. DNA
   e. ATP

---

6-8: Match the description of nutrient transport with the mechanism's name (use no answer twice)

A. Passive Diffusion
B. Active Transport
C. Group Translocation
D. Facilitated Diffusion

_____ 6. Responsible for the entrance into cells of oxygen, nitrogen, water, fatty acids, lipid-soluble materials.

_____ 7. Cannot create higher concentrations inside cell than outside; uses a membrane-based carrier.

_____ 8. Requires expenditure of energy; accumulates materials to much higher concentrations inside the cell than outside. Uses permeases.

9-13: Match the activity with the photosystem directly responsible for its performance. If both photosystems participate equally, choose answer "C". Answers can be used more than once.

A. Photosystem I
B. Photosystem II
C. Both
D. Neither

_____ 9. Performs the photolysis of water.

_____ 10. Reduces $NADP^+$ to NADPH.

_____ 11. Performs cyclic phosphorylation.

_____ 12. Produces oxygen gas (as a waste product).

_____ 13. Produces ATP by cyclic or noncyclic phosphorylation.

---

14-16: Match the metabolic type with its description.

A. Chemoheterotrophs
B. Chemoautotrophs
C. Photoheterotrophs
D. Photoautotrophs

_____ 14. Organism gets its carbon from carbon dioxide, its energy from oxidizing inorganic compounds (e.g. *Thiobacillus*).

_____ 15. Organism gets its energy from light, its carbon from organic compounds (e.g. *Rhodospirillum*).

_____ 16. Organism gets its energy from light, its carbon from carbon dioxide (e.g. *Chlorobium*).

---

17-19: Match the metabolic type with its description.

A. Aerobic (respiratory)
B. Anaerobic (fermentative)
C. Anaerobic (respiratory)

_____ 17. Organism use an inorganic material other than oxygen for its final electron acceptor.

_____ 18. Organism uses organic molecules as its final electron acceptor.

_____ 19. Organism uses oxygen as its final electron acceptor.

20-25: Circle the choice that best answers the questions.

20. The Embden-Meyerhof pathway, performed by most organisms, converts one glucose molecule to:
    a. one ethyl alcohol molecule
    b. one lactic acid molecule
    c. two lactic acid molecules
    d. two pyruvic acid molecules
    e. six carbon dioxide molecules

21. The sole function of fermentation is to:
    a. produce vodka
    b. generate much ATP
    c. regenerate $NAD^+$
    d. produce NADPH
    e. produce endotoxins

22. The ATP produced during the Embden-Meyerhof pathway and during the tricarboxylic acid cycle are made by:
    a. oxidative phosphorylation
    b. cyclic photophosphorylation
    c. substrate phosphorylation
    d. noncyclic phosphorylation
    e. cyclic phosphorylation

23. Counting the ATPs mentioned in the previous question and those produced during the electron transport, oxidative phosphorylation pathways, how many ATPs are produced from one glucose?
    a. 2 c. 18 e. 56
    b. 4 d. 38

24. Anaerobic respiration includes all of the following types EXCEPT:
    a. sulfate reducers (e.g. *Desulfovibrio*)
    b. lactic acid bacteria (e.g. *Streptococcus*)
    c. nitrate reducers (e.g. *Escherichia*)
    d. methane bacteria (e.g. *Methanococcus*)

25. The breakdown of fat starts with digestion by lipases and ends by the processing of acetate (acetyl CoA) fragments through:
    a. Embden-Meyerhof pathway
    b. Electron Transport
    c. Glyoxylate Pathway
    d. Tricarboxylic Acid Cycle (Citric Acid Cycle)
    e. Hexose Monophosphate Shunt

ANSWERS TO LEARNING ACTIVITIES

Fill-in-the-blank questions:

1. Anabolism; 2. Oxidation; 3. Nicotinamide Adenine Dinucleotide; 4. Reduction; 5. Protons; 6. Protonmotive force; 7. Cytochromes; 8. ATPase; 9. Permeases; 10. Group translocation; 11. Passive diffusion; 12. Photosynthetic; 13. Electrons; 14. Cyanobacteria; 15. NADPH; 16. Chemolithotrophs (or Chemoautotrophs); 17. Heterotrophs (or Chemoheterotrophs); 18. Oxygen; 19. Stable fermentation products (organic molecules); 20. Anaplerotic sequences.

**MASTERY TEST ANSWERS**

| | | | | | | | | | | | | |
|---|---|---|---|---|---|---|---|---|---|---|---|---|
| 1<br>e | 2<br>b | 3<br>a | 4<br>c | 5<br>e | 6<br>A | | 7<br>D | 8<br>B | 9<br>B | 10<br>C | 11<br>A | 12<br>B |
| 13<br>C | 14<br>B | 15<br>C | 16<br>D | 17<br>C | 18<br>B | 19<br>A | 20<br>d | 21<br>c | 22<br>c | 23<br>d | 24<br>b | 25<br>d |

# CHAPTER 7

## BACTERIAL GENETICS: GENE FUNCTION AND MUTATION

### CHAPTER SUMMARY

**DNA** (**d**eoxyribo**n**ucleic **a**cid) is a large double-stranded macromolecule with a shape described as a double helix. It is composed of subunits called **nucleotides** which are assembled by dehydration synthesis like all other macromolecules. Each nucleotide consists of a 5-carbon sugar (**2-deoxyribose**), a phosphate group attached to carbon 5' of the sugar, and a **nitrogenous base** attached to the 1' carbon of the sugar. The nitrogenous base is either a **purine** (**adenine** or **guanine**) or a **pyrimidine** (**thymine** or **cytosine**). The **5' carbon** of one **2-deoxyribose** is linked to the **3' carbon** of another 2-deoxyribose by a **phosphodiester bond**.

The two DNA strands are said to be **complementary**; wherever an A (Adenine) is found in one strand there is always a T (Thymine) **hydrogen bonded** to it on the other strand; wherever a C (Cytosine) is found on one strand there is always a G (Guanine) hydrogen bonded to it on the other strand. Adenine cannot hydrogen bond to another adenine, or to a guanine, or a cytosine. This complementary structure is directly related to the way DNA undergoes **replication** (copying).

The two DNA strands are **antiparallel** in addition to being complementary. One of the strands always runs from a 5' end towards a 3' end (**5' to 3'**), while the other strand is always running in the opposite direction, 3' toward 5' (**3' to 5'**). This structural detail is also important in replication.

Replication in bacteria always begins with the creation of two **replication forks** at a **specific origin** point on the chromosome and proceeds around the circular molecule in both directions. Because **DNA polymerase** can only operate in a **5' to 3' direction** and because the two strands of DNA are antiparallel, one strand is copied **continuously** while the other strand is copied **discontinuously**. The discontinuous strand is produced as series of short DNA pieces called **Okazaki fragments**. The fragments are sewn together by another enzyme, **DNA ligase**.

DNA replication ultimately produces two new molecules each of which contains one old strand and one complementary new strand. This is called **semiconservative replication**, because each new molecule conserves one half of the old molecule.

DNA is never used directly; instead it is always copied into **RNA** (**r**ibo**n**ucleic **a**cid) - usually **mRNA** (**messenger RNA**). RNA differs from DNA is several important ways: it is almost always single-stranded, it contains **uracil** (**U**) instead of thymine, and its pentose sugar is **ribose** instead of deoxyribose. Only one strand of DNA is used as a **template** for the production of RNA - the **positive strand**. It has specific sites on it called **promoter** regions which permit the binding of **RNA polymerase**. RNA polymerase opens up the DNA double helix into the **open promoter complex**, then polymerizes the ribonucleotides that **base-pair** on the positive DNA strand. In RNA U (uracil) base-pairs with A in DNA, A with T, C with G and G with C. RNA synthesis in eucaryotes is complicated by the presence of **introns** (**intervening sequences**) in the DNA. These are nucleotide sequences which must be cut out after transcription is completed, leaving the remaining **exons** as the functioning messenger RNA. There are no introns in procaryotic DNA.

Messenger RNA is used to direct the synthesis of protein, a process called **translation**. Because a "language change" occurs (going from a 4-letter nucleotide language to a 20-letter amino acid language), a "code" is needed for translation to occur. This is called the **genetic code** and consists of 64 unique **codons** - triplets of nucleotides on mRNA (see Table 7.1 in your textbook). The codons are read by another kind of RNA, **transfer RNA** (**tRNA**). Transfer RNA molecules bind to specific amino acids and bring them into position during translation by base-pairing with complementary codons using their **anticodons**.

Ribosomes complete the translation picture by forming a work surface on which protein synthesis occurs. Ribosomes come in two parts, the small subunit (called the **30S subunit**) and the large subunit (called the **50S subunit**). The 30S subunit initiates the translation process by binding to the mRNA molecule at a ribosome binding site. The 50S subunit then attaches to the small one and permits the binding of "**charged tRNAs**" (tRNAs carrying amino acids) to two binding sites on its surface. The ribosome then moves down the mRNA molecule, one codon at a time, adding amino acids to the growing peptide chain. The process stops when a **terminator codon** is encountered (UAA,UGA, or UAG). **Polysomes** (**poly**ribo**somes**) commonly result when more than one ribosome binds to a mRNA and begins synthesizing protein.

Bacterial cells have a single **chromosome**; eucaryotic cells typically have many chromosomes (e.g. 46 in humans). In most eucaryotes the chromosomes come in pairs, thus each **gene** is present twice. Such cells are said to be **diploid** (two sets). Bacteria, and some eucaryotes, have chromosomes that don't come in pairs and thus have only one copy of each gene; they are said to be **haploid** (one set). The **genotype** of an organism is its genetic endowment; its observed physical properties is its **phenotype**.

Genes may be present in a cell but not be **expressed**. Control of gene expression is a critical task for cells. Some genes are always expressed; such genes are said to be **constitutive**. Other genes, called **inducible genes**, are under transcriptional control. Some inducible genes are subject to **negative control**. A classic example is provided by the **lactose operon**, a set of genes controlled by the *lac I* regulatory gene. As long as a **repressor protein** (coded for by the *lac I* gene) is bound to the **operator site** (near the promoter region), no gene in the operon is transcribed. When **lactose** (a disaccharide) binds to the repressor protein and removes it from the promoter region, all genes in the operon are transcribed into a **polycistronic mRNA**.

Some genes are subject to active **repression**. In this case the complex of a repressor protein and a specific material binds to the operator site (near the promoter region) of an operon and shuts the genes down. An example of this is the tryptophan synthesis operon.

Some genes are subject to another kind of control, **positive control**. Such genes are only transcribed when a regulatory protein (present in the cytoplasm) binds to an inducer and then the complex binds to the promoter region of the gene. Only when the complex is bound can RNA polymerase transcribe the gene.

Both positive and negative control of genes has one major drawback - time lag. A system which regulates the enzyme molecule directly would involve no such time lag. Such a system is characteristic of **allosteric** enzymes. These enzymes have two binding sites on their surface; one normal active site and another site for the binding of specific activators or inhibitors. The inhibitors are often metabolites that come later on in the metabolic pathway than the enzyme under control.

The function of a gene can change if it suffers a mutation (a heritable genetic change). Mutations that are the result of replication errors are called **spontaneous mutations**, while mutations caused by outside influences (**mutagenic chemicals**, **ultraviolet light**, radiation) are called **induced mutations**. Mutagenic chemicals may induce mutations because they resemble natural nucleotides (e.g. 5-bromouracil), or because they are alkylating agents (e.g. nitrogen mustard, ethylene oxide). Ultraviolet light has its major impact in inducing thymine dimers (covalent bonds between adjacent thymines in DNA).

Mutations most commonly affect single nucleotides or pairs of nucleotides. One of the most common is the **base pair substitution**, in which one nucleotide is replaced by another (e.g. a T by a G). Such mutations, often called **missense mutations**, usually change one and only one amino acid in the polypeptide chain. Most of these mutations will be trivial unless they occur in critical regions or if they create **nonsense mutations** - mutations which create terminator codons and cause premature release of incomplete polypeptides. Base **insertion** and base **deletion** mutations are more likely to induce severe damage. They cause a **reading frame shift** to occur and will, in all probability, completely change the polypeptide being produced.

Systems exist in cells to correct mutations, but they are not always successful. Mutations caused by ultraviolet light (UV), for example, are often corrected by **photoreactivation**. Visible light activates an enzyme that removes thymine dimers created by UV light. Another class of repair enzymes are the **excision-repair system**. **Endonuclease** enzymes recognize errors and cleave the DNA strand prior to the error. **DNA polymerase I** binds to the cut area and replaces nucleotides complementary to the uncut strand. Another enzyme, DNA ligase, heals the nick. Less successful is the so-called **SOS repair** system, an inducible set of enzymes produced when DNA replication forks become blocked. They make it possible to resume replication at blocked forks, but do so at the cost of making numerous mistakes - they are **error-prone**.

Some mutations in higher organisms result in a uncontrolled cell division - cancer. Chemicals that cause cancer are called **carcinogens** and up to 80 percent of them are **mutagens** in bacteria. Tests for mutagenicity thus have a good chance of detecting potential carcinogens as well. The best known such test is the **Ames test** which uses mutant strains of *Salmonella typhimurium* to screen chemicals for mutagenicity. Any chemical which shows mutagenic activity in the Ames test should undergo further animal testing to determine its carcinogenic potential.

OBJECTIVES — The study of this chapter should provide a clear understanding of the following points:

1. The structure of DNA and the mechanism whereby DNA replicates itself so as to preserve the message encoded in the DNA.
2. The steps involved in the transcription of DNA into mRNA.
3. The mechanism whereby an mRNA is translated into protein.
4. The difference between the inducible expression and the repression of an operon.
5. The meaning of feedback inhibition and how it can control enzyme activity.
6. The various types of mutations that occur and how one can increase the rate of such mutations.
7. The purpose of the Ames test.
8. Mechanisms used by the cell for DNA repair.

## LEARNING ACTIVITIES

### Vocabulary

Having read the chapter, you should be able to define or cite the significance of the following terms. If you cannot, look them up in the text. Terms are presented in the order you will encounter them in the book.

DNA
2-deoxyribose
nucleotide

messenger RNA
promoter
termination site

*lac I* regulatory gene
repressor

nitrogenous base
purine
pyrimidine
adenine
guanine
thymine
cytosine
phosphodiester bonds
double helix
complementary
replication
DNA polymerase
template
semiconservative
antiparallel
5' to 3'
continuous
discontinuous
Okazaki fragments
DNA ligase
origin
replication fork
transcription
RNA
uracil
ribose
RNA polymerase
positive DNA strand
base pairing

open promoter complex
intervening sequences
introns
exons
translation
codon
transfer RNA
anticodon
ribosome
50S subunit
30S subunit
ribosome binding site
termination codon
polysome
chromosome
diploid
haploid
gene
genotype
phenotype
constitutive gene
inducible
ß-galactosidase
lactose operon
polycistronic mRNA
negative control

repression
positive control
feedback inhibition
allosteric enzyme
spontaneous mutation
base substitution
missense mutation
base insertion
base deletion
frame shift mutation
nonsense mutation
replica plating
mutagenic agents
induced mutations
5-bromouracil
alkylating agents
ultraviolet light
thymine dimer
photoreactivation
DNA repair systems
excision-repair system
DNA endonuclease
DNA polymerase I
SOS repair
carcinogen
epidemiological
Ames test
*his* mutation

Complete each of the following statements by supplying the missing word or words.

1. Nucleotides consist of a pentose sugar, a phosphate group, and a nitrogenous base.

2. Double Helix is the term used to describe the shape of the DNA molecule.

3. 2-deoxyribose is the name of the pentose sugar found in DNA nucleotides.

4. Complementary is the word used to describe the relationship between the two strands of DNA in terms of base-pairing of nucleotides.

5. antiparallel ______ is the word used to describe the relationship between the two strands of DNA in terms of the direction the nucleotides run (5' to 3' or 3' to 5').

6. DNA polymerase ______ is the name of the enzyme which directs the replication of DNA.

7. semiconservative ______ replication is the term used to describe DNA replication (each new molecule contains one old and one new strand).

8. Transcription ______ is the term used to describe the copying of DNA into RNA.

9. Uracil ______ is the pyrimidine that replaces thymine in RNA.

10. Introns ______ are intervening sequences found in the DNA of eucaryotes, but not of procaryotes. They must be excised before the mRNA becomes functional.

11. Translation ______ is the term used to describe the synthesis of protein based upon information in mRNA.

12. Condons ______ are the triplets of nucleotides on mRNA which are "read" by ribosomes and tRNA during protein synthesis.

13. * polysome ______ is a term used to describe a piece of messenger RNA with multiple ribosomes on it.

14. constitutive genes ______ are genes that are transcribed all the time, and whose coded polypeptides are therefore always being made.

15. operons ______ are contiguous groups of genes under common control of the same regulatory element.

16. inducible ______ genes are normally not being transcribed because a repressor protein is bound to the operator site (near the promoter). They are subject to negative control.

17. repression ______ of a gene normally being transcribed can occur if the product of the pathway binds to a repressor protein and the complex binds to the operator site (e.g. the tryptophan biosynthesis operon).

18. allosteric ______ enzymes are subject to direct control because they have two binding sites on their surfaces - one for their normal substrate, another for an activator or an inhibitor.

19. Spontaneous ____________________ mutations occur during normal growth and result mainly from replication errors.

20. Reading frame shift ____________________ is the term for the effect of both base insertion and base deletion mutations. The effect results in a total change in the peptide being coded for.

MASTERY TEST

1-6: Circle the choice that best answers the questions.

1. All of the following are found in DNA EXCEPT:
   a. Adenine
   b. Cytosine
   c. Guanine
   d. Thymine
   e. Uracil

2. The term "base pair" refers to the following combinations:
   a. A with T, C with G
   b. A with U, C with T
   c. A with G, C with T
   d. A with A, T with T
   e. A with T, G with U

3. All of the following are characteristic of DNA EXCEPT:
   a. double-stranded
   b. two strands are parallel
   c. two strands are complementary
   d. composed of 2-deoxyribonucleotides
   e. organized as a double helix

4. The bonds that hold together the nucleotides in DNA are:
   a. glycosidic bonds
   b. peptide bonds
   c. phosphodiester bonds
   d. 2' - 3' ester bonds
   e. carbonyl bonds

5. During replication one strand of DNA is copied continuously, the other discontinuously. The discontinuous strand is copied as a series of short pieces of DNA called:
   a. Chargaff chunks
   b. Watson pieces
   c. Crick segments
   d. Okazaki fragments
   e. Spallanzani sections

6. The enzyme which links the pieces described above is:
   a. DNA Polymerase
   b. RNA Polymerase
   c. DNA Ligase
   d. DNA Endonuclease
   e. DNA Helicase

7-14: Match the term with its description. (use no answer twice)

ANSWERS

| | | | | | |
|---|---|---|---|---|---|
| A. | 30S Subunit | F. | DNA Polymerase | K. | Replication |
| B. | 50S Subunit | G. | Origin | L. | RNA Polymerase |
| C. | Antiparallel | H. | Parallel | M. | Terminator |
| D. | Codons | I. | Positive Strand | N. | Transcription |
| E. | Complementary | J. | Promoter | O. | Translation |

N 7. DNA --------------> RNA (process)

O 8. RNA --------------> Protein (process)

I 9. Strand of DNA which is copied into RNA.

C 10. Relationship between two DNA strands in terms of nucleotide orientation (5' to 3' or 3' to 5').

G 11. Region on bacterial chromosome where replication begins.

J 12. Region on bacterial chromosome where transcription begins.

A 13. Ribosome subunit which first binds to mRNA molecule.

D 14. Triplets of nucleotides on mRNA.

---

15-25: Circle the choice that best answers the questions.

15. In eucaryotes genes contain information which is not used in the final messenger RNA molecule. The unused material is the introns (intervening sequences). The remaining sequences are used in messenger RNA and are called:
   a. exons
   b. outrons
   c. textrons
   d. ailerons
   e. anticodons

16. The genetic code consists of triplets of nucleotides where each position could be one of four nucleotide types. This produces _______ possible combinations of 4 nucleotide types in triplets.
a. 8 b. 16 c. 32 d. 64 e. 128

17. Three of the possible triplets (UAA, UAG, and UGA) are special in that they do not specify an amino acid; they are called:
a. initiators
b. promoters
c. origins
d. terminators
e. anticodons

18. Transfer RNA molecules (tRNA), which are able to specifically bind to amino acids, locate their proper position during the translation process by the base-pairing of their _____ with the _____ in mRNA.
a. codon ... anticodon
b. anticodon ... codon
c. anticodon ... anticodon
d. initiator ... terminator
e. promoter ... repressor

19. Cells that have chromosomes in pairs and therefore have two copies of every gene are said to be:
a. diploid
b. haploid
c. aneuploid
d. polyploid
e. celluloid

20. Which of the following best describes the function of the *lac I* regulatory gene in the lac operon?
a. makes a cytoplasmic protein which can bind to lactose and derepress the operon
b. makes a repressor protein which binds to the operator site and prevents transcription of the operon
c. makes a protein which can bind to lactose and then bind to the operator site and promote transcription of the operon
d. occupies the first position in the operon and contains an inactive promoter region which lactose can activate directly

21. The messenger RNA molecules which are made from operons contain copies of several genes. Such mRNA molecules are said to be:
a. polyoperonic
b. polyplatonic
c. polycistronic
d. polyphonic

22. A gene under positive control is transcribed whenever the regulatory gene product combines with the substance the operon exists to metabolize. This complex of regulatory protein plus metabolite binds to:
a. the operator site
b. the origin site
c. the cistronic site
d. the terminator site
e. the promoter site

23. When an enzyme is subject to direct repression by a metabolite from the end of a pathway, it is undergoing:
   a. feedback inhibition
   b. noncompetitive inhibition
   c. allosteric activation
   d. anaplerotic reactivation

24. A mutation which is deadly under one set of circumstances but not deadly under more permissive conditions is said to be a ____________________ mutation.
   a. capricious
   b. conditional lethal
   c. nonsense
   d. missense
   e. frame shift

25. Most DNA repair systems are of total benefit to organisms. Which of the following is a useful system, but does considerable harm, too, due to its error-prone behavior?
   a. photoreactivation
   b. excision-repair system
   c. DNA Polymerase I
   d. SOS repair

## ANSWERS TO LEARNING ACTIVITIES

Fill-in-the-blank questions:

1. Nucleotides; 2. Double helix; 3. 2-Deoxyribose; 4. Complementary; 5. Antiparallel; 6. DNA polymerase; 7. Semiconservative; 8. Transcription; 9. Uracil; 10. Introns; 11. Translation; 12. Codons; 13. Polysome; 14. Constitutive; 15. Operons; 16. Inducible; 17. Repression; 18. Allosteric; 19. Spontaneous; 20. Reading frame shift.

**MASTERY TEST ANSWERS**

| | | | | | | | | | | | | |
|---|---|---|---|---|---|---|---|---|---|---|---|---|
| 1 e | 2 a | 3 b | 4 c | 5 d | 6 c | | 7 N | 8 O | 9 I | 10 C | 11 G | 12 J |
| 13 A | 14 D | 15 a | 16 d | 17 d | 18 b | 19 a | 20 b | 21 c | 22 e | 23 a | 24 b | 25 d |

## CHAPTER 8

# BACTERIAL GENETICS: THE NATURE AND TRANSFER OF GENETIC MATERIAL

## CHAPTER SUMMARY

Mendelian genetics was founded over 125 years ago and achieved some tremendous accomplishments with no knowledge of the nature of genetic material. The 1928 experiments of **Frederick Griffith** provided one of the earliest clues to the chemical nature of genes. Griffith discovered that avirulent, "rough", nonencapsulated Type II *Streptococcus pneumoniae* could undergo **transformation** to encapsulated, virulent Type I *Streptococcus pneumoniae* when placed in proximity to heat-killed Type I cells. Avery, MacLeod and McCarty proved 16 years later that the transforming material was DNA.

*Streptococcus* and other **gram-positive** bacteria must be **competent** in order to be transformed. This occurs naturally when cultures are in late log growth phase or in early stationary phase. Cells in this condition have surface proteins that can bind foreign (but similar) double-stranded DNA (dsDNA), partly degrade it to a single-stranded form (ssDNA), and transport that ssDNA into the cell. Once in the cell the foreign DNA locates a complementary region on the cell's chromosome and undergoes a process called **homologous recombination**. In this process the "foreign" strand replaces part of one strand of the host chromosome, aided by cellular enzymes. **Gram-negative** bacteria are always competent. They can bind and absorb foreign DNA at all stages of growth and can also practice homologous recombination and incorporate the DNA into their own chromosome.

Transformation is unlikely to be of much importance in nature, but it has proved to be of immense value in recombinant DNA technology (genetic engineering).

**Transduction** is a process whereby genes can be transferred from cell to cell by viruses (**bacteriophages**). **Restricted (specialized) transduction** involves the transfer of one of only two possible genes, **generalized transduction** involves the transfer of virtually any gene. Which type occurs depends upon the behavior of the bacteriophage.

Typical bacteriophages enter a cell, take it over, enzymatically digest the host chromosome into tiny fragments, produce new viruses, then kill (**lyse**) the cell to effect viral release. Such viruses are called **lytic phages**. Occasionally, when virus particles are being assembled, tiny fragments of the bacterial chromosome get into the virus coat instead of its own genes. These bacterial genes can then be transferred to another bacterial cell by means of the viral adsorption process. The process is totally random and any of the original host cell's genes could be transferred in this manner. This is **generalized transduction**.

Some bacteriophages invade a cell and, instead of replicating themselves, insert their DNA into the host chromosome at a specific site. These are called **temperate phages**; the incorporated version of the phage is called the **prophage**, and the bacteria that harbor prophages are referred to as **lysogenic**. These phages can be induced to become lytic and "loop out" of the chromosome. When they do, they sometimes mistakenly take along a bacterial gene (leaving one or more of their own genes behind). This gene is not randomly selected but rather is always one of two possibilities - the genes between which the virus incorporated in the first place. This is **restricted (specialized) transduction**.

Another way that bacteria can exchange genes is by means of **conjugation**. This process is quite common among gram-negative bacteria but quite rare among gram-positives. Typically, small extrachromosomal pieces of DNA called **plasmids** are transferred from **donor** cells (males) to **recipient** cells (females) via a structure called a **sex pilus** (in gram-negatives, not in gram-positives). Plasmids are self-replicating pieces of DNA which often contain genes responsible for **antibiotic resistance**, fimbriae, resistance to ultraviolet light, **hemolysin** production, **enterotoxin** production, and **exotoxin** production. Plasmids that engage in conjugation activities have, in addition, genes responsible for their transmissibility (*tra* genes). During conjugation, the donor cell produces a sex pilus which contacts a recipient cell (of the same species or even other species). The cells then are drawn close together and a **conjugal bridge** is formed. A ***tra*-gene-encoded DNA endonuclease** then nicks the donor's plasmid, one strand of which then feeds through the conjugal bridge (5' end first). The recipient cell thus receives the *tra* genes along with the rest of the plasmid genes - it becomes a donor cell!

In some cases the transmissible plasmid becomes incorporated into the cell's chromosome. In *E. coli* the normal donor cell is called $\mathbf{F^+}$ (the normal recipient is $\mathbf{F^-}$). The incorporated version of the $F^+$ is called **Hfr** (**h**igh **fr**equency of chromosomal recombinants). Hfr cells conjugate readily but attempt to transfer the entire chromosome to the recipient cell. It takes almost two hours to complete this task, so it is rarely accomplished (and the $F^+$ genes are the last to be copied, so the recipients are rarely transformed to Hfr). The $F^+$ plasmid which is incorporated in Hfr cells can also become excised from the chromosome. When this process occurs, mistakes are sometimes made and the plasmid may carry off a few chromosomal genes (leaving some of its own behind). Such modified plasmids are called **F'** plasmids.

Genes may not only be transferred between cells, they may also move about within the cell. These unusual genes, called **transposons**, have the ability to migrate to new locations on the chromosome, from the chromosome to a plasmid, from a plasmid to the chromosome, etc. They are, however, incapable of independent replication, so they must be incorporated into a **replicon** (replication unit such as a plasmid or a chromosome). The simplest transposons are called **insertion sequences**; they consist of the **inverted repeats** (mirror-image repetitive nucleotide sequences) at both ends that all transposons have plus a gene coding for an enzyme called **transposase**. Each transposon has its own transposase which can recognize the unique inverted repeats of its own transposon and catalyze the ligation of the transposon into its target site (on the chromosome, on a plasmid, on a phage, etc.). Transposons are also found in eucaryotes and viruses.

Despite appearances, bacteria are actually always on guard against the invasion of their cytoplasm by foreign DNA. Each species of bacterium makes a unique enzyme called a **restriction DNA endonuclease** whose job it is to recognize foreign DNA and to destroy it. The cell's own DNA is **methylated** in a unique pattern by **DNA modification enzymes** and the endonuclease looks for DNA that lacks this methylation pattern. When it finds foreign DNA it looks for particular sequences of nucleotides and, usually, performs a **"staggered cut"** in the DNA. This leaves each DNA fragment with a short single-stranded segment which is complementary to the short single-stranded segment left on the other piece. Such short, complementary segments can base-pair with one another; they are called **sticky ends**. That is normally the end of the matter - unless all of this is occurring in a test tube.

Genetic engineers use restriction enzymes to create complementary sticky ends on the DNA of two species of organism (e.g. human and *Salmonella*). These two kinds of DNA are then mixed together and allowed to reanneal. **DNA ligase** is then added to the DNA; it will attach together any annealed segments, and **recombinant DNA molecules** are created (DNA molecules containing regions derived from two species of organism). If these **hybrid DNA** molecules (often plasmids) can be incorporated in living microbial cells and if the foreign genes are expressed, then microbes may synthesize human gene products (e.g. human insulin, human interferon, human growth hormone, etc.).

One tricky point involves the inability of bacteria to deal with DNA containing **introns**. Human genes incorporated into bacteria must be purged of all **intervening sequences**. This is most easily done by isolating the mRNA version of the human gene (all introns already gone) and converting it into DNA by means of a **retrovirus** enzyme, **reverse transcriptase**. Such DNA is called **cDNA** (DNA **c**omplementary to mRNA).

<u>OBJECTIVES</u> After studying this chapter, you should:

1. Understand the nature of transformation and be familiar with the importance of the techniques used in recombinant DNA technology.
2. Know the difference between restricted and general transduction.

3. Be able to list the major steps involved in both plasmid and chromosome transfer through conjugation.
4. Be able to list a variety of functions that are usually encoded in plasmids.
5. Comprehend what is a transposable element.
6. Know what restriction enzymes are and how these are used to clone segments of foreign DNA.
7. Understand why a cDNA must be used when cloning human genes in a bacterium.
8. Be able to list several human genes that have been cloned in *E. coli*, as well as to suggest a few new possibilities for cloned genes.

## LEARNING ACTIVITIES

### Vocabulary

Having read the chapter, you should be able to define or cite the significance of the following terms. If you cannot, look them up in the text. Terms are presented in the order you will encounter them in the book.

Mendel
mendelian genetics
somatic
recessive
dominant
Griffith
*Streptococcus pneumoniae*
virulent
encapsulated
nonencapsulated
transformation
competent
homologous recombination
heterologous DNA
recombinant DNA
transduction
lytic phage
temperate phage
prophage
lysogenic
restricted transduction
general transduction
lambda phage ($\lambda$)
lysogenization
conjugation
plasmids
self-transmissible plasmid
sex pilus
conjugal bridge
$F^+$ cell
$F^-$ cell
Hfr
*tra* genes
antibiotic resistance
ultraviolet light resistance
enterotoxins
exotoxins
transposon
replicon
inverted repeats
transposase
insertion sequences
DNA endonuclease
restriction endonuclease
DNA modification enzyme
genetic engineering
recombinant DNA technology
hybrid plasmid
sticky ends
reverse transcriptase
cDNA
retrovirus

Complete each of the following statements by supplying the missing word or words.

1. ____________________ performed critical experiments in 1928 which led to the discovery of the role of DNA in heredity.

2. ____________________ was the organism used by the individual discussed in question #1; avirulent, "rough" versions of the bacterium were transformed to encapsulated, virulent "smooth" bacteria.

3. Gram-____________________ bacteria must be in late log growth phase or early stationary phase for transformation to be possible.

4. ____________________ is the process by which the foreign DNA is incorporated into the host chromosome during transformation.

5. ____________________ is the general term for transfer of genes from bacterium to bacterium *via* a bacteriophage.

6. ____________________ is the term which is used for the transfer of one of two possible genes from one bacterium to another *via* a bacteriophage.

7. ____________________ phages can only perform generalized transduction.

8. ____________________ bacteria harbor temperate bacteriophages in their prophage form.

9. ____________________ is the term used to describe the exchange of DNA between donor gram-negative cells and recipient gram-negative cells via a sex pilus.

10. ____________________ are by far the most common type of DNA being exchanged by the mechanism discussed in question #9. Entire chromosomes are rarely involved.

11. ____________________ strains in *E. coli* are one of the relatively rare examples of organisms that attempt to transfer entire chromosomes to recipient cells.

12. ____________________ are sequences of DNA which have the ability to relocate themselves to other parts of the cell's genome; from chromosome to plasmid, from plasmid to chromosome, etc.

13. ____________________ are mirror-image repetitive nucleotide sequences found at the two ends of the structures discussed in question #12.

14. ____________________ enzyme genes are always present in even the smallest transposons, the insertion sequences.

15. ____________________ recombination is the term which describes the incorporation of things like transposons, prophage genomes, etc. in the DNA of a cell.

16. ____________________ DNA endonuclease enzymes perform a defensive function in cells, guarding against the invasion of foreign DNA.

17. ____________________ cuts in DNA by restriction enzymes create "sticky ends" in the DNA being digested. Only DNA without the normal methylation patterns will be attacked by the enzymes.

18. ____________________, or genetic engineering, is the field of endeavor that is attempting to create hybrid plasmids which will allow bacteria to produce human gene products.

19. ____________________ (complementary DNA) is created by using a viral enzyme to convert eucaryotic mRNA to DNA.

20. ____________________ is the name of the viral enzyme that can convert RNA to DNA.

## MASTERY TEST

1-5: Circle the choice that best answers the questions.

1. Which of the following recombination mechanisms was discovered by means of an experiment involving *Streptococcus pneumoniae*?
   a. conjugation
   b. generalized transduction
   c. restricted transduction
   d. transformation
   e. genetic engineering

2. Which of the following is a process that involves the transferal of virtually any gene from one bacterium to another *via* a virus?
   a. conjugation
   b. generalized transduction
   c. restricted transduction
   d. transformation
   e. genetic engineering

3. Strains of *E. coli* which carry the $F^+$ factor practice ____________ with strains of *E. coli* which are $F^-$.
   a. conjugation
   b. generalized transduction
   c. restricted transduction
   d. transformation
   e. genetic engineering

4. When a "temperate" phage is incorporated into the chromosome of its bacterial host it is termed:
   a. a prophage
   b. a lysogenic phage
   c. a lytic phage
   d. an "f" factor
   e. none of these

5. Cells of gram-positive bacteria must be in late log growth phase or early stationary phase in order to successfully undergo transformation. Cells in this condition are said to be:
   a. transformable
   b. competent
   c. inducible
   d. restricted
   e. allopathic

6-10: Match the name of the individual with his major discovery.

ANSWERS

A. Avery, MacLeod, McCarty
B. Griffith
C. Lederberg and Tatum
D. Mendel
E. Watson and Crick
F. Zinder and Lederberg

_____ 6. Founded the science of genetics with a paper published in 1865.

_____ 7. Credited with demonstrating that the agent of transformation in bacteria is DNA.

_____ 8. Worked out the structure of DNA.

_____ 9. Discovered transduction in 1952

_____ 10. Discovered conjugation in 1946.

---

11-25: Circle the choice that best answers the questions.

11. Which of the following can be used to artificially prepare cells for transformation?
   a. $CaCl_2$
   b. $H_2O$
   c. NaCl
   d. $CH_3OH$
   e. $C_6H_{12}O_6$

12. A bacteriophage which reproduces in its host cell and then kills it is termed a(n) ________________ phage.
    a. temperate
    b. avirulent
    c. lytic
    d. prophage
    e. lambda ($\lambda$) phage

13. Specialized transduction results from a mistake in excision of the viral genome; in the case of the $\lambda$ (lambda) phage of *E. coli*, the _______ gene is most commonly carried off by the phage.
    a. *lac*
    b. *tra*
    c. *inxs*
    d. *rem*
    e. *gal*

14. Small, extrachromosomal pieces of DNA which can replicate themselves and which often carry genes for antibiotic resistance are called:
    a. transposons
    b. replicons
    c. plasmodesmata
    d. plasmids
    e. insertons

15. Transmissible plasmids, plasmids that can participate in conjugation, always carry a set of genes of the _____ class.
    a. *lac*
    b. *tra*
    c. *inxs*
    d. *rem*
    e. *gal*

16. An especially long member of the fimbriae class of bacterial structures which participates in the conjugation process in gram-negative bacteria is called the:
    a. conjugal bridge
    b. sex pilus
    c. fimbri-o-rama
    d. cilium
    e. flagellum

17. All of the following are known to be present on plasmids EXCEPT:
    a. genes coding for essential DNA repair enzymes
    b. genes coding for enterotoxin production
    c. genes coding for antibiotic resistance
    d. genes coding for ultraviolet light resistance
    e. genes coding for exotoxin production

18. All of the following are true of transposons EXCEPT:
    a. they are incapable of autonomous replication
    b. they always have inverted repeats at their ends
    c. their integration can occur at many sites in target DNA
    d. they always include a gene for production of the transposase enzyme
    e. they always include terminator codons early in their nucleotide sequences

19. Transposons (transposable elements) can insert themselves at random in chromosomes, plasmids, viral genomes, etc. by a process called:
    a. nonhomologous recombination
    b. homologous recombination
    c. heteroduplex formation
    d. restriction sequence formation
    e. all of the above

20. Reverse transcriptase is an enzyme derived from retroviruses which:
    a. copies protein to RNA
    b. copies DNA to RNA
    c. copies RNA to RNA
    d. copies RNA to DNA
    e. copies DNA to DNA

21. Insertion sequences are:
    a. large, complex sequences of nucleotides which participate in heteroduplex formation
    b. small transposons with two inverted repeats and one gene for a transposase enzyme
    c. antibiotic resistance transposon which frequently jump from species to species
    d. complex transposons which contain normal bacterial genes in multiple copies

22. Restriction endonuclease enzymes are believed to serve what natural function?
    a. normal repair enzymes used to fix breaks in DNA
    b. DNA polymerase enzymes used in the replication of plasmids
    c. DNA polymerase enzymes used in the replication of transposons
    d. DNA polymerase enzymes used in the replication of the chromosome
    e. degradative enzymes that prevent entry of foreign DNA

23. The value of restriction endonucleases is that they create "sticky ends" in any DNA to which they are exposed. These sticky ends are automatically produced because:
    a. the enzymes synthesize sticky ends on the 5' terminals of all DNA
    b. the enzymes always break the DNA at specific nucleotide sequences
    c. the enzymes create heteroduplexes with cellular DNA, automatically creating sticky ends
    d. the enzymes synthesize sticky ends onto the 3' terminals of all DNA

24. Besides the enzyme discussed in the above question, what other enzyme is absolutely required for recombinant DNA technology experiments?
    a. DNA endonuclease
    b. DNA ligase
    c. DNA gyrase
    d. RNA polymerase
    e. DNA polymerase

25. When recombinant DNA techniques are used, the source DNA is most effectively cloned if it is very pure and lacks introns. One technique used is to synthesize the gene that is desired from cellular mRNA using the viral enzyme:
a. restriction endonuclease
b. DNA gyrase
c. reverse transcriptase
d. RNA-Dependent RNA synthetase
e. DNA modification enzymes

ANSWERS TO LEARNING ACTIVITIES

Fill-in-the-blank questions:

1. Frederick Griffith; 2. *Streptococcus pneumoniae*; 3. -positive; 4. Homologous recombination; 5. Transformation; 6. Specialized (restricted) transformation; 7. Lytic; 8. Lysogenic; 9. Conjugation; 10. Plasmids; 11. Hfr; 12. Transposons; 13. Inverted repeats; 14. Transposase; 15. Nonhomologous; 16. Restriction; 17. Staggered; 18. Recombinant DNA technology; 19. cDNA; 20. Reverse transcriptase.

**MASTERY TEST ANSWERS**

| | | | | | | | | | | | | |
|---|---|---|---|---|---|---|---|---|---|---|---|---|
| 1<br>d | 2<br>b | 3<br>a | 4<br>a | 5<br>b | 6<br>D | | 7<br>A | 8<br>E | 9<br>F | 10<br>C | 11<br>a | 12<br>c |
| 13<br>e | 14<br>d | 15<br>b | 16<br>b | 17<br>a | 18<br>e | 19<br>a | 20<br>d | 21<br>b | 22<br>e | 23<br>b | 24<br>b | 25<br>c |

## CHAPTER 9

## METHODS FOR THE CONTROL OF MICROORGANISMS

### CHAPTER SUMMARY

In barely a century we have progressed from a world rife with epidemic diseases to one in which once-common diseases are now rare. Starting with the pioneering work of **Pasteur** in convincing medical science that germs could cause disease, the past century has seen a seemingly never-ending set of advances in our understanding of infection and contagion. **Semmelweis** made the connection between lack of handwashing by doctors and infections in their patients; **Koch** discovered the causes of many diseases and made possible the discovery of many more with his "postulates". **Lister** pioneered the use of phenol as an antiseptic during surgery, and so on.

Hospitals are vastly today improved over their predecessors in the 19th Century, but still have persistent problems with **nosocomial** (hospital-acquired) infections. **Antibiotic resistance** is an increasing problem made worse by the ability of microbes to spread resistance around.

**Disinfection** (the destruction of potentially disease-producing organisms on inanimate surfaces) and **sterilization** (the destruction of *all* forms of life within a given area) have been the most important tools in controlling the spread of infectious diseases in medical settings. Both can be accomplished by a variety of **physical** or **chemical** means.

Heat is one physical method of sterilization; its most likely means of killing is the inactivation (**denaturation**) of critical cell **proteins** and enzymes. Normal **vegetative cells** of bacteria and fungi are relatively easy to kill - they typically succumb at temperatures of **80°C**, which is below the boiling point of water. Much harder to eliminate are the **endospores** of pathogenic bacteria which can survive long periods of boiling water temperatures without damage.

Critical variables for heat sterilization include the amount of heat (temperature), the length of time of the treatment, and the environment in which the treatment is occurring (organic environments high in protein protect microbes from heat damage). The most reliable way to ensure sterilization of materials by heat is by using the **moist heat** of an **autoclave**. In these machines **air is**

**evacuated**, then the chamber filled with **pressurized steam** at 15 lb/in$^2$; **121°C**. If sufficient **time** is allowed an autoclave can completely sterilize practically anything. The lower temperatures of boiling water can sometimes be used if 2 percent **sodium carbonate** or detergents are added to the solution.

Sometimes it is inconvenient or impractical to use moist heat sterilization. Glassware, powders, and oily substances can be sterilized, instead, by **dry heat**. Higher temperatures (**170°C**) and longer time courses (hours instead of fractions of hours) are required.

**Pasteurization** is a well-known method of killing bacteria which is *not* an example of true sterilization. The purpose of pasteurization is to destroy disease-producing organisms and to reduce the numbers of spoilage organisms to increase shelf-life of products such as milk.

**Desiccation** (lack of water) is another physical mechanism that kills some bacteria, although endospores and some vegetative cells (and many viruses) are highly resistant. Many bacteria can, in fact, be *preserved* by dryness. **Lyophilization (freeze-drying)** is a well-known preservation method which can maintain bacteria in a viable state for years.

Still another physical mechanism for effecting sterilization is **radiation**. **Ionizing radiations (X-rays, gamma rays**, etc.) kill largely by damaging DNA. This is accomplished in part by generating **free radicals** (extremely reactive fragments of molecules) and **peroxides** in water. **Ultraviolet light** (UV) also damages DNA; the specific site of its action is on adjoining thymine nucleotides, which form covalently bonded thymine dimers. Although cellular enzymes can repair the damage, sometimes the repair is error-prone and mutations result. The biggest drawback of ultraviolet light, however, is its lack of penetration into objects. The main utility of UV **germicidal lamps** is reducing numbers of air-borne bacteria.

**Filtration** is a mechanical means of removing microbes from air and other fluids. Membrane filters are available in a variety of **pore sizes** and can be used to sterilize many types of fluids which would be damaged by other methods of sterilization. Alternatively, membrane filters can be used to separate bacteria and fungi from their fermentation products, or from viruses (which pass through the filters).

The last physical sterilization mechanism is high **osmotic pressure**. If the environment is more concentrated than the cell's cytoplasm, the cell loses water by osmosis, resulting in lethal **plasmolysis**. This is the principle behind salted foods and high-sugar preserves.

**Chemical agents** for microbial control range from **antiseptics** (which inhibit or destroy bacteria on the human body), **disinfectants** (which destroy vegetative cells on inanimate objects), **bacteriostatics** (which prevent the growth of bacteria without killing them), **bactericides** (which kill bacteria), and **sanitizers** (agents that reduce the number of microbes to safe levels on food preparation surfaces).

The major variables in the use chemical disinfectants includes the **concentration** of the material (high generally more effective than low), the **time** during which it can act (the longer the better), the **temperature** at which it is used (the higher the better), the number and type of microbe present, and the **environment** in which it is used (proteins and other organics protect microbes from damage). The **mechanism** by which disinfectants work is one of three main possibilities: damage to the **cytoplasmic membrane**, damage to **enzymes**, damage to structural proteins. Damage to the membrane would make the cell "leak" essential nutrients and/or prevent absorption of nutrients. **Surface-active** agents such as **phenol**, **cresols**, and **alcohols** have their main effect on membranes. Strong **acids**, **alkalies**, **heavy metals** and **oxidizers** tend to damage proteins. The site of action is often the **sulfhydryl (-SH)** groups in proteins, which are particularly susceptible to heavy metal damage.

**Phenol** (carbolic acid) was the first disinfectant used. At usable levels (0.1 to 2 percent) it causes membranes to leak and damages membranes. It is effective against **vegetative bacteria**, **fungi**, and **enveloped viruses**; it is ineffective against spores and naked viruses. **Hexylresorcinol** and **hexachlorophene** are derivatives of phenol with lower toxicity to human tissues. **Chlorhexidine** is a still another compound which has good activity against bacteria and is very low in toxicity to human tissues. It is not absorbed through the skin and thus can be used as an antiseptic.

**Cresols** are coal derivatives which are effective disinfectants even in the presence of organic materials. Because of their toxicity to human tissues they are not suitable as antiseptics. **Alcohols** have mild antiseptic properties by means of protein denaturation. The larger alcohols, like propyl alcohol, are the most effective. Unlike most disinfectants, their activity is actually higher at 80 percent than at 100 percent.

**Halogens** (**chlorine** and **iodine**) are potent disinfectants. Chlorine gas is widely used to purify water. **Hypochlorite** (HClO) formation in water results in rapid oxidation of sulfhydryl groups on essential proteins. **Iodine** and its organic derivatives the **iodophors** (Betadine, etc.) are effective antiseptics and disinfectants. Their most likely activity is protein damage *via* binding to the amino acid tyrosine.

**Heavy metal** salts (mercury, silver, arsenic) are potent bactericides. All three bind to the sulfhydryl groups in proteins. Organic mercury compounds are commonly used as antiseptics or skin disinfectants (e.g. merthiolate).

Gram-positive bacteria are sensitive to certain **basic dyes**, such as **crystal violet**. Such materials are mostly used in microbiologic media as selective agents. **Quaternary ammonium** compounds are also much more effective against gram-positive bacteria than against gram-negatives. They are often used in combination with detergents to disinfect large surfaces. They damage cytoplasmic membranes and proteins. **Detergents** and **soaps**, acting alone, are effective at inhibiting or killing fragile bacteria. More effective against gram-positive bacteria, their primary action is damage to the cytoplasmic membrane. **Formaldehyde** and **glutaraldehyde** are strong alkylating agents which damage proteins and DNA. They are both effective at sterilizing materials and in disinfection. Formaldehyde even kills endospores.

**Hydrogen peroxide** is a mild antiseptic effective mostly against **anaerobic** bacteria which lack the enzyme **catalase** (which converts hydrogen peroxide to water and oxygen gas). **Ethylene oxide** is a widely used disinfectant both for its effectiveness and for its ability to penetrate into and through any substance not sealed against it. It kills bacteria, spores, molds and viruses. It is, however, quite **toxic**, very irritating to skin, and is explosively **flammable**. Oxygen-free mixtures of ethylene oxide in gas form are thus most commonly employed. An additional awkward trait is the requirement for long time periods both for action of the material (4 to 12 hours) and for decontamination (another 4 to 12 hours). Its main effect seems to be replacing hydrogen atoms with the hydroxyethyl radical ($-CH_2CH_2OH$).

**Betapropiolactone** is similar in action to ethylene oxide but is a liquid instead of a gas; it is also effective in much shorter periods of time. It is highly unstable and spontaneously hydrolyzes in a few hours, thus no lengthy decontamination period is required.

No matter what material or physical process is being used for disinfection, the **death** of the microbial population occurs in a **logarithmic** fashion; when populations are high, huge numbers of cells die, but as numbers decrease, the number dying also declines dramatically. Such behavior is referred to as a **first-order reaction.**

Many chemical disinfectants are compared in their effectiveness to phenol, using the **phenol coefficient**. This numerical value is determined by taking the highest dilution of a disinfectant that kills the organism in 10 minutes and dividing this by the highest dilution of phenol that gives the same result. Another method is the **use dilution test** in which test organisms are allowed to dry on glass rods or rings and these are then exposed to disinfectant; growth of cells from the glass rods or rings then gives you data on the killing rate for each disinfectant.

OBJECTIVES After studying this chapter, you should:

1. Be able to define sterilization, disinfection, lyophilization, antiseptic, germicide, and disinfectant.
2. Be familiar with the term *nosocomial infections*.
3. Know the many ways in which heat is used to sterilize an object.
4. Be able to describe pasteurization and to differentiate it from sterilization.
5. Know the types of radiation used to control microorganisms and be able to describe how ultraviolet light kills a cell.
6. Know the type of filter that is most commonly used to remove bacteria from a solution.
7. Know how disinfectants act to kill microorganisms and what are the major variables involved in disinfection.
8. Be able to list the commonly used chemical disinfectants.
9. Understand the kinetics of the disinfection process.
10. Know the meaning of the term phenol coefficient.

## LEARNING ACTIVITIES

### Vocabulary

Having read the chapter, you should be able to define or cite the significance of the following terms. If you cannot, look them up in the text. Terms are presented in the order you will encounter them in the book.

Pasteur
Semmelweis
Koch
Lister
phenol (carbolic acid)
nosocomial infections
*Escherichia coli*
*Klebsiella pneumoniae*
disinfection
physical sterilization
chemical sterilization
moist heat
autoclave
spore-strip-set
boiling water
dry-heat
Pasteurization
desiccation
ionizing radiation
free radicals
ultraviolet light
germicidal lamps
thymine dimers
Berkefeld filters
Sietz filters
membrane filters
osmotic pressure
lyophilization
freeze drying
antiseptic
disinfectant
bacteriostatic
bactericide
germicide
sanitizer
cytoplasmic membrane
protein denaturation
enzyme inactivation
sulfhydryl groups
phenol
substituted phenols
hexylresorcinol
hexachlorophene
chlorhexidine
cresols
alcohols
halogens
chlorine
chloramines
hypochlorite
oxidizing agent
iodine
iodophor
heavy metals
mercury
silver
arsenic
BAL (British antilewisite)
crystal violet
malachite green
brilliant green
quaternary ammonium compounds
soap
cationic detergent
anionic detergent
formaldehyde
hydrogen peroxide
ethylene oxide
betapropiolactone
logarithmic death
phenol coefficient
use dilution test

Complete each of the following statements by supplying the missing word or words.

1. ___Lister___ is famous for apparently being the first to use disinfectants during surgery (phenol, or carbolic acid).

2. nosocomial infections are hospital-acquired.

The following table has scrambled the definitions for the terms in the left column. Rearrange the terms to fit the definitions.

| TERM | DEFINITION |
|---|---|
| Sterilizing agent | An agent that kills bacteria Bactericide |
| Disinfectant | A disinfectant used on food-handling equipment sanitizer |
| Antiseptic → | Identical to disinfectant but may be only bacteriostatic; also, this term is usually restricted to chemicals used on skin and mucous membranes. |
| Sanitizer | Use of a chemical to destroy the growth of potential disease-producing organisms. May not kill endospores or viruses. Term is usually restricted to chemicals used on inanimate objects disinfectant |
| Bactericide | Agent that inhibits the growth of bacteria but does not kill the organisms Bacteriostatic agent |
| Bacteriostatic agent | Chemical that destroys all forms of life within a given area (sterilizing agent |

9. endospores are the hardest microbial stages to kill; most sterilization regimes have them in mind.

10. Autoclaves can produce steam temperatures of 121 °C, which is sufficient to sterilize most objects in an hour or less.

11. Damage to the cytoplasmic cell membrane, enzymes or structural proteins is the most common mechanism by which sterilization agents work. Some work directly at the DNA level, but they are relatively rare.

12. Pasteurization is not really a sterilization method, but rather one that attempts to destroy disease-causing bacteria in liquids.

13. Ionizing radiation and ultraviolet light inflict most of their damage on the genetic (DNA) level of the cell. This is not typical of most sterilization agents.

14. membrane filters with pore sizes of 0.22$\mu$m are usually effective in removing all bacteria from a fluid.

15. ___Lyophilization___ or freeze-drying is an excellent preservation method for many species of bacteria.

16. ___chemical agents___ vary in their mode of destroying bacteria; some damage the cytoplasmic membrane, others damage enzymes, still others mainly damage structural proteins.

17. ___phenol___ was the first chemical disinfectant used and is still the basis of comparison for chemical agents (remember the ___phenol___ coefficient)

18. ___Hexachlorophene___ was once widely used as an antiseptic, until it was shown that it was easily absorbed through the skin and that it was capable of producing brain damage in newborn animals.

19. ___Halogens___ such as chlorine and iodine are widely used disinfectants. Their effects are similar to those achieved by the heavy metals (mercury, silver, arsenic).

20. ___Betapropiolactone___ is a promising disinfectant which has the convenient property of self-destructing and therefore disappearing in just a few hours. This eliminates the need for decontamination that might otherwise be required.

## MASTERY TEST

1-13: Circle the choice that best answers the questions.

1. Which of the following is a specific term for hospital-acquired infections?
   a. postoperative infections
   b. antibiotic-resistant staphylococci infections
   c. nosocomial infections
   d. indwelling catheter-induced infection

2. Many patients who become infected in modern hospitals are particularly susceptible because their ___Immune___ systems have become altered by anticancer chemotherapy, antiinflammatory drugs or antirejection drugs.
   a. reproductive
   b. circulatory
   c. digestive
   d. immune
   e. respiratory

3. Sterilization (the killing of all forms of life in a given area) can be accomplished by two main means, physical and chemical ________________.

a. spiritual
b. bacteriostatic
c. thermal
d. osmotic
e. chemical

4. Moist heat temperatures of ______ are sufficient to kill normal vegetative cells of bacteria, but endospores can only be killed by ______ temperatures.

a. 25°C ... 50°C
b. 45°C ... 71°C
c. 80°C ... 121°C
d. 100°C ...150°C
e. 137°C ...215°C

5. Heat kills cells by inactivating proteins; its effectiveness is subject to several variables including all of the following EXCEPT:

a. environment (amount of fat)
b. amount of heat (temperature)
c. treatment length (time)
d. environment (amount of protein)
e. volume or mass of material being sterilized

6. Autoclave testing by weekly spore-strip-set tests are recommended by the Centers for Disease Control. Incubation of the test material should produce no growth of:

a. *Staphylococcus epidermidis*
b. *Streptococcus pyogenes*
c. *Klebsiella pneumoniae*
d. *Bacillus stearothermophilus*

7. All of the following can accomplish true sterilization (of bacteria and endospores) of a material EXCEPT:

a. moist heat of 121°C for 60 minutes
b. Pasteurization
c. dry heat of 170°C for 2 hours
d. moderate doses of ionizing radiation
e. membrane filtration (pore size .22$\mu$m)

8. Germicidal lamps, which reduce the numbers of air-borne bacteria in operating rooms, restaurants, bakeries, laboratories, etc. emit:

a. cathode rays
b. ultraviolet light
c. gamma rays
d. beta particles
e. visible light

9. The key activity which serves to preserve salted meats and high-sugar fruit preserves is:
   a. high osmotic pressure
   b. potent bacteriostatic effect of salt and sugar
   c. disinfectant effect of salt and sugar
   d. damage to cytoplasmic membranes by salt, sugar

10. Disinfectants can often be used as antiseptics, as long as:
   a. they effectively kill bacteria on inanimate objects
   b. they do not become spontaneously inactivated on contact with air
   c. they remain effective at the alkaline pH of skin
   d. they do not irritate skin and mucous membranes
   e. they kill fungi and bacteria equally well

11. Many chemical disinfectants work by damaging the cytoplasmic membrane of treated cells. The main effect of this is the inability of damaged cells to:
   a. retain their water
   b. synthesize their cell walls
   c. secrete digestive exoenzymes
   d. produce exotoxins efficiently
   e. retain their essential ions, coenzymes, sugars

12. Which of the following disinfectants does NOT have its main effect on damaging the cytoplasmic membrane?
   a. benzalkonium
   b. phenol
   c. cresols
   d. soap
   e. mercury

13. Phenol, like many chemical disinfectants, can be effective against all of the following EXCEPT:
   a. vegetative bacteria
   b. endospores
   c. vegetative fungi
   d. fungal spores
   e. enveloped viruses

---

14-19: TRUE-FALSE: (T for true, F for false)

T 14. Hexylresorcinol and hexachlorophene are technically described as substituted phenols.

F 15. Chlorhexidine has largely replaced the chlorinated phenols because it can be easily absorbed through the skin and thus can fight deep-seated infections.

____ 16. Lysol is an effective disinfectant based upon a coal distillate mixed with soap.

____ 17. Alcohols have their highest antiseptic power when 100 percent concentrated; weaker concentrations are markedly less effective.

____ 18. Halogens (chlorine and iodine) are basically oxidizing agents and have a germicidal effect based upon their ability to react with susceptible parts of proteins.

____ 19. There is no antidote for mercury poisoning.

---

20-23: Match the described disinfectant with its name. (use no answer twice)

ANSWERS

A. Basic Dyes
B. Betapropiolactone
C. Ethylene Oxide
D. Formaldehyde
E. Hydrogen Peroxide
F. Soaps

____ 20. Extremely toxic alkylating agent; often used as a preservative; quite effective in closed areas as a bactericide and fungicide.

____ 21. Normally used in gaseous form, this material is highly flammable, requires long periods of time to perform its work and equally long periods of time to evaporate to harmless levels. Despite these drawbacks, the agent is widely used due to its unparalleled ability to penetrate materials.

____ 22. Much more effective against gram-positive bacteria than gram-negatives. Often added to media to deter growth of gram-positives.

____ 23. Generally only effective against anaerobic bacteria which lack catalase, an enzyme that can detoxify this material.

---

24-25: Circle the choice that best answers the questions.

24. If a particular disinfectant kills cells at a 1:100,000 dilution just as effectively as phenol kills at a 1:250 dilution, the "phenol coefficient" is:
   a. 250
   b. 400
   c. 800
   d. 0.0025

25. The death rates for bacteria undergoing attack by a physical or chemical sterilization process is described as a "first order process". This means that:

a. cells die in a linear fashion
b. cells die in a parabolic fashion
c. rate of killing is dependent upon the number of viable cells present
d. more cells die at the end of the process than at the beginning
e. cells die at an accelerating rate as the process continues

ANSWERS TO LEARNING ACTIVITIES

Fill-in-the-blank questions:

1. Lister; 2. Nosocomial;

| TERM | DEFINITION |
|---|---|
| ~~Sterilizing agent~~<br>Bactericide | An agent that kills bacteria |
| ~~Disinfectant~~<br>Sanitizer | A disinfectant used on food-handling equipment |
| Antiseptic | Identical to disinfectant but may be only bacteriostatic; also, this term is usually restricted to chemicals used on skin and mucous membranes. |
| ~~Sanitizer~~<br>Disinfectant | Use of a chemical to destroy the growth of potential disease-producing organisms. May not kill endospores or viruses. Term is usually restricted to chemicals used on inanimate objects |
| ~~Bactericide~~<br>Bacteriostatic agent | Agent that inhibits the growth of bacteria but does not kill the organisms |
| ~~Bacteriostatic agent~~<br>Sterilizing agent | Chemical that destroys all forms of life within a given area |

9. Endospores; 10. Autoclaves; 11. Cytoplasmic membrane; 12. Pasteurization; 13. Ionizing; 14. Membrane filters; 15. Lyophilization; 16. Chemical agents; 17. Phenol; 18. Hexachlorophene; 19. Halogens; 20. Betapropiolactone.

## MASTERY TEST ANSWERS

| | | | | | | | | | | | | |
|---|---|---|---|---|---|---|---|---|---|---|---|---|
| 1<br>c | 2<br>d | 3<br>e | 4<br>c | 5<br>a | 6<br>d | | 7<br>b | 8<br>b | 9<br>a | 10<br>d | 11<br>e | 12<br>e |
| 13<br>b | 14<br>T | 15<br>F | 16<br>T | 17<br>F | 18<br>T | 19<br>F | 20<br>D | 21<br>C | 22<br>A | 23<br>E | 24<br>b | 25<br>c |

# CHAPTER 10

## SURGICAL AND MEDICAL ASEPSIS

### CHAPTER SUMMARY

**Asepsis** means the absence of any infectious agent. Under ideal conditions, hospitals would be able to maintain asepsis; in the real world they can't. 6 to 10 percent of hospital patients acquire an infection during their stay; such infections are called **nosocomial infections**. One reason for such statistics is the fact that hospitals are the one place where sick people (with their infectious agents) are concentrated. This risk factor can be dealt with to some degree by **isolation**, a precaution often used with patients suffering from communicable infectious (see Figure 10.1 in your textbook for sample isolation policies).

A second contributing factor is that many hospital patients are particularly vulnerable to infections due to breaks in their normal **anatomical barriers** (surgical incisions, wounds, burns). Other patients may have an **impaired immune response** due to **drug therapy, malignancies** or **extremes of age** (very young or very old). Such patients are often made ill by members of the patient's normal flora. Such bacteria and fungi are called **opportunists** because they can't normally cause infections, unless given an opportunity (surgical wound or burn; impaired immune system; implantation *via* catheter, syringe, respirator).

Breaks in the skin (or mucous membranes) are major risk factors. Severely **burned patients** have a 75 percent nosocomial infection rate; the only group to approach this level are **general surgery** patients (11 percent). **Surgical aseptic technique** is aimed at preventing infective agents from reaching the surgical wound.

1. Patient's skin is **shaved**, cleansed with **alcohol** or other cleaning agent; then an **antiseptic** (usually **providone-iodine**) is applied (sometimes along with or replaced by an **antibiotic** such as **ampicillin** or **cephaloridine**);
2. **Surgeons** and other operating room personnel are **scrubbed** (thorough hand-washing with germicidal agents), and wear **sterile gowns**, **masks**, **caps** or **turbans**, and sterile **rubber gloves**.
3. **Instruments** all must be **sterilized** in an autoclave or by some chemical means (which may require hours to complete).

4. **Sterile dressings** are applied without being handled by bare hands.

**General medical asepsis** aims to destroy pathogens as well as to reduce the number of microorganisms in the environment. This process includes general **housekeeping**, **dust** control, thorough cleaning of **dishes**, control of potential **carriers** of infectious agents, and care of patient **equipment**. All personnel must be thorough in their **handwashing** and guard against contamination through contact with patient **body secretions** which can be potent sources of infectious agents. Particular care must be taken when handling **blood** or **syringes** that can be sources of infection of **hepatitis B** or **HIV** (**h**uman **i**mmunodeficiency **v**irus - the cause of **AIDS**). Another problem of significant magnitude is the disposal of **solid waste**, which can amount to 40 pounds per patient per day. 25 to 30 percent of this material is likely to be contaminated with virulent organisms and must be disinfected prior to disposal by means of: (1) **incineration**, or (2) grinding and disposal *via* **sewage system** or, (3) burial in **land fills**.

Soiled **dressings** generally should be incinerated, although autoclaving followed by disposal is often substituted. **Body discharges** that contain pathogens should also be incinerated, but thorough disinfection with phenol or cresol or chlorine compounds may be sufficient provided that adequate amounts of **time** are allotted to the process. Safe disposal of **used syringes** and **needles** is essential to reduce the risk of accidental spread of hepatitis or AIDS.

A **committee on infection control** is a mandated activity for every hospital. Such committees are responsible for **reporting** and **evaluating infections** in patients, personnel and discharged patients. The committee is charged with determining which infections are nosocomial and to determine the **source** and **mode of transmission** of each nosocomial infection.

OBJECTIVES — A study of this chapter should provide a clear understanding of:

1. Nosocomial infections and how they can be minimized.
2. The objectives and procedures of surgical asepsis.
3. The problems of disposal of waste material.
4. General procedures involved in medical asepsis.
5. The responsibilities and functions of an infection control committee.

## LEARNING ACTIVITIES

### Vocabulary

Having read the chapter, you should be able to define or cite the significance of the following terms. If you cannot, look them up in the text. Terms are presented in the order you will encounter them in the book.

| | | |
|---|---|---|
| asepsis | cleansing | blood |
| nosocomial | antiseptic | individual equipment |
| CDC | providone-iodine | syringes |
| anatomical barriers | gown | hepatitis B |
| drug therapy | mask | HIV |
| predisposing factors | cap | AIDS |
| communicable | turban | solid waste |
| isolation | rubber gloves | handwashing |
| flora | medical asepsis | infection control committee |
| opportunists | dust control | |
| surgical asepsis | carriers | |
| | body secretions | |

Complete each of the following statements by supplying the missing word or words.

1. ____________________ infections are picked up by 6 to 10 percent of hospital patients.

2. ____________________ is the absence of any infectious agent.

3. The presence of ____________________, and the elimination of normal anatomical barriers to infection as a result of hospital procedures are the two main reasons that nosocomial infections are so common.

4. ____________________ is the term used to describe the control exercised over patients suffering from communicable infections.

5. Impaired ____________________ systems result from some drug therapies, malignancies, and the extremes of age (very young or very old patients).

6. ____________________ are members of a patient's normal flora which can cause infections when given a chance.

7. ____________________ units always experience the highest rates of nosocomial infections - often exceeding 75 percent of the patients in the unit.

8. ____________________ is a medical procedure that always results in the risk of infection because it always breaks normal anatomical barriers, thus great care must be taken to ensure asepsis before, during and after the procedure.

9. ____________________ are much more widely used than antibiotics to reduce skin bacterial levels. Two reasons for this are the potential for development of patient allergy to antibiotics and the potential for development of antibiotic-resistant strains of bacteria.

10. Providone-____________________ is the most widely-used pre-surgical disinfectant.

11. Proper ____________________-washing is one of the very most important aseptic techniques that surgeons and all other medical personnel can follow.

12. ____________________ should never be handled with bare hands, but rather with sterile forceps. This can dramatically reduce the chances of a post-surgical infection.

13. ____________________ are people who are able to transmit an infectious agent even though they do not exhibit any symptoms of disease.

14. ____________________ aims to destroy pathogens as well as to reduce the number of microorganisms in the environment; its agencies include housekeeping, dish washing, and waste disposal.

15. Contact with ____________________ is an important potential source of spread of poliomyelitis, hepatitis A, typhoid fever, and dysentery.

16. Contact with ____________________ or syringes carries with it a serious potential risk of contracting hepatitis B or AIDS.

17. The presence of ____________________ dramatically slows down the disinfection process, thus materials such as sputum or feces must be disinfected for extended periods of time.

18. ____________________ is the disposal method of choice for soiled dressings and contaminated body discharges.

19. ____________________ patients must be given protective isolation not to protect others but to protect them; they are the most common severely compromised patients present in hospitals.

20. ____________________ are established in all hospitals to keep track of nosocomial infections and to attempt to determine the sources and mode of transmission of such infections. Their aim is to reduce the frequency of nosocomial infections.

MASTERY TEST

1-12: Circle the choice that best answers the questions.

1. Which of the following is NOT true of nosocomial infections?
   a. acquired during a hospital stay
   b. affect 6 to 10 percent of patients
   c. occur at dramatically declining rates each year
   d. affect approximately 2 million patients per year
   e. cost the nation approximately $2 billion annually.

2. Not all patients are equally likely to acquire a nosocomial infection; those with ________________ are more likely to become infected.
   a. predisposing factors
   b. high body weight
   c. previous hospitalization
   d. heart disease
   e. poor eyesight

3. Intact ________________ is the best barrier to infection and any breaks invite infection.
   a. heart valves
   b. immune systems
   c. digestive tracts
   d. skin
   e. circulatory systems

4. Members of a patient's own microbial flora which take advantage of circumstances to cause infections are called:
   a. opportunists
   b. true pathogens
   c. virulent pathogens
   d. pneumocistic
   e. allelopathic

5. The best way to handle the risk posed by patients suffering from communicable infectious diseases like influenza or typhoid is to:
   a. discharge them
   b. isolate them
   c. group them together with others suffering the same infection
   d. dose them heavily with antibiotics

6. Which of the following is the most common cause of nosocomial infections regardless of the predisposing factor (just look at Table 10.2 in your text).
   a. *Streptococcus*
   b. *Escherichia*
   c. *Mucor*
   d. *Pseudomonas*
   e. *Staphylococcus*

7. Which of the following is NOT a contributing factor to the development of a nosocomial infection?
   a. patients with impaired immune systems
   b. patients with breaks in anatomical barriers
   c. patients undergoing antibiotic therapy
   d. patients with implanted catheters or respirators

8. Which of the following has the highest rate of nosocomial infections?
   a. general surgery
   b. neurosurgery
   c. obstetrics
   d. burn unit
   e. ophthalmology

9. Which of the following has the second-highest rate of nosocomial infections?
   a. general surgery
   b. neurosurgery
   c. obstetrics
   d. burn unit
   e. ophthalmology

10. Which of the following is NOT an important part of surgical asepsis?
   a. pre-surgical removal of any hair in the operation area
   b. thorough hand-washing by surgeon and all other participating personnel
   c. thorough dust removal of hallways, recovery room, etc.
   d. antiseptic treatment of patient's skin with providone-iodine

11. General medical asepsis aims to destroy pathogens as well as to reduce the number of ________________ in the environment.
   a. unnecessary personnel
   b. microorganisms
   c. incautious visitors
   d. nonsterile liquids
   e. unused machines

12. People who are capable of transmitting an infectious microorganism but who have no apparent symptoms themselves are called:
   a. sick people
   b. spurious pathogens
   c. fallacious reporters
   d. covert sources
   e. carriers

---

13-20: TRUE-FALSE: (T for true, F for false)

_____ 13. Patient equipment, if disposable, can be safely discarded in ordinary trash.

_____ 14. Poliomyelitis, hepatitis A, and typhoid fever are easily spread by contact with contaminated sputum.

_____ 15. Hepatitis B and the HIV organism can be spread by contact with blood products and used syringes.

_____ 16. Typical hospital patients generate 10 to 40 pounds of solid waste per day.

_____ 17. Disposal of solid waste is ideally carried out by incineration but can also be achieved by burial in local landfills.

_____ 18. Surgical scrubs are no different from regular handwashing, except for the use of bactericidal soaps and alcohol rinses.

_____ 19. All smooth-surfaced metal instruments **must** be sterilized in an autoclave.

_____ 20. Properly attended to, the skin can be rendered truly sterile, although this condition is very short-lived due to contamination from the environment.

---

21-25: Circle the choice that best answers the questions.

21. Dressings to be used in surgical procedures should be:
    a. sterilized in an autoclave
    b. sterilized by intense radiation
    c. sterilized by a chemical disinfectant
    d. sterilized by an infusion of antibiotics

22. Infectious body discharges are particularly hard to render safe with disinfectants due to their high content of:
    a. water
    b. sodium ions
    c. calcium ions
    d. chloride ions
    e. organic material

23. Which of the following is NOT a disease requiring enteric precautions?
    a. cholera
    b. diarrhea
    c. pertussis
    d. gastroenteritis
    e. typhoid fever

24. Protective isolation is required for patients suffering all of the following EXCEPT:
   a. extensive burns
   b. agranulocytosis
   c. immunosuppressive therapy
   d. measles
   e. lymphomas, leukemia

25. Which of the following is responsible for the reporting and evaluating of infections in patients, personnel, and discharged patients?
   a. hospital administrator
   b. CEO of hospital board
   c. chief epidemiologist
   d. infection control committee
   e. pharmacist

ANSWERS TO LEARNING ACTIVITIES

Fill-in-the-blank questions:

1. Nosocomial; 2. Asepsis; 3. sick people; 4. Isolation; 5. immune; 6. Opportunists; 7. Burn; 8. Surgery; 9. Chemical disinfectants; 10. iodine; 11. hand; 12. Sterile dressings; 13. Carriers; 14. General medical asepsis; 15. feces; 16. blood; 17. organic material; 18. Incineration; 19. Burn; 20. Infection control committee.

**MASTERY TEST ANSWERS**

| | | | | | | | | | | | | |
|---|---|---|---|---|---|---|---|---|---|---|---|---|
| 1<br>c | 2<br>b | 3<br>d | 4<br>a | 5<br>b | 6<br>e | | 7<br>c | 8<br>d | 9<br>a | 10<br>c | 11<br>b | 12<br>e |
| 13<br>F | 14<br>F | 15<br>T | 16<br>T | 17<br>T | 18<br>F | 19<br>F | 20<br>F | 21<br>a | 22<br>e | 23<br>c | 24<br>d | 25<br>d |

## CHAPTER 11

## ANTIMICROBIAL AGENTS IN THERAPY

### CHAPTER SUMMARY

**Chemotherapy**, the treatment of disease with chemical compounds, dates to the 1908 introduction of an anti-syphilis compound called **arsphenamine** by Paul Ehrlich. Synthetic chemotherapeutic agents are outnumbered by **antibiotics** (byproducts of the metabolic activity of bacteria and fungi). The perfect chemotherapeutic agent should be: **selectively toxic** (low in **toxicity** for the host, highly toxic to disease agent); non-allergenic (the host should not easily develop an **allergy** to the agent); the disease agent should not become readily **resistant** to the drug; the host should not destroy, neutralize or **excrete** the drug rapidly; and the drug must reach the **site of infection**.

The first widely-used synthetic chemotherapeutic agents were based on the red dye **Prontosil**. From this dye was developed the sulfonamide ("sulfa") drugs, a group of easily absorbed drugs with only moderate toxicity. They exerted a bacteriostatic effect by interfering with the synthesis of **folic acid**. Unlike humans, who absorb this B vitamin from their food, most bacteria synthesize it from scratch. Sulfonamides interfere with this synthesis by acting as **competitive inhibitors** of the enzyme that converts **paraaminobenzoic acid** (PABA) to folic acid. Some bacteria (especially gram-negatives) have become **resistant** to the drugs by producing mutant versions of the condensing enzyme, by decreasing uptake of the sulfonamides, or by overproducing PABA. They remain the drug of choice for some infections.

**Trimethoprim** is an antibiotic that also affects folic acid synthesis, but at an earlier step in the pathway than that affected by sulfonamides. Its effect (blocking the action of an enzyme called **dihydrofolate reductase**) also results in reduced production of **thymine** (an essential component of DNA). Trimethoprim and sulfonamides act **synergistically** on bacteria since they act on different steps of the same pathway.

**Isoniazid** (INH or **i**so**n**icotinic acid **h**ydrazide) has a structure very similar to the B vitamin **pyridoxine** and acts as a competitive inhibitor of this coenzyme in many reactions. It is particularly effective against *Mycobacterium tuberculosis* (the causative agent of tuberculosis) and is often used in combination with **ethambutol** (a synthetic) or **streptomycin** in treating this disease.

**Antibiotics** are products of the metabolism of bacteria and fungi which have selective toxicity toward microorganisms. The first one, **penicillin**, was discovered in 1929 by **Alexander Fleming** and its production was promoted by **Howard Florey** in the war years (World War II). The second antibiotic, **streptomycin**, was discovered in 1941 by Selman Waksman, *et.al.* Dozens more have been discovered since then, and all have activity against one of four possible cellular targets: **cell wall** synthesis, **protein** synthesis, **cell membrane** integrity, or **DNA** or **RNA** synthesis.

**Peptidoglycan** is a unique material found only in the cell walls of bacteria. It has no analogue in eucaryotic cells, and includes in its structure some pretty unusual ingredients. Among them are **L** and **D amino acids** (normal amino acid are all L forms) and two amino sugars, ***N*-acetylglucosamine** (NAGA) and ***N*-acetylmuramic acid** (NAMA). Anything that can attack peptidoglycan or prevent its synthesis will have selective toxicity against bacteria alone. **Fosfomycin** attacks early in the pathway by preventing the synthesis of NAMA. Fosfomycin is referred to as a **broad-spectrum antibiotic**, since it affects both gram-negative and gram-positive cells.

**Penicillin**, however, remains the best-known inhibitor of peptidoglycan synthesis. It is bactericidal because of its effects in weakening the cell wall and exposing the cells to osmotic damage. The penicillin structure includes a region called a **ß-lactam** which is similar enough to a portion of the building-block of peptidoglycan (**D-alanyl-D-alanine**) that it can bind to an enzyme, **transpeptidase** (an example of a PBP - **p**enicillin-**b**inding **p**rotein). Transpeptidase normally forms **cross-links** in the peptidoglycan by removing one D-alanine and bonding the other to a glycine. This action is blocked by penicillin. **Vancomycin** and **Ristocetin**, two very different antibiotics, have their effect in this same general region of cell wall synthesis; they **bind to D-alanyl-D-alanine** and prevent the transpeptidase reaction.

**Natural penicillin** has three main limitations: it is damaged by stomach acids; it is subject to destruction by **penicillinase** (**ß-lactamase**) enzymes, and it is mainly effective only against gram-positive bacteria. A number of modified forms and **semisynthetic derivatives** of penicillin have been developed to overcome the deficiencies of the natural product (e.g. **benzyl penicillin, penicillin G, penicillin V, methicillin, ampicillin**). These derivatives may be more resistant to damage by stomach acids, more resistant to enzymatic degradation, or more persistent in the system.

**Cephalosporins** represent another group of **ß-lactam** antibiotics whose effect is inhibition of peptidoglycan synthesis. These drugs, however, are quite **resistant** to penicillinase damage, and show improved effects against **gram-negative bacteria**. Again, they have been modified by semisynthetic manipulation of their structures and are now in their third generation - the **oxacephalosporins**.

**Monobactams** (monocyclic ß-lactams) are produced by bacteria, rather than fungi. Their basic effect is similar to that of the penicillins and cephalosporins, but they tend to be very resistant to destruction by ß-lactamase enzymes.

**Aztreonam**, the first semisynthetic monobactam, seems to be very effective against a variety of gram-negative bacteria.

**Bacitracin** is a very different antibiotic produced by *Bacillus licheniformis*. It is a peptide whose effect on cell wall synthesis is interference with the **dephosphorylation** of a **lipid carrier** responsible for moving the building blocks of peptidoglycan across the bacterial membrane. Without the lipid carrier, wall synthesis can't carry on.

Interference with protein synthesis can attack at various levels, by interfering with ribosome function or by interfering with enzyme function. **Chloramphenicol**, a broad-spectrum antibiotic produced by *Streptomyces venezuelae*, has its effect in binding with the **50S** (large) **ribosome subunit** and inhibiting the enzyme **peptidyl transferase** which forms the peptide bonds in the growing peptide chain. Protein synthesis stops dead in its tracks but can resume later (chloramphenicol is bacteriostatic, not bactericidal). Chloramphenicol has very **high toxicity** and can cause irreversible **aplastic anemia** in humans.

**Macrolide** antibiotics (**erythromycin, oleandomycin, carbomycin, spiromycin**) which have a large **lactone ring** in their structure, all prevent protein synthesis by binding to the **50S** ribosome subunit. Erythromycin, at least, seems to interfere with the **translocation** step (movement of the ribosome down the mRNA molecule). **Lincomycin** and **Clindamycin** (a semisynthetic derivative of Lincomycin) both also bind to the 50S ribosome subunit, interrupting protein synthesis.

The **tetracyclines** are a group of related very **broad-spectrum** antibiotics which exert a bacteriostatic effect on all bacteria except the mycobacteria. They bind to the **30S** ribosome subunit and prevent binding of the tRNA-amino acid complex, thus blocking protein synthesis. Another group of protein-synthesis blocking antibiotics that affect the **30S** subunit are the **aminoglycoside antibiotics** such as **streptomycin**, **neomycin**, **kanamycin**, **gentamicin** and **spectinomycin**. These tend to be bactericidal, rather than merely bacteriostatic. Their main effect is to block the **translocation** of the ribosome down the mRNA, thus **freezing the initiation complex**. In some cases protein synthesis continues to occur but the **mRNA is misread**. An important side effect of prolonged use of these antibiotics is **eighth cranial nerve damage** (hearing impairment).

**Polymyxins** are **peptides** with one end **hydrophilic** (soluble in water) and the other end **hydrophobic** (soluble in lipids). This structure allows these materials to embed themselves in cell membranes and create a **pore** through which materials can move into or out of the cell freely. They are **equally damaging to eucaryotic** membranes and thus have high **toxicity**. Somewhat more useful are the **polyene** antibiotics, **nystatin** and **amphotericin B,** which also damage membranes. These materials combine with **sterols** in the membrane, again creating pores that permit the membranes to **leak**. They are only effective against cells that have sterols in their membranes, which includes **all eucaryotes** (including fungi) and only the **mycoplasmas** in the procaryotic group. Their primary use is in the treatment of **fungal infections**.

The **imidazole** molecule has been modified to produce drugs which prevent the synthesis of **ergosterol**, an essential component of fungal membranes.

**Ketoconazole** can be taken orally, **miconazole** is used topically or intravenously, **clotrimazole** topically only due to its high toxicity.

**Mitomycin** and **actinomycin** bind to **DNA** and thus prevent **replication** and **transcription**. Much too toxic to be used against bacteria, they have been utilized as **antitumor** chemotherapy agents. **Nalidixic acid** and **novobiocin** both block DNA replication by inhibiting an enzyme called **DNA gyrase** which is involved in initiating the DNA replication process. **Fluoroquinolones** (broad-spectrum) and **ciprofloxacin** are derivatives of nalidixic acid and are hundreds of times more effective than it is. Working in a different way is **rifampin** (a type of rifamycin). This antibiotic inhibits **DNA to RNA transcription** by binding to the RNA polymerase enzyme. It is particularly valuable in treating **tuberculosis** and **leprosy**.

**Drug resistance** is a serious and increasing problem. There are three main ways for an organism to become drug resistant: it may develop an ability to **destroy** the antibiotic, it may develop a changed metabolic pathway to **bypass** the sensitive step, or it may become **impermeable** to the antibiotic. **Penicillinase (ß-lactamase)** enzymes are an example of the first mechanism. Many bacteria have apparently modified the transpeptidase enzyme that penicillin normally inhibits into one that destroys the antibiotic.

Multiple drug resistance was first reported in 1956 in *Shigella*; the organism was resistant to sulfonamide, streptomycin, chloramphenicol and the tetracyclines. Plasmid-based **resistance factors** (genes) are extensively passed around among gram-negative bacteria by means of **conjugation**. Similar effects are achieved by gram-positive organisms by means of **transformation**. Sometimes a simple mutation can result in total resistance to an antibiotic, as for example one in *E. coli* which changed one amino acid in the S-12 protein in the 30S ribosome subunit and thereby abolished the cell's sensitivity to streptomycin.

Overuse of antibiotics is one of the main reasons that resistance is progressing so quickly. An especially risky behavior is the use of **subtherapeutic** amounts of broad-spectrum antibiotics to enhance the growth of **farm animals**. This procedure is banned in Europe but continues in the U.S. with the result that food animals are the source of 69 percent of outbreaks of resistant *Salmonella typhimurium*.

When treating human patients it is generally advisable to use **doses** of antibiotics that are **high enough** to knock out the infection as fast as possible to reduce the likelihood of resistant forms developing. It is often desirable to treat the infection with **two or more drugs simultaneously** because a mutant that is resistant to one drug will still be vulnerable to the other one. It is also desirable to know which antibiotics a given infectious agent are sensitive to and which it is resistant to. Two main tests exist for this determination: the **Kirby-Bauer Susceptibility Test**, and the **Tube Dilution Assay**. In the Kirby-Bauer test a single high-strength filter paper **antibiotic disk** is placed on a petri dish containing Mueller-Hinton medium. The test organism is then spread over the surface of the medium. A **ring-shaped zone of inhibition** will develop around the disk if the organism is at all sensitive to the agent.

The **tube dilution assay** is more **quantitative** but also more time-consuming. A series of tubes with progressively decreasing amounts of antibiotic are inoculated with the test organism. The **MIC** (**m**inimal **i**nhibitory **c**oncentration) is the minimal concentration of antibiotic that prevents growth. To determine whether growth was prevented (**bacteriostatic** effect) or whether the organism was killed (**bactericidal** effect), one must subculture the tubes to fresh media to give the organism a chance to grow.

All of this advance work will not prevent the patient from developing an **allergic reaction** (hypersensitivity) or other side effect from the antibiotic. Allergies can range in severity from mild skin rashes to **anaphylactic shock** resulting in death. Other side effects include deafness (streptomycin), kidney damage (polymyxins), and superinfections (clindamycin, ampicillin). In a superinfection one resistant organism may overgrow to a dangerous degree because all of its competitors have been killed off (e.g. *Candida albicans, Clostridium difficile, Proteus*).

None of the agents so far discussed has any significant effect on viruses, largely because they depend on the host cell's own enzymes and metabolic pathways for most of their needs. There are, however, some antiviral agents. **Interferons** are natural products of cells infected by viruses. Their main effect is in preventing the subsequent infection of noninfected cells (the already-infected ones can't be saved). **Purine** and **pyrimidine analogues** are another class of antiviral agents. Their effect is to interfere with DNA replication. An example is **acyclovir**, an analogue of guanine. It is currently used to treat **herpesvirus** infections. **AZT** (**az**ido**t**hymidine, or zidovudine) is an effective inhibitor of the **reverse transcriptase** enzyme of HIV (**h**uman **i**mmunodeficiency **v**irus - the cause of AIDS) and other **retroviruses**.

**Amantadine** is yet another antiviral drug which works in a very different fashion from the others. Its effect is prophylactic, as it can **prevent the release of viral RNA** from the virus particle into cells before infection has occurred! It is particularly effective against the **Type A influenza** virus.

<u>OBJECTIVES</u> Study of this chapter should provide a clear understanding of:

1. The mechanism of action of the sulfonamides, trimethoprim, and isoniazid.
2. How various antibiotics inhibit cell wall synthesis.
3. The mechanism whereby penicillinase destroys penicillin.
4. How various antibiotics inhibit protein synthesis.
5. How polymyxin, nystatin, and amphotericin B affect cell membranes.
6. Antibiotics that bind to nucleic acids or inhibit their transcription.
7. The mechanism of transfer of drug resistance from one organism to another.
8. The problems associated with the use of subtherapeutic levels of antibiotics in animal feeds.
9. Laboratory tests for antibiotic susceptibility.
10. How some of the antiviral compounds exert their effects.

## LEARNING ACTIVITIES

### Vocabulary

Having read the chapter, you should be able to define or cite the significance of the following terms. If you cannot, look them up in the text. Terms are presented in the order you will encounter them in the book.

chemotherapy
arsphenamine
antibiotics
chemotherapeutic agent
selective toxicity
allergic
hypersensitive
resistant
sulfonamides
Prontosil
sulfanilamide
sulfisoxazole
competitive inhibition
folic acid
PABA
trimethoprim
dihydrofolate reductase
ethambutol
isonicotinic acid hydrazide
isoniazid
pyridoxine
Fleming
Florey
penicillin
Waksman
streptomycin
peptidoglycan
fosfomycin
muramic acid
broad-spectrum antibiotic
bactericidal
ampicillin
transpeptidization
transpeptidase
D-alanyl-D-alanine
PBPs
cephalosporin C
oxacephalosporins
oxa-ß-lactams
ß-lactamases
monocyclic ß-lactams
monobactams
aztreonam
bacitracin
vancomycin
ristocetin
50S subunit
30S subunit
70S ribosome
translocation
translocase
chloramphenicol
peptidyl transferase
aplastic anemia
macrolide antibiotics
lactone ring
erythromycin
lincomycin
clindamycin
ulcerative colitis
tetracyclines
aminoglycoside antibiotic
streptomycin
polyene antibiotics
imidazole derivatives
ergosterol
ketoconazole
miconazole
chlortrimazole
mitomycin
actinomycin
replication
transcription
nalidixic acid
novobiocin
DNA gyrase
fluoroquinolones
ciprofloxacin
griseofulvin
chitin
rifamycin
rifampin
drug resistance
multiple-drug resistance
synergistic effect
drug diffusion tests
tube dilution assays
Kirby-Bauer Susceptibility Test
susceptible
MIC
anaphylactic
pseudomembranous colitis

benzyl penicillin
probenecid
procaine
penicillin G
penicillinase
phenoxyacetic acid
penicillin V
ß-lactam
methicillin
initiation complex
neomycin
kanamycin
gentamicin
spectinomycin
eighth cranial nerve
polymyxins
nystatin
amphotericin B
sterols
superinfections
interferon
arabinose
herpesvirus
acyclovir
analogue
retrovirus
reverse transcriptase
AZT (zidovudine)
amantadine

## Fill-In-the-Blank Questions

Complete each of the following statements by supplying the missing word or words.

1. Paul Ehrlich ______ pioneered the field of chemotherapy with the 1906 introduction of arsphenamine, a synthetic treatment for syphilis.

2. Antibiotics ______ are natural or semisynthetic byproducts of the metabolic activity of bacteria or fungi.

3. Sulfonamides ______ are a group of synthetic chemotherapeutic agents based on a red dye called Prontosil.

4. Competitive inhibition ______ of an enzyme involved in the synthesis of folic acid is the mechanism of action of the agents discussed in question #3.

5. Trimethoprim ______ is a synthetic agent that also interferes with folic acid synthesis, but at an earlier step in the pathway. This agent interferes with the reduction of dihydrofolate to tetrahydrofolate.

6. Isonicotinic acid hydrazide ______ (INH) competitively inhibits enzymes using pyridoxine as a coenzyme.

7. Alexander Fleming ______ discovered penicillin, Howard Florey and others pioneered its production.

In the following chart, fill in the information in the blank blocks, using the filled-in blocks as a guide.

| ANTIBIOTIC NAME | GENERAL EFFECT | SPECIFIC EFFECT |
|---|---|---|
| Penicillin | Inhibits peptido-glycan synthesis | Blocks trans-peptidase enzyme |
| Cephalosporin | 8. | Blocks trans-peptidase enzyme |
| Vancomycin | Inhibits peptido-glycan synthesis | 9. |
| Macrolide anti-biotics (e.g. Erythromycin) | 10. | Binds to 50S ribosome subunit; blocks trans-location |
| Tetracyclines | Inhibit protein synthesis | 11. |
| Aminoglycoside antibiotics (e.g. Streptomycin) | 12. | Binds to 30S ribosome subunit; freeze initiation |
| Polyene anti-biotics (e.g. Nystatin) | Damage cell mem-branes; promote material leakage | 13. |
| Actinomycin and Mitomycin | Block replication and transcription | 14. |
| Nalidixic acid and Novobiocin | 15. | Bind to DNA gyrase and inhibit its activity |
| Rifampin | 16. | Binds to RNA polymerase and inhibits its action |

17. Penicillinases are enzymes which specifically attack penicillin.

18. β-lactamases are enzymes capable of destroying both penicillin and some of the cephalosporins.

19. The Tube dilution assay is the most precise way to ascertain antibiotic resistance of microbes.

20. AZT (azidothymidine) is the name of the antiviral agent effective against retroviruses (including HIV).

## MASTERY TEST

1-9: Circle the choice that best answers the questions.

1. Which of the following is NOT a desirable trait for a chemotherapeutic agent?
   a. the drug should show selective toxicity toward disease agent, low toxicity toward host
   b. the host should not easily become allergic to the agent
   c. the disease agent should not readily become resistant to the drug
   d. the host must be able to easily excrete the drug and rapidly clear it from its system
   e. the drug should be able to reach the site of infection

2. The selective toxicity of sulfonamides on bacteria is based on the fact that:
   a. humans do not synthesize folic acid
   b. the bacterial enzyme is high-affinity, the human one is low affinity
   c. bacteria use a different starting material to synthesize folic acid than humans do
   d. all of these are true

3. Bacteriostatic agents:
   a. kill bacteria slowly
   b. kill bacteria quickly
   c. do not kill bacteria, but prevent their growth
   d. do not kill bacteria, but slow down their growth

4. A broad-spectrum antibiotic kills:
   a. many species of related bacteria
   b. gram-positive and gram-negative bacteria
   c. bacteria and fungi
   d. bacteria, fungi and Helminths

5. Trimethoprim is said to operate synergistically with the sulfonamides because:
   a. they both inhibit the same pathway
   b. bacteria resistant to one are always sensitive to the other
   c. bacteria are killed by one, fungi by the other
   d. one operates at the enzyme level, the other at the gene level

6. Streptomycin was discovered by:
   a. Alexander Fleming
   b. Louis Pasteur
   c. Paul Ehrlich
   d. Howard Florey
   e. Selman Waksman

7. Fosfomycin is an inhibitor of cell wall synthesis that operates by inhibiting the:
   a. transport of peptidoglycan building blocks across the membrane
   b. the synthesis of *N*-acetylglucosamine (NAGA)
   c. the cross-linking of peptides in peptidoglycan
   d. the synthesis of *N*-acetylmuramic acid (NAMA)

8. Semisynthetic derivatives of penicillin have been developed to try to overcome all of the following shortcomings of natural penicillin EXCEPT:
   a. easy destruction of penicillin by stomach acids
   b. destruction by penicillinase enzymes
   c. virtual limitation of effectiveness to gram-negative organisms
   d. virtual limitation of effectiveness to gram-positive organisms

9. The key step in cell wall synthesis that is blocked by penicillin is the:
   a. transpeptidase step linking alanine to glycine
   b. transpeptidase step linking alanine to alanine
   c. transpeptidase step linking alanine to glutamine
   d. transport of D-alanyl-D-alanine across the membrane

---

10-16: Match the antibiotics to their chemical class (use no answer twice)

ANSWERS

| | |
|---|---|
| A. Aminoglycoside group | E. Monobactam group |
| B. Cephalosporin group | F. Penicillin group |
| C. Imidazole group | G. Polyene group |
| D. Macrolide group | H. Tetracycline group |

F 10. Methicillin, ampicillin - Penicillin group

B 11. Moxalactam, cefotaxime, cefoperazone, cefriaxone CEPHALOSPORIN Gr

D 12. Erythromycin, oleandomycin, carbomycin, spiromycin macrolide gr

H 13. Chlorotetracycline, oxytetracycline Tetracycline gr

A 14. Streptomycin, neomycin, kanamycin, gentamicin Aminoglycoside gr

G 15. Nystatin, amphotericin B polyene gr.

---

16-25: Circle the choice that best answers the questions.

16. Multiple drug resistance, as occurs in *Shigella* and other gram-negative organisms derives from:
    a. extensive transformation of cells by free DNA from various resistant species
    b. extremely rapid rates of mutation
    c. extensive conjugation between different resistant species
    d. drug-induced plasmid formation

17. Some ß-lactamase enzymes (which hydrolyze the ß-lactam bond) are capable of destroying all of the following EXCEPT:
    a. penicillins
    b. cephalosporins
    c. semi-synthetic penicillins
    d. tetracyclines
    e. monobactams

18. Some antibiotic resistance involves a mutational change that prevents the cell from ______ the antibiotic.
    a. binding to
    b. absorbing
    c. metabolizing
    d. hydrolyzing
    e. excreting

19. The Kirby-Bauer Susceptibility Test is performed on which of the following types of media?
    a. TSA
    b. Sabouraud's Agar
    c. Kligler's Iron Agar
    d. Manson-Frome Agar
    e. Mueller-Hinton Agar

20. The inclusion of subtherapeutic amounts of antibiotics in animal feed is illegal in:
    a. all countries in the developed world
    b. all Asian countries
    c. the U.S. and Canada
    d. Europe
    e. the Soviet Union and South Africa

21. Using two chemotherapeutic agents simultaneously to achieve a greater effect than either alone is an example of:
    a. a fortuitous effect
    b. a synergistic effect
    c. a sympathetic effect
    d. extremely risky
    e. illegal

22. The tube dilutions assay enables one to determine the lowest concentration that prevents the growth of bacteria; this level is known as the:
    a. CAB
    b. FCC
    c. MIC
    d. MBC
    e. ABC

23. The development of an allergy to an antibiotic is an example of:
   a. prophylactic response
   b. hypersensitivity
   c. subtherapeutic activity
   d. hyperactivity
   e. bad luck

24. Some antibiotic treatments can be so effective in destroying most bacteria that one resistant species may be able to overgrow and reach huge populations. Such a response is called a(n):
   a. superinfection
   b. anaphylactic shock
   c. urticaria
   d. serum sickness
   e. blood poisoning

25. Which of the following is an antiviral substance manufactured by virus-infected cells?
   a. acyclovir
   b. AZT
   c. amantadine
   d. interferon
   e. histamine

## ANSWERS TO LEARNING ACTIVITIES

Fill-in-the-blank questions:

1. Paul Ehrlich; 2. Antibiotics; 3. Sulfonamides
4. Competitive inhibition; 5. Trimethoprim;
6. Isonicotinic acid hydrazide; 7. Alexander Fleming;(8-16 on next page)
17. Penicillinases; 18. ß-lactamases; 19. tube dilution assay; 20. AZT or azidothymidine.

| MASTERY TEST ANSWERS | | | | | | | | | | | | |
|---|---|---|---|---|---|---|---|---|---|---|---|---|
| 1 d | 2 a | 3 c | 4 b | 5 a | 6 e | | 7 d | 8 c | 9 a | 10 F | 11 B | 12 D |
| 13 H | 14 A | 15 G | 16 c | 17 d | 18 b | 19 e | 20 d | 21 b | 22 c | 23 b | 24 a | 25 d |

| ANTIBIOTIC NAME | GENERAL EFFECT | SPECIFIC EFFECT |
|---|---|---|
| Penicillin | Inhibits peptido-glycan synthesis | Blocks trans-peptidase enzyme |
| Cephalosporin | 8. Inhibits peptidoglycan synthesis | Blocks trans-peptidase enzyme |
| Vancomycin | Inhibits peptido-glycan synthesis | 9. Binds to D-alanyl-D-alanine |
| Macrolide anti-biotics (e.g. Erythromycin) | 10. Inhibits protein synthesis | Binds to 50S ribosome subunit; blocks trans-location |
| Tetracyclines | Inhibit protein synthesis | 11. Bind to 30S ribosome subunit |
| Aminoglycoside antibiotics (e.g. Streptomycin) | 12. Inhibits protein synthesis | Binds to 30S ribosome subunit; freeze initiation |
| Polyene anti-biotics (e.g. Nystatin) | Damage cell mem-branes; promote material leakage | 13. Bind to fungal membrane sterols |
| Actinomycin and Mitomycin | Block replication and transcription | 14. Bind to DNA |
| Nalidixic acid and Novobiocin | 15. Block DNA replication | Bind to DNA gyrase and inhibit its activity |
| Rifampin | 16. Blocks RNA transcription | Binds to RNA polymerase and inhibits its action |

# CHAPTER 12

## CLASSIFICATION SCHEMES FOR COMMON PROCARYOTES

### CHAPTER SUMMARY

**Taxonomy** is the branch of biology concerned with the identifying and classifying of organisms. Modern taxonomy is concerned with determining **relationships** between organisms. The field is said to have been founded in 1753 by **Carolus Linnaeus**. Linnaeus established the system of **binomial nomenclature** wherein each organism has a two-part name, the **genus** (always capitalized) and the **species** (always lower case). Linnaeus also established the basic hierarchical system of **taxons** still used today: the **species** is in a **genus**, the genus is in a **family**, the family is in an **order**, the order is in a **class**, the class is in a **division** (or phylum, for zoologists), and the division is in a **kingdom**. The kingdom is the broadest taxon, one in which all of its members share a small group of very basic characteristics.

Linnaeus was satisfied with only two kingdoms: the Kingdom **Plantae** (photosynthetic, nonmotile plants with rigid cell walls) and the Kingdom **Animalia** (motile, animals; nonphotosynthetic and without cell walls). In the mid-19th Century, Haeckel proposed a new, third kingdom, the Kingdom **Protista** (composed of unicellular algae, bacteria, fungi, and protozoa). R.H. **Whittaker** proposed a 5-kingdom system in 1969; the new kingdoms are the **Myceteae**, or **Fungi** (yeasts and molds) and the **Monera** (procaryotic cells); the Protista consist of eucaryotic algae and the protozoa. Carl **Woese**, in another departure based upon studies on **ribosomal RNA** and other biochemical data, suggested in 1979 that there should be only three kingdoms; the **Eubacteria**, the **Archaebacteria**, and the **Eucaryotes**.

**Phylogenetic** classification systems stress the **relationships** between organisms rather than trivial physical similarities. According to Woese, for example, the eucaroytic organisms have a common ancestry with the archaebacteria, yet their organelles, the mitochondria and chloroplasts, have strong affiliations with the eubacteria. It seems possible that some primitive **archaebacterial** organism had an **endosymbiotic** relationship with a **eubacterial** organism (mitochondrion or chloroplast) and this gave rise to the eucaryotic group.

The archaebacteria of today are unique organisms with unusual **RNA sequences**, no **peptidoglycan** in their cell walls, and lipids composed of **ether** linked carbon chains (versus the more common ester linkage). All archaebacteria live in hostile environments that may resemble conditions on the early Earth. The **methanogens** are a group of unusual obligate anaerobes that reduce carbon dioxide to methane; the extreme **halophiles** live in very saline environments (e.g. the Great Salt Lake, Utah); and the **thermoacidophiles** grow at extremely high temperatures and low pH levels (90°C and pH 2).

Identification of the eubacteria begins with determining the **shape** and **Gram reaction** of the cells. Other valuable information includes **oxygen requirements**, colony appearance, and biochemical behavior. **Serological** and genetic information may ultimately be required to finalize the identification. Still other information used in indentification includes data on specific **sugar metabolism** (e.g. growth on mannitol), the **end products** of metabolism (acids or alcohols, $CO_2$, or $H_2S$), **fatty acid** products of fermentation, and **enzyme** production (e.g. catalase, urease, ß-galactosidase).

**Adsonian analysis**, or **numerical taxonomy**, is a system in which one hundred or more **biochemical** and **morphological** characteristics are compared to determine a **similarity index** for each pair of organisms. *S* (the similarity index) = *NS* (the number of similarities) divided by (*NS* + *ND*) (the number of similarities plus the number of differences. The higher S is, the more closely related the organism are likely to be. An accurate result requires the comparison of so many characteristics that a computer is required for analysis.

**Serological classification** is an extremely sensitive means of distinguishing between species or even between varieties of a single species. **Antibody-antigen binding** is the key to these tests and they may include such sophisticated enhancements as **fluorescent antibody** techniques and the use of **monoclonal antibodies. Bacteriophage typing** is a technique that is at least as sensitive as serological classification. Phages are **extremely specific** as to the species and even strain of a single species that they will attack. Such testing is particularly valuable for important pathogens and opportunists (e.g. *Staphylococcus aureus*, *Salmonella typhi*, etc.). Such testing is often of great value to **epidemiologists** in tracing the origin of an outbreak of an infective agent.

**DNA homology** studies take advantage of the fact that **DNA melts** (separates into single strands) easily and can **reanneal** into double-stranded **duplexes** with its original complementary strand or with strands of closely related species. The **rate and extent** to which the test DNA will complex with that of the reference organism reveals the degree of **homology** between them. A cruder method is to compare the gross amounts of **G** and **C** (guanine and cytosine) in DNA. Organisms with large differences cannot be related; organisms that you already suspect to be related should have very similar G + C percentages.

*Bergey's Manual of Systematic Bacteriology* is not a taxonomic text but rather a guide to the identification of bacteria; it is mainly a series of "keys" to various groups of procaryotes. Bergey's is an example of a practical, rather than a phylogenetic classification system, based as it is on relatively easy-to-determine traits of organisms such as morphology and physiology.

OBJECTIVES Study of this chapter should provide a comprehension of

1. Past and present attempts to classify living organisms.
2. The five-kingdom system proposed by Whittaker.
3. The three-kingdom scheme proposed by Woese.
4. The use of rRNA sequences to establish phylogenetic relationships among living cells.
5. The properties of the archaebacteria that differentiate them from the eubacteria.
6. Procedures used for the identification of bacteria.
7. What types of biochemical information can be used for identification purposes.
8. What is meant by numerical taxonomy.
9. How specific antibodies or bacteriophages can be used to type microorganisms.
10. The use of genetic classifications such as plasmid exchange or DNA homology studies.
11. How the current *Bergey's Manual* has divided the procaryotes into different sections and the major characteristics for each section.

## LEARNING ACTIVITIES

### Vocabulary

Having read the chapter, you should be able to define or cite the significance of the following terms. If you cannot, look them up in the text. Terms are presented in the order you will encounter them in the book.

taxonomy
relationship
morphology
reproductive compatibility
Linnaeus
binomial nomenclature
genus
species
family
order
class
division

Haeckel
Protista
Whittaker
Myceteae
Monera
Woese
Archaebacteria
Eubacteria
Eucaryotes
phylogenetic
rRNA
endosymbionts
ether linkage
ester linkage

gas-liquid chromatography
fatty acid endproducts
*Bergey's Manual*
numerical taxonomy
similarity index
serological
antibodies
monoclonal antibodies
antigenic determinants
bacteriophage typing

| | | |
|---|---|---|
| phylum | methanogens | DNA homology |
| kingdom | halophiles | preferential |
| Animalia | thermoacidophiles | degradation |
| Plantae | urkaryote | G + C content |

Complete the following list of taxons **in order**.

Kingdom

1. ____________________

Class

2. ____________________

3. ____________________

Genus

4. ____________________

5-9: Unscramble the Whittaker kingdom descriptions in the following table.

| KINGDOM NAME | DESCRIPTION |
|---|---|
| ANIMALIA | Cells are universally procaryotic. |
| MYCETEAE | Cells have walls; metabolism is photosynthetic; organisms are multicellular. |
| MONERA | Cells lack walls; organisms are multicellular and generally motile |
| PLANTAE | Cells have walls, often of chitin; organisms are never photosynthetic |
| PROTISTA | Cells may have walls or lack them; metabolism may be photosynthetic or not; organisms unicellular or colonial |

Complete each of the following statements by supplying the missing word or words.

10. ____________________ proposes only three kingdoms; the archaebacteria, the eubacteria and the eucaryotes.

11. Determining ____________________ relationships is the goal of modern taxonomic workers.

12. ____________________ is the key molecule studied by Woese and others because of its presumed stability.

13. ____________________ lack peptidoglycan in their cell walls, have membrane lipids based on ether bonds, and generally are adapted to severe environments.

14. ____________________ are obligate anaerobes which reduce carbon dioxide to methane gas.

15. ____________________ are organisms which live in extremely salty environments.

16. ____________________ is an identification scheme that depends upon comparing one hundred or more traits in order to determine the similarity of two species of organism.

17. ____________________ typing depends upon the high degree of specificity showed by bacterial viruses in selecting and attacking their hosts.

18. ____________________ homology studies depend upon the ability of very similar types of molecules to adhere to one another, while different ones will not adhere.

19. ____________________ G + C amounts do not guarantee that two organisms are related, only that they might be.

20. ____________________*'s Manual of Systematic Bacteriology* is an extremely popular and valuable set of keys for the identification of bacteria.

MASTERY TEST

1-25: Circle the choice that best answers the questions.

1. Which of the following is generally regarded to be the founder of modern taxonomy?
   a. R.H. Whittaker
   b. Carolus Linnaeus
   c. Gregor Mendel
   d. Carl Woese
   e. Jacob Monod

2. Binomial nomenclature is the technique of giving an organism a name based upon its:
   a. class and family
   b. genus and order
   c. species and kingdom
   d. genus and species
   e. class and order

3. Which of the following is the correct way to represent the binomial for the human organism?
   a. *homo sapiens*
   a. homo Sapiens
   a. Homo sapiens
   d. *Homo sapiens*
   e. *Homo Sapiens*

4. Which of the following kingdoms was first proposed by Haeckel in the middle of the 19th Century?
   a. Animalia
   b. Myceteae (Fungi)
   c. Monera
   d. Plantae
   e. Protista

5. Which of the following is split into two kingdoms in the scheme of Woese?
   a. Animalia
   b. Myceteae (Fungi)
   c. Monera
   d. Plantae
   e. Protista

6. Which of the following is a proposed kingdom which includes the animals, plants, fungi, algae and protozoans?
   a. archaebacteria
   b. eubacteria
   c. protists
   d. eucaryotes
   e. prokaryotae

7. Which of the following contains organisms generally believed to be the most primitive living things on the planet?
   a. archaebacteria
   b. eubacteria
   c. protists
   d. eucaryotes
   e. prokaryotae

8. Which of the following molecules has been sequenced carefully by the Woese team?
   a. mRNA
   b. tRNA
   c. rRNA
   d. DNA
   e. cytochrome c

9. Which of the following is a group of primitive organisms which live only in very hot water regions, often with very low ambient pH levels?
   a. mesophiles
   b. halophiles
   c. anglophiles
   d. thermoalkalinophiles
   e. thermoacidophiles

10. Which of the following is the type of bond holding together the lipids in the archaebacteria?
   a. glycosidic
   b. peptide
   c. ester
   d. ether
   e. ß-lactam

11. The term used to describe the primitive eucaryotic cell type that existed before the acquisition of mitochondria and chloroplasts is:
   a. urkaryote
   b. archaecaryote
   c. archaebacterium
   d. archaemoneran
   e. prokaryote

12. Chloroplasts and mitochondria most closely resemble which of the following?
   a. archaebacteria
   b. protozoans
   c. eubacteria
   d. fungi
   e. viruses

13. Which of the following is NOT used in the classification and identification of bacteria?
   a. shape of cells
   b. Gram reaction
   c. oxygen requirements
   d. biochemical traits
   e. microtubule structure

14. Which of the following metabolic traits is usually assayed by means of a gas-liquid chromatograph?
   a. specific sugar metabolism
   b. hydrogen sulfide production
   c. fatty acid endproducts
   d. acetyl coenzyme A production
   e. carbon dioxide production

15. Enzyme production by bacteria is often of taxonomic importance. Which of the following enzymes is produced in high levels by *Proteus*, but not by most other members of the enteric bacterial group?
   a. catalase
   b. urease
   c. ß-galactosidase
   d. DNA gyrase
   e. ß-lactamase

16. In the formula S = NS/(NS + ND), the term "ND" refers to:
a. near departures
b. number of differences
c. number of similarities
d. similarity index
e. neutral density

17. If a pair of organisms have a very high value for "S" computed from the formula in #16, they:
a. are probably close relatives
b. are probably not related at all
c. might be close or distant relatives

18. In serological classification, specific ______________ are used to bind to specific ____________ on the surfaces of bacterial cells.
a. antigens ... antibodies
b. phages ... phage binding sites
c. antibodies ... phage binding sites
d. antibodies ... antigens
e. antigens ... phages

19. Fluorescent microscope analysis of serological studies depends upon the availability of:
a. fluorescent antibodies
b. fluorescent antigens
c. fluorescent phages
d. fluorescent bacteria
e. fluorescent peptides

20. Bacteriophage typing is particularly important in the study of:
a. food spoilage organisms
b. soil bacteria
c. pathogenic bacteria
d. soil fungi
e. milk-borne bacteria

21. Which of the following is the most likely professional to be involved in tracking down the spread of a nosocomial infection?
a. a dermatologist
b. a proctologist
c. a neurologist
d. an immunologist
e. an epidemiologist

22. DNA homology studies involve heating up double-stranded DNA until it:
a. disintegrates into free nucleotides
b. separates into single stranded DNA
c. changes into RNA
d. undergoes denaturation
e. becomes phosphorylated

23. G + C percentage analysis is:
    a. an extremely sensitive and accurate way to determine relatedness between 2 species
    b. a relatively sensitive and very accurate way to determine relatedness between 2 species
    c. a relatively crude and inaccurate way to determine relatedness between 2 species

24. The S1 nuclease enzyme
    a. preferentially degrades natural double-stranded DNA
    b. preferentially degrades hybrid double-stranded DNA
    c. preferentially degrades DNA-RNA hybrid molecules
    d. preferentially degrades single-stranded DNA
    e. preferentially degrades phage DNA

25. The main purpose of Bergey's Manual is:
    a. to be in the forefront in taxonomic data collection
    b. to be useful for identification of unknown bacteria
    c. to be useful for identification of unknown fungi
    d. to be consulted for antibiotic sensitivity analysis

## ANSWERS TO LEARNING ACTIVITIES

Fill-in-the-blank questions:

1. Phylum; 2. Order; 3. Family; 4. Species;

| KINGDOM NAME | DESCRIPTION |
|---|---|
| ~~ANIMALIA~~ MONERA | Cells are universally procaryotic. |
| ~~MYCETEAE~~ PLANTAE | Cells have walls; metabolism is photosynthetic; organisms are multicellular. |
| ~~MONERA~~ ANIMALIA | Cells lack walls; organisms are multicellular and generally motile |
| ~~PLANTAE~~ MYCETEAE | Cells have walls, often of chitin; organisms are never photosynthetic |
| PROTISTA | Cells may have walls or lack them; metabolism may be photosynthetic or not; organisms unicellular or colonial |

10. Carl Woese; 11. phylogenetic; 12. rRNA; 13. Archaebacteria; 14. Methanogens; 15. Halophiles; 16. Numerical taxonomy (Adsonian analysis); 17. Bacteriophage; 18. DNA; 19. Very similar; 20. *Bergey*

## MASTERY TEST ANSWERS

| | | | | | | | | | | | | |
|---|---|---|---|---|---|---|---|---|---|---|---|---|
| 1<br>b | 2<br>d | 3<br>d | 4<br>e | 5<br>c | 6<br>d | | 7<br>a | 8<br>c | 9<br>e | 10<br>d | 11<br>a | 12<br>c |
| 13<br>e | 14<br>c | 15<br>b | 16<br>b | 17<br>a | 18<br>d | 19<br>a | 20<br>c | 21<br>e | 22<br>b | 23<br>c | 24<br>d | 25<br>b |

## CHAPTER 13

## UNUSUAL PROCARYOTIC CELLS

### CHAPTER SUMMARY

The **rickettsiae** are a group of very small, unusual procaryotes which grow as **obligate intracellular parasites**. This means that they cannot survive outside of the cells of their hosts (animal cells). They are derived from **gram-negative** bacteria as is shown by their gram reaction and the presence of **diaminopimelic** acid in their cell walls. They cannot be cultured in normal media because they leak essential **intracellular metabolites** ($NAD^+$, coenzyme A, ATP) and ions ($K^+$ and $Mg^{2+}$). Although the rickettsiae do appear to have an intact **citric acid cycle**, and can oxidize glutamic acid, they are totally unable to metabolize sugar. Rickettsiae are studied by growing them in susceptible animals, in tissue cultures, or, most commonly, in **chick embryos**.

All known rickettsial diseases (with one exception - **Q fever**) are spread by means of the bite of an infected **arthropod vector**. **Vectors** are organisms that carry disease-producing agents from one host to another, **arthropods** are insects and arachnids such as ticks, lice, fleas, and mites. The arthropod may become a carrier of the agent after having bitten an **infected animal** or it may have been infected by means of a **transovarian route** from its mother. The **human body louse** is the only arthropod vector that is actually harmed by the rickettsial agent (in this case the cause of epidemic **typhus**, *Rickettsia prowazekii*).

**Chlamydiae** are, like the rickettsiae, obligate **intracellular parasites** derived from **gram-negative** bacteria. They are so small that they were once thought to be viruses. Their parasitism is enforced by a metabolic inability to produce ATP - they must live within another cell that provides them with energy. They are distinct from all other procaryotes by virtue of their totally unique mode of reproduction (called their **developmental cycle**). Host cells are infected by a small, dense stage called the **elementary body**. Once inside the host cell, the elementary body grows into a much larger, less dense stage called the **initial body** (or **reticulate body**). These cells are metabolically active, synthesize much RNA and protein, and reproduce by **binary fission**; they are, however, noninfectious. After 24 to 48 hours the initial bodies reorganize into the small dense **elementary body** stage again. At this point the host cell bursts open, freeing the new infective elementary bodies.

The chlamydiae are divided into two taxonomic groups: **group A** (a single species - *Chlamydia trachomatis*), and Group B. *Chlamydia trachomatis* causes a diverse group of human infections and forms compact inclusion bodies containing glycogen; they are inhibited by the sulfonamide drugs. **Group B**, which includes two species (*Chlamydia psittaci* and *Chlamydia pneumoniae*), does not produce a glycogen inclusion body and is resistant to sulfonamides. *C. psittaci* causes **psittacosis** (a virulent bird disease communicable to humans), while *C. pneumoniae* causes a human pneumonia.

**Mycoplasmas** are the smallest living cells capable of being cultured outside of host cells. They are the only group of procaryotes totally **lacking a cell wall** and thus having no reliable, defined shape (**pleomorphism**). They were once referred to as **PPLOs** (**p**leuro**p**neumonia**l**ike **o**rganisms), but are now placed in the division **Mollicutes** (soft skins). One family, the **Mycoplasmataceae**, demonstrates an absolute requirement for **cholesterol** in their diet. No procaryote can make this steroid, and no others need it. It appears to strengthen the cell membrane of these wall-less organisms. The second family, the **Acholeplasmataceae**, does not require cholesterol but appears to strengthen its membrane with **carotenoids** that it makes itself.

Being as small as they are, the mycoplasmas also produce extremely small colonies on agar media. One variety, however, makes colonies so tiny that they are called the **T strains** (**t**iny). These mycoplasmas demonstrate a requirement for **urea** in their diet and are now classified as the *Ureaplasma*.

There is no conclusive proof that mycoplasmas cause more than one type of human disease (**primary atypical pneumonia**), but they do cause disease in cattle (**pleuropneumonia**), **arthritis** in rats, and a **neurological** disorder in mice. There is suspicion that they may be involved in human arthritis and a variety of genitourinary ailments.

**L forms** were discovered in 1935 at the **L**ister Institute. They do not constitute a distinct group of procaryotes but rather a different form of normal bacteria. They differ from normal bacteria in their **lack of a cell wall**. This allows the organisms to adopt a variety of shapes and achieve very small cell sizes. In most cases the L forms retain the ability to **revert** (become normal, walled cells). It is possible that L forms represent a **survival** form of bacteria faced with cell-wall-damaging **antibiotic** exposure, as they are easily isolated from patients undergoing penicillin treatment. They are **not** mycoplasmas, as is seen by their capacity for **reversion**, their **lack of cholesterol** in membranes, and their very different G + C ratios.

**Bdellovibrios** are a remarkable group of bacterial parasites; they parasitize other bacteria! Very **tiny**, these **highly motile** organisms can "bore holes" in the cell walls of host bacteria and move into the space between the membrane and the cell wall (the so-called **periplasmic space**). There they grow in size at the expense of their host and eventually fragment into a number of new daughter cells.

Some bacteria produce an extracellular structure called a **sheath**. Almost all of these organisms are **aquatic** and incorporate an attachment device called a

**holdfast** to one end of their sheath. Some species deposit metal oxides (e.g. iron) in their sheaths. Reproduction results in the release of **motile "swarmer"** stages that swim off and establish new colonies elsewhere.

The **actinomycetes** are a diverse group of gram-positive, fungus-like bacteria that grow in the form of **branched filaments** of cells (like fungal mycelia). Most species are soil-dwelling **saprophytes** (agents of decay). The genus **Actinomyces** is a group of **non-spore-forming**, anaerobic or microaerophilic filamentous bacteria. When disturbed (as on a heat-fixed slide) the mycelia break up into **coccoid** and **bacillary fragments**. Only two species are significant pathogens: *Actinomyces israelii* causes **actinomycosis** in humans, *Actinomyces bovis* causes lumpy jaw in cattle.

*Nocardia* is a genus of aerobic, gram-positive, non-spore-forming mycelium-producing bacteria that, like the *Actinomyces*, fragments into a **pleomorphic** mass of coccoid and bacillary fragments. They can cause lung infections.

The *Streptomyces* differ from the other members of the actinomycetes in being **spore-formers** - they produce long chains of spores **(conidia)**. They are best known as the source of **streptomycin**, **actinomycin** and many other antibiotics.

*Caulobacter* is an example of an **appendage** bacterium, as it produces an outward **extension** of its cell wall called a **prostheca**. In this genus the main function of the prosthecae is to **attach the cell** to a solid surface; most species live in quick-moving freshwater streams and might be swept away without their "holdfast".

Almost all motile bacteria use flagella, but some are capable of "**gliding motility**". This motility mechanism requires the cell to be in contact with a **solid surface** and may involve the secretion of slime by the cells. The **Myxobacteriales** are a group of unicellular bacteria characterized by their **gliding motility** and their unique habit of forming multicellular **fruiting bodies** (containing **myxospores**) remarkably similar to those produced by some fungi. Most of these organisms are saprophytes. Other gliding bacteria are found in long filaments of cells; some of these are chemolithotrophs able to oxidize $H_2S$ or elemental sulfur for energy.

<u>OBJECTIVES</u> After studying this chapter you should:

1. Know what rickettsiae are and how to grow them.
2. Be aware of how rickettsial infections are acquired by humans.
3. Be familiar with the replication of the chlamydiae.
4. Comprehend the morphology and pathogenic significance of the mycoplasma and be able to differentiate them from L forms.
5. Be familiar with Bdellovibrios and sheathed bacteria.
6. Know the general morphology of the actinomycetes, as well as that of the appendage bacteria and the myxobacteria.

LEARNING ACTIVITIES

Vocabulary

Having read the chapter, you should be able to define or cite the significance of the following terms. If you cannot, look them up in the text. Terms are presented in the order you will encounter them in the book.

endosymbiont
atypical
rickettsiae
diaminopimelic acid
obligate intracellular parasites
intracellular metabolites
tissue cultures
chick embryos
yolk sac
Q fever
arthropod vector
human body louse
transovarian
chlamydiae
developmental cycle
infective
elementary body
initial body
reticulate body
group A
*Chlamydia trachomatis*
*Chlamydia psittaci*
psittacosis
*Chlamydia pneumoniae*
mycoplasmas
pleomorphism
pleuropneumonia-like organism
PPLO
Mollicutes
cholesterol
Mycoplasmataceae
Acholeplasmataceae
carotenoids
diphasic
T strains
*Ureaplasma*
primary atypical pneumonia
L forms
bdellovibrios
sheathed bacteria
holdfast
actinomycetes
saprophytes
*Actinomyces israelii*
actinomycosis
endogenous
*Nocardia*
*Streptomyces*
conidia
prostheca
*Caulobacter*
Myxobacteriales

Complete each of the following statements by supplying the missing word or words.

1. diaminopimelic __________ acid is found in the cell walls of the Rickettsiae - proof of the gram-negative origin of the group

2. animal __________ cells are the only hosts to Rickettsiae.

3. obligate __________ intracellular parasite is the description used to describe organisms like the Rickettsiae.

4. ____Intracellular____ metabolites apparently cannot be retained within the cells of the Rickettsiae, thus they quickly die when removed form their host cells.

5. ____glucose____ cannot be used as a substrate for the production of metabolic energy by members of the Rickettsiae.

6. ____chick embryos____ are the most widely used culture technique for maintaining the Rickettsiae.

7. ____chick Q____ fever is the only human rickettsial illness not spread by the bites of arthropods.

8. ____Vector____ is the term used to describe an animal that carries an infectious agent from one host to another.

9. The ____human body Louse____ is the only arthropod carrier of rickettsiae that seems to be harmed by the infectious agent (*Rickettsia prowazakii*, agent of epidemic typhus).

10. The ____chlamydiae____ are so tiny that prior to 1966 they were considered to be viruses. They cause a variety of diseases in the psittacosis-lymphogranuloma-trachoma group.

11. The ____elementary____ body is the infective stage of the group of organisms described in question #10; the reproductive stage is called the initial body.

12. ____ATP____ cannot be produced by the chlamydiae, thus they must live within the cells of their hosts which supply them with this essential metabolite.

13. ____Group A____ chlamydiae are probably all members of one species: *Chlamydia trachomatis*. These organisms are inhibited by sulfonamides and store glycogen.

14. ____Mycoplasma____ are the smallest organisms known to be capable of growth and reproduction outside of living host cells.

15. ____Mollicutes____, a term which translates as "soft skins" is the taxonomic class which includes the organisms described in question #14.

16. Lack of a ____cell wall____ results in the pleomorphism and the delicacy of the mycoplasmas.

17. cholesterol is required for the growth of members of the Mycoplasmataceae, it is not required by the Acholeplasmataceae.

18. L -forms were once confused with mycoplasmas, until it became clear that they were bigger, could "revert" to normal, and did not use cholesterol in their membranes.

19. Bdellovibrios are a bizarre group of tiny, motile bacteria that prey upon other bacteria.

20. Streptomyces are members of the actinomycetes which generate spores called conidia.

## MASTERY TEST

1-5: Circle the choice that best answers the questions.

1. The reason for the obligate intracellular parasitism of the Rickettsiae is the inability of the organism to:
   a. retain essential intracellular metabolites
   b. manufacture ATP by any metabolic means
   c. manufacture cholesterol, a necessary material
   d. manufacture their own ribosomes
   e. produce the carotenoids they need in membranes

2. The agent of Q Fever is the only human rickettsial disease which is not spread by:
   a. contaminated clothing
   b. arthropod vectors
   c. bats, skunks, foxes
   d. contaminated needles
   e. flea collars

3. Which of the following is NOT a human rickettsial disease?
   a. Rocky Mountain spotted fever
   b. epidemic typhus fever
   c. endemic typhus fever
   d. Q fever
   e. atypical primary pneumonia

4. The infective stage of a chlamydial organism is called the:
   a. mollicute
   b. reticulate body
   c. initial body
   d. elementary body
   e. L-form

5. One member of the Group B chlamydiae causes:

a. scrub typhus
b. psittacosis
c. smallpox
d. atypical pneumonia
e. pleuropneumonia

---

6-13: Match the bacterial variety with its description.
(use no answer twice)

ANSWERS

A. Actinomyces
B. Bdellovibrios
C. Caulobacter
D. Chlamydiae
E. L-Forms
F. Leptothrix
G. Mycoplasmas
H. Myxobacteriales
I. Nocardia
J. Rickettsias
K. Streptomyces
L. Xerophyces

Mycoplasmas 6. G Group that includes the smallest cells that can grow and reproduce outside of host cells.

Myxobacteriales 7. H Group characterized by "gliding motility" and the production of complex fruiting bodies.

chlamydiae 8. D Obligate intracellular parasites which have no capacity to produce ATP by metabolic means.

L-forms 9. E Lack cell walls but can "revert" to normal form of organism (complete with cell wall).

Actinomyces 10. A Group characterized by obligately anaerobic or microaerophilic physiology, growth as branched filaments, no spore production; one species causes "lumpy jaw" in cattle.

Caulobacter 11. C Aquatic "stalked" bacterium, uses its prostheca to attach itself to solid surfaces in fast-moving streams.

Nocardia 12. I Group of aerobic organisms that grow as branched filaments, do not produce spores; some species partially acid-fast; cause some lung disease.

leptothrix 13. F One of the "sheathed" bacteria, this organism is known for accumulating iron oxides in its sheath and staining itself brown.

---

14-25: Circle the choice that best answers the questions.

14. Which of the following is a term used to describe varying cell shape which may be due to lack of cell walls or fragmentation of filamentous mycelia?
   a. multimorphism
   b. pleomorphism
   c. polymorphism
   d. mesomorphism
   e. oligomorphism

15. Which of the following groups has demonstrated a total requirement for cholesterol?
   a. spiroplasmataceae
   b. Group A chlamydiae
   c. mycoplasmataceae
   d. Group B chlamydiae
   e. acholeplasmataceae

16. Which of the following is a group of mycoplasmas known for their extremely small colonies on solid media?
   a. lilliputionaformes
   b. T strains
   c. diphasic strains
   d. thermoplasma
   e. anaeroplasma

17. Mycoplasmas are known to cause all of the following EXCEPT:
   a. human pelvic inflammatory disease
   b. pleuropneumonia of cattle
   c. rolling disease in mice
   d. arthritis in rats
   e. they cause all of the above

18. Mycoplasmas that do not require cholesterol to strengthen their membranes instead use ______________ which they make themselves.
   a. peptidoglycan
   b. phospholipids
   c. carotenoids
   d. microtubules
   e. microfilaments

19. Myxospores are produced by which of the following groups?
   a. rickettsiae
   b. chlamydiae
   c. mycoplasmas
   d. myxoplasmas
   e. myxobacteria

20. The term saprophyte is used to describe organisms that obtain their energy from the:
   a. tissues of living host animals
   b. remains of plants and animals
   c. tissues of living host plants
   d. tissues of living bacterial cells

21. Which of the following has been suggested to be a "survival mechanism" for pathogens exposed to antibiotics such as penicillin?
   a. mycoplasmas
   b. sheathed bacteria
   c. L-forms
   d. stalked bacteria
   e. reticulate body

22. Which of the following is a parasite which preys upon other bacteria, not on eucaryotes?
a. *Bdellovibrio*
b. *Actinomyces*
c. *Streptomyces*
d. *Nocardia*

23. Which of the following produces long chains of aerial spores called conidia?
a. *Actinomyces*
b. *Nocardia*
c. *Rickettsia*
d. *Myxobacterium*
e. *Streptomyces*

24. The members of which of the following groups have shown the ability to produce over 500 different antibacterial compounds?
a. *Actinomyces*
b. *Nocardia*
c. *Rickettsia*
d. *Myxobacterium*
e. *Streptomyces*

25. The multicellular gliding bacteria, like *Leucothrix*, *Beggiatoa*, and *Thiothrix*, obtain their energy by oxidizing:
a. sugar
b. glutamic acid
c. methane
d. $H_2S$ and elemental S

ANSWERS TO LEARNING ACTIVITIES

Fill-in-the-blank questions:

1. Diaminopimelic; 2. Animal; 3. Obligate; 4. Intracellular; 5. Glucose; 6. Chick embryos; 7. Q; 8. Vector; 9. human body louse; 10. chlamydiae; 11. elementary; 12. ATP; 13. Group A; 14. Mycoplasmas; 15. Mollicutes; 16. cell wall; 17. Cholesterol; 18. L; 19. Bdellovibrios; 20. Streptomyces.

| MASTERY TEST ANSWERS | | | | | | | | | | | | |
|---|---|---|---|---|---|---|---|---|---|---|---|---|
| 1<br>a | 2<br>b | 3<br>e | 4<br>d | 5<br>b | 6<br>G | | 7<br>H | 8<br>D | 9<br>E | 10<br>A | 11<br>C | 12<br>I |
| 13<br>F | 14<br>b | 15<br>c | 16<br>b | 17<br>a | 18<br>c | 19<br>e | 20<br>b | 21<br>c | 22<br>a | 23<br>e | 24<br>e | 25<br>d |

## CHAPTER 14

## VIRUSES

### CHAPTER SUMMARY

**Viruses** are not truly alive, since in isolation they have no capacity to make **ATP** nor can they **synthesize proteins**. They can, however, **reproduce** when they invade a living procaryotic or eucaryotic cell; they are **obligate intracellular parasites**. A viral infection most commonly results in a **cell's death**, although other effects are possible, including **proliferation** of cells (warts and tumors), and **altered cell differentiation** (**rubella** virus on fetal humans). Some viral infections are apparently **asymptomatic**.

A **virion** (virus particle) at its simplest consists of a **nucleocapsid**: a piece of **nucleic acid** (DNA **or** RNA) surrounded by a protein **capsid**. The genetic material of viruses is **NEVER** both DNA and RNA; it is always one or the other. Some viruses contain normal double-stranded DNA (**dsDNA**), others contain single-stranded DNA (**ssDNA**), still others contain double-stranded RNA (**dsRNA**), while many more contain single-stranded RNA (**ssRNA**). The RNA is sometimes present as several to many separate pieces - the so-called **segmented genome**.

The capsid is composed of protein units called **capsomeres**, produced under the control of viral genes. Some capsids contain **enzymes** that the virus needs for replication of its nucleic acid. Some capsids may contain **glycoproteins** (protein + polysaccharide), in addition to the protein capsomeres. Capsids come in three main shapes: **icosahedral** (20-sided polygon with equilateral triangle faces); **helical** (or filamentous) which are long and thin, and a combination of the two (found in **bacteriophages**) in which an **icosahedral head** is bound to a **helical tail**.

Some viruses are further surrounded by a membrane-like **envelope**. The envelope represents **cell membrane** stolen from the previous host cell with the addition of **virus-specific proteins** and **glycoproteins**. These materials are produced under virus gene control and are transported to and incorporated into the host membrane at special areas. The virus **buds** off from these special areas.

Since viruses cannot grow and reproduce on their own, they must be grown in the presence of living cells. **Chick embryos** are a favorite means of growing viruses, but another method utilizes cells in **tissue culture**. **Primary cell cultures** are obtained directly from the animal tissue or organ. They have **brief life spans**, as they can be subcultured only five to six times. **Diploid cell strains** are much longer lived (forty to fifty subcultures); they are derived from human embryonic tissue. **Permanent cell lines** have unlimited life spans, but are not morphologically or genetically normal. Some are spontaneously produced in other types of cultures (probably by mutation) or they may be derived from **cancer tumors** or from cells that have been **transformed** by chemicals or **oncogenic (cancer-producing) viruses**. All animal tissue cultures require complex media to support their growth and all but the malignant tumor lines grow in monolayers over the bottom surface of a bottle; when all cells are in contact with one another, growth stops (**contact inhibition**).

Viral **infections** follow most of the same basic steps regardless of the nature of the host organism. **Adsorption** (skipped by plant viruses) is the first step and involves the specific binding of the virus to receptor sites on the host cell surface. **Penetration** follows adsorption and occurs by **engulfment** of the intact virion by animal cells, the **fusion of the envelope** with animal cell membranes, the entrance into **wounds** in plant cells, or the **hypodermic-like injection** of bacteriophages. **Uncoating** is the release of nucleic acid from the capsid, a process that may require host enzyme activity or that may be automatic. **Replication** of the nucleic acid then follows, using viral enzymes or cellular enzymes, depending on the genome type. **RNA viruses** use an RNA-Dependent **RNA polymerase** enzyme which they make on site (dsRNA or **plus strand viruses**) or which they carry into the cell with them (**negative strand viruses**). **Assembly** is an automatic process; the capsomeres self-assemble about the viral genomes. **Release** occurs by **lysis** of the cell in some cases, **budding** in enveloped viruses, and by a form of **exocytosis** (reverse phagocytosis) in still others.

**Viral populations** can be **enumerated** by using dilution techniques similar to those used for bacteria. The assay depends upon the destruction of tissue culture cells or of bacterial cells on plates. Viral replication results in the formation of cleared zones called **plaques** (areas where cells have been killed and lysed). One merely counts the plaques and multiplies the number by the **dilution factor** to determine the original density of viruses.

Viruses have a variety of effects on the infected cell; one of the more distinctive is the formation of **inclusion bodies** which develop during the assembly stage of a virus infection. **Cytolytic viruses** totally block host macromolecular synthesis. Some viruses may persist long after a **primary infection** seems to be over. Such **asymptomatic latent infections** are characteristic of the **herpesviruses** and can also occur with the measles virus.

Animal **viral taxonomy** is based, first, upon the **nature of the genome** (DNA *vs*. RNA). Secondary traits include the **shape of the capsid** (icosahedral, helical, complex), the **number of capsomeres**, the presence/absence of an **envelope**, the **size** of the virus, and the **nature and size of its genome** (segmented or not, ds or ss, etc.). Inspect Tables 14.3 and 14.4 in your textbook for examples of animal viruses.

**Bacteriophages** are viruses that attack bacteria. The DNA phages occur in two main capsid varieties: **filamentous** (helical) and "**complex**" (icosahedral "head" and helical "tail"). None of them are enveloped. Many of the filamentous forms enter their target cells through the hollow **sex pili** (F pilus), thus are male specific. The "complex" forms inject their DNA into the cell, leaving their capsids outside. Small, **icosahedral RNA phages** use the sex pilus as a route of entry, like the filamentous DNA phages.

**Virulent**, or **lytic** phages typically effect their release by producing **lysozyme** (an enzyme that digests peptidoglycan). **Icosahedral RNA** viruses always synthesize a **lysis protein** to kill their host cells, but filamentous DNA phage may migrate out of intact cells without lysing them. **Temperate** phages do not kill their host cells at all, under normal circumstances. They insert their genome into the host cell's chromosome, becoming a **prophage**, and replicate along with their host. The bacterium carrying a prophage is called a "**lysogenic cell**". Not all phage genes are dormant under these circumstances; some produce new surface proteins for the cell, others enable the cell to produce potent **exotoxins** (diphtheria, scarlet fever, botulism). Lysogenic cells that exhibit new traits are said to have undergone **lysogenic conversion**. Temperate phages do, on occasion, "break out" and go through a **lytic cycle**, behaving like typical cytolytic viruses.

**Oncogenic** viruses are capable of **transforming** normal cells into cancer cells. The first discovered were the **RNA retroviruses** like **Rous Sarcoma virus (RSV)** which were shown to cause leukemias and sarcomas in chickens in the early 1900s. Two known for humans are **HTLV-I** and **HTLV-II** (**h**uman **T**-cell **l**ymphoma **v**irus - close relatives of HIV, the cause of **AIDS**). The retroviruses enter the cell as **ssRNA** and use a viral enzyme, **RNA-dependent DNA polymerase** (**reverse transcriptase**) to produce ssDNA complementary to their RNA. The ssDNA is then converted to **dsDNA** and **integrates with the host chromosome**. Viral mRNA is then transcribed by host enzymes and translated on host ribosomes. Assembled virions are released by budding from specific areas of the membrane where viral glycoproteins are found. The **oncogenic principle** of such viruses is a gene called *src* (**an example of an oncogene**, *onc*) which produces a **protein kinase** which phosphorylates cell proteins and somehow results in their transformation to tumor cells. The viral gene (*v-src*) is identical to the cell's own gene (*c-src*); the oncogenic result seems to be a **dose effect**. The extra copy of the gene results in overactivity. Some retroviruses, called **defective transforming viruses**, can't even replicate in cells without the simultaneous infection of the cell by a **helper virus**. Yet these viruses can still cause transformation because they carry an oncogene (*onc*).

**Nonacute leukemia viruses** are different from other retroviruses. Their genome does not include an *onc* gene. Their effect (which is delayed in time) appears to involve activation of an existing cellular **protooncogene**. Such genes are normally inactive (or active at very low levels) but become much more active as a result of **downstream promotion** (the incorporated viral genome serving as a promoter to genes "downstream" of its position). Other protooncogenes can be activated by chromosomal mutations called **translocations**.

What are these **protooncogenes**? Most encode for **factors that regulate normal cellular growth**, or produce the **receptors** for those growth factors. Others may work less directly, like the protein kinase of the *src* system. Some are activated by "downstream promotion", others are brought into the cell by retroviruses. How did the **retrovirus** acquire these mammalian genes? It probably occurred by **mistake**; when the retrovirus transcribes its DNA to RNA it must occasionally **transcribe** a host gene or two; if the host gene is a protooncogene the viral genome will now contain it.

**Tumor suppressor genes** (**antioncogenes**) are the exact opposite of protooncogenes; their **loss** results in transformation. The first discovered is involved in a hereditary cancer of the eye called **retinoblastoma**. This disorder results from the loss of a gene called the **Rb1 locus**. The same defect seems to be involved in **osteosarcoma** (bone cancer) and human small-cell **lung cancer**. A second antioncogene called **p53** has been implicated in lung cancer, colon cancer and bone cancer. Chromosomal mutations can result in the loss of such genes, and certain **DNA viruses** can produce materials that **form stable complexes with tumor-suppressor gene products**. Such seems to be the case for the **T antigens** (**t**umor antigens) of **SV40** and **adenovirus**, which bind to p53.

Viruses can undergo mutation, too. Such mutations often result in the production of **attenuated** or nonpathogenic strains of normally disease-causing viruses. Such attenuated (**nonvirulent**) strains are often used in **immunization** treatments (along with **killed viruses**). Recombinant DNA technology has made possible the **cloning** of virus genes and the production of vaccines that are totally virus-free, containing only "**immunogens**" derived from the virus.

**Plant viruses** are mostly ssRNA, although other genome types exist. Their names are generally derived from the type of plant they infect and the disease they cause (e.g. **TMV** or **t**obacco **m**osaic **v**irus). The adsorption step does not occur in plant virus infections; all plant viruses gain entrance to their host *via* **wounds** (usually caused by **arthropod vectors** such as aphids and leafhoppers). Some plant viruses (e.g. **alfalfa mosaic** and **cucumoviruses**) have a **segmented genome** consisting of two to four strands of RNA. What makes this unusual is that each must be assembled into its **own capsid**. Successful infections thus must involve all **four different capsid types** invading a host cell! Typical plant viruses have helical (filamentous) or icosahedral shapes. Effects of **virus infections** include defects in **chlorophyll** production, tissue **necrosis**, **tumor**-like growths, and defective **growth hormone** production (resulting in **stunted** growth). Some extremely unusual plant diseases are caused by **naked RNA** agents called **viroids**. No capsid is produced by these organisms.

**Prions** (proteinaceous infectious particles) are infectious agents which appear to be pure **protein**. They are extremely resistant to **heat** but are easily destroyed by **proteinase** enzymes. Diseases caused by these organisms have extremely **long incubation periods** and thus are often called **slow virus** diseases. **Kuru** and **Creutzfeldt-Jakob** disease in humans and **scrapie** in sheep are all terminal **neurological** illnesses apparently caused by these controversial agents.

OBJECTIVES A study of this chapter should provide you with a comprehension of:

1. The nature and structure of animal viruses.
2. Types of cell cultures used to grow viruses.
3. The mechanism of replication of DNA and RNA viruses.
4. Ways to enumerate viruses.
5. The reaction of the host cell to virus infection.
6. A classification of animal viruses.
7. The structure and replication of bacteriophages.
8. The mechanism of lysogeny and lysogenic conversion.
9. The mechanism of replication of the retroviruses and how their gene structure is correlated with their ability to cause cell transformation.
10. What protooncogenes are and how they are activated to induce cell transformation.
11. The normal functions of protooncogenes.
12. The role of tumor-suppressor genes in oncogenesis.
13. The role of RNA and DNA viruses in human cancer.
14. The nomenclature and types of plant viruses.
15. The transmission and replication of plant viruses.
16. The structure of plant viruses.
17. The nature of a viroid and a prion.

## LEARNING ACTIVITIES

### Vocabulary

Having read the chapter, you should be able to define or cite the significance of the following terms. If you cannot, look them up in the text. Terms are presented in the order you will encounter them in the book.

virus
transformation
cell differentiation
virion
capsid
glycoproteins
binding sites
receptor sites
icosahedral viruses
inclusion bodies
cytolytic viruses
Adenoviridae
Herpetoviridae
Hepadnaviruses
Poxviridae
Papovaviridae
Parvoviridae
Picornaviridae
Togaviridae
Orthomyxoviridae
*src* gene
dose effect
oncogene (*onc*)
protein kinase
transformation
downstream promotion
chromosomal translocation
transfect
*c-ras* gene
cell growth

capsomeres
helical viruses
nucleocapsid
dsDNA
ssDNA
dsRNA
ssRNA
segmented genome
envelope
primary cell cultures
diploid cell strains
permanent cell line
oncogenic
contact inhibition
adsorption
penetration
uncoating
assembly
release
lysis
budding
plus strand viruses
negative strand viruses
plaques
Paramyxoviridae
Rhabdoviridae
Arenaviridae
Bunyaviridae
Coronaviridae
Retroviridae
Reoviridae
bacteriophages
filamentous DNA phages
lysogeny
virulent
prophage
lysogenic
temperate phage
lytic cycle
exotoxins
lysogenic conversion
oncogenic viruses
protooncogenes
retroviruses
reverse transcriptase
RNA-dependent DNA polymerase
nondefective virus
defective virus
RSV
regulators
cell growth regulator receptors
*v-ras* gene
*v-sis* gene
etiologic agent
HTLV-I; HTLV-II
tumor suppressors
antioncogenes
retinoblastoma
Rb1 locus
tumor-suppressor p53
herpesvirus
papillomavirus
hepatitis B virus
SV40
polyomavirus
T-Ags (Tumor antigens)
attenuated (nonvirulent) viruses
immunogens
viroids
prions
Kuru
Creutzfeldt-Jakob disease

Complete each of the following statements by supplying the missing word or words.

1. virion ________ is a term used to describe a single virus particle.

2. capsid ________ is the name of the protein and glycoprotein structure that surrounds the genetic material of the virus.

3. icosahedral ________ is a structure with 20 faces (each an equilateral triangle).

4. capsomeres ________ are the protein subunits which self-assemble to produce the viral capsid.

5. Segmented _________ genomes are found in some RNA viruses which have up to 11 different pieces of dsRNA.

6. The envelop _________ is a membrane-like surrounding structure found outside the capsid of some viruses.

7. primary _________ cell cultures are derived directly from the tissue or organ of an animal; they can only be subcultured five to six times.

8. oncogenic _________ (cancer-producing) chemicals or viruses can transform normal cells into tumor cells which do not exhibit contact inhibition or any limit to the number of times they can be subcultured.

9. Adsorption _________ is a very specific process in which capsid proteins or glycoproteins bind to receptor sites on the host cell.

10. Plus _________ strand viruses do not need to bring an RNA-dependent RNA polymerase into the cell with them; their genome can act directly as a messenger RNA molecule.

11. plaques _________ form in a monolayer of animal cells in culture or on lawns of bacteria when lytic viruses are allowed to attack. Counting such clear zones and multiplying their number by the virus dilution factor allows enumeration of virus levels.

12. Asymptomatic Latent _________ virus infections can recur - sometimes many times and sometimes years after recovery from a primary infection.

13. Lysogenic _________ conversion is a term used to describe new genetic capacities conferred upon a bacterium by the prophage it is playing host to.

14. Retroviruses _________ are viruses which use reverse transcription to produce ssDNA complementary to their ssRNA. Some of them are oncogenic viruses.

15. Rous Sarcoma Virus _________ (RSV) is a nondefective virus that causes cancer in chickens.

16. Oncogene _________ is a gene which can cause transformation of a normal cell into a tumor cell. An example is the *src* gene of retroviruses.

17. Defective _________ transforming viruses lack the genetic ability to reproduce on their own; they need helper viruses to coinfect the cell and aid their replication. Despite their inability to reproduce, however, they can cause cancer.

18. protooncogene can be involved in transformation if they are subjected to "downstream promotion" (the insertion of a nonacute leukemia virus genome "upstream" from the gene in question).

19. Tumor Suppressors (also called antioncogenes) have been implicated in at least one hereditary human cancer (retinoblastoma) and in the cancer-causing abilities of SV40 and the adenoviruses.

20. PRions are hypothetical, pure protein infectious agents which have been implicated in Kuru and scrapie.

## MASTERY TEST

1-13: Circle the choice that best answers the questions.

1. Viral infections are known to do all of the following EXCEPT:
   a. kill the host cells outright
   b. interfere with cell differentiation
   c. fill the body of the host with endotoxins
   d. cause cell proliferation
   e. cause asymptomatic latent infections

2. Viral genomes consist of all of the following EXCEPT:
   a. dsDNA
   b. ssDNA
   c. dsRNA
   d. ssRNA
   e. all are possible

3. Which of the following is a viral capsid type characterized by 20 faces (each an equilateral triangle)?
   a. icosahedral
   b. helical
   c. rhabdo
   d. complex
   e. viroidal

4. Capsids are made from:
   a. pilin
   b. flagellin
   c. tubulin
   d. capsomeres
   e. capselin

5. Viruses which leave their host cell by budding are always equipped with:
   a. a cytoplasmic membrane
   b. reverse phagocytosis
   c. an envelope
   d. a nucleocapsid
   e. a capsid

6. The viral genome plus the capsid constitute:
   a. the nucleus
   b. the envelope
   c. the capsid
   d. the nucleocapsid
   e. the prion

7. Glycoproteins are complexes between protein and ________________. They are frequent components of viral capsids and envelopes.
   a. polysaccharides
   b. lipids
   c. DNA
   d. RNA
   e. ribosomes

8. A permanent cell line differs from primary cell cultures and diploid cell strains in that it can be subcultured:
   a. 40 to 50 times
   b. 100 to 125 times
   c. an unlimited number of times
   d. only 5 to 6 times

9. Which of the following stages in a virus infective cycle involves such terms as lysis, budding, reverse phagocytosis?
   a. adsorption
   b. penetration
   c. uncoating
   d. assembly
   e. release

10. ssRNA viruses may or may not need to bring along an RNA-dependent RNA polymerase enzyme with them when they penetrate a host cell. Plant viruses never do, but ________________ animal viruses always do.
   a. retrovirus
   b. negative strand
   c. picornavirus
   d. positive strand
   e. herpesvirus

11. Which of the following uses the F pilus (sex pilus) of bacteria as its entry portal to the cell?
   a. dsDNA poxviruses
   b. "complex" bacteriophages
   c. prions
   d. filamentous bacteriophages

12. Lytic phages produce which of the following enzymes as a means of getting out of their host cell?
   a. protein kinase
   b. lysozyme
   c. proteinase
   d. RNA polymerase
   e. reverse transcriptase

13. A lysogenic bacterial cell:
   a. is occupied by a lytic phage
   b. is immune to lytic phages
   c. is occupied by a prophage
   d. is occupied by a bdellovibrio

---

14-20: Match the virus-related terms with their descriptions (use no answer twice)

ANSWERS

A. antioncogene
B. c-src
C. defective virus
D. dose effect
E. downstream promotion
F. HTLV-I
G. nonacute leukemia virus
H. nondefective virus
I. oncogene
J. protein kinase
K. protooncogene
L. retinoblastoma
M. retrovirus
N. SV40
O. T antigens
P. v-src

_____ 14. Which of the above is the general type of virus that could be described as a ssRNA virus that uses a viral RNA-dependent DNA polymerase to produce a ssDNA molecule complementary to its RNA?

_____ 15. An oncogenic virus which is unable to replicate without the coinfection of the cell by a "helper virus" is called a(n):

_____ 16. Which of the above is the oncogene carried by such retroviruses as Rous sarcoma virus?

_____ 17. Which of the above is the protein product of the gene described in question #16?

_____ 18. Which of the above is a known human oncogenic virus of the retrovirus type?

_____ 19. Some "nonacute leukemia viruses" do not themselves possess any oncogenes. Their effect is to activate existing genes in the cell called a(n):

_____ 20. The mechanism by which nonacute leukemia viruses activate existing cellular genes is called:

---

21. Lysogenic conversion proves that:
   a. some prophage genes are active and transcribed
   b. all prophage genes are inert and inactive
   c. ultraviolet light is mutagenic
   d. gamma rays kill incorporated prophages

22. Which of the following hereditary conditions led to the discovery of tumor suppressors (antioncogenes)?
   a. hemophilia
   b. sickle-cell anemia
   c. Down's Syndrome
   d. retinoblastoma

23. Vaccines against viral diseases are generally produced using killed viruses, cloned immunogens, or live, ______________ viruses.
   a. nonacute
   b. asymptomatic
   c. attenuated
   d. helper

24. The possible oncogenic mechanism of human DNA viruses (like SV40) is the production of T antigens that form stable complexes with:
   a. tumor suppressors
   b. protein kinases
   c. oncogenes
   d. downstream promoters

25. Plant viruses practice all of the following aspects of a typical viral infection EXCEPT:
   a. adsorption
   b. penetration
   c. assembly
   d. release

## ANSWERS TO LEARNING ACTIVITIES

Fill-in-the-blank questions:

1. Virion; 2. Capsid; 3. Icosahedron; 4. Capsomeres; 5. Segmented; 6. envelope; 7. Primary; 8. Oncogenic; 9. Adsorption; 10. Plus; 11. Plaques; 12. Asymptomatic latent; 13. Lysogenic; 14. Retroviruses; 15. Rous sarcoma virus; 16. Oncogene; 17. Defective; 18. Protooncogenes; 19. Tumor suppressors; 20. Prions.

**MASTERY TEST ANSWERS**

| | | | | | | | | | | | | |
|---|---|---|---|---|---|---|---|---|---|---|---|---|
| 1 c | 2 e | 3 a | 4 d | 5 c | 6 d | | 7 a | 8 c | 9 e | 10 b | 11 d | 12 b |
| 13 c | 14 M | 15 C | 16 P | 17 J | 18 F | 19 K | 20 E | 21 a | 22 d | 23 c | 24 a | 25 a |

## CHAPTER 15

## EUCARYOTIC MICROORGANISMS

### CHAPTER SUMMARY

Eucaryotic microorganisms include the algae, the fungi, the protozoa and the helminths. The **algae**, members of the Kingdom Protista, are photosynthetic organisms that use chlorophyll and other pigments to trap light energy. They lack **vascular tissue** and do not have multicellular reproductive structures. **Phytoplankton**, small floating algae in fresh water or the sea form the basis of the **food chain**. Most algae are **unicellular**, but some form multicellular **colonies**.

The Division **Chlorophyta** (the green algae) are the ancestors of higher plants. They have **cellulose** and **pectin** cell walls and store starch as a food reserve. A common unicellular form is the flagellated *Chlamydomonas*; a common colonial form is *Volvox*. The Division **Euglenophyta** includes organisms which **lack cell walls** but have the capacity to ingest food (thus they are **facultative chemoheterotrophs**); some group these organisms with the protozoans.

The Division **Chrysophyta** (the golden-brown algae) includes organisms that store oils as reserve food and have so much carotene that they look more gold than green. Among the most important groups in this division are the **diatoms** which have cell walls made of glass (**silica**); huge deposits of their empty cell walls can actually be mined for **diatomaceous earth**. The Division **Phaeophyta** (the brown algae) are also characterized by containing lots of accessory pigments, in their case **fucoxanthin**. Some of these marine algae get extremely large (the **kelps** are up to 100 meters long), others occupy large areas of the sea surface (e.g. *Sargassum*).

The Division **Pyrrophyta** includes a diverse group of unicellular organisms called the **dinoflagellates**. These organisms sometimes reach such high population densities that they stain the sea red (thus causing the "**red tides**"). If humans eat shellfish that have fed on these organisms **paralysis** of muscles and **toxemia** results. The Division **Rhodophyta** (the red algae) are of considerable importance as reef builders and as a source of **agar** (produced by *Gelidium*).

The **fungi**, members of the Kingdom Myceteae, lack chlorophyll, are generally nonmotile, and exist as unicells (**yeasts**) or as long, branched filaments called **hyphae (molds)**. Some **dimorphic** forms may be yeasts in one environment, molds in another. Fungal hyphae can be **septate** (broken by crosswalls, or septa) or **coenocytic** (no crosswalls). Masses of hyphae are called **mycelia**. Most fungi grow as **saprophytes** (agents of decay), although a few are parasitic. They can tolerate much **higher osmotic concentrations** and much lower pHs than bacteria, thus are more of a problem in attacking preserved foods.

Fungi reproduce **asexually** by cell division and **mitotic spore production**, or **sexually** by the fusion of two cells (**fertilization**) followed by **meiotic spore production**. The major taxonomic groups of fungi are the Division **Gymnomycota** (slime molds), the Division **Mastigomycota** (aquatic fungi with flagellated, motile spores), and the Division **Amastigomycota** (no motile forms at all). The Gymnomycota includes two classes: the **Myxomycetes (plasmodial slime molds)** and the **Acrasiomycetes (cellular slime molds)**. The plasmodial slime molds are large **multinucleate** amoeba-like organisms that engulf bacteria and other particulate foods. The **cellular** slime molds are **uninucleate** amoebae that, like the plasmodial forms, produce elaborate fruiting bodies under appropriate circumstances. A few of the cellular slime molds are **parasitic** on higher plants.

All fungal species pathogenic to humans are in the Division Amastigomycota. In the Class **Zygomycetes** hyphae are coenocytic and the sexual spores are called **zygospores**. They also produce asexual **sporangiospores** in structures called **sporangia**. *Rhizopus* and *Mucor* are opportunists that can cause pneumonia.

The Class **Ascomycetes** (the sac fungi) have septate hyphae and produce sexual spores in structures called **asci** (singular **ascus**). Asexual spores are produced in **microconidia** or **macroaleuroconidia**. Most yeasts are in this class, including the economically valuable **Saccharomyces** genus (used by brewers, winemakers, and bakers). The Class **Basidiomycetes** (the club fungi) also have septate hyphae and produce sexual spores on structures called **basidia**. They may also produce asexual spores on microconidia. Some of these fungi cause important plant diseases; others are edible (although some mushrooms are toxic).

The Class **Deuteromycetes** (or **Fungi Imperfecti**) have no ***known*** sexual form, reproducing solely by means of asexual spores. Periodically, members of this class are moved to one of the other three classes when a sexual stage is observed. Many species are human pathogens, causing **superficial infections**, **cutaneous infections** (penetrating infections of the skin, nails, hair, stratum corneum), or **subcutaneous** and **systemic** infections.

Fungi are of **economic value** far beyond their edible stages. They **produce drugs** (e.g. penicillin, ergot), organic compounds (enzymes, vitamins), and are used in the production of many foods. Their role in decomposition of dead plant and animal bodies is of paramount importance. **Lichens** are the prime source of food to domestic reindeer and wild caribou; they represent a **symbiotic association** between two different forms of life: fungi and algae. The fungal partner is usually an ascomycete, the alga is usually a member of the green algae.

**Protozoa** are animal-like members of the Kingdom Protista that are typically unicellular. They lack cell walls, having instead a tough covering called a **pellicle**. Most are **holozoic**, procuring their nutrients through the consumption of solid food.

Digestion takes place within the cell in **food vacuoles**. Most are free-living, but some are parasitic and a few cause serious diseases. Many species can form tough resting stages called **cysts**. The cyst is particularly important to parasites in allowing them to survive the hazardous process of transferring from one host to another. The main taxonomic feature for the group is **mode of locomotion**.

The Class **Mastigophora** (flagellates) move by means of flagella. Some are important **pathogens**: *Giardia lamblia* causes **giardiasis** (an intestinal infection), *Trichomonas vaginalis* produces **trichomoniasis** (a sexually-transmitted infection of the urogenital tract), *Trypanosoma gambiense* and *T. rhodesiense* cause **trypanosomiasis** (African sleeping sickness), *Trypanosoma soma cruzi* causes **Chagas' disease** (a myocardial infection), and *Leishmania* causes **Leishmaniasis**.

The Class **Sarcodina** consists of organisms that use **pseudopodia** to effect **amoeboid movement**. Most are naked unicells, but some produce hard coverings (e.g. the *Foraminifera*, whose chalky remains produced the White Cliffs of Dover). *Entamoeba histolytica* is a well-known pathogen responsible for **amoebiasis** (**amoebic dysentery**), a potentially fatal disease.

The Class **Sporozoa** consists entirely of **immotile** animal **parasites**. They cause some important diseases: **malaria** which is caused by members of the genus *Plasmodium* (spread by mosquitos), **Toxoplasmosis** which is caused by *Toxoplasma gondii* (spread by contact with cat feces), and pneumocystic **pneumonia** which is caused by *Pneumocystis carnii* (a common complication of AIDS). Some think the pneumocystis organism is an ascomycete fungus.

The Class **Ciliata** uses **cilia** for locomotion, and have two nuclei per cell. One nucleus, the **micronucleus**, is used for reproduction, the **macronucleus** is used to control metabolism. The only significant human parasite is *Balantidium coli* which causes dysentery.

The **helminths** are true animals that are often parasitic. The Phylum **Platyhelminthes** (**flatworms**) includes two significant groups of animal parasites: the Class **Cestoda** (**tapeworms**), and the Class **Trematoda** (**flukes**). The **cestodes** typically have two hosts: the **definitive host** in which the adult tapeworm develops, and the **intermediate host** in which the larval stages develop. The **trematodes** also have more than one host; all use **snails** as intermediate hosts. Their life cycle includes three (blood flukes only) to four different stages (other flukes). Eggs develop into a small ciliated form called the **miracidium** which burrows into the tissues of a snail. Inside the snail the **sporocyst** (a long tubular larva) develops and migrates to the liver. **Blood flukes** then develop directly into **cercariae**, which leave the snail and enter the water. If they contact human skin they bore into a surface blood vessel where they can then develop into the adult form of the worm. Other flukes undergo an intermediate stage between the sporocyst and the cercaria called the **redia**. Their cercariae leave the snail intermediate host and encyst themselves as a **metacercaria**. Ingestion of metacercariae by humans results in infestation with intestinal flukes, lung flukes, liver flukes, etc.

The Phylum **Aschelminthes** (**roundworms**) includes both free-living and parasitic members. The **intestinal nematodes** (e.g. *Trichinella*, *Ascaris*) develop into adults in the digestive tract, while their larval stages may be widely disseminated in the body. They are contracted by the ingestion of larvae or eggs of adult worms. The **blood and tissue nematodes** are spread from human to human by arthropod vectors (mosquitos, black flies, sand flies). Except for *Dracunculus medinensis* (the guinea worm), all of these worms are members of the "superfamily" **Filarioidea** and cause an infection called **filariasis.** They reproduce by giving birth to live young, the **microfilariae.**

OBJECTIVES After studying this chapter, you should:

1. Be able to list one or more properties for each of the six divisions of algae.
2. Be familiar with the term phytoplankton and know their role in our ecology.
3. Be able to differentiate between a yeast and a mold.
4. Know the types of sexual and asexual spores produced by each major class of fungi.
5. Be able to list important products that are the result of yeast or mold metabolism.
6. Be cognizant of what are slime molds and be familiar with their fruiting body and spore formation.
7. Be able to define a lichen.
8. Know the general morphological properties of each class of protozoa.
9. Be able to list one or more diseases caused by each class of protozoa.
10. Be familiar with morphology and replication of each of the parasitic classes of helminths.

## LEARNING ACTIVITIES

### Vocabulary

Having read the chapter, you should be able to define or cite the significance of the following terms. If you cannot, look them up in the text. Terms are presented in the order you will encounter them in the book.

| | | |
|---|---|---|
| algae | *Mucor* | *trypanosomiasis* |
| carotenoids | Ascomycetes | *Trypanosoma rhodesiense* |
| biloproteins | sac fungi | African sleeping sickness |
| vascular tissue | ascus | *Trypanosoma soma cruzi* |
| phytoplankton | microconidia | |
| food chain | conidiophore | |
| Chlorophyta | *Saccharomyces* | |

filamentous
cellulose
pectin
*Chlamydomonas*
unicellular
longitudinal
 fission
*Volvox*
colony
Euglenophyta
facultative
 chemoheterotroph
Chrysophyta
diatoms
Phaeophyta
fucoxanthin
kelps
*Sargassum*
Pyrrophyta
dinoflagellates
red tide
toxemia
Rhodophyta
algal reefs
*Gelidium*
blooms
fungi
yeast
mold
dimorphic
hyphae
septa
septate hypha
coenocytic hypha
mycelium
saprophyte
sexual spores
fertilization
meiosis
asexual spores
mitosis
Gymnomycota
Mastigomycota
Amastigomycota
Zygomycetes
zygospores

Basidiomycetes
basidiospores
basidia
mushrooms
Deuteromycetes
Fungi Imperfecti
chlamydoconidia
arthroconidia
blastoconidia
superficial
 infections
cutaneous
 infections
dermatophytes
subcutaneous
 infections
systemic
 infections
ascospores
budding
plasmodial slime
 molds
Myxomycetes
cellular slime
 molds
Acrasiomycetes
lichen
symbiotic
 relationship
Protista
protozoan
pellicle
contractile vacuole
obligate parasite
holozoic
food vacuole
cyst
Mastigophora
flagella
longitudinal binary
 fission
*Euglena viridis*
giardiasis
*Giardia lamblia*
trichomoniasis
*Trichomonas*

Chagas' disease
leishmaniasis
*Leishmania*
Sarcodina
pseudopodia
*Foraminifera*
*Entamoeba histolytica*
amoebiasis
amoebic dysentery
Sporozoa
malaria
*Plasmodium*
toxoplasmosis
*Taxoplasma gondii*
*Pneumocystis carnii*
Ciliata
micronucleus
macronucleus
*Paramecium caudatum*
*Balantidium coli*
helminths
Platyhelminthes
flatworms
Aschelminthes
roundworms
Cestoda
Trematoda
Nematoda
tapeworm
definitive host
intermediate
 host
*Taenia*
fluke
snail
blood fluke
miracidium
sporocyst
redia
cercariae
metacercaria
intestinal
 roundworms
blood and tissue
 roundworms
arthropod vector

sporangiospores
sporangium
*Rhizopus*
*vaginalis*
*Trypanosoma*
*gambiense*
Filarioidea
filariasis
microfilariae

Complete each of the following statements by supplying the missing word or words.

1. ____algae____ are a general group of eucaryotic, unicellular and colonial, photosynthetic microorganisms.

2. ____phytoplankton____ are microscopic forms of the group described in question #1 that are found floating in the upper layers of fresh and salt water.

3. ____chlorophyta____ are the division of algae most think are the ancestors of higher (land) plants.

4. ____Euglenophyta____ are a division of motile, unicellular algae which lack a cell wall and are capable of facultative chemoheterotrophy.

5. ____Diatoms____ are members of the Chrysophyta and are characterized by a two-part cell wall which contains silica. Deposits of their empty cell walls are mined.

6. ____phaeophyta____ is a division of algae which includes the kelps and *Sargassum*; they are known for containing the pigment fucoxanthin.

7. ____Red tides____ is the term used to describe the immense "blooms" of *Gonyaulax catanella* and *Ptychodiscus brevis* that can make shellfish unsafe to eat.

8. ____Rhodo phyta____ is a division of algae which has members that produce reefs and another member that is the source of agar.

9. ____Hyphae____ are long, branched filaments of algal cells. Masses of them constitute the mycelium.

10. ____Yeasts____ are fungi which consist mainly of unicells which reproduce (asexually) by budding.

11. ____cysts____ are protozoan resting stages which are able to survive harsh conditions; they are very valuable to parasitic forms in making the transfer between hosts.

12-16: The common name and description columns in the table below match. Rearrange the class names so that they match the columns to their right.

| CLASS | COMMON NAME | DESCRIPTION |
|---|---|---|
| ~~MYXOMYCETES~~ ACRASIOMYCETES | CELLULAR SLIME MOLDS | Uninucleate amoebae; produce complex fruiting bodies from slugs |
| ~~DEUTEROMYCETES~~ ASCOMYCETES | SAC FUNGI | Septate hyphae, produce sexual spores in asci. |
| ~~ACRASIOMYCETES~~ BASIDIOMYCETES | CLUB FUNGI | Septate hyphae, produce sexual spores in complex fruiting bodies often called mushrooms. |
| ~~BASIDIOMYCETES~~ DEUTEROMYCETES | FUNGI IMPERFECTI | Do not reproduce sexually. |
| ~~ASCOMYCETES~~ MYXOMYCETES | PLASMODIAL SLIME MOLDS | Multinucleate amoebae; produce complex fruiting bodies. |

17. Mastigophora are a class of protozoans which include the parasites *Giardia, Trichomonas, Trypanosoma*, and *Leishmania*.

18. Malaria is a protozoan infection caused by several species of the genus *Plasmodium*; it claims 150 million new victims each year, many of whom ultimately die of the disease.

19. Pneumocystis carnii causes a pneumonia which is a common complication of AIDS; there is reason to suspect that the organism is actually an ascomycete fungus, not a protozoan.

20. Helminths is a general term used to refer to the members of the Platyhelminthes and the Aschelminthes.

## MASTERY TEST

1-15: Circle the choice that best answers the questions.

1. Fungi which have filaments (chains of cells) that do not have crosswalls (septa) in them are said to have:
   a. complex mycelia
   b. septate hyphae
   c. simple mycelia
   d. coenocytic hyphae
   e. dimorphic hyphae

2. Fungi which exist as yeasts and as molds (depending upon their cultural conditions) are said to be:
   a. schizophrenic
   b. dimorphic
   c. biphasic
   d. amphipathic
   e. coenocytic

3. Fungi are generally maintained in nature by the consumption of dead or decaying organic matter. They are thus called:
   a. scavengers
   b. holozoic
   c. lithotrophs
   d. amphipaths
   e. saprophytes

4. Sexual spore production in fungi always involves (at some time during the life cycle) both the fusion of cells (fertilization) and __________________ cell division.
   a. longitudinal binary fission
   b. meiotic
   c. mitotic
   d. transverse binary fission

5. The fungal division Mastigomycota is distinct from other fungi in the ability of its members to produce:
   a. flagellated spores
   b. multinucleate hyphae
   c. dimorphic growth forms
   d. amoebic cells
   e. fruiting bodies

6. *Rhizopus* and *Mucor* are opportunistic members of the Class:
   a. Ascomycetes
   b. Basidiomycetes
   c. Deuteromycetes
   d. Zygomycetes

7. Sporangiospores and conidiospores are examples of:
a. sexual mitotic spores
b. asexual meiotic spores
c. sexual meiotic spores
d. asexual mitotic spores

8. The most common and important yeasts are in the genus *Saccharomyces* and in the Class:
a. Ascomycetes
b. Basidiomycetes
c. Deuteromycetes
d. Zygomycetes

9. The Ascomycetes and Basidiomycetes differ from the Zygomycetes in various ways, but one nonreproductive difference is the presence of _______________ in the Zygomycetes.
a. conidiospores
b. coenocytic hyphae
c. septate hyphae
d. amoebic cells

10. Which of the following is a symbiotic association between an alga and a fungus?
a. kelp
b. irish moss
c. lichen
d. cellular slime molds

11. If it has proved impossible to determine the mode of sexual reproduction practiced by a fungus, the organism is placed into the Class:
a. Ascomycetes
b. Basidiomycetes
c. Deuteromycetes
d. Zygomycetes

12. Protozoans never have cell walls; most make do with a tough covering called a(n):
a. pellicle
b. cyst
c. outer membrane
d. capsule

13. Which of the following is a sexually transmitted disease caused by a flagellated protozoan?
a. trichomoniasis
b. trypanosomiasis
c. syphilis
d. giardiasis

14. Which of the following is a disease more commonly known as "African sleeping sickness"?
a. trichomoniasis
b. trypanosomiasis
c. filariasis
d. giardiasis

15. *Entamoeba histolytica* causes which of the following diseases?
a. amoebic meningitis
b. filariasis
c. elephantiasis
d. amoebic dysentery
e. malaria

16-21: Match the taxonomic group with its description (use no answer twice)

ANSWERS

| | | |
|---|---|---|
| A. Aschelminthes | D. Mastigophora | G. Sarcodina |
| B. Cestoda | E. Nematoda | H. Sporozoa |
| C. Ciliata | F. Platyhelminthes | I. Trematoda |

D 16. Protozoan group capable of locomotion by means of flagella; includes many parasitic forms.

G 17. Protozoan group that is characterized by amoeboid movement; the shells of one group (*Foraminifera*) produced the White Cliffs of Dover.

A 18. Members of this PHYLUM are often called roundworms.

I 19. This class of worms includes a group of organisms called "flukes".

H 20. Members of this protozoan group are immotile and are exclusively parasites of animals.

E 21. This class includes the parasitic round worms.

---

22-25: Circle the choice that best answers the questions.

22. Toxoplasmosis, caused by the sporozoan *Toxoplasma gondii*, is most likely to be acquired by contact with which of the following animal groups?
    a. dogs
    b. arthropods
    c. snails
    d. cats
    e. raccoons

23. The development of an adult parasitic worm from a larval stage occurs in the:
    a. alternate host
    b. intermediate host
    c. definitive host
    d. casual host
    e. terminal host

24. Blood flukes enter the human body in which of the following stages of development?
    a. miracidium
    b. sporocyst
    c. redia
    d. cercaria
    e. metacercaria

25. Except for *Dracunculus medinensis* (the guinea worm), all blood and tissue nematodes are in the following superfamily:
   a. cestoda
   b. filarioidea
   c. trematoda
   d. nematoda
   e. sporozoa

ANSWERS TO LEARNING ACTIVITIES

Fill-in-the-blank questions:

1. Algae; 2. Phytoplankton; 3. Chlorophyta; 4. Euglenophyta; 5. Diatoms; 6. Phaeophyta; 7. Red tides; 8. Rhodophyta; 9. Hyphae; 10. Yeasts; 11. Cysts

| CLASS | COMMON NAME | DESCRIPTION |
|---|---|---|
| ~~MYXOMYCETES~~ ACRASIOMYCETES | CELLULAR SLIME MOLDS | Uninucleate amoebae; produce complex fruiting bodies from slugs |
| ~~DEUTEROMYCETES~~ ASCOMYCETES | SAC FUNGI | Septate hyphae, produce sexual spores in asci. |
| ~~ACRASIOMYCETES~~ BASIDIOMYCETES | CLUB FUNGI | Septate hyphae, produce sexual spores in complex fruiting bodies often called mushrooms. |
| ~~BASIDIOMYCETES~~ DEUTEROMYCETES | FUNGI IMPERFECTI | Do not reproduce sexually. |
| ~~ASCOMYCETES~~ MYXOMYCETES | PLASMODIAL SLIME MOLDS | Multinucleate amoebae; produce complex fruiting bodies. |

17. Mastigophora; 18. Malaria; 19. *Pneumocystis carnii*; 20. Helminths.

| MASTERY TEST ANSWERS | | | | | | | | | | | | | |
|---|---|---|---|---|---|---|---|---|---|---|---|---|---|
| 1 d | 2 b | 3 e | 4 b | 5 a | 6 d | | 7 d | 8 a | 9 b | 10 c | 11 c | 12 a |
| 13 a | 14 b | 15 d | 16 D | 17 G | 18 A | 19 B | 20 H | 21 E | 22 d | 23 c | 24 d | 25 b |

# CHAPTER 16

## INFECTION AND BACTERIAL INVASIVENESS

### CHAPTER SUMMARY

**Infection** by microorganisms is a natural consequence of human life; our **normal flora** constitutes a harmless and usually beneficial infection. **Disease** begins when organisms move from their natural location or when an organism demonstrating **pathogenicity** invades the body. **Virulent** pathogens cause disease easily, weakly virulent ones rarely do. Some diseases are **communicable** (or **contagious** - spread from one individual to another), others are contracted from animals, still others develop from **soil saprophytes** (usually contracted *via* wounds). Diseases which are always present (usually at low rates) are said to be **endemic**. Diseases which are not usually present (especially ones occurring at high rates) are called **epidemic** diseases. Very widespread epidemics, often worldwide, are called **pandemics**. If a disease occurs very infrequently it is referred to as **sporadic**.

Invasion by a pathogen does not immediately result in a symptomatic infection; generally an **incubation period** (ranging from days to years) is required. Eventually **illness** (**symptomatic infection**) results and, if the individual is fortunate, **convalescence** leads to recovery. Some people may recover from an illness (or may never even reach the symptomatic stage) and yet continue to harbor the causative agent; such people are called **carriers**. Carriers of **typhoid** fever, bacillary **dysentery**, amebic dysentery, bacterial **diarrhea**, and viral **hepatitis** are fairly common. Disease can be spread in a similar fashion by people suffering from an **undiagnosed infection** - one mild enough to escape detection but productive of contagious agents of disease. An **inapparent infection** is similar to a mild, undiagnosed one. Often people contract **hepatitis A** or **poliomyelitis** and never exhibit any symptoms yet later demonstrate antibody produced against the agent. A **reservoir** is a continuing source of infectious agents; it may be a wild animal population, or other humans.

Infections which develop **rapidly**, are of **short** duration, and which commonly result in **high fevers** are called **acute infections** (e.g. scarlet fever, toxic shock syndrome). **Slowly** developing, relatively **milder** infections which have a **prolonged** course are called **chronic infections** (e.g. leprosy, tuberculosis). Infections which remain confined to the area of initial invasion are called **local infections** (e.g. boils or furuncles). Some local infections have general effects if the agent produces potent **toxins** (e.g. **tetanus** and **diphtheria**). Infections which spread from the initial site of invasion are called **systemic infections** (e.g. **Lyme disease**, mumps). Some systemic infections spread from a localized source, called a **focal infection** (often an abscess). If the systemic infection is being spread by the blood stream it is called a **bacteremia**; if the disease organism actually multiplies in the blood it is called **septicemia** (or **viremia** if a virus is the agent). **Toxemia** is a condition in which bacterial toxins (**endotoxins** or **exotoxins**) are present in the blood.

**Primary infections** are caused by true pathogens which possess the capacity called **invasiveness** (ability to overcome normal body defenses and cause an overt infection). **Opportunists** (organisms that lack invasiveness) may take advantage of the effects of a primary infection to cause a **secondary infection** (e.g. staphylococcal pneumonia which often follows primary respiratory infections like measles and influenza).

Demonstrating the cause of a disease is usually a straightforward procedure which can be achieved by following **Koch's postulates**. Some diseases prove harder to document because the agent can't be grown in culture (e.g. the causative agents of leprosy and syphilis: *Mycobacterium leprae* and *Treponema pallidum*) or because of a lack of suitable experimental animals to test the agent against (e.g. the causative agent of AIDS, **HIV**).

Typical pathogens have a characteristic **portal of entry** into the body and a **portal of exit** from the body. Some important portals of entry include: the **mouth** and/or the **nose** (portals for **respiratory** infections and **gastrointestinal** infections), the **skin** and **mucous membranes** (portals of entry for localized **skin infections** and some systemic diseases), the mucous membranes of the **genital tract** (portals of entry for **sexually transmitted diseases** and **urinary tract** infections), and the **blood** - usually *via* **arthropod vectors** but also by means of contaminated needles and **blood transfusions** - the portal of entry of many **systemic diseases** such as malaria, bubonic plague, tularemia, and AIDS. In most cases the **portal of exit** is the same as the portal of entry; an important exception is **gastrointestinal infections** which enter via the mouth and exit via the **anus**.

True **pathogens** can gain entry to the body of their host unaided, opportunists cannot. **Virulence factors** are what set the true pathogens apart. The **capsule** is an important virulence factor for many bacteria, acting as an **antiphagocytic** agent. Unless specific antibodies are bound to the capsule, bacteria like *Streptococcus pneumoniae* cannot be controlled by **leukocytes** (white blood cells). **Fimbriae (pili)** are another virulence factor whose main effect seems to be enhancing the ability of bacteria to attach to one another and to the membranes of host cells. Mutant strains of *E. coli, Neisseria gonorrhoeae*, and *Neisseria meningitidis* which lack fimbriae also lack virulence.

**Exotoxins** (toxins excreted by bacteria) may be responsible for the **symptoms** of a disease (e.g. diphtheria, pertussis, cholera), or the cause of **food**

**poisoning** (e.g. botulism, staphylococcal food poisoning), or they may be important virulence factors if they **permit cells (including leukocytes) to be killed**. **Hemolysins** (e.g. streptolysin and staphylolysin) kill and lyse red blood cells (and other cells), **leukocidins** kill white blood cells, **necrotizing factor (necrotoxin)** kills tissue cells. Some **enterotoxins** (toxins that affect the cells lining the intestine and that result in dysentery and diarrhea) work by **killing intestinal epithelial cells** by blocking protein synthesis in the cells (e.g. **diphtheria toxin** from *Corynebacterium diptheriae* and **Shiga toxin** from *Shigella dysenteriae*).

Other virulence factors include **hyaluronidase**, an enzyme which digests **hyaluronic acid** (an important intracellular material), allowing the bacterium to spread within tissues. **Collagenase**, which digests collagen, has a similar but more drastic effect, allowing the rapid progression of clostridial cells in **gas gangrene**. **Streptokinase** (made by *Streptococcus*), and the similar **staphylokinase** (made by *Staphylococcus*) both **dissolve blood clots** by activating a proteolytic enzyme called **plasmin**. **Coagulase** (manufactured by *Staphylococcus*) has the opposite effect; it **causes the coagulation** of plasma, producing a fibrin clot. This may **prevent phagocytosis** of the bacterium by creating a **fibrin barrier** between it and the host's defenses. **Siderophores** are a final virulence factor; their function is to liberate **iron** from the vertebrate carriers **lactoferrin** and **transferrin**.

Many disease symptoms are directly attributable to toxins produced by the disease agent. **Enterotoxins** cause diarrhea and dysentery by causing the death (diphtheria and shigellosis, discussed above) or leakage of fluid (cholera) from intestinal epithelial cells. **Fluid leakage** is typically accomplished by stimulating the **overproduction of cAMP** (cyclic AMP) by the affected cells. Similar effects on cells are caused by the **pertussis toxin** (whooping cough) and the **anthrax** toxin. **Neurotoxins** affect the nervous system or neuromuscular communication (e.g. **botulism** toxin and **tetanus** toxin). **Endotoxins**, the **lipopolysaccharide** components of **gram-negative** cell walls, cause two main effects: **fever** and **shock**. They apparently work by **stimulating the release** of a **cytokine** called **tumor necrosis factor alpha (TNF-$\alpha$)** by macrophages (a white blood cell). TNF-$\alpha$ itself can cause severe **hypotension** by stimulating the release of another cytokine, **interleukin-1**, from macrophages and epithelial cells.

<u>OBJECTIVES</u> After a study of this chapter, you should:

1. Be able to differentiate among acute, chronic, local, systemic, and inapparent infection.
2. Be familiar with how communicable diseases are transmitted to a susceptible individual.
3. Know how to use Koch's postulates to establish the causes of a disease.
4. Be able to recognize any properties possessed by a bacterium that contribute to its ability to produce disease.
5. Know what is meant by such terms as *portal of entry, virulence*, and *vector*.

## LEARNING ACTIVITIES

### Vocabulary

Having read the chapter, you should be able to define or cite the significance of the following terms. If you cannot, look them up in the text. Terms are presented in the order you will encounter them in the book.

symptomatic infections
pathogenicity
virulence
communicable disease
contagious disease
endemic
epidemic
pandemic
sporadic
incubation period
illness
convalescence
carriers
reservoir
acute infection
chronic infection
local infection
systemic infection
focal infection
primary infection
invasiveness
opportunists
secondary infection
inapparent infection
bacteremia
septicemia
viremia
endotoxin
toxemia
Koch's postulates
discharges
portal of entry
portal of exit
respiratory
gastrointestinal
skin and mucous membranes
furuncle
genitourinary
blood
virulence factors
capsule
antiphagocytic
fimbriae
exotoxins
endotoxins
hemolysins
leukocidins
leukocyte
hyaluronidase
hyaluronic acid
streptokinase
plasmin
staphylokinase
coagulase
fibrin barrier
collagenase
collagen
necrotizing factor
hypothermic factor
edema-producing substance
siderophore
lactoferrin
transferrin
chelated
enterotoxins
neurotoxins
cAMP-producing toxins
protein-synthesis-inhibiting toxins
endotoxins
fever
shock
cytokine
tumor necrosis factor alpha
interleukin-1
prostaglandins

Complete each of the following statements by supplying the missing word or words.

1. Pathogenicity__________ is the ability of a microorganism to cause disease.

2. Communicable__________ (contagious) diseases are spread from human to human.

3. Endemic diseases are constantly present in an area, usually at relatively low rates.

4. Pandemic are extremely widespread epidemics, often worldwide.

5. * Carriers are asymptomatic but can transmit such diseases as typhoid fever, bacillary dysentery, amebic dysentery, bacterial diarrhea, and viral hepatitis.

6. Bacteremia are diseases which are spread throughout the body by the bloodstream.

7. Local infections are confined to the region of the body where the infectious organism first penetrated host defenses.

8. Focal infections act as a nucleus for the spread of the infectious agent to other sites; surgical removal of the nucleus is often required.

9. Opportunists are bacteria (or fungi) that are incapable of invading the host's body on their own but will often follow after a true pathogen and cause a secondary infection.

10. Koch's postulates lay out a logical method for establishing the causative agent of a disease. They do not work for all diseases.

11. Mycobacterium Leprea and *Treponema pallidum* are two agents of disease which have never been grown in the laboratory and therefore fail the second postulate mentioned above.

12. The portal of entry is the blood for such diseases as malaria, yellow fever, bubonic plague, tularemia, and Lyme disease (in all cases aided by an arthropod vector).

13. Virulence factors are the mechanisms used by true pathogens to evade host defenses and to establish an overt infection.

14. Capsules seem to operate mainly as antiphagocytic agents, preventing successful engulfment by leukocytes.

15. Fimbriäe aid pathogens in binding to the membranes of host cells.

16. *Hemolysins* are secreted by some pathogens and have the effect of lysing red blood cells and some other mammalian cells.

17. *Coagulase* is an agent secreted by *Staphylococcus* which causes blood plasma to clot and forms a "fibrin barrier" that protects the bacterium from host defenses.

18. *Siderophores* are agents that are able to "steal" iron atoms from vertebrate carriers such as lactoferrin and transferrin.

19. *Exotoxins* are secreted mostly by gram-positive bacteria; some are neurotoxins, others are enterotoxins.

20. *Endotoxins* are produced exclusively by gram-negative bacteria and are lipopolysaccharides.

## MASTERY TEST

1-12: Circle the choice that best answers the questions.

1. A pathogen which causes disease easily is said to be highly *virulent*; one that causes disease only with difficulty is weakly ____________.
   a. opportunistic
   b. virulent
   c. parasitic
   d. resistant
   e. communicable

2. A disease occurring in excess of normal expectancy is called:
   a. endemic
   b. contagious
   c. pandemic
   d. sporadic
   e. epidemic

3. Carriers **most commonly** harbor and transmit:
   a. respiratory agents
   b. intestinal agents
   c. genitourinary agents
   d. blood-borne agents
   e. skin infection agents

4. Viral hepatitis and ____________ are the two diseases most commonly transmitted *via* blood products and body secretions.
   a. syphilis
   b. gonorrhoea
   c. AIDS
   d. hemophilia

5. A common opportunist that causes a secondary pneumonia after a measles or influenza primary infection is:
a. *Staphylococcus*
b. *Streptococcus*
c. *Bacillus*
d. *Mycobacterium*
e. *Escherichia*

6. Which of the following is the term applied to an infection in which the agent is actually multiplying in the blood?
a. bacteremia
b. toxemia
c. hepatitis
d. septicemia
e. focal infection

7. Which of the following is the term applied to an illness characterized by bacterial poisons (exo- and endo-) in the blood?
a. bacteremia
b. toxemia
c. hepatitis
d. septicemia
e. focal infection

8. An infection which develops rapidly, is of short duration, and which typically results in a high fever is called a(n) ______________ infection.
a. chronic
b. asymptomatic
c. acute
d. undiagnosed
e. septicemic

9. An example of a localized (local) infection which has general symptoms is:
a. furuncle
b. mumps
c. Lyme disease
d. diphtheria
e. leprosy

10. The classic use of Koch's postulates breaks down when one attempts to discover the causes of diseases generated by ________________ like viruses, rickettsiae, and chlamydiae:
a. virulent pathogens
b. obligate extracellular pathogens
c. obligate intracellular pathogens
d. obligate anaerobes

11. The portal of entry and portal of exit is the same for all of the following except:
a. respiratory infections
b. gastrointestinal infections
c. skin and mucous membrane infections
d. genitourinary infections
e. blood infections

12. The most common mechanism by which blood infections are transmitted is by means of:
   a. arthropod vectors
   b. anthropoid vectors
   c. contaminated needles
   d. blood transfusions
   e. bad food

---

13-19: Match the virulence factor with its description (use no answer twice)

ANSWERS

A. capsules
B. coagulase
C. collagenase
D. enterotoxins
E. exotoxins
F. fimbriae
G. hemolysins
H. hyaluronidase
I. leukocidins
J. neurotoxins
K. siderophores
L. streptokinase

H 13. Hyaluronidase digests intercellular material in ordinary tissues, allowing pathogenic cells to move through the tissue.

C 14. collagenase digests the main protein in cartilage, bone and other connective tissues.

D 15. enterotoxins are toxins that damage intestinal epithelial cells, killing them or causing them to leak fluids.

I 16. Leukocidins kills white blood cells.

L 17. streptokinase is an agent that activates a blood protein called plasmin, causing it to break down blood clots.

E 18. exotoxins are a **general** group of toxic materials excreted by bacteria into their environment.

G 19. hemolysins are toxic materials that cause the lysis of red blood cells.

---

20-25: Circle the choice that best answers the questions.

20. The physical symptoms of food poisoning caused by *Clostridium botulinum, Staphylococcus aureus*, and *Bacillus cereus* are all due to:
   a. endotoxins
   b. hemolysins
   c. enterotoxins
   d. exotoxins
   e. $\alpha$-amylases

21. Enterotoxins that act on cAMP production result in:
a. fluid leakage
b. massive cell death
c. fever
d. fermentation

22. Endotoxins are chemically:
a. peptides and proteins
b. glycoproteins
c. lipoproteins
d. lipopolysaccharides

23. Endotoxins produce fever and shock by triggering the release of ____________ (a cytokine) from macrophages.
a. N-acetylglucosamine
b. TNF-α Tumor Necrosis Factor α
c. necrotoxin
d. prostaglandins

24. Which of the following is NOT a source of infectious agents?
a. other human beings
b. marine saprophytes
c. wild and domestic animals
d. soil saprophytes

25. Protozoan parasites can often survive for long periods of time outside the body of their hosts by forming:
a. endospores
b. conidiospores
c. ascospores
d. basidiospores
e. cysts

## ANSWERS TO LEARNING ACTIVITIES

Fill-in-the-blank questions:

1. Pathogenicity; 2. Communicable; 3. Endemic; 4. Pandemics; 5. Carriers; 6. Bacteremia; 7. Local; 8. Focal; 9. Opportunists; 10. Koch; 11. *Mycobacterium leprae*; 12. portal of entry; 13. Virulence; 14. Capsules; 15. Fimbriae (pili); 16. Hemolysins; 17. Coagulase; 18. Siderophores; 19. Exotoxins; 20. Endotoxins.

**MASTERY TEST ANSWERS**

| | | | | | | | | | | | | |
|---|---|---|---|---|---|---|---|---|---|---|---|---|
| 1<br>b | 2<br>e | 3<br>b | 4<br>c | 5<br>a | 6<br>d | | 7<br>b | 8<br>c | 9<br>d | 10<br>c | 11<br>b | 12<br>a |
| 13<br>H | 14<br>C | 15<br>D | 16<br>I | 17<br>L | 18<br>E | 19<br>G | 20<br>d | 21<br>a | 22<br>d | 23<br>b | 24<br>b | 25<br>e |

# CHAPTER 17

# NONSPECIFIC HOST RESISTANCE

## CHAPTER SUMMARY

**Resistance** to infection is a complex set of **reactions** and **defenses** that host animals utilize against microorganisms. Resistance is categorized into two types: (1) **nonspecific (natural)** resistance and (2) **specific (acquired)** resistance. **Susceptibility** is defined as a lack of resistance; susceptibility to pathogens **varies widely** between species and even within a species. Some of these differences are due to **genetic** or **racial factors**, others may have more to do with diet and lifestyle.

The first line of defense in nonspecific resistance involves **mechanical** and **chemical barriers**. **Intact skin** constitutes an excellent mechanical barrier to infection, but its effectiveness is greatly increased by chemical means. **Saturated** and **unsaturated fatty acids**, highly toxic to bacteria and fungi, are secreted onto the skin by the **sebaceous glands**. **Propionic acid** released by normal skin flora reduces the **pH** of skin below that favored by many microbes.

**Mucous membranes** constitute a mechanical and chemical barrier as well. The **mucous entraps** dust and microbes, and the **cilia** on the surface of the cells sweeps both up and out of the lungs. Many secretions like tears and mucous contain **lysozyme**, an enzyme which **hydrolyzes peptidoglycan**. The enzyme is found in blood and tissue fluids as well. **Acids** produced in the stomach and vagina **reduce the pH** in these regions well below that favored by most microbes.

**Interferons**, produced by virus-infected cells or by activated white blood cells, constitute another type of nonspecific chemical defense - this time **against viruses**. Their general effect is to **inhibit viral replication** in the species of animal that produces the interferon. Three main **types** of interferon are produced by various tissues: **leukocyte interferon (IFNα)** is produced by **leukocytes**, **fibroblast interferon (IFNß)** is produced by **tissue cells**, and **immune interferon** (or **T-cell interferon, IFNγ**) is produced by **lymphocytes**. IFNα and IFNß both are induced by **double-stranded RNA**, a uniquely viral product. IFNγ is induced by contact between a **sensitized T-cell lymphocyte** and a **specific antigen**; less specific inducers such as bacterial endotoxins (a **mitogen**) may also work.

IFN$\gamma$ functions mainly as a **lymphokine**, regulating the action of other members of the leukocyte population. Its specific effect seems to be directed at **natural-killer-cells** (which kill tumor cells) and at **macrophages**. IFN$\alpha$ and IFN$\beta$ have their effect on normal, **uninfected tissue cells**. They stimulate these cells to produce two new products, one of which is a **protein kinase**, which phosphorylates an initiation factor used in protein synthesis. The effect of this is to **reduce the rate of translation** on mRNA. The other new product is **oligoadenylate** (a polymer of adenylic acid) which activates a cellular endonuclease enzyme, **RNase L**, which then **hydrolyzes viral mRNA** (and host mRNA, too). Interferons have shown **limited therapeutic use** against virus infections (e.g. herpesvirus, hepatitis B, papilloma virus) and against some tumors.

The second line of defense is the **nonspecific phagocytosis** of invading microorganisms by members of the leukocyte (white blood cell) population called **phagocytes**. The most numerous member of this group is the **polymorphonuclear neutrophil** (otherwise known as a **granulocyte**, a **PMN** or a **poly**). They make up **60-70** percent of total leukocyte population. Some infections cause a huge **increase** in poly population, a response known as **leukocytosis**; in other infections (typically gram-negative) their number **drops** - this is called **leukopenia**. Similar in appearance to neutrophils but less numerous and more involved with allergies are the **basophils** and **eosinophils**. Circulating **monocytes** look quite different from polys; when they leave the bloodstream and move into tissues they are called **macrophages (mononuclear phagocytes)**. The **mononuclear phagocyte system** (or **reticuloendothelial system**) comprises macrophages in fixed locations: liver, spleen, bone marrow, lungs, and in lymph nodes. They scrutinize circulating fluids for invading microorganisms. **Lymphocytes**, the last group of leukocytes, are **nonphagocytic** and participate in specific (acquired) immunity.

The activities of phagocytes are often preceded by the inflammatory response. This complex phenomenon consists of (1) **dilation of blood vessels** near the site of injury (**vasodilation**) accompanied by **increased permeability** of the capillary wall (both phenomena are induced by **vasoactive amines** like **histamine, serotonin**, and **bradykinin** - all released by damaged cells); (2) the **adherence of leukocytes** to the walls of blood vessels followed by (3) the **movement of leukocytes** out of the blood into the damaged tissues. The net result of the inflammatory response is **edema** (swelling) of the injured area and a rapid influx of leukocytes. The first cells to arrive are typically **neutrophils** which die in great numbers; they are followed up by **mononuclear macrophages**. The attraction of leukocytes to injured areas is called **chemotaxis**, a chemical attraction process dependent upon some bacterial products (endotoxins especially), products of damaged tissue cells, components released by the complement system, etc.

Phagocytosis may be hindered by some **bacterial defenses** such as **capsules** and **fimbriae**; some bacteria can even kill leukocytes with products called **leukocidins**. There are even some bacteria which can **survive inside leukocytes** after being engulfed by phagocytosis (e.g. agents of tuberculosis, leprosy, brucellosis, tularemia). Most bacteria, however, are susceptible to being phagocytized and, once brought into the leukocyte, being killed. The killing process involves an organelle discovered in 1955 by Christian **de Duve** - the **lysosome**. These are bags of **hydrolytic enzymes** which merge with the **phagosome** (containing the engulfed bacterium) to produce the **phagolysosome**. This fusion process is called **degranulation** (phagocytes have large numbers of lysosomes in them which results in their being referred to as granulocytes). Among the lethal materials liberated from lysosomes are: **lysozyme, lactoferrin, phagocytin, leukin**, and much **acid** that results in the phagolysosome having a pH of 3 to 4. People suffering from the genetic disorder **Chediak-Higashi syndrome (CHS)** have a defect in the ability of lysosomes to fuse with phagosomes.

The "respiratory burst" is another lethal activity which is correlated with phagocytosis. Shortly after engulfing the microorganism, the phagocyte mobilizes its **glycogen** reserves to produce large quantities of **NADPH**. This is further metabolized *via* the enzyme **NADPH oxidase** to produce **hydrogen peroxide** (**$H_2O_2$**). The hydrogen peroxide is further processed by the enzyme **myeloperoxidase (MPO)** to produce **hypochlorite (HClO$^-$)** - a lethal material. People suffering from **chronic granulomatous disease (CGD)** cannot produce these lethal materials due to a **defective NADPH oxidase enzyme**.

OBJECTIVES This chapter is designed to introduce you to:

1. The role of mechanical and chemical mechanisms in our first line of defense.
2. The nature of interferons, including their induction and mode of action.
3. The kinds of cells involved in the phagocytosis of invading organisms.
4. The mechanism by which phagocytic cells kill microorganisms.
5. Genetic defects in the ability to carry out phagocytosis.

## LEARNING ACTIVITIES

### Vocabulary

Having read the chapter, you should be able to define or cite the significance of the following terms. If you cannot, look them up in the text. Terms are presented in the order you will encounter them in the book.

resistance
nonspecific resistance
natural-killer-cell
lymphokine
inflammatory response
vasodilation

natural
 resistance
specific
 resistance
acquired
 resistance
susceptibility
genetic factors
racial factors
mechanical barrier
fatty acids
sebaceous glands
cilia
mucous
chemical defenses
lysozyme
acids
interferon
leukocyte
 interferon
fibroblast
 interferon
T-cell interferon
IFNα, IFNβ, IFNγ
double-
 stranded RNA
antigen
mitogen

protein kinase
initiation factor
oligoadenylate
RNase L
leukocyte
phagocytosis
phagocyte
polymorphonuclear
 neutrophil
granulocyte
PMN
poly
leukocytosis
leukopenia
Metchnikoff
monocyte
macrophage
mononuclear
 phagocyte
basophil
eosinophil
lymphocytes
mononuclear
 phagocyte system
reticulo-
 endothelial
 system
edema

vascular
 permeability
vasoactive amines
histamine
serotonin
bradykinin
chemotaxis
de Duve
lysosome
degranulation
phagolysosome
NADPH
NADPH oxidase
hydrogen peroxide
myeloperoxidase
hypochlorite
lactoferrin
phagocytin
leukin
capsule
fimbriae
chronic
 granulomatous
 disease (CGD)
Chediak-
 Higashi
 syndrome (CHS)
leukocidins

Complete each of the following statements by supplying the missing word or words.

1. Nonspecific________ or natural resistance consists of a variety of mechanical, chemical and cellular mechanisms.

2. Susceptibility________ (lack of resistance) is related to genetic and racial factors, but also to environmental and nutritional ones as well.

3. The skin________ and mucous membranes provide an effective mechanical barrier against invasion by microorganisms.

4. Interferon________ is a protein secreted by virus-infected cells that helps uninfected cells avoid invasion.

5. Acid ____________ production in the stomach, vagina, and on the skin is an effective chemical defense against most bacteria.

6. sebaceous ____________ glands release saturated and unsaturated fatty acids onto the skin which are quite lethal to many bacteria and fungi.

7. Double stranded RNA ____________ is the main inducer of both IFN$\alpha$ and IFN$\beta$; it is a characteristically viral product.

8. RNase L ____________ is an endonuclease whose activity is affected by interferon *via* the intermediary of oligoadenylate.

9. A phagocyte ____________ is a cell which performs phagocytosis.

polymorphonuclear

10. Neutrophil ____________ (PMN or poly) is the most common of all types of leukocytes.

11. Eosinophils ____________ and basophils bear a physical resemblance to the cell discussed above, but are involved mostly in allergic responses.

12. Macrophages ____________ (mononuclear phagocytes) are what becomes of monocytes that leave the bloodstream and move out into tissues.

13. The inflammatory response ____________ involves vasodilation, and increased vascular permeability; it results in edema.

14. Histamine ____________, serotonin, and bradykinin are three "vasoactive amines" which are involved in producing the response described above.

15. Chemotaxics ____________ is the chemical attraction process that results in the migration of neutrophils and macrophages into injury sites.

16. Capsules ____________ and fimbriae are two important antiphagocytic devices used by some pathogens in evading host defenses.

17. Lysosomes ____________ fuse with phagosomes to produce phagolysosomes.

18. degranulation ____________ is the term applied to the process described in question #17.

19. chronic granulomatous disease ____________ is a genetic disorder in which the NADPH oxidase enzyme is defective, and therefore hypochlorite is not produced in phagocytes.

20. Chediak - higashi syndrom ____________________ is a hereditary disorder in which lysosomes do not properly fuse with phagosomes in phagocytes, allowing pathogens to survive and grow inside of leukocytes.

## MASTERY TEST

1-9: Circle the choice that best answers the questions.

1. The apparent resistance to malaria evidenced by black Americans, and the extreme susceptibility to tuberculosis evidenced by the guinea pig are both examples of:
   a. acquired resistance
   b. genetic factors
   c. specific resistance
   d. chemical resistance

2. The sebaceous glands add to the mechanical barrier of skin a chemical barrier of:
   a. fatty acids
   b. propionic acid
   c. saponified esters
   d. lysozyme

3. Mucous membranes constitute a mechanical barrier which is enhanced by the presence of mucous and the action of ______________ which move(s) the mucous and its trapped particles away from the tissue.
   a. amoeboid cells
   b. flagella
   c. mastigophores
   d. cilia

4. Tears, blood, and tissue fluids all contain ______________, an enzyme which digests (hydrolyzes) peptidoglycan.
   a. penicillin
   b. streptomycin
   c. lysozyme
   d. lysosomes
   e. complement

5. Low pH is a key antimicrobial chemical attribute of the stomach, the skin, and the ____________________.
   a. lungs
   b. penis
   c. cornea
   d. colon
   e. vagina

6. Interferons are **always** effective in:
   a. protecting uninfected cells from virus attack
   b. inducing natural-killer-cell attack on tumors
   c. enabling virus-infected cells to throw off the attack
   d. directly killing bacteria and fungi
   e. assisting the reticuloendothelial system

7. Mouse interferon directed against smallpox virus will be ______________ against a measles virus infection of mice.
   a. less effective than human anti-measles interferon
   b. about as effective as rat anti-smallpox interferon
   c. more effective than anti-influenza mouse interferon
   d. very effective
   e. totally ineffective

8. The production of IFN$\gamma$ (T-cell interferon) is usually induced by contact with specific ______________.
   a. antibodies
   b. antigens
   c. antisera
   d. antibiotics
   e. thymogens

9. One of the important effects of interferons is the induction of a protein kinase in uninfected cells. This enzyme phosphorylates an "initiation factor" which, in turn, reduces the:
   a. likelihood that viral RNA will be replicated
   b. transcription of DNA into RNA
   c. reverse transcription of RNA to DNA
   d. assembly of virions from genomes and capsomeres
   e. translation of mRNA

10. Another effect of interferon is the induction of oligoadenylate, which acts as a positive effector to activate an inactive enzyme which destroys:
   a. viral DNA exclusively
   b. viral RNA exclusively
   c. viral and host cell DNA
   d. viral and host cell RNA

11. Leukocytosis is the effect of many infections; it is the ______________ in polymorphonuclear neutrophil populations.
   a. total obliteration
   b. dramatic increase
   c. drastic decrease
   d. lack of change
   e. rightward change

12. Some gram-negative bacterial infections result in a change in neutrophil populations that is the reverse of that described in question #11; this effect is called:
   a. neutrophilia
   b. necrophilia
   c. leukocide
   d. leukopenia
   e. acidophilus

13. The normal function of natural-killer-cells is apparently to destroy:
   a. bacteria
   b. fungi
   c. protozoan parasites
   d. viruses
   e. tumor cells

14. ____________________ make up 25 to 35 percent of leukocyte populations and are generally involved in specific (acquired) immunity.
    a. neutrophils
    b. lymphocytes
    c. monocytes
    d. eosinophils

15. Monocytes, when they move into tissues, transform into:
    a. neutrophils
    b. lymphocytes
    c. macrophages
    d. eosinophils

16. Cells of the type discussed in question #15 are commonly found in the liver, the spleen, the bone marrow, the lungs, and in lymph nodes; all of these are parts of the:
    a. mononuclear phagocyte system.
    b. T-cell lymphocyte group
    c. B-cell lymphocyte group
    d. gut associated lymphoid tissue

17. The main physical effect of the inflammatory response is a localized swelling called:
    a. lymphoma
    b. furuncle
    c. edema
    d. Babinski reaction

18. Histamine, serotonin, and bradykinin are collectively referred to as:
    a. antibacterials
    b. chemotaxic agents
    c. neurotoxins
    d. prostaglandins
    e. vasoactive amines

19. All of the following are suspected to be involved in the chemotaxis response of leukocytes EXCEPT:
    a. supernates from damaged tissue cells
    b. mycobacterial cell wall fatty acid residues
    c. components produced during activation of complement
    d. antibody-antigen complexes

20. All of the following are known to avoid phagocytosis by means of thick capsules EXCEPT:
    a. *Streptococcus pneumoniae*
    b. *Haemophilus influenzae*
    c. *Klebsiella pneumoniae*
    d. *Neisseria gonorrhoeae*
    e. *Bacillus anthracis*

21. The fusing of lysosomes with phagosomes in phagocytes results in the process of:
    a. degranulation
    b. defenestration
    c. deforestation
    d. denaturation
    e. debilitation

22. Christian de Duve discovered ________________ in 1955. He eventually came to call them "suicide bags".
a. mycoplasmas
b. lysosomes
c. natural-killer-cells
d. phagosomes

23. The action of NADPH oxidase on NADPH results in the **direct** production of:
a. large amounts of ATP
b. hypochlorite
c. lysozyme
d. endotoxins
e. $H_2O_2$

24. Chronic granulomatous disease (CGD) results in repeated bacterial infections. It is caused by a genetic flaw that results in:
a. the inability of phagocytes to perform phagocytosis
b. the lack of production of neutrophils by bone marrow
c. the ineffective fusion of lysosomes and phagosomes
d. the autolysis of phagocytes on contact with bacteria
e. the inability to produce hypochlorite

25. The ability of some bacteria to directly kill phagocytic cells is due to their production of:
a. hemolysins
b. leukocidins
c. capsules
d. fimbriae

ANSWERS TO LEARNING ACTIVITIES

Fill-in-the-blank questions:

1. Nonspecific; 2. Susceptibility; 3. skin; 4. Interferon; 5. Acid; 6. Sebaceous; 7. Double-stranded RNA; 8. RNase L; 9. phagocyte; 10. Polymorphonuclear neutrophil; 11. Eosinophils; 12. Macrophages; 13. inflammatory response; 14. Histamine; 15. Chemotaxis; 16. Capsules; 17. Lysosomes; 18. Degranulation; 19. Chronic granulomatous disease; 20. Chediak-Higashi Syndrome (CGS).

**MASTERY TEST ANSWERS**

| | | | | | | | | | | | | |
|---|---|---|---|---|---|---|---|---|---|---|---|---|
| 1<br>b | 2<br>a | 3<br>d | 4<br>c | 5<br>e | 6<br>a | | 7<br>d | 8<br>b | 9<br>e | 10<br>d | 11<br>b | 12<br>d |
| 13<br>e | 14<br>b | 15<br>c | 16<br>a | 17<br>c | 18<br>e | 19<br>b | 20<br>d | 21<br>c | 22<br>b | 23<br>e | 24<br>e | 25<br>b |

## CHAPTER 18

## ANTIGENS AND ANTIBODIES

### CHAPTER SUMMARY

**Specific (acquired) immunity** is a state of being resistant to a specific organism. Involved in this process is a recognition of a **foreign** agent, and the ability to distinguish **self from nonself**. The detection of "foreign" agents is the detection of **antigens (Ag)** or **immunogens**. **Antibody-mediated immunity** involves the binding of specific proteins called **antibodies (Ab)** to the antigen. **Cell-mediated immunity** involves the capacity of sensitized immune cells to **kill other cells**.

**Antigens** are always large molecules and can be proteins, polysaccharides, glycoproteins, nucleoproteins, or glycolipids. They may be free (**soluble**) or bound (**particulate**). Particulate antigens are often components of bacterial **capsules** or **cell walls**, viral **capsids**, or even the **membranes** and **cell coats** of mammalian cells. **Proteins** (e.g. diphtheria toxin) are very **strong antigens** and induce strong responses. The more "foreign" a material is, the more antigenic it will be.

Even though antigens must be large molecules, the actual region to which antibodies bind is rather small. This region is called the **determinant group** or **epitope**, and it is usually only 200 to 1000 daltons in weight. One antigen, such as a large protein, may in fact have **multiple** separate **epitopes. Haptens** are **small** molecules that could not, themselves, serve as antigens but can if they bind to a larger molecule, such as a protein.

**Antibodies (immunoglobulins**, or **Ig)** are large glycoproteins found in the **γ (gamma) globulin** fraction of blood plasma. There are five different **classes** of antibodies: **IgG, IgA, IgD, IgE**, and **IgM**. A typical antibody such as IgG consists of **four polypeptide** chains joined together with disulfide bonds; **two "light" chains** (L-chains), and **two "heavy" chains** (H-chains). The enzyme **papain** (derived from papaya fruits) splits IgG into two major parts, the **Fab** (**a**ntigen **b**inding **f**raction) and the **Fc** (**c**rystallizable **f**raction).

The light chains come in two different versions, the **kappa (κ-chain)** and the **lambda (λ-chain)**; each of the five classes of immunoglobulins can contain two κ-chains or two λ-chains. Both light and heavy chains have **amino terminal** regions which are **highly variable** ($V_L$ and $V_H$ respectively). These **variable regions constitute the binding site** of the antibody, and their variability is responsible for the incredibly diverse antigens which antibodies can respond to. Light and heavy chains also have **constant** regions which are the same from antibody to antibody.

Of the major classes of antibodies, **IgG** is the **most common**, accounting for 80 percent of circulating immunoglobulins. It is the only class that can **cross the placental wall** and thus transmit **immunity** to the fetus. It has two antigen-binding sites and is effective at **binding complement**. **IgA** exists in two forms; a small IgG-like molecule in blood, and a **larger form in secretions** (saliva, milk, tears, seminal fluid, gastrointestinal and genitourinary secretions). The larger form has **four binding sites** and consists of two monomers linked together by a **J chain** and a **secretory component** which permits the molecule to pass across epithelial cell layers. IgA is our **first line of defense** against invading microorganisms in body orifices and in the lungs and, *via* breast-feeding, is a major source of immune support to **newborns**. IgA does not bind complement.

**IgM** is by far the **largest** antibody and is the very **first form secreted** during a new infection. It has ten antigen binding sites but is usually only able to **bind to five antigens** of moderate size; the ten sites are too close together (sterically restricted). IgM is extremely effective at **binding complement** and thus effectively **kills gram-negative bacteria**. **IgD** is mainly found on the surface of **B lymphocytes** where it may serve as a **cell surface receptor** for antigens. It cannot bind complement.

**IgE** is largely found attached to the membranes of **mast cells** and is found in much higher concentration in the bodies of people suffering from **allergies**. This is not surprising, since IgE is the active player in allergies. When IgE binds to the antigen it is complementary to (pollen, bee venom, penicillin, food constituents) it triggers the massive release of **histamine** and other **vasoactive** materials from the mast cell.

Synthesis and release of antibody is a cooperative process involving three cell types: **APCs** (**antigen presenting cells**), **B lymphocytes**, and **T lymphocytes**. APCs can be **macrophages** or **dendritic** cells. Their responsibility is to **engulf** the foreign organism by phagocytosis, enzymatically degrade its surface structures, then **present the antigen** on the cells' surface coupled to a **MHC Class II peptide** (MHC stands for **m**ajor **h**istocompatibility **c**omplex, the cell surface antigen group that must be matched in transplants). This combination can be recognized by the **antigen-specific receptors** on the surface of **T cells**. B cells can deal with intact antigens, taking them in, processing them, and displaying them on their surfaces (again in association with MHC Class II antigens).

The "B" in B cell derives from the **Bursa of Fabricius**, a lymphatic organ in **birds** in which this class of cells matures. Mammals do not have a bursa, thus this class of cells is sometimes called "**bursa-equivalent**". The sole function of B cells is the manufacture and release of **antibodies**.

**T cells** are named for the **thymus** gland, in which they mature. T cells are a diverse group that includes: (1) **helper T cells (Th)** which are involved in the activation of B cells; (2) **delayed-type hypersensitivity T cells (Tdth)** and

**cytotoxic T cells (Tc)**, both of which are involved in **cell-mediated immunity**; and (3) **suppressor T cells** (Ts), which are responsible for **winding down** immune responses. Except for a few rare "**T-independent antigens**", Th cells are required for eventual antibody synthesis and release. Unable to process raw antigen themselves, all members of the T cell group depend upon **APCs**. **T-dependent antibody synthesis** begins with the absorption and processing of antigen by an APC (at the same time specific B cells bind, process, and display the same antigen on their surface). The **APC presents the antigen** on its surface, where it is available for binding to the specific receptor on a Th cell; upon binding, the APC releases **interleukin-1**. Interleukin-1 stimulates cell division and additional **lymphokine** secretion in the Th cell. Ultimately one of the activated Th cells contacts the displayed antigen on the surface of a **B cell**; the Th cell then releases lymphokines that stimulate **rapid cell division in the B cell** and results in the production of (1) antibody secreting **plasma cells** and (2) **memory B cells**. Without Th intervention, the B cell does nothing.

A **primary antibody response** results in measurable antibody in about 5 days and reaches a peak in 2 to 3 weeks. A **secondary antibody response** to a later invasion by the same organism produces measurable antibody in 1 to 3 days and reaches levels **10 to 15 times higher** than the primary response. This remarkable performance is made possible by persistent **memory B and T cells** that were formed during the primary response.

**Monoclonal antibodies** are a relatively recent development made possible by the **fusion** of **myeloma** cells with **B cells** in tissue cultures containing polyethylene glycol. **Hybridomas** result from this fusion, some of which produce usable antibody in culture. Many of these monoclonal antibodies are used in sensitive diagnostic tests; others are combined with powerful drugs to form **immunoconjugates** - used to target tumor cells. As marvelous as the immune system seems to be, it is not perfect. One of its defects is occasional attacks on the body's own cells - **autoimmune disease**. **Sequestered antigens** are one problem area; cell structures which are not freely exposed during fetal development when "self" vs. "not self" determinations are made. Mature **sperm cells**, **myelin** in the central nervous system, and **eye lens** cells all have antigens that are not recognized as "self". **Altered self** is a mechanism that creates trouble when a metabolic product changes to a material that reacts with the immune system even though an earlier product did not (e.g. thyroglobulin). Lack of, or defective behavior of **suppressor T cells** can result in autoimmune disorders as well.

Major defects in the immune system are also possible; **selective IgA deficiency** affects 2 of every 1000 people. Many who suffer this disorder have repeated respiratory infections. **Sex-linked agammaglobulinemia** results in a complete absence of mature B cells (and consequent lack of antibody-mediated immunity). This disorder shows up almost exclusively in males. Worst of all is **SCID** (**s**evere **c**ombined **i**mmunodeficiency **d**isease); the famous "boy in the bubble" was a victim of this disorder. People with SCID have neither B cells nor T cells and rarely live very long.

OBJECTIVES After studying this chapter, you should be familiar with the:

1. Nature of specific or acquired immunity.
2. Properties a substance must possess to be an antigen.
3. Definition of determinant group and hapten.
4. General structure of each class of antibody.
5. Principal functions of each class of antibody.
6. Origin and role of B cells and T cells in antibody synthesis.
7. Role of the macrophage in antibody synthesis.
8. Kinetics of antibody synthesis.
9. Meaning of adjuvants and monoclonal antibodies.
10. Several models of autoimmune diseases.

## LEARNING ACTIVITIES

### Vocabulary

Having read the chapter, you should be able to define or cite the significance of the following terms. If you cannot, look them up in the text. Terms are presented in the order you will encounter them in the book.

specific immunity
acquired immunity
foreign
self vs. nonself
immunogens
antigens (Ag)
antibody-mediated immunity
cell-mediated immunity
determinant group
epitope
hapten
gamma ($\gamma$) globulin
immunoglobulins
light (L) chain
heavy (H) chain
papain
Fab fragment
steric restriction
B lymphocytes
cell surface receptor
allergies
mast cell
histamine
variable-light ($V_L$)
constant-light ($C_L$)
variable-heavy ($V_H$)
constant heavy
hinge region
alloantigens
major histocompatibility complex (MHC)
suppressor T (Ts)
T-independent antigens
interleukin-1
lymphokines
plasma cell
memory cell
primary antibody response
secondary antibody response
adjuvant
monoclonal antibodies
myeloma
hybridomas
autoimmune disease
sequestered antigens

Fc fragment
multiple myeloma
IgG
IgM
IgA
IgE
IgD
κ (kappa) chain
λ (lambda) chain
complement
placental wall
ß-globulin
secretory component
J chain

MHC Class I antigens
MHC Class II antigens
Bursa of Fabricius
bursa-equivalent
T-cell
APC (antigen-presenting cell)
macrophage
dendritic cell
Thymus
helper T (Th)
delayed-type hypersensitivity T cells (Tdth)

altered self
suppressor T cell defect
antibody deficiency syndrome
hypogamma-globulinemia
agammaglobulinemia
selective IgA deficiency
sex-linked agamma-globulinemia
severe combined immunodeficiency disease (SCID)

Complete each of the following statements by supplying the missing word or words.

1. ____________________ or acquired immunity is the resistance to certain invading organisms.

2. The recognition of ____________________ vs. nonself forms the basis for the system discussed above.

3. ____________________ (also called immunogens) are materials to which we become immune (or allergic).

4. ____________________-mediated immunity and cell-mediated immunity are the two main varieties of specific immunity.

5. ____________________, especially if very foreign, make the best antigens.

6. The ____________________ (or epitope) is the part of an antigen molecule to which an antibody binds; there may be more than one per antigen molecule.

7. A ____________________ is too small to serve as an antigen on its own, but it can become effective by binding to a large carrier like a protein.

8. ____________________ (Ig) is the proper name by which antibodies are known.

9-13: The order of the antibody class names has been scrambled in the following table; unscramble them.

| CLASS | PRINCIPLE FUNCTION |
|---|---|
| IgA | Principal circulating Ab; passes placental wall to newborn; fixes complement and lyses gram-negative bacteria; binds to gram-positive bacteria and provides receptors for phagocytes. |
| IgD | First Ab synthesized after Ag stimulation; more efficient than IgG in its ability to fix complement and to lyse gram-negative bacteria. |
| IgE | Occurs in serum as a monomer and is found externally as a dimer bound to a secretory piece and a J chain; first line of Ab defense against organisms entering the body through the mucous membranes; major Ab in breast milk and provides newborn with preformed antibody. |
| IgG | Occurs almost exclusively on the surface of B cells; is believed to be involved in the regulation of B cell differentiation. |
| IgM | Binds very tightly to mast cells and leukocytes; when cross-linked by their specific Ag, mast cells release pharmacologically active substances (such as histamine), which results in various allergic reactions to the antigen in question. |

14. The ____________________ region of light and heavy Ab chains is where the antigen binding site is formed.

15. ____________________ (MHC) is a group of extremely important cell surface antigens that must be matched if a transplant is to succeed.

16. The ____________________ is the site of B cell formation in birds.

17. ____________________ production is what B cells do.

18. ____________________ (APCs) are required by T cells because they cannot interact with intact antigens on their own.

19. ____________________ B and T cells are the key to the highly effective secondary antibody response.

20. ____________________ antigens is the term applied to normal antigens that the immune system may class as "nonself" since it did not have access to them during fetal development (e.g. eye lens).

MASTERY TEST

1-25: Circle the choice that best answers the questions.

1. Two things are absolutely required for an antigen to be effective; first it must be foreign, second it must be:
   a. a protein
   b. large
   c. a polysaccharide
   d. small
   e. sequestered

2. The basic activity of leukocytes in cell-mediated immunity is:
   a. secretion of antibody
   b. processing of antigen
   c. persistence in lymph nodes
   d. killing of other cells

3. Which of the following, assuming they are all equally foreign, would generally make the best (strongest) antigen?
   a. protein
   b. polysaccharide
   c. glycoprotein
   d. glycolipid
   e. nucleoprotein

4. The determinant group (or epitope) is always a(n) ________ portion of the whole antigen
   a. large
   b. major
   c. internal
   d. small

5. Which of the following is the blood protein fraction that contains the largest concentration of antibodies?
   a. $\alpha$ globulin
   b. ß globulin
   c. $\gamma$ globulin
   d. $\kappa$ globulin

6. Which of the following is the fragment of IgG produced by papain digestion which contains the antigen binding sites?
   a. Fc
   b. SCID
   c. MHC
   d. Fav
   e. Fab

7. Which of the following classes of antibodies has 5 to 10 antigen binding sites?
   a. IgA  b. IgD  c. IgE  d. IgG  e. IgM

8. Which of the following classes of antibodies has the ability to pass across the placenta into the fetus?
   a. IgA  b. IgD  c. IgE  d. IgG  e. IgM

9. Which of the following classes of antibodies is the major player in allergies?
a. IgA b. IgD c. IgE d. IgG e. IgM

10. Which of the following cells types releases histamine when an allergy attack is underway?
a. mast cells
b. eosinophils
c. neutrophils
d. T lymphocytes
e. B lymphocytes

11. The _______________ region (domain) of light and heavy Ab chains are the variable ones responsible for forming the antigen binding site.
a. κ (kappa)
b. λ (lambda)
c. amino terminal
d. carboxyl terminal
e. γ (gamma)

12. The antigen binding site of an antibody is a convoluted surface that is _______________ to the antigenic determinant to which it binds.
a. antiparallel
b. complementary
c. identical
d. amphipathic
e. enantiomeric

13. The B in B cell is derived from which of the following?
a. Bone Marrow
b. Bubo
c. Bands of Giacomini
d. Bursa of Fabricius
e. Babinski Reaction

14. The T in T cell is derived from which of the following?
a. Thymus
b. Thyroid
c. Thalamus
d. Tonsils

15. Antigens that are very similar to ones on body cells but may differ very slightly since they are from another individual of the same species are called:
a. alloantigens
b. heteroantigens
c. Freund's antigens
d. homoantigens

16. The _______________ MHC antigen is used by B cells and by APC cells when presenting their processed antigens.
a. primary
b. major
c. Class I
d. Class IV
e. Class II

17. Which of the following is the cell type absolutely required for B cell synthesis and release of antibody (except for those rare T-independent antigens)?
a. Th
b. Tdth
c. Tc
d. Ts

18. Which of the following is involved in cell-mediated immunity?
   a. Th
   b. Teth
   c. Tc
   d. Ts

19. The **lack of** which of the following has been implicated as being involved in the development of some autoimmune diseases?
   a. Th
   b. Tdth
   c. Tc
   d. Ts

20. Which of the following is a typical example of an APC (antigen presenting cell)?
   a. T lymphocyte
   b. B lymphocyte
   c. monocyte
   d. dendritic cell
   e. neutrophil

21. Interleukin-1, released by an APC, causes rapid cell division of Th cells and also results in the release of ______________ (soluble growth factors) by the Th cell.
   a. erythropoetins
   b. thymogens
   c. thyroglobulins
   d. lymphocidins
   e. lymphokines

22. The fusion of a B cell with a myeloma cell results in the production of a(n):
   a. hybridoma
   b. sarcoma
   c. fibroblastoma
   d. lymphoma
   e. mongreloma

23. The cell type discussed above can be a useful producer of which of the following products?
   a. interferon
   b. lymphokines
   c. monoclonal antibodies
   d. interleukin-2
   e. interleukin-1

24. Persons unfortunate enough to be suffering from the immune disorder called SCID lack which of the following immune cells?
   a. B cells
   b. IgA cells
   c. T cells
   d. B and T cells
   e. B, T, and APC cells

25. Which of the following is NOT an example of a sequestered antigen?
   a. eye lens
   b. sperm cells
   c. heart valve
   d. myelin

ANSWERS TO LEARNING ACTIVITIES

Fill-in-the-blank questions:

1. Specific; 2. self; 3. Antigens; 4. Antibody;
5. Proteins; 6. determinant group; 7. hapten;
8. Immunoglobulins;

| CLASS | PRINCIPLE FUNCTION |
|---|---|
| ~~IgA~~<br>IgG | Principal circulating Ab; passes placental wall to newborn; fixes complement and lyses gram-negative bacteria; binds to gram-positive bacteria and provides receptors for phagocytes. |
| ~~IgD~~<br>IgM | First Ab synthesized after Ag stimulation; more efficient than IgG in its ability to fix complement and to lyse gram-negative bacteria. |
| ~~IgE~~<br>IgA | Occurs in serum as a monomer and is found externally as a dimer bound to a secretory piece and a J chain; first line of Ab defense against organisms entering the body through the mucous membranes; major Ab in breast milk and provides newborn with preformed antibody. |
| ~~IgG~~<br>IgD | Occurs almost exclusively on the surface of B cells; is believed to be involved in the regulation of B cell differentiation. |
| ~~IgM~~<br>IgE | Binds very tightly to mast cells and leukocytes; when cross-linked by their specific Ag, mast cells release pharmacologically active substances (such as histamine), which results in various allergic reactions to the antigen in question. |

14. variable; 15. Major histocompatibility complex;
16. Bursa of Fabricius; 17. Antibody; 18. Antigen presenting cells; 19. Memory;
20. Sequestered.

| MASTERY TEST ANSWERS | | | | | | | | | | | | |
|---|---|---|---|---|---|---|---|---|---|---|---|---|
| 1<br>b | 2<br>d | 3<br>a | 4<br>e | 5<br>c | 6<br>e | | 7<br>e | 8<br>d | 9<br>c | 10<br>a | 11<br>c | 12<br>b |
| 13<br>d | 14<br>a | 15<br>a | 16<br>e | 17<br>a | 18<br>c | 19<br>d | 20<br>d | 21<br>e | 22<br>a | 23<br>c | 24<br>d | 25<br>c |

# CHAPTER 19

## MEASUREMENT OF ANTIBODIES AND THEIR ROLE IN IMMUNITY AND HYPERSENSITIVITY

### CHAPTER SUMMARY

**Serology** is the study of antigen-antibody reactions and may involve **blood typing, tissue typing**, or measurement of **antibody titer**. Two of the primary reactions used by serologists is the **precipitin reaction** (precipitation of soluble antigen by antibody) and the **agglutination reaction** (clumping together of particulate antigens by antibody). Other tests may focus on specific antibody activities such as **antitoxins** (neutralize toxins), **neutralizing antibodies** (neutralize viruses), and **opsonins** (enhance phagocytosis by leukocytes).

The **precipitin reaction** involves mixing together solutions of antigen and antibody and looking for the appearance of a cloudy precipitate. The precipitate will only appear if the **right concentrations** of Ag and Ab are mixed together - a ratio called the **equivalence point**. The same basic reaction can also be carried out in a **semi-solid medium** containing agar. Solutions of antigen and antibody are placed in separate wells and allowed to **diffuse** through the agar; where they meet a line of precipitate forms. **Double diffusion** tests challenge the same antibody with two antigens; the shape and exact position of the lines of precipitate that form allow one to **distinguish between different antigens**.

**Immunoelectrophoresis** depends upon **separating** the components of a mixture of **antigens** from one another by electrophoresis, then challenging the separated antigens with antibody. A complex set of precipitin bands will often form which indicates the distribution of antigens and the purity of the original mixture.

The **agglutination reaction** is a much more sensitive technique than the precipitin reaction due to the **particulate** nature of the antigen. **Whole cells** (or, sometimes, plastic beads) are used, thus very little antibody can produce a visible reaction. This technique is commonly used for **blood typing**, making **tentative diagnoses** of infectious diseases, etc. A semiquantitative measure of antibody level can be achieved by exposing a fixed amount of cells to a serial dilution of serum. The **antibody titer** is the reciprocal of the lowest dilution to demonstrate agglutination.

**Opsonins** are antibodies that promote ingestion of bacteria by **phagocytes** (despite, or even because of the presence of antiphagocytic capsules or fimbriae on the bacterium). The key part of the antibody for this activity is the Fc (crystallizable fraction) end to which phagocytes can bind. **Neutralizing antibodies** bind to toxins and nullify their toxic effect (**antitoxins**) or bind to viruses and prevent their capacity to adsorb to host cells and induce infection.

The **hemagglutination inhibition test** is an indication of viral neutralization, since it depends on antibody **preventing** the agglutination of red blood cells by viruses that normally do so. **Fluorescent antibody tests** can be direct or indirect. In the **direct type** antibodies bound to fluorescent dyes are exposed to suspect cells; if the **cells are visible** under the fluorescent microscope, they have specifically bound to the antibody. The **indirect method** involves two steps: (1) known antigen is incubated with human serum which **may** contain antibodies to the antigen, (2) the sample is then exposed to **fluorescent antihuman immunoglobulin** (antibodies against human antibodies); fluorescence then proves that **human antibodies** to the antigen were present. Such tests are routinely conducted against *Treponema pallidum* (causative agent of syphilis).

**Neufeld typing**, or the **Quellung reaction** depends upon the phenomenon of **capsule swelling** in the presence of specific antibody to the capsular material. Differences in pathogenicity are related to strain differences in capsule antigens. **Passive agglutination reactions** make the high sensitivity of agglutination reactions usable on soluble antigens. **Polysaccharide** and **lipopolysaccharide** antigens spontaneously bind to RBCs, **protein** antigens will bind readily to RBCs previously exposed to **tannic acid** (tanned cells). The "marked" RBCs can then be exposed to diluted antibody for agglutination testing.

Antibodies directly neutralize viruses and toxins, but have no **direct** effect on bacteria. The **Fc portion**, however, serves as an **opsonin**, promoting phagocytosis; it also serves as a site of initiation for the **complement cascade**, which leads to **lysis** of many cells, enhanced **phagocytosis** of others, and also leads to local **inflammation**. The **complement system** consists of at least 16 proteins which interact with antibodies in the **classical pathway** of complement activation.

1. The trigger for the classical pathway is the Fc portion of an antibody. Complement component **C1q** binds to the antibody, leading to the formation of the **recognition unit** at **Site I** on the membrane. **C1r** binds to C1q, becoming an enzyme which **converts C1s** to a protease enzyme that triggers the next step.
2. **C1s** cleaves **C4** into two pieces: C4a and C4b. **C4b** binds to **Site II** on the membrane, leading to the formation of the **activation unit**. **C1s** *also* cleaves **C2** into two fragments, **C2a** and C2b; **C2a binds to C4b** at Site II producing an active enzyme called **C3 convertase**. **C3** is split into C3a and **C3b**; C3b binds to C4bC2a on Site II, producing a new enzyme called **C5 convertase** (C4bC2aC3b - the complete **activation unit**).
3. C5 convertase splits C5 into **C5a** (**anaphylatoxin**, a potent **inflammation promoter** and **chemotactic** agent for leukocytes) and **C5b**. **C5b** binds to **Site III** on the membrane, leading to the formation of the **membrane attack**

**complex**. **C6**, **C7**, **C8**, and **C9** bind to C5b (producing the C5b6789 attack complex), ultimately producing a **hole** in the cell membrane of susceptible cells, leading to **lysis** of **gram-negative bacteria** and many types of eucaryotic cells. **Gram-positive bacteria** are NOT lysed by complement, but **C3b** does bind to their cell surface, promoting enhanced phagocytosis.

An **alternate**, antibody-independent pathway exists for complement activation. It is triggered by a plasma protein called **properdin**. Properdin nonspecifically splits **C3** into C3a and C3b, which results in the splitting of **C5** into C5a and C5b, formation of the **membrane attack complex** (with C6789), and lysis of susceptible cells. Note that C1 (q,r and s), C2 and C4 are not utilized in this alternate pathway.

Antibody production always follows exposure to antigen - with one prominent exception. The exception is the production of **alloantibodies** against the **alloantigens** of the ABO blood groups. **Antigen A** is found only on the RBCs of **Type A** and **Type AB** people; **Antigen B** is found only on the RBCs of **Type B** and **Type AB** people. **Type O** people have neither antigen. Alloantibodies are made - **without prior exposure** - to any of these antigens a person doesn't have. Type As make Anti-B, Type Bs make Anti-A, Type Os make **Anti-A and Anti-B** (Type ABs do not make either). **Fatal transfusion reactions** can result if a person receives a blood type which he makes antibodies against (e.g. Type A receiving Type B). Alloantibody binds to transfused cells, complement binds and lyses the cells.

**Rh factor** is like all normal antigens - one must be exposed first in order to produce antibodies. An Rh-negative person receiving an Rh-positive transfusion will suffer no ill effects, the first time. If a repeat mismatched transfusion is performed, however, hemolytic disease will result. The most common problem involving the Rh factor, however, involves **Rh-negative mothers** of Rh-positive offspring. Prior exposure being necessary, the first child usually suffers no difficulty. Mixing of blood during delivery, however, leads to the mother's production of anti-Rh antibodies which, being mostly IgG, can diffuse across the placenta and cause **erythroblastosis fetalis** in any subsequent Rh-positive offspring. Testing for anti-Rh antibody must be done using the **Coombs antiglobulin test** (which uses antihuman immunoglobulin) because anti-Rh antibody fails to agglutinate RBCs.

**Natural active immunity** is any immune response derived from an actual infection. Such immunity may be **life-long** (e.g. against measles, yellow fever, etc.), may last a **few years** (e.g. influenza, diphtheria), or have **no apparent persistence** (e.g. the common cold). **Artificial active immunity** is an immune response derived from the receipt of a **vaccine** or **toxoid** injection. **Passive immunity** is an immune response derived from the receipt of **preformed antibodies**; it is called **artificial** if the antibodies (usually from horses) are injected, and **natural** if they are derived from transplacental transfer or from breast milk. Such immunity is immediate, but is short-lived.

**Allergies** are **hypersensitive** reactions to typically nonthreatening antigens called **allergens**. Two classes exist: **immediate hypersensitivity**, which is due to circulating **antibodies**, and **cell-mediated hypersensitivity** (often called delayed-type). **Anaphylaxis** is a **potentially fatal** hypersensitivity which often develops in response to **insect venoms** and certain drugs such as **penicillin**. **IgE** bound to circulating or fixed **mast cells** is the active agent; binding of antigen (allergen) to the IgE results in the massive release of **vasoactive amines** (primarily **histamine**) which cause smooth muscle contraction in the lungs, followed by **suffocation**. Prompt administration of epinephrine or antihistamines may be life-saving. **Leukotrienes** (formerly called **SRS-A**, or slow-reacting substance of anaphylaxis) are also involved in this type of response. **Desensitization treatments** are aimed at building up circulating **IgG** and **IgA** antibodies to the allergen (so-called **blocking antibodies**) which will bind the allergen before it reaches IgE.

The **Arthus reaction** involves **IgG**, **IgM** and **complement**, rather than IgE. This localized reaction is much slower to develop than anaphylaxis but can involve massive tissue destruction. Allergen combines in tissues with antibodies that leak out of capillaries; complement is bound, killing cells and attracting polymorphonuclear leukocytes. Leukocytes consume the antigen-antibody complexes, die and release lysosomal enzymes which destroy more cells and create more inflammation. **Serum sickness** is basically a **whole-body Arthus reaction**; complexes between antigen and high levels of antibody cause complement activity in the blood and in kidney glomeruli, followed by massive activity by leukocytes. Acute **glomerulonephritis**, and **rheumatoid arthritis** can result from such activities. The stimulus may be a second injection of a foreign protein (such as tetanus antitoxin), or a Group A streptococcal infection.

<u>OBJECTIVES</u> The completion of this chapter should make the reader familiar with:

1. A number of techniques used in the laboratory to detect and measure specific antibodies.
2. Terms such as opsonins, neutralizing antibodies, and quellung reactions.
3. The mechanism whereby antibodies protect the body from toxins, viruses, gram-negative bacteria and gram-positive bacteria.
4. The nature of the complement system and its role in the immune system.
5. The ABO system of classification of red blood cells and the role of alloantibodies in transfusion reactions.
6. The nature of the Rh factor and the conditions under which a newborn might be subjected to anti-Rh antibodies received from its mother.
7. A method for assaying anti-Rh antibodies.
8. The difference between active and passive immunity.
9. The types of allergic reactions resulting from immediate-type hypersensitivity.
10. The series of events leading to anaphylaxis.
11. The role of antibodies and complement in the induction of serum sickness or the Arthus reaction.

## LEARNING ACTIVITIES

### Vocabulary

Having read the chapter, you should be able to define or cite the significance of the following terms. If you cannot, look them up in the text. Terms are presented in the order you will encounter them in the book.

serology
blood typing
tissue typing
agglutination
precipitin reaction
antitoxin
neutralizing antibody
opsonins
equivalence point
double diffusion
Ouchterlony Technique
immunoelectrophoresis
agglutination reaction
titer
hemagglutination inhibition test
fluorescent antibody
Neufeld Typing
quellung reaction
passive agglutination
complement system
classical pathway
cascade
recognition unit
Site I
activation unit
Site II
membrane attack complex
Site III
alternate pathway
properdin
alloantigens
alloantibodies
ABO
ABO-hemolytic disease
Rh factor
erythroblastosis fetalis
Coombs antiglobulin test
antihuman immunoglobulin
natural active immunity
artificial active immunity
passive immunity
allergy
immediate hypersensitivity
cell-mediated hypersensitivity
allergen
anaphylaxis
vasoactive amines
SRS-A
leukotrienes
desensitization
blocking antibodies
Arthus reaction
serum sickness
acute glomerulonephritis
rheumatoid arthritis

Complete each of the following statements by supplying the missing word or words.

1. ____________________ is the study of antigen-antibody reactions.

2. The ____________________ is a reaction between soluble antigen and antibody.

3. ____________________ is the interaction between antibody and particulate (cell-bound) antigen.

4. ____________________ antibody activity is directed against bacterial secretions such as botulinin.

5. A virus can be ____________________ by antibody.

6. ____________________ make bacteria more easily engulfed by phagocytic cells.

7. ____________________ in agar makes it possible to compare two potentially-identical antigen samples.

8. Antibody ____________________ is the reciprocal of the highest dilution that causes clumping in the agglutination test.

9. The ____________________ fluorescent antibody test uses fluorescent antihuman immunoglobin as an indicator.

10. ____________________ is a set of 16 proteins which interact with some susceptible cells to cause lysis.

11. The ____________________ (on Site I) consists of Antigen-Antibody + C1qrs.

12. C4b2a3b comprise the ____________________, which is found at Site II on the target cell membrane.

13. The ____________________ on Site III includes C5b6789.

14-17: Fill in the alloantibody column in this table on blood types, alloantigens, and alloantibodies.

| BLOOD TYPE | ALLOANTIGEN ON RBC | ALLOANTIBODY IN SERUM |
|---|---|---|
| A | A | |
| B | B | |
| AB | AB | |
| O | NONE | |

18. ____________________ is the term used to describe the hemolytic disease that can result if an Rh-negative mother is carrying an Rh-positive fetus.

19. ____________________ immunity is an immune response due to injected preformed antibodies.

20. The ____________________ reaction is a form of immediate hypersensitivity that involves a localized interaction between allegen, IgG, IgM and complement.

## MASTERY TEST

1-25: Circle the choice that best answers the questions.

1. Which of the following terms applies to the enhanced potential for phagocyte ingestion conferred by antibody?
   a. antitoxin
   b. agglutination
   c. neutralizing
   d. precipitin
   e. opsonin

2. Which of the following is the source of the most sensitive test of antibody activity?
   a. antitoxin
   b. agglutination
   c. neutralizing
   d. precipitin
   e. opsonin

3. Proper proportions of antigen and antibody result in the equivalence point in which of the following antibody tests?
   a. antitoxin
   b. agglutination
   c. neutralizing
   d. precipitin
   e. opsonin

4. The measurement of antibody concentration achieved in the agglutination test is:
   a. semiquantitative
   b. extremely consistent
   c. highly quantitative
   d. totally unreliable

5. Passive agglutination tests on protein antigens require pre-treatment of RBCs by:
   a. strong alkali
   b. complement
   c. tannic acid
   d. lipopolysaccharide
   e. alloantibody

6. The __________ portion of the antibody is critical to its ability to act as an opsonin and to trigger complement.
   a. Fab
   b. heavy chain alone
   c. light chain alone
   d. Fc
   e. variable light chain

7. Antibodies are capable of neutralizing all of the following except:
a. endotoxins
b. exotoxins
c. gram-negative bacteria
d. viruses

8. The hemagluttination inhibition test depends upon the ability of _______________ to cause agglutination of human RBCs; an effect nullified by specific antibody.
a. endotoxins
b. exotoxins
c. gram-negative bacteria
d. viruses

9. Neufeld typing, which involves the quellung reaction, depends upon changes in the ____________ when cells are mixed with specific antibody.
a. cytoplasmic membrane
b. capsule
c. cell wall
d. nuclear envelope
e. bacterial flagellum

10. Binding of specific antibody to bacterial cells can result in all of the following effects EXCEPT:
a. direct killing of the bacterial cell
b. enhanced phagocyte englufment of the cell
c. binding of complement with possible consequent lysis
d. localized inflammation and leukocyte infiltration

11. C1q of complement binds to the Fc portion of antibodies; C1r binds to Ag-AbC1q. C1r then develops into an enzyme which acts upon:
a. C2
b. C4
c. C1s
d. C5

12. C5b binds to Site III on the target cell membrane where it becomes the focus for the formation of the binding of C6, C7, C8, and C9. C5b6789 constitute the:
a. recognition unit
b. alternate pathway
c. activation unit
d. C5 convertase enzyme
e. membrane attack complex

13. The "trigger" for the alternate complement pathway is a circulating plasma protein called:
a. prolapsin
b. properdin
c. anaphylatoxin
d. C3 convertase
e. alloantigen

14. The key to the alternate pathway is not that it skips C1, C4 and C2 but that it can act in a(n) _____________ way.
a. highly specific
b. nonspecific
c. extremely rapid
d. highly lethal

15. Complement activity can directly kill which of the following?
   a. gram-negative bacteria
   b. gram-positive bacteria
   c. viruses
   d. all of these

16. The antigens found on the surfaces of Type A, Type B, and Type AB red blood cells are referred to as:
   a. alloantibodies
   b. allografts
   c. alloantigens
   d. allopathic substances
   e. auxotrophs

17. The main reason that ABO-hemolytic disease of the newborn is rare is the nature of the antibody involved in ABO immunity. Which of the following classes comprises the antibodies in question?
   a. IgA
   b. IgD
   c. IgE
   d. IgG
   e. IgM

18. The main reason that erythroblastosis fetalis can result in the case of Rh-negative mother and Rh-positive fetus is the nature of the antibody involved. Which of the following classes comprises the antibodies in question?
   a. IgA
   b. IgD
   c. IgE
   d. IgG
   e. IgM

19. Anti-Rh antibodies perform poorly in agglutination tests. A modified test which uses antihuman immunoglobulins to enhance the agglutination reaction is named after which of the following individuals?
   a. Coombs
   b. Landsteiner
   c. Neufeld
   d. Ouchterlony
   e. Quellung

20. Which of the following types of immune responses results from an experience with a given disease?
   a. artificial active immunity
   b. artificial passive immunity
   c. natural active immunity
   d. natural passive immunity

21. Which of the following types of immune responses results from an injection of preformed antibody?
   a. artificial active immunity
   b. artificial passive immunity
   c. natural active immunity
   d. natural passive immunity

22. Local immediate hypersensitivity can result from or produce all of the following EXCEPT:
    a. hay fever
    b. food allergies
    c. asthma
    d. anaphylaxis
    e. ragweed sensitivity

23. An material once known as SRS-A (slow-reacting substance of anaphylaxis) is:
    a. histamine
    b. bradykinin
    c. epinephrine
    d. serotonin
    e. leukotriene

24. Serum sickness commonly results from:
    a. injection of a foreign antiserum for the first time
    b. staphylococcal infections
    c. injection of a foreign antiserum for the second time
    d. mycobacterial infections

25. A not unusual complication of serum sickness is:
    a. anaphylaxis
    b. acute glomerulonephritis
    c. Arthus lesions of the lung
    d. hemolytic disease

---

ANSWERS TO LEARNING ACTIVITIES

Fill-in-the-blank question:

1. Serology; 2. precipitin reaction; 3. Agglutination; 4. Antitoxin; 5. neutralized; 6. Opsonins; 7. Double diffusion; 8. titer; 9. indirect; 10. Complement; 11. recognition unit; 12. activation unit; 13. membrane attack unit.

| BLOOD TYPE | ALLOANTIGEN ON RBC | ALLOANTIBODY IN SERUM |
|---|---|---|
| A | A | Anti-B |
| B | B | Anti-A |
| AB | AB | None |
| O | NONE | Anti-A, Anti-B |

18. Erythroblastosis fetalis; 19. Artificial passive; 20. Arthus.

**MASTERY TEST ANSWERS**

| | | | | | | | | | | | | |
|---|---|---|---|---|---|---|---|---|---|---|---|---|
| 1<br>e | 2<br>b | 3<br>d | 4<br>a | 5<br>c | 6<br>d | | 7<br>c | 8<br>d | 9<br>b | 10<br>a | 11<br>c | 12<br>e |
| 13<br>b | 14<br>b | 15<br>a | 16<br>c | 17<br>e | 18<br>d | 19<br>a | 20<br>c | 21<br>b | 22<br>d | 23<br>e | 24<br>c | 25<br>b |

# CHAPTER 20

## CELLULAR IMMUNITY

### CHAPTER SUMMARY

**Cell-mediated immunity** is dependent upon the function of living lymphocyte cells from the **T lymphocyte** group and from the **LGL (large granular lymphocyte**) group. **Th cells (helper T cells**), **Tdth cells** (involved in **delayed-type hypersensitivity**, or **DTH**), and **Tc cells (cytotoxic T cells**) are all members of the T lymphocyte group. **NK cells (natural killer cells**), and **K cells (killer cells**) are both members of the large granular lymphocyte (LGL) group.

Delayed-type hypersensitivity is a pronounced inflammatory response that develops 24 to 48 hours after exposure to the antigen, and is totally dependent upon the activities of Th, Tdth and **macrophage** cells. Like the Th cell, Tdth cells must be activated by an **antigen-presenting cell (APC**), typically a macrophage carrying antigen on a Class II MHC protein. Contact between Tdth and **macrophage** causes the macrophage to release **interleukin-1** which, combined with **interleukin-2** released by **Th cells,** gives rise to proliferation and differentiation of Tdth cells into two classes: **activated Tdth** and **memory Tdth**. Further development of delayed-type hypersensitivity depends upon the release of soluble **lymphokines** by the activated Tdth cells. These compounds are all directed at macrophages, which cause the actual events called DTH.

**Migration inhibition factor** (**MIF**) is one lymphokine released by activated Tdth cells. It prevents macrophages from leaving the area of inflammation. A second lymphokine called the **chemotactic factor for macrophages** draws monocytes into the inflamed area where they undergo rapid cell division and differentiate into macrophages. A third lymphokine secreted by Tdth cells is the **macrophage activating factor** which causes **macrophage activation** (they increase their phagocytic and metabolic activity, and build up increased numbers of lysosomes). Activated macrophages are sometimes called **enraged macrophages**. Other lymphokines *not* involved in DTH include **lymphotoxin** (LT, secreted by cytotoxic lymphocytes) and **IFNγ (immune interferon** released by T cells and effective in stimulating natural killer cells).

The **normal functional role of DTH** seems to be in dealing with **fungal** infections, infections by **viruses** that leave the host cell by **budding**, and with infections of **intracellular parasites** such as those that cause **leprosy**, **tuberculosis**, **tularemia**, etc. Testing involves the intradermal injection of antigen or the application of an antigen-impregnated patch against the skin. Such **skin tests** are routinely performed for tuberculosis.

Like antibody-mediated immunity, cell-mediated immunity can "go wrong". **Allergic contact dermatitis** is an example, in which an **innocuous foreign antigen** (like poison ivy catechols, cosmetics, etc.) can trigger a destructive hypersensitivity response.

**Tc cells** (cytotoxic T cells) have the ability to directly **kill target cells** *via* the secretion of **lymphotoxins**. Tc cells must first be aroused by contact with **specific antigen** combined with Class I or Class II MHC peptides (MHC stands for **major histocompatibility complex**, sometimes called the **HLA**, for **human leukocyte antigen**). Tc cells bind to the target cell (which may be a **tumor cell**, a **transplanted cell**, or a **virus-infected cell**), secrete lymphotoxin, then move off. The target cell quickly dies by means of **membrane disorganization** and leakage of intracellular components.

Tc cells thus play a critical role in tumor immunity and defense against some viral infections. Their role in **transplant rejection**, however, has given rise to a variety of ways to suppress their activity. **Steroids**, **azathioprine**, and **cyclosporin** are all examples of compounds used to prevent transplant rejection; **antilymphocyte serum** (**ALS**) and **monoclonal anti-T-cell antibodies** are somewhat more complex means to the same end. All have the drawback of making the recipient more vulnerable to viral, bacterial and fungal infections as well as prone to develop certain tumor types. Graft rejection is a nonexistent problem with **autografts** (grafts from one area to another in same person), and **isografts** (grafts between identical twins). Rejection can be serious with **allografts** (between members of same species) and even worse for **xenografts** (between two species).

**Natural killer cells** (**NK cells**) are not T cells or B cells (some call them **null lymphocytes**, or LGL). They kill like Tc cells but **do not require exposure to specific antigen**. Their major role seems to be in **immune surveillance** and in killing **tumor cells**. **Killer cells** (K cells) have an Fc (antibody) receptor on their surface and can kill any cell coated by antibody. This response is called **antibody-dependent cell-mediated cytotoxicity** (ADCC) and occurs even though the cells have no prior exposure to the antigen.

**Immunological tolerance** is the lack of a specific immune response resulting from a exposure to an antigen. The most important example is tolerance to self. According to the **clonal deletion** model of Burnet any immune cell responding to self antigens during fetal development is destroyed. Another source of tolerance is the **suppressor T cell** population, which specifically promotes tolerance to selected antigens.

OBJECTIVES The material in this chapter will familiarize you with:

1. The types of cells taking part in cell-mediated immunity.
2. The nature and types of lymphokines involved in delayed-type hypersensitivity.
3. The mechanisms whereby delayed-type hypersensitivity cells provide their immune function.
4. The way in which cytotoxic T cells kill foreign target cells.
5. The difference between natural killer cells and killer cells.
6. The cellular aspects of transplantation rejection.
7. The role of tumor antigens in immune surveillance.
8. The mechanisms of immunological tolerance.

LEARNING ACTIVITIES

Vocabulary

Having read the chapter, you should be able to define or cite the significance of the following terms. If you cannot, look them up in the text. Terms are presented in the order you will encounter them in the book.

cell-mediated immunity
T cells
Tdth cells
delayed-type hypersensitivity
DTH
Tc cells
LGL
natural killer cells
killer cells
Th
APC
activated Tdth cells
memory Tdth cells
lymphokines
macrophage
monokines
migration inhibition factor (MIF)
chemotactic factor
macrophage activating factor
lymphotoxin (LT)
interferon (IFN$\gamma$)
allergic contact dermatitis
poison ivy
cytotoxic T lymphocytes (Tc)
MHC; HLA
suppression of cell-mediated response
steroids
azathioprine
cyclosporin
antilymphocyte serum (ALS)
large granular lymphocytes
NK cells
antibody-dependent cell-mediated cytotoxicity
ADCC
transplantation rejection
autografts
isografts
allografts
xenografts
thymus
tumor antigens
immune surveillance
clonal deletion
suppressor T cells

Complete each of the following statements by supplying the missing word or words.

1. ____________________ differs from antibody-mediated immunity in a number of ways, but most importantly on its dependence upon living lymphocyte cells.

2. ____________________ are members of the T lymphocyte population intimately involved in delayed-type hypersensitivity.

3. ____________________ cells are also members of the T lymphocyte group but have the capacity to directly kill target cells.

4. The ____________________ group includes non T and non B lymphocytes such as the natural killer and killer cells.

5. ____________________ is an inflammatory response to fungal, viral, and bacterial antigens that may develop 24 to 48 hours after contact with the antigen.

6. ____________________ are the real active players in DTH, once they have been activated by Tdth cells.

7. ____________________ (MIF) is a material secreted by an activated Tdth cell which restricts the movement of leukocytes from the inflamed area.

8. ____________________ are soluble materials released by lymphocytes with effects on other members of the leukocyte population.

9. ____________________, or activated macrophages, develop after exposure to macrophage activating factor.

10. ____________________ is a material released by a Tc cell which has the ability to disorganize the membranes of target cells and leads to their death.

11. ____________________ (IFN$\gamma$) stimulates natural killer cells to higher activity levels.

12. ____________________ is an example of cell-mediated immunity gone wrong, as it is a response to innocuous or non-threatening antigens (like cosmetics).

13. ____________________ catechols are famous for their ability to produce the destructive inflammatory response discussed in the above question.

14. ____________________ (MHC) antigens are the major ones of concern in "tissue typing" before conduction of a transplant.

15. ____________________ is a cyclic peptide derived from fungi which has proven effective in suppressing tissue rejection phenomena.

16. ____________________ are involved in killing any antibody-coated cell they encounter, without any requirement for prior exposure or Th activation.

17. ____________________ is the term used to describe the activity of Tc and NK cells in "looking for" the appearance of tumor cells in the body.

18. ____________________ are grafts between members of the same species; unless very carefully matched, rejection is a major problem.

19. ____________________ is the theory of Burnet which attempts to explain the immunological tolerance for "self" antigens.

20. ____________________ T cells are probably also heavily involved in immunological tolerance.

## MASTERY TEST

1-17: Circle the choice that best answers the questions.

1. Which of the following is NOT a member of the T-cell group?
   a. Th helper cells
   b. Tk killer cells
   c. Tdth cells
   d. Tc cytotoxic cells
   e. all are T cells

2. Which of the following is NOT involved in the delayed-type hypersensitivity response?
   a. Th cells
   b. macrophages
   c. Tdth cells
   d. B lymphocytes
   e. monocytes

3. Delayed-type hypersensitivity was discovered by:
   a. Hans Gram
   b. Karl Landsteiner
   c. Robert Koch
   d. Merril Chase
   e. Walter Reed

4. Tdth cells can interact with antigen
   a. only when presented by an APC
   b. in its natural state
   c. only after complement fixation
   d. only when bound to antibody

5. Antigen-bearing macrophages release which of the following lymphokines when interacting with Tdth cells?
   a. lymphotoxin
   b. MIF
   c. interleukin-2
   d. immune interferon
   e. interleukin-1

6. Which of the following lymphokines is secreted by activated Tdth cells to restrict movement of macrophages from the site of inflammation?
   a. lymphotoxin
   b. MIF
   c. interleukin-2
   d. immune interferon
   e. interleukin-1

7. Which of the following is NOT involved in macrophage activation?
   a. increased capacity for phagocytosis
   b. increased metabolic activity
   c. increased production of lymphotoxin
   d. increased numbers of lysosomes
   e. increased quantities of lysosomal enzymes

8. The main target of the lymphokine IFN$\gamma$ (immune interferon) is:
   a. Th cells
   b. NK cells
   c. Tdth cells
   d. Tc cells
   e. Ts cells

9. Which of the following is NOT a main natural target of delayed-type hypersensitivity?
   a. fungal infections
   b. viral infections involving budding
   c. intracellular bacterial infections
   d. viral-induced tumors

10. The catechols produced by poison ivy plants act as ____________ in the production of allergic contact dermatitis.
    a. haptens
    b. intact antigens
    c. transfer factors
    d. lymphokines

11. The term MHC is synonymous with which of the following?
    a. IUD
    b. MIF
    c. HUD
    d. IFN
    e. HLA

12. The effect of lymphotoxin secretion on target cells is:
   a. lysis of the cell
   b. opsonization of the cell; future phagocytosis
   c. enhanced complement fixation on cell
   d. future recognition of the cell by memory cells

13. Which of the following is NOT an immune suppressor used to enhance transplant success?
   a. cyclosporin
   b. cephalosporin
   c. steroids
   d. azathioprine
   e. antilymphocyte serum

14. Which of the following is the main target of the drugs and treatments discussed in the above question?
   a. Th cells
   b. Tdth cells
   c. Tc cells
   d. NK cells
   e. Killer cells

15. The major natural function apparently performed by NK (natural killer) cells is the destruction of:
   a. protozoan parasites
   b. fungal parasites
   c. tumor cells
   d. bacterial parasites
   e. deteriorated red blood cells

16. Which of the following is capable of destroying antibody-coated cells with no prior exposure to the cells?
   a. Th cells
   b. Tdth cells
   c. Tc cells
   d. NK cells
   e. Killer cells

17. Which of the following would you expect to experience the most severe and lasting rejection phenomena?
   a. allografts
   b. autografts
   c. isografts
   d. xenografts

---

18-25: TRUE-FALSE: (T for true, F for false)

_____ 18. Drugs or other treatments that reduce the likelihood of rejection phenomena have no significant side effects.

_____ 19. Animals whose thymus gland has been removed at birth have unimpaired cell-mediated immune responses.

_____ 20. The HLA complex in humans is totally irrelevant to tissue typing and of no interest to those performing transplants.

_____ 21. Tumor antigen occurring on the cancer cells of any polyoma-induced cancer are always the same, regardless of the organ or tissue of origin.

_____ 22. Immunological tolerance is an abnormal development that occurs only in some inbred strains of nude mice.

_____ 23. A positive "patch test" for the tuberculin antigen proves that a patient has an active case of tuberculosis.

_____ 24. The main, active cell involved in the inflammatory response called delayed-type hypersensitivity is the polymorphonuclear neutrophil.

_____ 25. The mechanism of action of lymphotoxin is completely understood.

---

## ANSWERS TO LEARNING ACTIVITIES

Fill-in-the-blank questions:

1. Cell-mediated immunity; 2. Tdth cells; 3. Tc; 4. large granular lymphocytes; 5. Delayed-type hypersensitivity; 6. Macrophages; 7. Migration inhibition factor; 8. Lymphokines; 9. Enraged; 10. Lymphotoxin; 11. Immune interferon; 12. Allergic contact dermatitis; 13. Poison ivy; 14. Major histocompatibility complex; 15. Cyclosporin; 16. Killer cells; 17. Immune surveillance; 18. Allografts; 19. Clonal deletion; 20. Suppressor.

**MASTERY TEST ANSWERS**

| | | | | | | | | | | | | |
|---|---|---|---|---|---|---|---|---|---|---|---|---|
| 1<br>b | 2<br>d | 3<br>c | 4<br>a | 5<br>e | 6<br>b | | 7<br>c | 8<br>b | 9<br>d | 10<br>a | 11<br>e | 12<br>a |
| 13<br>b | 14<br>c | 15<br>c | 16<br>e | 17<br>d | 18<br>F | 19<br>F | 20<br>F | 21<br>T | 22<br>F | 23<br>F | 24<br>F | 25<br>F |

# CHAPTER 21

## ANTISERA AND VACCINES

### CHAPTER SUMMARY

**Variolation** was apparently the first **attempt to induce immunity** against an infectious disease. It was practiced in ancient China and India and involved exposing susceptible individuals to the dried scabs from mild cases of smallpox. Modern **vaccines** are safer and more effective than variolation, but they are not perfect. The **perfect vaccine** would (1) stimulate **lifelong immunity**, (2) be completely **safe**, (3) require only **one administration** (no boosters), (4) be **easy to produce**, and (5) be **stable** in storage.

Vaccines may be prepared from **killed** or **inactivated** pathogens, **attenuated living** **(avirulent)** pathogens, **inactivated exotoxins** **(toxoids)**, or clonal **fragments of antigens** from pathogens. **Killed** bacterial cell vaccines include those for pertussis, typhoid, paratyphoid, and plague. **Living** attenuated vaccine against tuberculosis and tularemia has been used in humans; anthrax and brucellosis in farm animals. **Capsule material** (no whole cells at all, live or dead) can effectively immunize against *Streptococcus pneumoniae* and *Neisseria meningitidis*.

Potent **exotoxins** are often the main cause of symptoms of bacterial disease. Treatment of the toxin with **formaldehyde** destroys its toxic effect yet leaves it productively antigenic. Such modified toxins are called **toxoids**, and they are often prepared as alum precipitates to increase their persistence in the body. Prominent toxoids used in vaccines include **diphtheria** and **tetanus**.

Killed **rickettsial** cells are used in vaccines against Rocky Mountain Spotted Fever, typhus, and others. The organisms are generally grown in chick yolk sacs, but can be prepared in tissue cultures. Cells are killed and preserved with formaldehyde.

Viral vaccines, like bacterial ones, may be of the killed (inactivated) virus type or prepared from living, attenuated viruses. **Live** virus vaccines produce a much **more prolonged immunity** than do killed virus vaccines, yet not all viruses have been obliging enough to produce **stable avirulent strains** for our use. Some that have include the **polio** virus, the **measles** viruses, the **yellow fever** virus and the **mumps** virus. One that hasn't is the **influenza** virus, whose vaccine still contains inactivated viruses. **Recombinant DNA technology** is giving rise to a new class of vaccines called **split** or **subunit vaccines**. Such vaccines consist of one or two viral antigens (proteins or glycoproteins) produced by bacterial or yeast cells which have been given the genes for the antigens. Totally virus-free vaccines are thus produced.

The **vaccinia** virus, long used in smallpox vaccinations, is now being utilized in a new way. Genes for **foreign antigens** from other viruses are being incorporated into the **vaccinia genome**, so that **hybrid vaccinia** viruses now produce antigens from hepatitis B virus, influenza virus, herpesviruses, and the rabies virus.

Vaccines vary in their effectiveness in providing **prolonged active immunity**. Live agents are more effective because (1) the living agent may stimulate **cellular immunity**, not just antibody-based immunity, (2) the living agent grows in the individual thus producing a **larger mass of antigen**, and (3) the living organism probably **persists** much longer then the killed forms. The drawback of using living agents is, however, that they may **mutate to a virulent form** and cause active disease (as happens with the poliovirus). Vaccines may cause **problems** for the recipient in ways other than causing active disease. Those prepared form agents grown in **chick embryos** can produce dangerous allergic responses in recipients **allergic to eggs**; traces of **penicillin** are often present in vaccines, posing a risk to anyone hypersensitive to this antibiotic. Another problem involves **toxic properties of the vaccine** itself. The most prominent example of this is the **pertussis vaccine** which contains killed organism, toxin, and hemagglutinin. The vaccine produces a local reaction in many recipients, serious systemic toxic reactions leading to **brain damage or death** in a very few.

**Antisera** were once a main line of defense against important infectious diseases like pneumonia. Their use has declined due to adverse reactions (mainly **serum sickness**) and the development of better treatments such as vaccines and antibiotics. One advantage antisera have over all other types of therapy is the **speed** with which effective levels of antibody can be reached. Current use is mainly for **antitoxin** treatment (e.g. tetanus), although post-exposure treatment for **hepatitis A** and **measles** remains important. The major source of antisera is from **horses** experimentally immunized to various antigens, and from **pooled human serum**. The risks inherent in using human sera (hepatitis, AIDS) makes this form of therapy less attractive today. The typical duration of passive immunity from antisera is 4 to 6 weeks.

<u>OBJECTIVES</u> A study of this chapter should familiarize you with:

1. The general types of vaccines presently in use.
2. How recombinant DNA techniques are being exploited for the preparation of safer vaccines.

3. The expected duration of immunity from the administration of killed versus living attenuated vaccines.
4. Some of the hazards associated with the use of the current pertussis and polio vaccines.
5. What situations would require the use of specific antiserum rather than a vaccine for disease prevention.
6. The source of specific antisera and the potential hazards associated with its employment.
7. The duration of passively acquired immunity as compared to actively acquired immunity.

## LEARNING ACTIVITIES

### Vocabulary

Having read the chapter, you should be able to define or cite the significance of the following terms. If you cannot, look them up in the text. Terms are presented in the order you will encounter them in the book.

variolation
vaccine
killed pathogen
inactivated pathogen
avirulent
attenuated
toxoids
clonal fragments
pertussis
capsular antigen
formaldehyde
inactivated
recombinant DNA techniques
split vaccine
subunit vaccine
hybrid vaccinia
epitopes
egg protein allergy
DTP vaccine
antiserum
antitoxin
pooled serum
serum sickness

Complete each of the following statements by supplying the missing word or words.

1. ______________________, practiced in ancient China and India, attempted to confer resistance to smallpox.

2. ______________________ consist of killed or inactivated cells, live attenuated cells, or fragments of cells.

3. ______________________ are inactivated toxins used to induce immunity in humans and animals.

4. ______________________ cells are used in the vaccines for pertussis, typhoid and the plague.

5. ______________________ cells are used in the vaccines for tuberculosis and tularemia.

6. ______________________ material can effectively immunize people against *Streptococcus pneumoniae.*

7. ______________________ is used to convert toxins to toxoids and to kill rickettsial organisms.

8. ______________________ virus vaccines are much more effective at stimulating prolonged immunity.

9. ______________________ vaccine is a commonly administered vaccine which depends upon killed (inactivated) virus.

10. ______________________ has made possible the production of so-called "split" or "subunit" vaccines produced from cloned viral genes in bacteria or yeasts.

11-17: The following table contains scrambled vaccines and examples; match the right vaccine with the right examples.

| VACCINE | SELECTED EXAMPLES |
|---|---|
| Capsular material | Typhoid fever, pertussis, rickettsial diseases |
| Living attenuated virions | Brucellosis, anthrax, tuberculosis |
| Killed whole cells | Pneumococcal pneumonia, *Haemophilus influenzae, Neisseria meningitidis* |
| Split virion components | Diphtheria, tetanus |
| Living attenuated cells | Influenza, adenoviruses, polioviruses, rabies |
| Inactivated toxins | Measles, rubella, polioviruses, mumps, yellow fever |
| Killed whole virions | Influenza, rabies, herpesviruses, Hepatitis B, foot-and-mouth disease |

18. ____________________ vaccine is hazardous to the health of a significant fraction of its recipients.

19. ____________________ have the advantage of producing a very rapid protective level of antibody activity.

20. The ____________________ is the most common animal used to prepare antisera for use against bacterial toxins.

## MASTERY TEST

1-25: Circle the choice that best answers the questions.

1. Variolation, practiced in ancient India and China, was an attempt to induce immunity to ____________________.
   a. malaria
   b. influenza
   c. plague
   d. measles
   e. smallpox

2. An ideal vaccine should have all of the following attributes EXCEPT:
   a. stimulate lifelong immunity
   b. stimulate only cell-mediated immunity
   c. be completely safe to use
   d. require only one administration
   e. be stable under a variety of storage conditions

3. All of the following are used to produce vaccines EXCEPT:
   a. pooled serum from human volunteers
   b. killed whole cells and virions
   c. inactivated exotoxins
   d. live, attenuated cells and virions
   e. capsular material from some bacteria

4. All of the following vaccines are typically made using killed organism EXCEPT:
   a. pertussis
   b. typhoid
   c. tuberculosis
   d. paratyphoid
   e. plague

5. Bacterial exotoxins treated with formaldehyde to reduce their toxicity are called:
   a. endotoxins
   b. antitoxins
   c. alkaloid toxins
   d. toxoids

6. Toxins treated with formaldehyde are usually precipitated on __________ to prolong their residence in the system.
   a. alum
   b. iron
   c. resins
   d. nickel
   e. protein

7. Rickettsial organisms grown in __________ produce vaccines that have an additional risk factor due to common allergies.
   a. horse serum
   b. human tissue culture
   c. synthetic media
   d. chick embryos
   e. goat serum

8. An example of a rickettsial disease for which a vaccine exists is:
   a. typhoid fever
   b. paratyphoid
   c. plague
   d. leprosy
   e. Rocky Mountain spotted fever

9. Recombinant DNA technology now can transfer genes for viral antigens to bacterial or yeast cells and produce a new class of vaccine called:
   a. toxoid vaccine
   b. antiserum vaccine
   c. split or subunit vaccine
   d. hybrid variola vaccine

10. All of the following are currently available as live (attenuated) virus vaccines EXCEPT:
   a. influenza
   b. poliomyelitis
   c. red measles
   d. yellow fever
   e. mumps

11. Live (attenuated) vaccines are generally __________ killed virus vaccines.
   a. much less effective than
   b. slightly less effective than
   c. about as effective as
   d. slightly more effective than
   e. much more effective than

12. There is very little prospect that a successful vaccine for ________________ will be developed due to the multiplicity of viral agents responsible for this malady.
   a. hepatitis A
   b. hepatitis B
   c. AIDS
   d. common cold
   e. rabies

13. The ____________________ virus has been used for years to immunize people against smallpox. It is now being used by genetic engineers to produce "hybrid" viruses bearing foreign virus antigens on its surface.
   a. yellow fever
   b. chickenpox
   c. vaccinia
   d. herpes
   e. smallpox

14. All of the following probably help to explain the enhanced effectiveness of live virus vaccines EXCEPT:
   a. it mutates to virulent form, causing mild disease
   b. it stimulates cellular immunity
   c. it grows and produces a greater mass of antigen
   d. it grows and therefore persists longer in the body

15. There is reason for concern that all of the following diseases may have a "comeback" due to failure of parents to obtain immunizations for their children EXCEPT FOR:
   a. measles
   b. smallpox
   c. poliomyelitis
   d. diphtheria
   e. pertussis

16. Which of the following vaccines has exhibited a persistent tendency to show reversion of attenuated viruses to virulent form?
   a. measles
   b. smallpox
   c. poliomyelitis
   d. diphtheria
   e. pertussis

17. Which of the following vaccines causes a local reaction in many infants and, more rarely, causes serious systemic toxic reactions including brain damage and death?
   a. measles
   b. smallpox
   c. poliomyelitis
   d. diphtheria
   e. pertussis

18. The single largest disadvantage to the historic use of antisera was its:
   a. extreme toxicity
   b. lack of specificity
   c. specificity
   d. hepatitis A content
   e. high cost

19. Antisera are used today for:
   a. routine protection from influenza in the elderly
   b. protection from potent bacterial toxins
   c. protection from rabies virus after animal bites
   d. desensitization from poison ivy toxin

20. The one overwhelming advantage of antisera as compared to all other immune enhancers is its:
   a. low cost
   b. speed of effectiveness
   c. low toxicity
   d. broad action spectrum
   e. few side effects

21. Pooled human serum should be effective against all of the following EXCEPT:
   a. rabies
   b. influenza
   c. measles
   d. chickenpox
   e. all of these

22. One major potential side effect of standard antiserum treatments, particularly if it is a repeat treatment, is:
   a. hepatitis A
   b. hepatitis B
   c. tetanus
   d. diphtheria
   e. serum sickness

23. The use of pooled human serum carries with it the risk of spreading all of the following diseases EXCEPT:
   a. hepatitis A
   b. hepatitis B
   c. AIDS
   d. hemophilia

24. Antiserum treatments typically protect the recipient from infectious disease for:
   a. 4 to 6 days
   b. 2 to 3 weeks
   c. 4 to 6 weeks
   d. 4 to 6 months
   e. 4 to 7 years

25. A sophisticated antiserum use which is currently being tested for reduction in organ transplant rejection is:
   a. antilymphocyte serum
   b. antihuman immunoglobulin serum
   c. antineutrophil serum
   d. antithymus serum

---

ANSWERS TO LEARNING ACTIVITIES

Fill-in-the-blank questions:

1. Variolation; 2. Vaccines; 3. Toxoids; 4. Killed; 5. Live, attenuated; 6. Capsular; 7. Formaldehyde; 8. Live, attenuated; 9. Influenza; 10. Recombinant DNA technology; 11-17 below; 18. Pertussis; 19. Antisera; 20. horse.

| VACCINE | SELECTED EXAMPLES |
|---|---|
| ~~Capsular material~~<br>Killed whole cells | Typhoid fever, pertussis, rickettsial diseases |
| ~~Living attenuated virions~~<br>Living attenuated cells | Brucellosis, anthrax, tuberculosis |
| ~~Killed whole cells~~<br>Capsular material | Pneumococcal pneumonia, *Haemophilus influenzae, Neisseria meningitidis* |
| ~~Split virion components~~<br>Inactivated toxins | Diphtheria, tetanus |
| ~~Living attenuated cells~~<br>Killed whole virions | Influenza, adenoviruses, polioviruses, rabies |
| ~~Inactivated toxins~~<br>Live attenuated virions | Measles, rubella, polioviruses, mumps, yellow fever |
| ~~Killed whole virions~~<br>Split virion components | Influenza, rabies, herpesviruses, Hepatitis B, foot-and-mouth disease |

**MASTERY TEST ANSWERS**

| | | | | | | | | | | | | |
|---|---|---|---|---|---|---|---|---|---|---|---|---|
| 1<br>e | 2<br>b | 3<br>a | 4<br>c | 5<br>d | 6<br>a | | 7<br>d | 8<br>e | 9<br>c | 10<br>a | 11<br>e | 12<br>d |
| 13<br>c | 14<br>a | 15<br>b | 16<br>c | 17<br>e | 18<br>c | 19<br>b | 20<br>b | 21<br>a | 22<br>e | 23<br>c | 24<br>c | 25<br>a |

# CHAPTER 22

## INTRODUCTION TO THE PATHOGENS

### CHAPTER SUMMARY

In the past century the fields of **epidemiology** and **immunology** have worked in concert with the development of **chemotherapeutic agents** and **antibiotics** to drastically reduce the incidence of most major infectious diseases. At least in the developed world such agents as typhoid fever, yellow fever, diphtheria, pertussis, tetanus, smallpox, and polio have either been eliminated or had their incidence dramatically reduced. **Antibiotic resistance** continues to be a problem for many bacterial pathogens.

Previously **rare** or even **unknown infections** caused by organisms thought to be members of the "**normal flora**" or **nonpathogenic** are *increasing* in incidence. Such **opportunistic infections** are, in part, due to some of the activities and methods of modern medicine. Some examples are (1) the use of **immunosuppressants** to prevent organ transplant rejection, (2) the use of **cancer chemotherapy** and **irradiation**, (3) the use of kidney **dialysis machines, heart pumps** and **urethral catheters**, and (4) the use of **antibiotics** which disturbs the normal ecological balance of flora.

**Epidemiology** is the study of disease occurrence in human populations (all diseases, including heart disease, cancer, etc.). **Epidemiologists** attempt to determine (1) who gets a particular disease, (2) how the disease is acquired, and (3) how the spread of the disease can be prevented. Often they are required to trace the **origin of an epidemic** outbreak, such as typhoid, legionnaires' disease, etc. The **Centers for Disease Control** (**CDC**) have the responsibility to collect data on about 50 different infections and track any increases in incidence. The CDC is responsible for setting up immunization programs for any outbreaks of illness that can be dealt with in this manner.

Before one can do any epidemiological studies, or even recommend any therapy, one must first diagnose the cause of an illness. A **clinical diagnosis** is frequently sufficient, if the illness is one with characteristic signs and symptoms like chickenpox, or mumps. **Specific antibody response** can often be checked during the course of an illness to give one a retrospective diagnosis. The **best**

**diagnosis**, however, remains the **isolation and identification** of the causative organism from the infected individual. This, in turn, requires the proper collection of, care of, and culture of **specimens**.

The single most important variable in specimen handling is the **time** between collection and culturing in the laboratory. This time must be as **short as possible** to prevent (1) the death of delicate pathogens, and (2) the overgrowth by normal flora that may contaminate the specimen. It is sometimes necessary to introduce the specimen directly into culture medium immediately after collection.

**Blood specimens** must be collected with full attention to disinfecting the intervening skin as thoroughly as possible. Very often the specimen should be immediately inoculated into suitable medium at bedside. Deep **respiratory tract** specimens are often contaminated by normal flora resident in the upper respiratory tract. It is sometimes necessary to use **transtracheal aspiration** to obtain specimens from the lower lung.

**Wound and abscess** specimens are best collected with a sterile syringe and needle, both to obtain a sufficient quantity of material and to protect the typically **anaerobic** agents from contact with oxygen. Specimens of this type are often transported in bottles containing oxygen-free gas. **Intestinal pathogens** are also often anaerobic and are, furthermore, quite delicate. A **stool preservative** containing a buffer to maintain neutral pH is essential unless the specimen can be immediately cultured in **gram-negative enrichment broth**.

Most common urinary tract infections are derived from **normal-flora enterics**. **Urethral catheterization** may yield contamination-free samples but carries a **considerable risk** of introducing urethral contaminants into the bladder. **Voided samples** are much safer for the patient and, with suitable precautions such as cleansing the external genitalia, quite reliable.

<u>OBJECTIVES</u> After a study of this chapter, you should be able to:

1. Discuss the changing patterns of disease over the past century and list the factors responsible for these alterations.
2. Explain why infections by normal flora or organisms usually considered to be nonpathogens are more prevalent now than 30 to 50 years ago.
3. Define epidemiology and outline the types of problems that the epidemiologist is called on to solve.
4. Describe the major responsibilities of the Centers for Disease Control.
5. Discuss the different methods for diagnosing an infection.
6. Describe the procedures for the collection of various specimens and be aware of any precautions that must be taken to preserve them until they are delivered to the diagnostic laboratory.

LEARNING ACTIVITIES

Vocabulary

Having read the chapter, you should be able to define or cite the significance of the following terms. If you cannot, look them up in the text. Terms are presented in the order you will encounter them in the book.

| | | |
|---|---|---|
| epidemiology | irradiation | clinical diagnosis |
| immunology | dialysis | specific antibody response |
| opportunistic infections | catheters | transtracheal aspiration |
| immuno-suppressants | legionnaires' disease | nasopharyngeal |
| chemotherapy | CDC | |
| | specimen | |

Complete each of the following statements by supplying the missing word or words.

1. Better ____________________ can be credited with curtailing typhoid fever and dysentery.

2. ____________________ has largely been eliminated from urban areas by mosquito control.

3. The field of ____________________ is generally credited with developing techniques of artificially inducing specific immunity for such diseases as diphtheria, pertussis, tetanus and polio.

4. ____________________ infections are now occurring with increasing frequency, caused by members of the normal flora or by organisms once thought to be nonpathogenic.

5. ____________________ are materials used to reduce transplant rejection that have the side effect of promoting infections.

6. Cancer ____________________ treatments also have the effect of damaging the immune system and making opportunistic infections more likely.

7. ____________________ tend to promote the incidence of urinary tract infections.

8. ____________________ disturb the ecological balance of normal flora, making it possible for some organisms to "overgrow" and create problems.

9. ____________________ are those who study disease occurrence in human populations.

10. ____________________ fever is often transmitted by carriers working in the food preparation industry.

11. The ____________________ collects information on 50 bacterial, fungal, viral and parasitic infections.

12. A ____________________ is made on the basis of the symptoms of a disease; it is often sufficient.

13. ____________________ during the course of an illness can give one a retrospective diagnosis of a disease.

14. The ____________________ between collection of a specimen and delivery to the laboratory is often the critical factor involved in a successful or unsuccessful identification.

15. The ____________________ is a nonsterile barrier through which blood specimens must be obtained.

16. ____________________ is a technique used to obtain deep respiratory specimens from very young, very old, or comatose patients.

17. ____________________ are poorly adapted for collecting specimens from wounds and abscesses, since they cannot collect enough material and they dry out quickly, allowing the pathogens to die.

18. ____________________ bacteria or less per milliliter from voided urine is considered to be insignificant.

19. ____________________ are the most common causes of urinary tract infections (e.g. *Escherichia*, *Klebsiella*, *Enterobacter*).

20. ____________________ is used by the textbook as the primary means of presenting pathogens.

## MASTERY TEST

1-14: Circle the choice that best answers the questions.

1. Which of the following terms is used to describe infections caused by normal body flora or other organisms not considered true pathogens?
   a. random
   b. productive
   c. opportunistic
   d. fulminating
   e. acute

2. Which of the following is NOT one of the possible reasons for the current increased incidence of the infections described in question #1?
   a. use of immunosuppressants in transplant cases
   b. evolution of new capacities in common organisms
   c. AIDS
   d. use of dialysis machines, heart pumps, catheters
   e. use of antibiotics

3. Which of the following specialists is responsible for studying disease occurrence in human populations?
   a. ecologists
   b. immunologists
   c. pathologists
   d. sanitary engineers
   e. epidemiologists

4. An epidemic of *Salmonella muenchen* in 1981 was eventually traced to:
   a. two restaurant workers in San Antonio
   b. contaminated kangaroo meat at fast food outlets
   c. contaminated eggs from Iowa
   d. contaminated marijuana
   e. defective sewage treatment equipment

5. The causative agent of Legionnaires' disease was:
   a. a well-known normal member of the nasal flora
   b. a newly-discovered bacterium unlike any other
   c. an unusual strain of a normal pharyngeal species
   d. a long-ignored strain newly antibiotic resistant

6. Which of the following is considered to be the best type of diagnosis?
   a. clinical diagnosis
   b. specific antibody response
   c. isolation and identification of causative organism
   d. computerized autodiagnosis

7. Which of the following specimens is considered to be normally sterile?
   a. blood
   b. sputum
   c. wound exudate
   d. feces
   e. urine

8. Which of the following is NOT a normal contributor to the organisms collected from the respiratory tract?
   a. mouth
   b. nose
   c. throat
   d. stomach
   e. lungs

9. Specimens from throat vesicles and ulcers should be promptly inoculated into/onto:
   a. gram-negative enrichment broth
   b. 100 ml of McConkey's medium
   c. blood agar
   d. oxygen-free media of low pH

10. Most of the causative agents of abscesses and deep infections are:
    a. obligate aerobes
    b. microaerophiles
    c. facultative anaerobes
    d. obligate anaerobes
    e. all of these, depending on the species

11. Intestinal pathogens are:
    a. generally very fragile
    b. generally very tough
    c. typically gram-positive
    d. generally strict anaerobes

12. Which of the following is NOT a typical cause of urinary tract infections?
    a. *Escherichia*
    b. *Klebsiella*
    c. *Enterobacter*
    d. *Pseudomonas*
    e. *Staphylococcus*

13. Which of the following techniques carries quite a large risk of introducing infectious organisms into regions that they do not normally inhabit?
    a. syringes
    b. catheters
    c. hemodialysis equipment
    d. heart pumps
    e. all of these have that potential

14. Which of the following government agencies has the responsibility to set up immunization programs for newly discovered epidemic situations?
    a. HHS
    b. FCC
    c. CDC
    d. EPA

15-25: Match the taxonomic group with the specific examples given. (use no answer twice)

ANSWERS

A. Actinomycetes
B. Chlamydiae
C. Endospore-forming rods
D. Gram - anaerobic rods
E. Gram - aerobic rods
F. Gram - facultative rods
G. Gram - cocci
H. Gram + cocci
I. Mycoplasmas
J. Non-spore-forming gram +
K. Rickettsias
L. Spirochetes

| CLASSIFICATION | SOME EXAMPLES |
|---|---|
| 15. | *Brucella abortus, Pseudomonas aeruginosa* |
| 16. | *Escherichia coli, Klebsiella pneumoniae* |
| 17. | *Bacteroides fragilis, Fusobacterium necrophorus* |
| 18. | *Staphylococcus aureus, Streptococcus pyogenes* |
| 19. | *Neisseria meningitidis, Neisseria gonorrhoeae* |
| 20. | *Bacillus anthracis, Clostridium tetani* |
| 21. | *Mycobacterium leprae, Mycobacterium tuberculosis* |
| 22. | *Treponema pallidum, Borelia recurrentis* |
| 23. | *Rickettsia rickettsiae, Coxiella burnetii* |
| 24. | *Chlamydia trachomatis, Chlamydia psittaci* |
| 25. | *Mycoplasma pneumoniae, Mycoplasma hominis* |

ANSWERS TO LEARNING ACTIVITIES

Fill-in-the-blank questions:

1. sanitation; 2. Yellow fever; 3. immunology; 4. Opportunistic;
5. Immunosuppressants; 6. chemotherapy or irradiation; 7. Urethral catheters;
8. Antibiotics; 9. Epidemiologists; 10. Typhoid fever; 11. CDC;
12. clinical diagnosis; 13. Specific antibody response; 14. time; 15. skin;
16. Transtracheal aspiration; 17. Swabs; 18. $10^3$; 19. Normal-flora enterics;
20. Portal of entry.

**MASTERY TEST ANSWERS**

| | | | | | | | | | | | | |
|---|---|---|---|---|---|---|---|---|---|---|---|---|
| 1<br>b | 2<br>b | 3<br>e | 4<br>d | 5<br>b | 6<br>c | | 7<br>a | 8<br>d | 9<br>c | 10<br>d | 11<br>a | 12<br>e |
| 13<br>e | 14<br>c | 15<br>E | 16<br>F | 17<br>D | 18<br>H | 19<br>G | 20<br>C | 21<br>A | 22<br>L | 23<br>K | 24<br>B | 25<br>I |

## CHAPTER 23

## THE NORMAL FLORA OF THE HUMAN BODY

### CHAPTER SUMMARY

**Symbiosis** is a term that literally means "living together"; it accurately describes the interaction between us and our **normal flora** (the microorganisms that live in or on our bodies). Symbiosis takes a number of different forms, including **mutualism**, **commensalism**, and **parasitism**. Many of the microbes that constitute our normal flora are **mutualistic symbionts** - they are actually beneficial to us. Some intestinal bacteria produce excess amounts of **vitamin K** and members of the **vitamin B complex** which we absorb across the wall of the large intestine. The microbes benefit by having nutrients delivered to them and a place to live. Other bacteria (on the skin, in the vagina) produce **acids** which impede the growth of other bacteria. Still other microbes benefit the host by competing with potential pathogens for nutrition and space; when they are eliminated by **antibiotic therapy** serious overgrowths can occur. Examples include the overgrowth of *Candida albicans* in the intestine and vagina, and *Clostridium difficile* in the intestine.

**Commensals** are **harmless** to their host, but they're not beneficial either. Many of the inhabitants of the skin, the intestines, and the respiratory tract are truly commensal during normal circumstances. Many commensals are also **opportunists** when conditions permit, moving from a harmless interaction to a harmful **parasitism**. *Staphylococcus aureus* is an example, living harmlessly in the nose and throat but rapidly causing a **secondary pneumonia** following a measles or influenza attack. Other examples are *Escherichia coli* and *Proteus vulgaris* which are harmless in the intestine but cause bladder infections if introduced by catheterization. The **Bacteroidaceae** are obligately anaerobic inhabitants of the intestine which cause serious **peritonitis** if they are accidentally introduced into the peritoneal cavity. **AIDS patients**, and others with **impaired immune systems**, suffer from a plethora of opportunistic infections caused by a variety of microbes usually thought of as commensals.

True **pathogens** also find a place in the normal flora of some members of the population. *Neisseria meningitidis*, *Streptococcus pneumoniae*, and ß-hemolytic streptococci are all common members of the **respiratory tracts** of **carriers**.

Even viruses appear to be members of the "normal flora". They can be detected by means of their **cytopathic effect** on tissue culture cells, and are especially common in the digestive tract where they do not normally appear to cause disease. A large group of such viruses are now known as **echoviruses** (short for **e**nteric **c**ytopathic **h**uman **o**rphan viruses); another group cultured from tonsils and adenoids are known as the **adenoviruses**.

Most parts of the body are occupied by a typical flora; **exceptions** include the **blood**, which is usually sterile, the **lower respiratory tract** which is protected by the filtering action of the upper respiratory tract and by its own ciliary action, and the **stomach**, kept largely sterile by high acidity. The **skin** is richly endowed with bacteria, concentrated in the openings to **hair follicles** (especially in moist areas such as the axilla and the groin). *Propionibacterium acnes* is a dominant member of the skin flora; its secretion of **propionic acid** not only contributes to the acidity of the skin but is also toxic to many microorganisms.

The **eye** is protected by the high levels of **lysozyme** (a peptidoglycan-digesting enzyme) in tears, yet still harbors a collection of resident bacteria including staphylococci and streptococci. The **upper respiratory tract** contains many organisms **filtered out** of inhaled air, as well as normal resident flora. A **tracheostomy**, which bypasses the filtering action of the upper respiratory tract, invites contamination of the lower respiratory tract.

The **mouth** and **oropharynx** are occupied by large numbers of microorganisms including gram-positive and gram-negative bacteria as well as yeasts. **Poor dental hygiene** contributes to excess population sizes of these microbes. The **stomach** and **upper small intestine** are normally rather sterile. The lower small intestine becomes progressively more populated as it nears connection with the **large intestine**, which is itself occupied by a huge, diverse population of microbes. Most of these organisms are anaerobic and are dominated by the gram-negative *Bacteroides* and *Fusobacterium* species.

The urinary tract, with the exception of the urethra, is normally sterile. The urethra frequently harbors a variety of nonpathogenic bacteria and opportunistic mycoplasmas. *Mycobacterium smegmatis* is a common resident of the external genitalia in both sexes. Between puberty and menopause the **vagina** is occupied by **acid-loving bacteria** and yeasts including the dominant *Lactobacillus*. Alkaline secretions before puberty and after menopause result in a total change in flora, as is shown in Table 23.1 in your text.

The **blood** is normally devoid of bacteria but is not infrequently contaminated by viruses, including **HIV** (causes AIDS) and **hepatitis B** and **C** viruses. These may be present before any symptoms of the disease are apparent or, in the case of hepatitis, long after apparent recovery. These viruses pose a distinct threat to the blood supply and result in inadvertent transfer during transfusions.

OBJECTIVES — This chapter is designed to contribute to your understanding of:

1. The categories of microorganisms that constitute our normal flora and their role as helpful, harmless, or opportunistic agents.
2. Situations in which our opportunistic flora can cause disease.
3. The factors that influence the kinds and numbers of microorganisms in various body areas.
4. Which organisms are found normally in each of our body areas.
5. The mechanism whereby the lower respiratory tract remains free of microorganisms.
6. Why certain diseases can be transmitted via blood transfusions obtained from seemingly healthy individuals.

## LEARNING ACTIVITIES

### Vocabulary

Having read the chapter, you should be able to define or cite the significance of the following terms. If you cannot, look them up in the text. Terms are presented in the order you will encounter them in the book.

normal flora
symbiotic relationship
mutualistic
commensals
opportunists
parasitism
peritoneal cavity
pathogenic
ß-hemolytic streptococci
carriers
cytopathic effect
echoviruses
adenoviruses
enterotoxin
*Candida albicans*
pseudomembranous colitis
*Propionibacterium*
lysozyme
tracheostomy
hepatitis B
hepatitis C

Complete each of the following statements by supplying the missing word or words.

1. ____________________ is the term used to describe the microorganisms which live on and in our bodies.

2. ____________________ relationships involve two organisms living in an association with one another.

3. ____________________ symbionts are beneficial to their host.

4. ____________________ are organisms that do not harm, nor do they help their host.

5. ____________________ are organisms that can cause infections when normal barriers break down, or when the host's immune system is damaged.

6. ____________________ and vitamins of the B complex are produced by some intestinal bacteria and absorbed across the wall of the intestine into the blood.

7. ____________________ is the term applied to an interaction in which the microbe thrives at the expense of the host.

8. ____________________ is a good example of an opportunist, as it lives harmlessly in the nose and throat yet can cause pneumonia after respiratory infections such as measles or influenza have weakened the host.

9. ____________________ are a group of obligately anaerobic gram-negative bacteria which can cause opportunistic infections if they gain access to the peritoneal cavity.

10. ____________________ are people who harbor pathogens.

11. ____________________ are a group of apparently non-disease-producing viruses found in the enteric system.

12. ____________________ treatment can result in an overgrowth of resistant organisms such as *Candida albicans* and *Clostridium difficile*.

13. The ____________________ nature of stomach and vaginal secretions tends to deter the growth of most microorganisms in these body regions.

14. ____________________, a bacteriostatic, is produced by the *Propionibacteria* on the skin.

15. *Staphylococcus* ____________________ is a common resident of human skin.

16. ____________________ in tears protects the eye from many potentially harmful bacteria.

17. ____________________ creates a dramatically increased opportunity for microbes to penetrate into the lower respiratory tract.

18. The ____________________ is one part of the small intestine which is normally free of bacteria.

19. The ____________________ is the only part of the urinary tract which normally harbors bacteria; usually harmless species but including opportunistic mycoplasmas.

20. ____________________ now accounts for 90 percent of posttransfusional hepatitis infections.

<u>MASTERY TEST</u>

1-25: Circle the choice that best answers the questions.

1. Which of the following do no harm but do not help their host either?
   a. commensals
   b. mutualists
   c. parasites
   d. symbionts

2. Which of the following generally aid their hosts, while benefiting themselves.
   a. commensals
   b. mutualists
   c. parasites
   d. symbionts

3. Opportunists are normally commensals or even mutualists, but have the capacity to become ______________ when the opportunity arises.
   a. predators
   b. pathogens
   c. parasites
   d. symbionts

4. Many commensals are really ____________ since their very presence deters the growth of true pathogens by competing for nutrients and space.
   a. communists
   b. mutualists
   c. parasites
   d. symbionts

5. Which of the following is a true pathogen, not an opportunist?
   a. *Neisseria meningitidis*
   b. *Staphylococcus aureus*
   c. *Escherichia coli*
   d. *Proteus vulgaris*

6. Which of the following is NOT a mechanism which creates a chance for an opportunist to cause an infection?
   a. catheterization
   b. abdominal trauma
   c. AIDS
   d. tracheostomy
   e. stomach acid secretion

7. A _____________ is someone who has pathogenic bacteria growing in their bodies but who suffer no harm from them.
   a. symbiont
   b. mutualist
   c. carrier
   d. parasite

8. Which of the following is a term used to describe the damage done by viruses to cells growing in tissue culture?
   a. lysogenation
   b. cavitation
   c. encapsulation
   d. cytopathic effect
   e. ß-hemolysis

9. Non-disease-causing viruses from the digestive tract are called echoviruses, similar viruses isolated from tonsils and adenoids are called:
   a. tonsivoviruses
   b. togaviruses
   c. adenoviruses
   d. adenosiloviruses

10. Pseudomembranous colitis is caused by the administration of antibiotics (especially clindamycin and lincomycin) and the overgrowth of _____________ in the intestine.
    a. *Candida albicans*
    b. *Escherichia coli*
    c. *Proteus vulgaris*
    d. *Clostridium difficile*

11. The main cause of the gastroenteritis produced by the agent discussed in question #10 is a(n)
    a. enterotoxin
    b. endotoxin
    c. neurotoxin
    d. cytopathic effect

12. Which of the following tissues or body regions is NOT normally devoid of microorganisms?
    a. bladder
    b. blood
    c. pharynx
    d. stomach
    e. lower respiratory tract

13. The skin normally has a pH which is:
    a. acidic
    b. alkaline
    c. neutral
    d. strongly basic

14. Which of the following is not a normal resident of human skin?
    a. *Staphylococcus epidermidis*
    b. *Staphylococcus aureus*
    c. *Corynebacterium sp.*
    d. *Bacteroides sp.*
    e. *Mycobacterium sp.*

15. Which of the following is a major protective agent in the eye?
   a. lysozyme
   b. lactoferrin
   c. transferrin
   d. properdin

16. The upper respiratory tract:
   a. is basically sterile
   b. contains agents filtered out of the inhaled air
   c. contains a variety of enteric bacteria
   d. contains purely mutualistic species

17. The lower respiratory tract:
   a. is basically sterile
   b. contains agents filtered out of the inhaled air
   c. contains a variety of enteric bacteria
   d. contains purely mutualistic species

18. Which of the following is considered to be a **normal** member of the mouth flora?
   a. *Streptococcus pyogenes*
   b. *Streptococcus faecalis*
   c. *Streptococcus pneumoniae*
   d. viridans streptococci

19. Which of the following has been implicated in causing infections in the epithelial lining of the stomach and possibly contributing to the formation of peptic ulcers?
   a. *Streptococcus gastritis*
   b. *Halicobacter pylori*
   c. *Halobacterium cardiacii*
   d. *Haemophilus influenzae*

20. Which of the following is the dominant type found in the large intestine?
   a. *Bacteroides sp.*
   b. *Escherichia sp.*
   c. *Streptococcus sp.*
   d. *Clostridium sp.*
   e. *Fusobacterium sp.*

21. Which of the following regions is usually not populated with bacteria?
   a. rectum
   b. colon
   c. duodenum
   d. ileum
   e. jejunum

22. Which of the following has been implicated as a common cause of inflammatory infections of the urethra?
   a. *Mycobacterium sp.*
   b. *Rickettsia sp.*
   c. *Streptococcus sp.*
   d. *Micrococcus sp.*
   e. *Mycoplasma sp.*

23. Which of the following is a common member of the normal flora on external genitalia?
   a. *Mycobacterium sp.*
   b. *Rickettsia sp.*
   c. *Streptococcus sp.*
   d. *Micrococcus sp.*
   e. *Mycoplasma sp.*

24. The pH of the vagina shifts from __________ to __________ at puberty and makes the reverse shift at menopause.
   a. neutral ... alkaline
   b. acid ... alkaline
   c. alkaline ... acid
   d. alkaline ... neutral
   e. acid ... neutral

25. Which of the following is of NO CONCERN when blood transfusions are being performed?
   a. Hepatitis A
   b. Hepatitis B
   c. Hepatitis C
   d. HIV (AIDS virus)
   e. syphilis

ANSWERS TO LEARNING ACTIVITIES

Fill-in-the-blank questions:

1. Normal flora; 2. Symbiotic; 3. Mutualistic; 4. Commensals; 5. Opportunists; 6. Vitamin K; 7. Parasitism; 8. *Staphylococcus aureus*; 9. Bacteroidaceae; 10. Carriers; 11. Echoviruses; 12. Antibiotic; 13. acid; 14. Propionic acid; 15. *epidermidis*; 16. Lysozyme; 17. Tracheostomy; 18. duodenum; 19. urethra; 20. Hepatitis C.

**MASTERY TEST ANSWERS**

| | | | | | | | | | | | | |
|---|---|---|---|---|---|---|---|---|---|---|---|---|
| 1<br>a | 2<br>b | 3<br>c | 4<br>b | 5<br>a | 6<br>e | | 7<br>c | 8<br>d | 9<br>c | 10<br>d | 11<br>a | 12<br>c |
| 13<br>a | 14<br>d | 15<br>a | 16<br>b | 17<br>a | 18<br>d | 19<br>b | 20<br>a | 21<br>c | 22<br>e | 23<br>a | 24<br>c | 25<br>a |

## CHAPTER 24

## BACTERIA AND FUNGI THAT ENTER THE BODY VIA THE RESPIRATORY ROUTE

### CHAPTER SUMMARY

The **respiratory system** serves as the **portal of entry** of a large variety of infectious agents, but is quite effective at denying entrance to most microorganisms. Those which make it past the nasal hairs and mucous coats are still confronted with the "**mucociliary escalator**" that effectively removes bacteria that have gained access to the lower respiratory tract. Among those that successfully evade the physical and chemical defenses are the pathogenic members of the gram-positive genus *Streptococcus*. These bacteria cause **acute infections**, but even more importantly, they can produce **severe complications**. The genus is named for its **cell shape** and the **arrangement** of the cells; the cells are round cocci that typically come in chains (the strepto- arrangement). Their classification depends upon both **biochemical** and **antigenic** characteristics and is currently based on the work of **Lancefield** who divided up **Sherman's** four groups into 13 (**Groups A through O**).

One of the taxonomic criteria for the streptococci concerns their behavior on blood agar. **α-hemolytic** strains produce a hemolysis that results in a greenish-brown discoloration around the colony. Such organisms are known as the **viridans streptococci** (a Sherman class). **ß-hemolytic** streptococci secrete a **hemolysin** which totally lyses the red blood cells in the agar and leaves a clear zone around the colony. Almost all of the Lancefield groups are ß-hemolytic. The trait is related to one of two possible hemolysins secreted by the cells: **streptolysin S** (soluble in serum) and **streptolysin O** (inactivated by oxygen).

Streptolysin O is a large molecule capable of serving as an antigen (**ASO** is antistreptolysin O antibody). The molecule binds to **cholesterol** in the **erythrocyte membrane** and causes lysis; it also binds to sterols in **leukocyte** membranes ultimately killing the cell. This **leukocidin** activity is combined with **chemotaxis suppression** and inhibition on leukocyte mobility. Streptolysin S is a small, diffusible peptide not big enough to serve as an antigen. It binds to **phospholipids** in cell membranes and causes lysis of erythrocytes and leukocytes; it is also **antiphagocytic** and inhibits chemotaxis.

The Lancefield classification scheme is based on the antigenic nature of a material extracted from the cell walls of all streptococci except the viridans group. This is the **C carbohydrate**, of which 13 varieties have been identified (A through O). **Group A** (*Streptococcus pyogenes*) is by far the most important group of human pathogens. Over 50 different **types (strains)** of this group are based upon antigenic differences in the **M protein** in the cell wall. This protein is toxic to leukocytes and antiphagocytic. Antibodies to the M protein are **type specific** and rapidly lead to phagocytosis of the cells.

Streptococci are such important and effective pathogens because of a variety of products they secrete: **hemolysins** (lyse cells), **DNAse** (digests DNA), **NADase** (digests NAD), **hyaluronidase** (digests hyaluronic acid), **streptokinase** (dissolves blood clots), an **erythrogenic toxin** (causes skin rash), and **leukocidins** (kill leukocytes). The two primary acute diseases caused by group A streptococci are **pharyngitis** ("strep throat") and **impetigo** (a skin infection sometimes called **streptococcal pyoderma**). Group A streptococci are also responsible for **puerperal sepsis**, a once-common infection of the uterus which followed childbirth.

Pharyngitis can lead to **scarlet fever** if the infection involves a strain that secretes **erythrogenic toxins** (aka **streptococcal pyrogenic exotoxins**). These toxins are due to **lysogenic conversion** of the cells (the bacteria harbor a prophage which brought the toxin gene with it), and are related to the staphylococcal toxins that cause **toxic shock syndrome**. In fact, streptococcal infections sometimes involve a toxic-shock-like syndrome with a 30 percent mortality rate.

**Late nonsuppurative** (non-pus-forming) **sequelae** (complications) of group A streptococcal infection include **rheumatic fever** and **glomerulonephritis**. Rheumatic fever involves **joint inflammation** and, more importantly, damage to the **heart**. The joint involvement is probably due to the buildup of antigen-antibody complexes in the joints and is reversible. The heart damage, which is permanent, seems to involve an **autoimmune response** due to cross-reaction between streptococcal antigens and surface antigens on heart cells. People who have recovered from rheumatic fever are particularly vulnerable to recurrence.

Glomerulonephritis is an inflammation of the **glomeruli** in the kidney and may result in **hematuria** (bloody urine) as its main symptom. The disease is thought to be an autoimmune response due to cross-reactivity between streptococcal antigens and kidney cells or due to the buildup of antigen-antibody complexes in the glomeruli. Recurrence is not a serious problem.

**Group B** streptococci, such as *Streptococcus agalactiae* are normally parasites of cows but often occur in the human vagina and can lead to **postpartum endometritis** (infection of the endometrium). **Diabetics** and **immunosuppressed individuals**, as well as **newborns**, are subject to **bacteremia** (blood infections) and **meningitis**. Newborns, additionally, are subject to **pneumonia** with mortality rates as high as 50 to 70 percent; survivors often suffer permanent neurological handicaps.

**Subacute bacterial endocarditis** is an infection of the heart often caused by $\alpha$-hemolytic streptococci such as *Enterococcus*. Such infections are particularly likely in individuals with congenital heart valve damage or damage due to a previous episode of rheumatic fever. *Streptococcus mutans*, another α-hemolytic viridans streptococcus, is the principle agent involved in the production of **dental caries**. They use **sucrose** as a raw material to produce a large **dextran** complex called a **glycocalyx** on the tooth surface, which serves as a mechanism for bacterial attachment (resulting in **dental plaque**). In the process, the bacteria liberate **fructose**, which is fermented by the streptococci to **organic acids**, which **decalcify** the tooth enamel. Plaque formation can eventually lead to **gingivitis** and **periodontal disease** by becoming calcified (**tartar** or **calculus**) and irritating the gum tissue.

*Streptococcus pneumoniae* are α-hemolytic organisms that produce **leukocidins** and a hyaluronidase in addition to the hemolysin. They are the chief cause of **lobar pneumonia** and often result in **bacteremia**. They are the second-most common cause of **adult meningitis**, and result in the production of about half of all childhood **middle ear infections**. They are very similar to the viridans streptococci but can be distinguished on the basis of their "**bile solubility**" (exposure to bile salts triggers an **autolytic** enzyme system in the cells). Another detection system is the **optochin disk**; pneumococci are extremely susceptible to Optochin and will not grow in its presence, while the viridans group will grow.

**Epidemic meningitis** is caused by *Neisseria meningitidis*, a serious disease which can spread rapidly in **crowded conditions** (e.g. military trainees). The causative gram-negative cocci are quite delicate, and can best be cultured on the rich **chocolate blood agar** medium under high-carbon dioxide conditions. It is apparently a benign resident in the nasopharynx of **carriers**, and starts its infection as a mild nasopharyngeal infection. In some cases it spreads into the blood and develops into an explosive **meningococcemia** which can kill in a matter of hours. In other cases it merely uses the bloodstream as a route to the brain, where it causes **meningitis** by infecting the **meninges**. A primary virulence factor of this organism is a **proteolytic enzyme** which destroys **IgA**, the main microbial defense in the nasopharynx. Resistance to sulfonamides has increased so much that treatment is now achieved *via* penicillin, erythromycin or chloramphenicol.

**Whooping cough**, once a big killer, is currently staging a minor comeback due to low rates of immunization. *Bordetella pertussis*, the causative agent, is a delicate gram-negative coccobacillus whose major pathogenic effect is by means of toxins and other secretions. The organism never invades the bloodstream, but remains localized in the respiratory mucosa. **Pertussis toxin** is an enzyme which **hydrolyzes NAD** and transfers the ADP-ribose fragment to a host protein which regulates the host enzyme **adenylate cyclase**. This results in massive intracellular **cyclic AMP** production from ATP. Increased intracellular cAMP levels **activate protein kinases**, which phosphorylate host proteins creating (1) a **histamine-sensitizing effect**, promoting **anaphylaxis**; (2) an increased **insulin** synthesis and resultant **hypoglycemia**; (3) a lymphocytosis-promoting effect leading to **excess circulating lymphocytes**. The toxin also enables the bacterium to stick to host cell cilia. *C. diphtheriae* also secretes its own **extracytoplasmic adenylate cyclase** which produces still more cAMP, reducing the effectiveness of neutrophils, monocytes, and natural killer cells. A final product called **tracheal cytotoxin** (a breakdown derivative of peptidoglycan) directly kills ciliated respiratory cells. By far the best management is by vaccination, although toxic side effects have resulted in decreased use.

*Haemophilus influenzae*, a pleomorphic gram-negative "coccobacillus" is a major cause of **meningitis** and **acute epiglottitis**. The organism displays a strict cultural requirement for **hematin (X factor)** and **NAD (V factor)**; only the **encapsulated type b** organism is pathogenic, moving from the nasopharynx where it exists asymptomatically into the blood, thence to the brain. Survivors of meningitis often suffer irreversible **organic brain damage**. Acute epigottitis can create lethal respiratory distress by causing the epiglottis to swell into an obstructive blockage. *H. influenzae* is a major cause of middle ear infections, and can cause septic arthritis in children. A relative, *Haemophilus aegyptius*, causes **conjunctivitis (pinkeye)**. An unusual strain of this species recently caused a series of severe and often fatal infections called **Brazilian purpuric fever** characterized by overwhelming endotoxemia and irreversible shock.

*Corynebacterium diphtheriae*, a gram-positive pleomorphic organism (often club-shaped), causes **diphtheria**, a severe, acute infection which often obstructs the airway *via* the formation of a **pseudomembrane** constructed of dead tissue, leukocytes, erythrocytes and bacteria. Tracheotomy is often required to bypass the obstruction. All of the symptoms can be duplicated by the purified **diphtheria toxin**. Like the **erythrogenic toxins** of the streptococci, the diphtheria toxin is due to **lysogenic conversion** of the bacterium; phage-free strains fail to produce toxin. The toxin functions by **hydrolyzing NAD** and using the ADP-ribose portion to immobilize host cell **translocase enzymes**. This freezes the ribosome on the mRNA and prevents host cell protein synthesis; this kills the cell. **Antitoxin** remains an important therapeutic agent against this disease; immunization with toxoid is the best management technique available.

**Tuberculosis**, the "white plague" is caused by the acid-fast pleomorphic gram-positive organism *Mycobacterium tuberculosis*. Like other members of the genus, this organism has mycolic acids and other fatty materials in its cell wall which gives it its unusual staining behavior and, probably, serves as a virulence factor. **Cord factor** is a complex fatty acid linked to polysaccharide which results in growth of the bacteria in long, multilayered chains (resembling cords); only **virulent** mycobacteria produce this material. Cord factor stimulates the synthesis of **cachectin** (tumor necrosis factor alpha) in mice, leading to wasting. The **cachexia** (wasting away) of tuberculosis patients may be related to this phenomenon. In humans, infection with *M. tuberculosis* results in a **primary infection** producing lung lesions called **tubercles**, which may expand in an active infection to produce massive lung tissue destruction called **caseation necrosis**. If the organism makes it into the bloodstream it can result in **miliary tuberculosis** with lesions all over the body (in the brain it can cause **tuberculous meningitis**). Many of the bacteria in this stage of the disease grow **within** macrophages. Later, once cellular immunity develops, all of the bacteria are found growing extracellularly. In many patients the primary lesions are walled off by lymphoid and fibrous tissue; *M. tuberculosis* cells within these tubercles can remain viable for decades, subject to **reactivation infections**.

**Leprosy** is caused by another member of the Mycobacterium genus, *M. leprae* (**Hansen's bacillus**). **Lepromatous leprosy** only develops in people with defective cellular immunity; it infects every organ in the body, but concentrates in the skin, nerves, testes, and the eye. Untreated, it is invariably fatal. **Tuberculoid leprosy**, which produces skin lesions and nerve damage, is generally self-limiting due to cellular immune responses to the bacilli.

**Primary atypical pneumonia** is the one human disease known to be caused by a mycoplasma, *M. pneumoniae*. It is apparently a common disease, especially under crowded conditions; severe complications are due to an **autoimmune response**. Repeated infections produce exaggerated **pulmonary histopathology** which does not occur in immunosuppressed patients.

**Legionnaires' Disease** (Legionellosis) is caused by an unusual gram-negative organism called *Legionella pneumophila*. The organism apparently grows in warm, moist areas world-wide and is associated with **air-conditioning cooling towers, hot-water heaters**, and **shower heads**. It is capable of causing a severe, often fatal **pneumonia** which may have gastrointestinal involvement. The organism is relatively well controlled by erythromycin or rifampin.

**Psittacosis** (parrot fever or **ornithosis**) is a potentially fatal **pneumonia** which is transmitted by **birds** (especially members of the parrot family). The causative agent is *Chlamydia psittaci*, an intracellular parasite which is frequently encountered by poultry slaughterhouse workers and pet bird owners. *C. pneumoniae* (first identified in Taiwan) is a human-reservoir agent of pneumonia which may prove to be the most common chlamydial infection in humans.

*Coxiella burnetii* is the only rickettsial parasite of humans that does not require an arthropod vector to spread it. It causes **Q fever**. Its unusual resistance to dry conditions (and to heat) may be explained by an **endospore stage** (the so-called **SCV**, or **small-cell variant**). Ticks are the reservoir, often the vector, although Q fever can be acquired from the inhalation of dried tick feces or from the huge quantities shed by cattle during the birth process. Q fever may go through an active phase then become quiescent only to be reactivated by x-irradiation or multiple cortisone injections.

**Deep mycoses** are systemic diseases caused by **fungi**. Except for cryptococcosis, all are caused by **dimorphic fungi** (**yeasts** in humans, **filamentous** in nature). All begin *via* the inhalation of fungus spores. **Blastomycosis** is caused by *Blastomyces dermatitidis*, an Ascomycete. The fungus grows in nature in moist highly organic areas contaminated with animal feces. **Primary pulmonary blastomycosis** is the first phase of the disease and leads to **lobar pneumonia**. The organism then moves into the blood and spreads to the skin where it causes **ulcerated granulomas**. Internal organs are sometimes invaded and bone invasion can lead to bone destruction and arthritis. Intravenous amphotericin B is the treatment of choice.

**Histoplasmosis**, caused by the Ascomycete *Histoplasma capsulatum*, is common in the central and midwestern U.S. The organism is encountered *via* contact with contaminated **bird** and **bat feces** and is common in bat caves and bird roosts. Primary lung infection is followed by movement of the agent into the blood. **Healed lung lesions** resemble calcified tuberculous lesions. The infection is subject to **reactivation** late in life, indicating that viable cells are harbored by the calcified lesions. Recovery is generally spontaneous.

**Coccidioidomycosis**, caused by *Coccidioides immitis* is common in the southwestern U.S. and in northern Mexico; the organism is found in arid soils. As usual, the primary infection occurs in the **lungs** following inhalation of spores. Migration *via* the blood stream to the **meninges**, **internal organs** or the **skin** occurs in some cases. Recovery is generally spontaneous although chronic cases may need treatment with amphotericin B, or even surgical removal of lung cavities.

*Cryptococcus neoformans* is not a dimorphic fungus, but exists in nature and as a pathogen in the form of a yeast. When inhaled from contaminated pigeon feces it can cause **cryptococcosis**. Typically causing an asymptomatic primary lung infection, the organism occasionally moves to the brain and meninges *via* the blood stream. Untreated **meningitis** is always fatal, but amphotericin B is usually effective.

OBJECTIVES After studying this chapter, you should:

1. The classification and characteristics of group A streptococci.
2. The types of infections caused by group A streptococci.
3. A characterization of the late, nonsuppurative complications that may follow group A streptococci infections.
4. A description of group B streptococcal infections and their danger to the newborn.
5. The role of streptococci in dental caries and periodontal disease.
6. A description of *Streptococcus pneumoniae* and its role in human disease.
7. The serological classification of *Neisseria meningitidis* and the epidemiology and control of meningococcal meningitis.
8. The molecular basis and control of whooping cough.
9. The classification of *Haemophilus influenzae* and the types of infections caused by these organisms.
10. The mechanism of disease production and control of *Corynebacterium diphtheriae*.
11. The epidemiology, control, and diagnostic procedures for tuberculosis and leprosy.
12. A characterization of infections caused by *Mycoplasma pneumoniae* and *Legionella pneumophila*.
13. The systemic mycoses, which include blastomycosis, histoplasmosis, coccidioidomycosis, and paracoccidioidomycosis.
14. The occurrence of infections by opportunistic fungi such as *Geotrichum* and *Aspergillus*.
15. The type and source of infections caused by *Cryptococcus neoformans*.
16. The epidemiology of avian-borne and non-avian-borne psittacosis.
17. The reason why *Coxiella burnetii* is more resistant to heat and desiccation than are the other rickettsia.

## LEARNING ACTIVITIES

### Vocabulary

Having read the chapter, you should be able to define or cite the significance of the following terms. If you cannot, look them up in the text. Terms are presented in the order you will encounter them in the book.

mucociliary escalator
*Streptococcus*
rheumatic fever
acute glomerulonephritis
Sherman
biochemical classification
pyogenic
Lancefield
antigenic classification
hemolysins
α-hemolytic
viridans
ß-hemolytic
streptolysin S
streptolysin O
ASO
Group A Streptococci
γ-hemolytic
C carbohydrate
antigenic types
*Streptococcus pyogenes*
M protein
DNase, NADase
hyaluronidase
streptokinase
erythrogenic toxin
leukocidins
subacute bacterial endocarditis
dental plaque
acquired pellicle
*S. mutans*
dextransucrase
glycocalyx
periodontal disease
gingiva
calculus
tartar
*S. pneumoniae*
bile solubility
optochin disks
lobar pneumonia
epidemic meningitis
chocolate blood agar
*Bordetella pertussis*
whooping cough
filamentous hemagglutinin
tracheal cytotoxin
cAMP
protein kinase
anaphylaxis
hypoglycemia
*Haemophilus influenzae*
pleomorphism
tuberculosis
acid-fast
Ziehl-Neelsen
mycolic acids
cord factor
cachectin
cachexia
primary infection
quiescent infection
tubercle
caseation necrosis
miliary tuberculosis
reactivation infection
delayed-type hypersensitivity
*Mycobacterium bovis*
atypical mycobacteria
*Mycobacterium leprae*
leprosy
Hansen's bacillus
lepromatous leprosy
tuberculoid leprosy
MIF
*Mycoplasma pneumoniae*
primary atypical pneumonia
*Legionella pneumophila*
legionellosis
Legionnaires' Disease
*Chlamydia psittaci*

pharyngitis
impetigo
scarlet fever
pyrogenic
 exotoxins
toxic shock
 syndrome
streptococcal
 shock-
 like syndrome
puerperal
 sepsis
hematuria
autoimmune
 disease
Group B
 streptococci
*S. agalactiae*
bacteremia
meningitis
*Enterococcus*

X factor
V factor
acute
 epiglottitis
*Haemophilus*
 *aegyptius*
conjunctivitis
pinkeye
Brazilian
 purpuric
 fever
*Corynebacterium*
 *diphtheriae*
diphtheria
pseudomembrane
lysogenic
 conversion
translocase
Shick test
*Mycobacterium*
 *tuberculosis*

psittacosis
ornithosis
*Chlamydia*
 *pneumoniae*
*Coxiella*
 *burnetii*
Q fever
LCV
SCV
mycoses
dimorphic
primary
 pulmonary
 blastomycosis
histoplasmosis
coccidioido-
mycosis
cryptococcosis
paracoccidioido-
 mycosis
geotrichosis

Complete each of the following statements by supplying the missing word or words.

1. ____________________ and Lancefield are the two main figures associated with the taxonomy of the genus Streptococcus.

2. ____________________ on blood agar plates is characteristic of the so-called viridans streptococci.

3. ____________________ is a term used to describe bacterial traits due to genes introduced by temperate phages (many exotoxins are produced this way).

4. ____________________ is a term used to describe fungi which exist in two forms: a yeast form which is pathogenic, and a filamentous form which is found growing in nature. In human fungal pathogens this form of growth behavior is almost universal.

5-20: The following chart of organisms, diseases and controls has had the organisms scrambled; unscramble them.

| ORGANISM | DISEASE | CONTROL |
|---|---|---|
| *B. pertussis* | Scarlet fever, Rheumatic fever | Penicillin |
| *B. dermatitidis* | Neonatal septicemia & meningitis | Immunize mothers |
| *C. diphtheriae* | Lobar pneumonia | Polysaccharide vaccine |
| *C. immitis* | Epidemic meningitis | Vaccine for groups A,C,Y |
| *S. pneumoniae* | Whooping cough | Heat-killed vaccine |
| *C. pneumoniae* | Meningitis and epiglottitis | No vaccine available |
| *C. psittici* | Diphtheria | Toxoid vaccine |
| Group A streptococci | Tuberculosis | Vaccine in Europe |
| Group B streptococci | Leprosy | Treat active cases |
| *H. capsulatum* | Primary atypical pneumonia | Vaccines |
| *H. influenzae* | Legionnaires' disease | None available |
| *L. pneumophila* | Ornithosis | None available |
| *M. leprae* | Pneumonia | None available |
| *M. pneumoniae* | Blastomycosis | Amphotericin B |
| *M. tuberculosis* | Histoplasmosis | Amphotericin B |
| *N. meningitidis* | Coccidioidomycosis | Amphotericin B |

MASTERY TEST

1-25: Circle the choice that best answers the questions.

1. Secretions of Group A streptococci which cause the lysis of red blood cells are called:
   a. erythrogenic toxin
   b. leukocidins
   c. hemolysins
   d. viridans
   e. NADase

2. A zone of total clearing around a colony on a blood agar plate represents:
   a. $\alpha$-hemolysis
   b. ß-hemolysis
   c. $\gamma$-hemolysis
   d. $\lambda$-hemolysis

3. Which of the following is a large material which binds to cholesterol in membranes and thereby kills cells?
   a. Streptolysin S
   b. Streptolysin B
   c. Streptolysin O
   d. Streptolysin G

4. The bacterial compound used by the Lancefield classification system for organizing the streptococci is:
   a. C carbohydrate
   b. M protein
   c. O antigen
   d. coagulase enzyme
   e. diphtheria toxin

5. Which of the following exhibits a powerful antiphagocytic activity which protects *Streptococcus pyogenes* from leukocyte attack?
   a. C carbohydrate
   b. M protein
   c. O antigen
   d. coagulase enzyme
   e. diphtheria toxin

6. Which of the following is NOT a product of Group A streptococci?
   a. DNase
   b. NADase
   c. hyaluronidase
   d. erythrogenic toxin
   e. enterotoxin A

7. Group A streptococci can directly or indirectly cause all of the following except:
   a. pharyngitis
   b. impetigo
   c. scarlet fever
   d. meningitis
   e. rheumatic fever

8. The effects of rheumatic fever on the heart are most likely due to:
   a. an autoimmune reaction
   b. erythrogenic toxin effect on heart cells
   c. direct cytotoxic effect by streptococci
   d. Group B streptolysins

9. The inflammation of the kidney which sometimes follows a Group A streptococcal infection of the skin is called:
   a. hematuria
   b. renal atrophy
   c. renal hilus disfunction
   d. glomerulonephritis
   e. miliary tuberculosis

10. Subacute bacterial endocarditis is most commonly due to:
   a. Group A streptococci
   b. Group B streptococci
   c. *Staphylococcus aureus*
   d. *Enterococcus*
   e. *Neisseria meningitidis*

11. Which of the following is the main culprit in the production of dental caries?
   a. *Streptococcus pyogenes*
   b. *Streptococcus faecalis*
   c. *Streptococcus sanguis*
   d. *Streptococcus pneumoniae*
   e. *Streptococcus mutans*

12. One highly unusual virulence factor possessed by *Neisseria meningitidis* is a proteolytic enzyme whose only known substrate is:
   a. IgA
   b. IgD
   c. IgE
   d. IgG

13. Which of the following can cause serious disease without ever entering the blood or even crossing a layer of epithelial cells?
   a. *Streptococcus pyogenes*
   b. *Neisseria meningitidis*
   c. *Bordetella pertussis*
   d. *Staphylococcus aureus*
   e. *Mycobacterium leprae*

14. *Neisseria meningitidis*, like many pathogens, can enter the bloodstream and move from there to other parts of the body. An infection involving bacteria in the blood is called a(n):
   a. hematin
   b. hematuria
   c. streptolysin
   d. pyogenic infection
   e. bacteremia

15. Pertussis toxin is actually an enzyme which hydrolyzes ________ and binds the ADP-ribose fragment to a host cell protein.
a. DNA
b. FAD
c. ATP
d. MAC
e. NAD

16. The effect of pertussis toxin is to cause uncontrolled production of ________ within the affected cells, which in turn results in phosphorylation of many cellular proteins with effects including anaphylaxis, and hypoglycemia.
a. DNAse
b. FADH
c. cAMP
d. MAC
e. NADPH

17. Which of the following terms is used to describe bacteria whose shapes vary, resulting in difficulty in assigning a precise shape classification?
a. polymorphonuclear
b. heterosis
c. polymorphism
d. pleomorphism
e. heterogeneity

17. Which of the following recently developed into a form which causes an overwhelming endotoxemia rather than a rather trivial eye infection?
a. *Haemophilus influenzae*
b. *Corynebacterium diphtheriae*
c. *Streptococcus pneumoniae*
d. *Haemophilus aegyptius*
e. *Mycobacterium tuberculosis*

18. One of the life-threatening effects of infections caused by ____________ is the production of a pseudomembrane in the trachea which may block respiratory pathways and require a tracheotomy.
a. *Haemophilus influenzae*
b. *Corynebacterium diphtheriae*
c. *Streptococcus pneumoniae*
d. *Haemophilus aegyptius*
e. *Mycobacterium tuberculosis*

19. Which of the following organisms is acid-fast?
a. *Haemophilus influenzae*
b. *Corynebacterium diphtheriae*
c. *Streptococcus pneumoniae*
d. *Haemophilus aegyptius*
e. *Mycobacterium tuberculosis*

20. The development of lepromatous leprosy is tied to a defect in the victim's:
   a. antibody production
   b. histamine production
   c. cell-mediated immunity
   d. phagocyte activity
   e. $H_2O_2$ production

21. It appears that the most severe effects of primary atypical pneumonia are due to:
   a. toxins secreted by the causative agent
   b. secondary infections by *Staph. aureus*
   c. massive antigen-antibody deposits in the lung
   d. an autoimmune response
   e. persistent reactivation infections

22. Legionnaires' disease is caused by an organism which is very commonly found growing in:
   a. hot-water heaters
   b. heating ducts
   c. old automobile tires
   d. pigeon feces
   e. beaver lodges

23. The causative agent of psittacosis might well be isolated from:
   a. hot-water heaters
   b. heating ducts
   c. old automobile tires
   d. pigeon feces
   e. beaver lodges

24. The marked resistance to high temperatures and the ability to be transmitted by the respiratory route are both related to the ___________ form of *Coxiella burnetii*.
   a. ATV
   b. SCV
   c. LCV
   d. MTV

25. All of the following exist as dimorphic forms EXCEPT:
   a. *Blastomyces dermatitidis*
   b. *Histoplasma capsulatum*
   c. *Coccidioides immitis*
   d. *Cryptococcus neoformans*
   e. *Geotrichum candidum*

<u>ANSWERS TO LEARNING ACTIVITIES</u>

Fill-in-the-blank questions:

1. Sherman; 2. α-hemolysis; 3. Lysogenic conversion; 4. Dimorphic.
5-20: see below

| ORGANISM | DISEASE | CONTROL |
|---|---|---|
| ~~*B. pertussis*~~<br>Group A streptococci | Scarlet fever, Rheumatic fever | Penicillin |
| ~~*B. dermatitidis*~~<br>Group B streptococci | Neonatal septi-cemia & meningitis | Immunize mothers |
| ~~*C. diphtheriae*~~<br>*S. pneumoniae* | Lobar pneumonia | Polysaccharide vaccine |
| ~~*C. immitis*~~<br>*N. meningitidis* | Epidemic meningitis | Vaccine for groups A,C,Y |
| ~~*S. pneumoniae*~~<br>*B. pertussis* | Whooping cough | Heat-killed vaccine |
| ~~*C. pneumoniae*~~<br>*H. influenzae* | Meningitis and epiglottitis | No vaccine available |
| ~~*C. psittici*~~<br>*C. diphtheriae* | Diphtheria | Toxoid vaccine |
| ~~Group A streptococci~~<br>*M. tuberculosis* | Tuberculosis | Vaccine in Europe |
| ~~Group B streptococci~~<br>*M. leprae* | Leprosy | Treat active cases |
| ~~*H. capsulatum*~~<br>*M. pneumoniae* | Primary atypical pneumonia | Vaccines |
| ~~*H. influenzae*~~<br>*L. pneumophila* | Legionnaires' disease | None available |
| ~~*L. pneumophila*~~<br>*C. psittici* | Ornithosis | None available |
| ~~*M. leprae*~~<br>*C. pneumoniae* | Pneumonia | None available |
| ~~*M. pneumoniae*~~<br>*B. dermatitidis* | Blastomycosis | Amphotericin B |
| ~~*M. tuberculosis*~~<br>*H. capsulatum* | Histoplasmosis | Amphotericin B |
| ~~*N. meningitidis*~~<br>*C. immitis* | Coccidioidomycosis | Amphotericin B |

| MASTERY TEST ANSWERS | | | | | | | | | | | | |
|---|---|---|---|---|---|---|---|---|---|---|---|---|
| 1<br>c | 2<br>b | 3<br>c | 4<br>a | 5<br>b | 6<br>e | | 7<br>d | 8<br>a | 9<br>d | 10<br>d | 11<br>e | 12<br>a |
| 13<br>c | 14<br>e | 15<br>e | 16<br>c | 17<br>d | 18<br>b | 19<br>e | 20<br>c | 21<br>d | 22<br>a | 23<br>d | 24<br>b | 25<br>d |

## CHAPTER 25

## VIRUSES THAT ENTER THE BODY VIA THE RESPIRATORY TRACT

### CHAPTER SUMMARY

Many viruses enter the body *via* the respiratory route; some remain there to cause a **localized infection**, others spread to cause a **generalized infection**. One of the most common general types of localized infection is known as the **common cold syndrome**, caused by such a large variety of viruses that developing a vaccine against the syndrome is a highly unlikely event. The **rhinoviruses** (a member of the RNA **picornavirus** group) constitute the largest number of common cold viruses - over **100 serological types**. Humans are the only hosts of these viruses, none of which cause any generalized infections.

The **parainfluenza viruses** have also been implicated in causing the common cold; a mild disease in adults, a potentially more serious **pneumonia** in children and infants. Infants are also subject to develop **laryngotracheobronchitis** (**croup**). These RNA viruses are members of the **paramyxovirus** group. A prominent characteristic of the group is the production of a **hemagglutinin** (binds to and causes clumping of red blood cells) and a **neuraminidase** (enzyme which attacks neuraminic acid in cell membranes). The natural function of these agents is to allow the virus to bind to host cells (hemagglutinin) and to penetrate into the host cell (neuraminidase).

The **respiratory syncytial virus** (**RSV**) is also associated with the common cold syndrome. RSV is a member of the **paramyxoviruses**, like the parainfluenza viruses. It causes a mild disease in adults but a much more serious set of lower respiratory tract infections in **infants**. **Bronchiolitis** and **pneumonia** both occur in epidemic form in infants, some with high mortality. The **coronaviruses** are small RNA viruses that cause about 15 percent of common colds. The **reoviruses** (**r**espiratory **e**nteric **o**rphan viruses) are the last group that has been linked to the common cold syndrome. Unusual in having a **segmented genome** consisting of 10 separate pieces of **double-stranded RNA**, these viruses are very widespread.

The **adenoviruses** are double-stranded DNA viruses that exist in at least 41 antigenic types, some of which are **oncogenic** in animals (none has been implicated in humans). They may occur as very slow growing "**latent**" residents of the **adenoids**, or may cause acute respiratory disease and **ocular** infections, especially in children. Up to 19 percent of **febrile upper respiratory infections** in children are caused by adenoviruses. They may also be involved in **diarrhea** in children. **Fatal disseminated infections** sometimes occur in immunosuppressed renal transplant patients.

The **influenza viruses** are RNA viruses that are members of the orthomyxovirus group. They have a segmented genome consisting of eight distinct pieces of RNA. The capsid is surrounded by a membrane-like **envelope** in which is embedded two types of "spikes" - **neuraminidase** spikes and **hemagglutinin** spikes. Antibodies against the hemagglutinin are effective in neutralizing the virus. The disease produced by these viruses involves fever, chills, headache, generalized muscular aching, and loss of appetite. **Fatalities** are sometimes due to virus-induced pneumonia, but more commonly are caused by **secondary invasions by bacteria** (especially *Staphylococcus aureus*). An occasional complication of influenza is **Reye's Syndrome**, which has been associated with **aspirin** use during influenza, chickenpox, rubella, measles, poliovirus, and adenovirus infections.

Three distinct types of influenza virus exist, **Type A, Type B**, and **Type C**. Types B and C are known only from humans, but **Type A** also infects **birds** and **mammals** such as **swine**. Within each type, **antigenic strains** can be distinguished on the basis of neuraminidase and hemagglutinin differences (e.g. $H_1N_1$, $H_2N_3$, etc.). The influenza virus causes **periodic epidemics** largely due to its ability to **change** its surface antigens in unpredictable ways. All types have the capacity to accomplish minor changes by mutation, a mechanism called **antigenic drift**. Type A has a unique ability to undergo **recombination** if two different strains infect the same cell. The **segmented genome** makes possible the direct production of a brand new strain of the virus combining traits from the bird and the mammal viruses in one. This process is called **antigenic shift**, and can readily give rise to pandemics. These events occur most commonly in China which is on the flyway from Australia to the arctic and which also harbors large numbers of swine.

Current influenza **vaccines** are based on **killed virus** and have the disadvantage of causing **side effects** and being unable to stimulate the production of IgA. A **live attenuated vaccine** based on a **cold-adapted strain** is under development; **split-virus vaccines** (using purified neuraminidase and hemagglutinin fragments) are available but are not as effective as the killed virus vaccine. One hopes that new vaccines will not only be more effective than current ones, but also that they will not be associated with serious side effects such as **Guillain-Barré** syndrome.

**Mumps** is caused by another member of the RNA-genome paramyxovirus group. This virus has an affinity for cells of the brain, the meninges, the pancreas, the testes, the heart, and, of course, the **parotid gland**. Primary infection is of the parotid glands (which swell) but movement to the blood stream (**viremia**) allows spread to other parts of the body. In adult males the testes are a target, resulting in a severe and painful infection (**orchitis**). **Meningitis** is the most severe potential complication. Live, attenuated virus vaccine is available and is effective.

**Measles** (**rubeola** or **morbilli**) is another disease caused by a member of the paramyxoviruses, although this RNA virus does not produce a neuraminidase. This virus is one of the most communicable known and often causes severe epidemics. The disease is **potentially serious**, as it can result in **encephalitis** which often causes permanent neurological injury and sometimes death. **Secondary bacterial infections**, including pneumonia and ear infections, are common. An effective live attenuated virus vaccine is available.

**German measles**, or **rubella**, is caused by another RNA virus. The disease in children and adults is generally mild and is not associated with serious complications. **Fetal infection** *in utero*, especially if during the first trimester, is another story entirely. **Rubella syndrome** includes a host of congenital defects including mental retardation, cerebral palsy, cataracts, microcephaly, and heart abnormalities. The effect seems to be related to an interference with normal cell differentiation during embryonic development. Live, attenuated virus vaccines exist but must not be administered to pregnant women.

**Varicella-zoster** is a double name for a single virus that causes two distinct diseases: **chickenpox** (**varicella**) and **shingles** (**zoster**). This **DNA virus** is related to the herpesviruses and causes a primary infection which can be quite severe in adults. The virus apparently persists in **nerve tissue** after recovery from chickenpox and can reactivate years later to produce the nerve disease, shingles. The reactivation is particularly common in patients suffering from leukemia or other malignancies. **Acyclovir** and **vidarabine** are antivirals which have some utility against shingles; cortisone and other steroids dramatically increase the severity of the infections. An attenuated virus vaccine is being tested.

**Smallpox** was caused by the double-stranded DNA **variola** virus; the past tense is used because this disease is **extinct** in nature. **Vaccinations** derived from the cowpox (**vaccinia**) virus effectively eliminated this agent from the entire human population.

OBJECTIVES Completion of this chapter should familiarize you with:

1. The kinds of viruses involved in the common cold syndrome.
2. What is meant by a "latent" virus infection.
3. How influenza virus makes drastic changes in its surface antigens.
4. The types of vaccines available for viruses causing respiratory infections.
5. Complications that may follow measles and mumps.
6. Why rubella infections are so serious in pregnant women.
7. The relationship between chickenpox and zoster.

## LEARNING ACTIVITIES

### Vocabulary

Having read the chapter, you should be able to define or cite the significance of the following terms. If you cannot, look them up in the text. Terms are presented in the order you will encounter them in the book.

generalized infection
common cold syndrome
rhinoviruses
picornavirus
interferon
parainfluenza virus
paramyxoviruses
hemagglutinin
neuraminidase
laryngotracheo-bronchitis
croup
respiratory syncytial virus
*Pneumovirus*
coronavirus
reovirus
segmented genome
adenovirus
cytopathic effect
antioncogenes
influenza virus
orthomyxovirus
neuraminic acid
Type A
Type B
Type C
secondary bacterial invader
Reye's syndrome
antigenic drift
recombination
antigenic shift
pandemic
swine influenza
cold-adapted strain
split-virus vaccine
mumps virus
viremia
orchitis
measles virus
rubeola
morbilli
Koplik spots
rubella
German measles
rubella syndrome
varicella-zoster
chickenpox
zoster
shingles
variola virus
smallpox
Guarnieri body
vaccinia

Complete each of the following statements by supplying the missing word or words.

1. ____________________ infections involve a spread from the site of primary infection to other areas of the body.

2. ____________________ infections remain confined to the site of the primary infection.

3. ____________________ are the most numerous viruses that cause the common cold.

4. ____________________ against the common cold are extremely unlikely to be achieved due to the huge number of agents that can produce the syndrome.

5. ____________________ is the most likely explanation for the fact that people are nonspecifically protected from colds for about a month after they recover from one.

6. ____________________ is the most important means of passing the cold virus from infected person to uninfected persons.

7. ____________________ are members of the paramyxovirus group, occasionally produce laryngotracheobronchitis (croup) in children, the common cold syndrome in adults.

8. ____________________, or RSV is another member of the paramyxovirus group associated with the common cold, as well as pneumonia and bronchiolitis in newborns.

9. ____________________ cause gastroenteritis in swine, hepatitis in mice, common colds in humans.

10. ____________________ are unique among the common cold viruses in having double-stranded RNA as their genetic material, along with a segmented genome.

11. ____________________ cause a variety of latent infections in adults, upper and lower respiratory infections in children, and cancer in hamsters, mice and rats.

12. ____________________ renal transplant patients may suffer fatal disseminated infections caused by adenoviruses.

13. ____________________ is a material which aids viruses in attaching to host cells; it causes red blood cells to clump together.

14. ____________________ is an enzyme which aids viruses in penetrating into the host cell.

15. ____________________ influenza viruses are capable of infecting humans, birds, and swine.

16. ____________________ is the result of recombination, a process which can produce an entirely new variety of an influenza virus to which no one will have resistance.

17. ____________________ is the most serious possible complication of a mumps infection.

18. _____________________ (also called rubeola or morbilli) is caused by an extremely contagious RNA virus which may cause a fatal encephalitis in some victims.

19. _____________________, rubella, is a relatively trivial infection as long as the victim is not a pregnant woman.

20. _____________________ is the term used to describe the virus which causes chickenpox; its other name, zoster, is associated with the other disease it causes, shingles.

## MASTERY TEST

1-25: Circle the choice that best answers the questions.

1. Which of the following are a group of RNA viruses classified in the paramyxovirus group that cause a trivial cold-like illness in adults but a more severe lower respiratory infection in children, often with larynx involvement?
   a. rhinoviruses
   b. parainfluenza viruses
   c. RSV
   d. coronaviruses
   e. reoviruses

2. Which of the following are the most numerous agents of the common cold, totally over 100 serological types?
   a. rhinoviruses
   b. parainfluenza viruses
   c. RSV
   d. coronaviruses
   e. reoviruses

3. Which of the following are characterized by a genome of double-stranded RNA and 10 separate molecules of genetic material in the capsid?
   a. rhinoviruses
   b. parainfluenza viruses
   c. RSV
   d. coronaviruses
   e. reoviruses

4. Which of the following are responsible for one half of all cases of infant bronchiolitis, one-fourth of all infant pneumonias, yet cause the common cold in adults?
   a. rhinoviruses
   b. parainfluenza viruses
   c. RSV
   d. coronaviruses
   e. reoviruses

5. Which of the following is an enzyme effective in aiding viral penetration into host cells?
   a. streptolysin
   b. neuraminidase
   c. hemagglutinin
   d. streptokinase
   e. myeloperoxidase

6. Antibodies directed against which of the following are highly effective at inactivating the influenza virus?
   a. streptolysin
   b. neuraminidase
   c. hemagglutinin
   d. streptokinase
   e. myeloperoxidase

7. Viruses which damage cells are said to have a ________________ effect.
   a. lytic
   b. cytopathic
   c. amphipathic
   d. agglutination
   e. hemolytic

8. When a virus infection spreads into the blood stream it is said to be a(n)
   a. bacteremia
   b. septicemia
   c. tularemia
   d. viremia

9. Which of the following seem to cause a "latent" or very slowly-reproducing infection in most adults?
   a. adenoviruses
   b. picornaviruses
   c. rhinoviruses
   d. reoviruses
   e. coronaviruses

10. The kind of antigenic changes that all types of the influenza virus can undergo are called:
   a. antigenic shifts
   b. antigenic slips
   c. antigenic drifts
   d. antigenic moves
   e. antigenic selection

11. The genome of influenza viruses consists of:
   a. double-stranded DNA
   b. single-stranded RNA in one circular piece
   c. double-stranded RNA in one circular piece
   d. single-stranded RNA in eight pieces
   e. double-stranded RNA in ten pieces

12. The major cause of death associated with influenza is:
   a. virus-induced pneumonia
   b. encephalitis
   c. bacterial-induced pneumonia
   d. meningitis
   e. pharyngitis

13. Reye's syndrome develops as people are apparently recovering from such viral infections as influenza, chickenpox, and the measles. It has been associated with treating the illness with:
a. Tylenol
b. erythromycin
c. cortisone
d. immunosuppressors
e. aspirin

14. China is the source of so many major new types of the influenza virus because it is on the flyway of migrating birds and because so many _______________ live in China.
a. Chinese
b. rats
c. ducks
d. swine
e. pandas

15. The mumps virus quickly moves into the bloodstream and can infect a variety of tissues in the body. Invasion of the testes causes an painful infection called:
a. testitis
b. viremia
c. pancreatitis
d. orchitis

16. The most prominent effect of the mumps virus in typical patients is inflammation of:
a. the meninges
b. the parotid glands
c. the sublingual gland
d. the heart
e. the pancreas

17. The measles (rubeola) virus is classified with the paramyxoviruses but lacks a surface antigen generally found on members of this group of viruses:
a. hemagglutinin
b. envelope
c. phospholipids
d. C carbohydrate
e. neuraminidase

18. The measles virus is _________________.
a. highly contagious
b. moderately contagious
c. not very contagious
d. contagious *via* intimate contact only

19. One of the diagnostic signs of the true measles virus is the appearance of:
a. Koplik spots
b. crops of rashes
c. purpural lesions
d. vesicular lesions
e. granulomas

20. The rubella syndrome includes all of the following EXCEPT:
   a. cerebral palsy
   b. severe limb deformation
   c. mental retardation
   d. cataracts
   e. heart abnormalities

21. Rubella infection during ______________ of pregnancy produces defects in 80 percent of fetuses.
   a. the second trimester
   b. the third trimester
   c. the first month
   d. the ninth month

22. The varicella-zoster virus has a genome consisting of:
   a. double-stranded DNA
   b. single-stranded RNA in one circular piece
   c. double-stranded RNA in one circular piece
   d. single-stranded RNA in eight pieces
   e. double-stranded RNA in ten pieces

23. Shingles occurs in:
   a. immunologically compromised infants
   b. adults who had chickenpox as children
   c. adults who never had chickenpox, exposed as adults
   d. children who have recovered from measles

24. Which of the following pioneered the use of vaccinia virus as a protective against smallpox?
   a. Robert Koch
   b. Sir Christopher Andrews
   c. Louis Pasteur
   d. Linus Pauling
   e. Edward Jenner

25. Cortisone treatment of individuals suffering a chickenpox or shingles infection:
   a. greatly lessens the severity of the illness
   b. provides protection from viremia
   c. dramatically shortens the course of the disease
   d. greatly increases the severity of the disease
   e. has no effect on the progress of the disease

ANSWERS TO LEARNING ACTIVITIES

Fill-in-the-blank questions:

1. Generalized; 2. Localized; 3. Rhinoviruses; 4. Vaccines; 5. Interferon; 6. Hand contact; 7. Parainfluenza viruses; 8. Respiratory syncytial viruses; 9. Coronaviruses; 10. Reoviruses; 11. Adenoviruses; 12. Immunosuppressed; 13. Hemagglutinin; 14. Neuraminidase; 15. Type A; 16. Antigenic shift; 17. Meningitis; 18. Measles; 19. German measles; 20. Varicella

| MASTERY TEST ANSWERS | | | | | | | | | | | | |
|---|---|---|---|---|---|---|---|---|---|---|---|---|
| 1<br>b | 2<br>a | 3<br>e | 4<br>c | 5<br>b | 6<br>c | | 7<br>b | 8<br>d | 9<br>a | 10<br>c | 11<br>d | 12<br>c |
| 13<br>e | 14<br>d | 15<br>d | 16<br>b | 17<br>e | 18<br>a | 19<br>a | 20<br>b | 21<br>c | 22<br>a | 23<br>b | 24<br>e | 25<br>d |

## CHAPTER 26

## PATHOGENS THAT ENTER THE BODY VIA THE DIGESTIVE TRACT

### CHAPTER SUMMARY

The **oral portal of entry** is taken advantage of by a diverse group of bacteria, viruses, protozoans, helminths and fungi. Three general types of maladies result from these agents, (1) **gastroenteritis**, (2) **systemic** or **neurological infections**, and (3) **oral lesions**. **Bacterial gastroenteritis** can be further subdivided into three classes of ailments, (1) food **intoxications** (or **food poisoning**) resulting from the ingestion of **preformed bacterial toxins** (e.g. botulism), (2) food **intoxications** caused by **noninvasive bacteria** that secrete toxins while adhering to the intestinal wall (e.g. cholera), and (3) food intoxications that follow an **intracellular invasion** of the intestinal cells (e.g. bacillary dysentery).

Bacteria that cause food intoxications are ubiquitous, so *certain foods must always be considered to be contaminated and must be treated accordingly.* ***Staphylococcus aureus*** is the most common agent of food intoxications, largely because at least 25 percent of the population are **carriers**, thus any food that is directly handled may become contaminated. Once introduced into food, the staphylococci must be allowed to grow (they require **warm conditions**) and produce their toxin - a quick-acting, **heat-stable enterotoxin**. Illness generally occurs within a few hours and lasts less than 24 hours.

*Bacillus cereus* produces **two forms of enterotoxin**, thus can produce two different forms of food poisoning. The first toxin is a **heat-labile** form which induces a **cholera-like** change in adenylate cyclase activity, resulting in excess **cAMP** production, leakage of electrolytes and fluid from intestinal cells, and **profuse diarrhea**. The second toxin is **heat stable** and results in vomiting. Both forms of illness are frequently due to eating contaminated rice.

**Botulism** is a high-mortality intoxication to the preformed exotoxin (a neurotoxin) of *Clostridium botulinum*. This gram-positive obligate anaerobe produces **endospores** that can withstand boiling water temperatures for hours. Inadequately sterilized home-canned foods are the most common source of the toxin. Smoked meats are occasionally contaminated with spores and can also become toxic. The toxin is heat-labile and can be destroyed by boiling contaminated food 15 minutes before serving. *C. botulinum* occasionally infects deep wounds, producing **wound botulism** when the toxins secreted by the bacteria are carried from the site of infection. Infants are subject to **infant botulism**; *C. botulinum* can grow in their digestive tracts and produce the toxin in sufficient quantities to cause paralysis and, occasionally, death.

*Clostridium perfringens* produces its toxin within the body when food contaminated with it is eaten; it does not, however, produce a true infection. The bacteria undergo spore formation in the digestive tract, a process that results in the release of toxin; this agent is most commonly found in improperly stored meat dishes.

Preformed fungal **mycotoxins** produce **mycotoxicosis** when ingested. The most common toxin today is **aflatoxin**, produced by *Aspergillus flavus*. A common contaminant of peanuts, rice, cereal grains, and even cow's milk, aflatoxin causes **liver damage**, **cirrhosis**, and is linked to **liver carcinoma**.

Many bacteria produce their toxins within the digestive tract which they colonize in a **non-invasive** fashion. These organisms adhere to the wall of the intestine, releasing their toxins on-site. Most are members of the **Enterobacteriaceae** or **Vibrionaceae**; all possess **colonization factors** (allowing them to bind to epithelial cells) and the ability to secrete one or more toxins. ***Escherichia coli***, often thought of as a commensal or mutualist, has pathogenic strains that cause disease. **Traveler's diarrhea** (**Montezuma's revenge**) is most commonly caused by *E. coli* and can be mild or potentially fatal. **ETEC** (**e**ntero**t**oxigenic *E. coli*) produce **fimbriae** that permit adhesion to epithelial cells and one or both of two different toxins: **LT** (heat **l**abile **t**oxin) and/or **ST** (heat **s**table **t**oxin). **LT** works just like cholera toxin; it stimulates **adenylate cyclase** which produces excess **cAMP**; this results in the active excretion of $Cl^-$ and inhibits the absorption of $Na^+$. The net effect is the creation of an electrolyte imbalance across the membrane and copious fluid loss. **ST** is a small peptide which stimulates the activity of **guanylate cyclase**, resulting in an overproduction of **cGMP** from GTP; this results in **reduced $Cl^-$ absorption** and fluid loss. The effect is milder than that produced by LT. The ability to produce both toxins resides on the same **transmissible plasmid**, thus can be passed to other strains of *E. coli*, and other genera within the Enterobacteriaceae.

**EHEC** (**e**nERO**h**emorrhagic *E. coli*) cause hemolytic inflammation of the intestine resulting in copious, **bloody diarrhea**. These organisms have a **fimbrial adhesin** that allows them to stick to the intestinal wall, and produce one of two distinct toxins, **Shigalike toxins I** and **II**. Both toxins kill epithelial cells by changing the 60S ribosome subunit and **blocking protein synthesis**. **EPEC** (**e**ntero**p**athogenic *E. coli*) produce an **adhesin factor** which allows them to stick to **enterocytes** in the small intestine. Their effect is inflammation, cell destruction, and fluid loss. Other members of the Enterobacteriaceae cause similar effects, including *Klebsiella pneumoniae, Serratia, Edwardsiella, Citrobacter, Proteus, Providencia*, and *Morganella*.

**Cholera** is caused by a small, curved gram-negative organism called *Vibrio cholerae*. Like the pathogenic strains of *E. coli*, they colonize the surface of the intestine, release toxin (called **choleragen**), and result in noninvasive disease.

Action of choleragen is indistinguishable from **LT** toxin of *E. coli*; by increasing production of cAMP it increases chloride loss, reduces absorption of sodium, and produces **copious fluid loss** and electrolyte imbalance. The toxin is composed of two parts: the **B subunit binds to receptors** on epithelial cell surfaces, and the **A subunit** enters the cell and catalyzes the **increased production of cAMP**. Immunization to the B antigen results in antitoxic and antibacterial effects which may be transferrable to other enteropathogenic genera. Therapy involves fluid and electrolyte replacement. *Campylobacter jejuni* is a very major cause of diarrheal disease and produces its effects by means of a toxin indistinguishable from the LT toxin of *E. coli*. *Helicobacter pylori* (formerly grouped in the genus Campylobacter) has recently been implicated as the etiological agent of chronic gastritis and duodenal ulcers in humans.

Many bacteria **invade and grow intracellularly** in the epithelial cells lining the intestine (although they rarely leave the intestine itself). Members of the genus *Shigella* (nonmotile gram-negative rods) produce **bacillary dysentery** and are often harbored by **carriers**. The bacteria invade the epithelial cells and secrete **Shiga toxin** which binds to the 60S ribosome subunit and prevents protein synthesis, killing the epithelial cells. The genetic ability to invade the epithelium is carried by a plasmid that has apparently been transferred to *E. coli*; **EIEC** (**e**ntero**i**nvasive ***E. c**oli*) strains invade the epithelial cells, secrete a Shigalike toxin, and kill cells.

**Salmonellosis** is an infection caused by members of the genus *Salmonella*. The genus has been subdivided according to several surface antigens, including the **O antigen (lipopolysaccharide** in outer membrane of wall), **H antigens** (flagellar antigens, phase 1 or 2) and **Vi antigen** (a polysaccharide outer membrane antigen which can cover up the O antigen). Literally hundreds of serotypes are recognized from as few as three species: **S. typhi**, **S. choleraesuis**, and **S. enteritidis**. All are common residents of the digestive tracts of humans, birds, farm animals, and reptiles (especially turtles). Poultry and eggs constitute the largest reservoir in the United States; anything containing **raw eggs** or **uncooked or undercooked chicken** is a potential source of infection.

Salmonella **gastroenteritis** is a common infection that develops 10 to 28 hours after ingestion of contaminated food and can last for 2 to 7 **days**. The bacteria live within the digestive tract, where they invade the epithelial lining and produce enterotoxins and cytotoxins which result in headache, abdominal pain, nausea, vomiting, and diarrhea. **Typhoid fever** (caused by *S. typhi*) is a **systemic disease** which results from migration of agents from the intestine to **regional lymph nodes** and from thence to the **bloodstream**. Once in the blood, *S. typhi* can colonize the liver, kidneys, spleen, bone marrow and heart. Once in the liver, the organism can take up residence in **bile ducts** and remain there **indefinitely**, resulting in the production of life-long **carriers** (like "Typhoid Mary"). Some salmonella infections (especially those caused by *S. choleraesuis*) result in **septicemia** (fulminating blood infection).

Members of the Enterobacteriaceae genus *Yersinia* are normally pathogens of animals but may occasionally parasitize humans, causing abdominal ailments or even **septicemia**. *Listeria monocytogenes*, a gram-positive facultative anaerobe, can cause an intracellular infection called **listeriosis**. It is most often derived from contact with domestic animals, but several outbreaks involving contaminated cheese and other dairy products have occurred recently. **Meningitis** is the most common manifestation, especially in immunologically compromised patients; other effects include endocarditis, urethritis, conjunctivitis, and abortions. **Neonatal listeriosis** can produce an early-onset pneumonia (probably acquired during passage through the birth canal) or a late-onset meningitis.

**Brucellosis** (**undulant fever**) is most commonly a disease of domestic animals which shed the bacterium in their milk. Contact with or consumption of **milk products** can produce disease in humans. The disease may be acute or chronic and generally results in systemic spread to the liver, spleen, or bone marrow. Growth of the organism occurs intracellularly. Antibiotic treatment is unsatisfactory; the best course is to **eliminate the animal carriers**.

99 percent of the residents of the human digestive tract are members of the genera *Bacteroides* and *Fusobacterium* (obligate anaerobes). Both are **opportunists** that can be extremely virulent if introduced to parts of the body where they are not normally resident. **Intraabdominal abscesses** follow contamination of the peritoneal cavity by fecal contents, resulting from trauma or surgical procedures. Trauma during delivery, induced abortion or even use of intrauterine contraceptive devices cam result in pelvic abscesses. In both cases the primary agent is *Bacteroides fragilis*; *B. melaninogenicus* is often involved in lung abscesses, and is a participant in periodontal disease. **Bacteroides bacteremia** has a mortality in excess of 30 percent. The **fusobacteria** are major causes of sinus, middle, ear and dental infections.

Protozoa, too, are involved in a variety of infections using the mouth as portal of entry. **Amebic dysentery** (**amebiasis**) is caused by *Entamoeba histolytica*. The active form of the organism is called a **trophozoite**; inactive forms which leave the body in feces are called **cysts**. The trophozoites invade the intestinal mucosa where they often ingest body cells, including red blood cells. The infection produces intestinal ulcers which may become secondarily infected by bacteria. Severe **bloody diarrhea** is the consequence of this form of the disease. In rare cases ulcers may erode into adjoining blood vessels, causing intraluminal bleeding and permitting the spread of the amebas to the liver, diaphragm, and lung. Asymptomatic infections occur much more often and can produce chronic **carriers**.

***Naegleria fowlerii*** is a free-living amoeboflagellate that causes a lethal meningoencephalitis. It enters the body through the nasal mucosa from the warm fresh water ponds in which it lives and can produce death in 3 to 6 days after initial symptoms develop. *Acanthamoeba* is another free-living amoeboflagellate which causes a severe keratitis which can result in blindness. Infection of the **cornea** is especially common in wearers of **contact lenses**.

***Balantidium coli*** is the causative agent of **balantidiasis**, an acute gastrointestinal illness similar to amebic dysentery. Trophozoites of *B. coli* are **ciliated** and are natural residents of the digestive tracts of swine. ***Giardia lamblia*** is a flagellated protozoan which causes an enteric ailment called **giardiasis**; it is acquired by the fecal-oral route and is often waterborne. **Toxoplasmosis** is a systemic illness caused by *Toxoplasma gondii* (a sporozoan); in immunocompromised hosts encephalitis, myocarditis and pneumonia are possible outcomes. If a **human embryo** is infected *in utero*, the infection may cause mental retardation, blindness, and convulsions. Pregnant women should avoid all contact with **domestic cats** to avoid contracting the agent that could do such damage to her offspring. *Cryptosporidium* is another sporozoan which enters the body *via* the oral route. It remains in the digestive tract where it causes acute gastroenteritis, especially in children and in victims of AIDS. **Cryptosporidiosis** contributes to the death of many immunocompromised individuals.

**Platyhelminth** (flatworm) parasites frequently enter the body through the mouth; the **cestodes (tapeworms)** always do. Such parasites develop into the typical intestinal tapeworm only in their **definitive host**; in any **intermediate hosts** they produce a **disseminated infestation**. *Taenia saginata* (the **beef tapeworm**), for example, produces widespread larvae (**cysticercus**) in cattle; each consisting of a fluid-filled bladder containing the invaginated **scolex** (head) of a worm. If improperly-cooked beef containing bladder worms is ingested by a human, the cysticercus develops into a tapeworm in the small intestine. *Taenia solium* (**pork tapeworm**) can develop into tapeworms in humans, but can also (if eggs are consumed instead of cysticerci) develop into disseminated larvae causing **cysticercosis,** which can be fatal. *Hymenolepsis nana* (**dwarf tapeworm**) is unusual in having no intermediate host. Eggs hatch in the intestine, enter the mucosa and develop into the larval state (cysticercoid). The larvae develop into adults that reenter the lumen of the intestine.

*Echinococcus granulosus* normally uses sheep or cattle as intermediate hosts but can use humans (acquired from contact with dogs, wolves, coyotes, fox). The eggs develop into larvae (**oncospheres**) which burrow out of the intestine into the lymphatics or bloodstream from whence they spread to the liver, the lungs, kidneys, bone or brain. Each larva forms a **hydatid cyst** (a fluid-filled bladder) in which many scoleces develop. **Hydatid disease** in humans generally involves a single cyst which is often mistaken for a tumor; surgical removal is required.

**Trematodes (flukes)** are flatworms that always (except for blood flukes) enter the body as **metacercaria larvae. Clonorchis sinensis** (Chinese liver fluke) is the most common human fluke, although **Fasciola hepatica** (normally a sheep liver parasite) and **Fasciolopsis buski** (normally an intestinal parasite of pigs) occasionally infest humans. *Paragonimus westermani* causes **paragonimiasis**, a human lung fluke infestation. Humans become infected by eating raw or improperly cooked crabs or crayfish.

Members of the **Phylum Nematoda** include some important human parasites. *Trichinella spiralis* causes the disseminated infestation **trichinosis** in humans that consume improperly cooked, contaminated **pork** or **bear** meat. Only the pregnant female worms leave the intestine, moving into the mucosa where her larvae are released into blood vessels. They travel to **skeletal muscle** (less commonly lungs, heart, eyelids, meninges and brain) and become encysted, causing pain, and tissue destruction. Death of the victim is a rare occurrence.

*Trichuris trichiura* is the agent of **whipworm disease**, common in the tropics (500 million victims). Adult worms live in the **caecum** for many years; heavy infestation produces **chronic diarrhea**, pain, vomiting, and anemia. Proper sanitation is the most effective control. *Ascaris lumbricoides* is another roundworm parasite of humans, involving almost one billion victims worldwide. The fecal-oral route is used by the eggs to reach the intestine where they hatch. Larvae move into the bloodstream and eventually reach the **lungs**, where they mature. Coughed up, the adult worm returns to the intestine where they breed; occasionally they reinvade the liver, bile ducts, and gall bladder. **Loeffler's syndrome**, an asthmalike condition, results from hypersensitivity to larvae in the lung. Again, proper sanitation is the best means of control. *Enterobius vermicularis*, the **pinworm**, is an exclusive parasite of humans. The most prominent symptom is intense **perianal itching** caused by eggs laid in this region by adult females. Scratching allows reinfection by means of hand-to-mouth contact.

**Viral gastroenteritis** has a incidence second only to the common cold and is caused by two main classes of viruses: the **Norwalk-like agents**, and the **rotaviruses**. The Norwalk-like agents cause an acute infectious gastroenteritis most commonly in children; symptoms include nausea and vomiting plus diarrhea. **Rotaviruses** (their capsid resembles a wheel) are related to the reoviruses and, like them, have a segmented genome consisting of multiple pieces of double-stranded RNA; they are widespread in the animal kingdom. Acute gastroenteritis can be **fatal** to infants due to **dehydration** and loss of electrolytes - only **cholera** carries a higher risk of dehydration.

Some enteric viruses go beyond the digestive tract to produce **systemic illness**. One of the best known and studied is the **polio virus**, a member of the **Picornaviridae** and the causative agent of **poliomyelitis**. The natural environment of this virus is the human **oropharynx** and **intestine**, where it most commonly causes **abortive polio**, a mild disease. In 0.1 percent of cases the virus spreads *via* the bloodstream to the meninges where it invades the nervous system and results in **paralytic polio**. In **bulbar poliomyelitis** cells controlling respiration are affected. Vaccines have largely controlled this illness in the developed world, although it is still quite common in less-developed countries.

The **coxsackieviruses** cause a variety of diseases from the common cold to lethal myocarditis of the newborn. **Herpangina** (severe sore throat), **pleurodynia** (Bornholm disease - pain in the chest), **summer grippe** (flu-like) and **aseptic meningitis** are the most common manifestations of infection by this group of viruses. The viruses apparently spread *via* the fecal-oral route. The **echoviruses** (**e**nteric **c**ytopathic **h**uman **o**rphan viruses) cause illness similar to those caused by the coxsackieviruses, including (1) aseptic meningitis, (2) respiratory infections similar to the common cold, (3) gastroenteritis, and (4) disseminated infections involving fever, rashes, etc.

**Hepatitis** is a term used to describe an inflammation of the liver. At least five major types of viral hepatitis have been identified: **hepatitis A**, **hepatitis B**, **hepatitis C**, **hepatitis E**, and **delta** ($\delta$) **virus hepatitis**. **Hepatitis A** is a **highly contagious** disease caused by a picornavirus which is very resistant to environmental hazards. The incubation period varies from 15 to 40 days followed by an acute phase involving fever, nausea, vomiting and, often, jaundice. Complete recovery may require 8 to 12 weeks but does not involve any persistent infection with continuous viremia. There are **no asymptomatic carriers** and the disease is not spread *via* blood transfusions.

**Hepatitis B** is a much more serious illness once called **serum hepatitis. Chronic, persistent infections** (some life-long) are not uncommon, and there is a strong relationship between hepatitis B infection and **cancer of the liver**. The intact virus is called a **Dane particle** and consists of a double-stranded DNA and protein core (the **$HB_CAg$**) surrounded by an outer coat of viral protein (the **$HB_SAg$**). Once thought to be spread exclusively **via** contaminated needles and blood transfusions, it is now known that the **fecal-oral** route and **sexual transmission** are involved in its spread. The virus is found in feces, urine, saliva, vaginal secretions, semen, and breast milk. Newborns often contract the disease from their infected mothers. Several vaccines are currently being evaluated.

**NANB** (non-A, non-B) hepatitis is responsible for the majority of transfusion-related hepatitis cases. **Hepatitis C** alone accounts for 90 percent of such illnesses. The disease also spreads sexually and by means of IV drug use. Like hepatitis B, C can result in chronic persistent infections. **Hepatitis E** (for enteric) spreads *via* the fecal-oral route and is a major cause of illness in the less-developed countries. Yet another cause of hepatitis is a defective agent called the **delta ($\delta$) virus (HDV)**; it is incapable of making its own virus coat proteins. The only way this virus can replicate is if it simultaneously infects a cell with **hepatitis B**, which provides it with capsid proteins. Chronic, persistent illness is common with these two viruses.

**Vincent's angina**, also called **trench mouth**, is an ulcerative mouth infection which may well be initiated by a **herpesvirus**. It is generally characterized by a secondary bacterial infection involving *Treponema vincenti* and *Bacteroides melaninogenicus*. **Thrush (oral candidiasis)** is an infection caused by *Candida albicans*, a yeast. The disease is relatively common in **diabetics**, children or adults with **avitaminosis** or endocrine defects, and can be a consequence of **corticosteroid or antibiotic therapy**.

**Herpes simplex Type 1** is a DNA virus which causes a lesions in or around the mouth, although the genitalia, the eye, the skin or even the central nervous system can be involved. Primary infection is followed by a **life-long latent infection** which can be reactivated by exposure to the sun, heat, cold, or emotional stress. A fatal encephalitis sometimes occurs in newborns. **Cytomegaloviruses (CMV)** are herpesviruses which cause a distinctive cytopathic effect on cells. They are probably acquired orally, but may spread through sexual contact. **Latent infections** are common. Their most serious consequence is infection of a **fetus** before birth in which they can (1) kill the fetus, (2) result in mental retardation and microcephaly, (3) produce CNS damage resulting in seizures and deafness, etc. Cytomegalovirus is the most common **lethal infection** following **bone marrow transplants** and is a major cause of morbidity and mortality in **AIDS** patients and those **immunosuppressed** after organ transplants.

The **Epstein-Barr virus** (EB virus) is associated with **Burkitt's lymphoma** (BL) and is known to cause **infectious mononucleosis** (IM). EB virus has also been associated with nasopharyngeal carcinoma. **Chronic fatigue syndrome** may be related to a chronic Epstein-Barr virus disease. **HHV 6** is a relatively new herpesvirus which attacks T cells and has been implicated in **exanthem subitum (Roseola infantum)**, a skin disease.

<u>OBJECTIVES</u> Study of this chapter should acquaint you with:

1. The bacteria that cause a food intoxication by growing and secreting toxins in prepared foods.
2. Bacteria that cause a noninvasive food infection through their ability to secrete toxins in the intestine.
3. The role of mycotoxins in human disease.
4. Organisms that result in localized invasion of intestinal epithelial cells followed by the destruction of such cells through their ability to secrete toxins.
5. The known molecular mechanism of action of all of the above toxins.
6. The vibrios that cause cholera as well as a number of other intestinal infections.
7. The mechanism of *Clostridium perfringens* food intoxication.
8. The pathogenesis of *Salmonella* gastroenteritis, *Salmonella* septicemia, and *Salmonella* enteric fevers.
9. The mechanism of disease production by the enteric yersiniae.
10. The epidemiology and pathogenesis of listeriosis and brucellosis.
11. The role of obligately anaerobic enterics in disease production.
12. The protozoan responsible for amoebic dysentery.
13. The role of *Naegleria fowleri* as the etiological agent of amoebic meningoencephalitis.
14. The epidemiology of balantidiases, cryptosporidioisis, and giardiasis.
15. The role of toxoplasmosis in congenital disease.
16. The various types of tapeworms that can infect humans.
17. The epidemiology of a hydatid cyst.
18. The diseases caused by intestinal, liver, and lung flukes.
19. The various types of roundworms that can infect humans.
20. The causative agents of viral gastroenteritis and their role in the production of diarrheal disease.
21. The epidemiology, pathogenesis, and prevention of polio.
22. The role of other enteric viruses, such as coxsackieviruses and echoviruses as disease agents.
23. The epidemiology, pathogenesis, and disease characteristics of hepatitis A, hepatitis B, non-A, non-B hepatitis, and delta virus hepatitis.
24. Oral infections caused by *Candida albicans*.

25. Oral infections resulting in Vincent's angina and actinomycosis.
26. Infections caused by herpes simplex and cytomegaloviruses.
27. The role of Epstein-Barr virus in Burkitt's lymphoma and infectious mononucleosis.

## LEARNING ACTIVITIES

### Vocabulary

Having read the chapter, you should be able to define or cite the significance of the following terms. If you cannot, look them up in the text. Terms are presented in the order you will encounter them in the book.

gastroenteritis
food intoxications
*Staphylococcus aureus*
enterotoxin
heat stability
*Bacillus cereus*
heat-labile
cAMP
preformed enterotoxins
*Clostridium botulinum*
exotoxin
wound botulism
infant botulism
*Clostridium perfringens*
mycotoxicosis
mycotoxins
aflatoxin
liver carcinoma
noninvasive food infections
Enterobacteriaceae
lactose fermentation
O antigen
B subunit
A subunit
*Campylobacter*
*Helicobacter pylori*
locally invasive food infections
*Shigella*
bacillary dysentery
Shiga toxin
EIEC (entero-invasive *E. coli*)
*Salmonella*
salmonellosis
Vi antigen
cytotoxin
*Salmonella typhi*
Typhoid Fever
*Listeria monocytogenes*
listeriosis
brucellosis
*Bacteroides*
*Fusobacterium*
*Entamoeba histolytica*
amebiasis
amebic dysentery
oncospheres
hydatid cyst
brood capsules
hydatid disease
trematodes
flukes
metacercaria
liver flukes
*Fasciola hepatica*
*Clonorchis sinensis*
*Paragonimus westermani*
paragonimiasis
Nematoda
*Trichinella spiralis*
trichinosis
*Trichuris trichiura*
whipworm disease
*Ascaris lumbricoides*
Loeffler's syndrome
*Enterobius vermicularis*
pinworms
Norwalk-like agents
Rotaviruses
Picornaviridae
enteroviruses
poliovirus
poliomyelitis

K antigens
H antigens
colonization factors
*E. coli*
traveler's diarrhea
Montezuma's revenge
ETEC (enterotoxigenic *E. coli*)
ST, LT
adenyl cyclase
cholera toxin
guanylate cyclase
cGMP
fimbriae
EHEC (enterohemorrhagic *E. coli*)
fimbrial adhesin
Shigalike toxins
EPEC (enteropathogenic *E. coli*)
*Klebsiella pneumoniae*
*Serratia*
nosocomial
*Vibrio cholerae*
cholera
choleragen
trophozoite
amebic meningoencephalitis
*Naegleria fowleri*
*Balantidium coli*
balantidiasis
*Giardia lamblia*
giardiasis
*Toxoplasma gondii*
toxoplasmosis
*Cryptosporidium*
cryptosporidiosis
Platyhelminthes
cestodes
tapeworm
definitive host
scolex
*Taenia saginata*
cysticercus
*Taenia solium*
*Diphyllobothrium latum*
coracidium
procercoid larva
pleroceroid
*Hymenolepsis nana*
*Echinococcus granulosus*
intermediate host
abortive polio
paralytic polio
fecal-oral route
Coxsakieviruses
echoviruses
hepatitis A
hepatitis B
serum hepatitis
Dane particles
$HB_SAg$
$HB_CAg$
NANB hepatitis
hepatitis C
Hepatitis E
Delta virus hepatitis
defective virus
superinfection
Vincent's angina
trench mouth
thrush
*Candida albicans*
herpesviruses
latent infections
cytomegaloviruses
Epstein-Barr virus
infectious mononucleosis
HHV 6

Complete each of the following statements by supplying the missing word or words.

1. ____________________ develop from the ingestion of preformed bacterial toxins in food.

2. ____________________, a gram-positive coccus, is the most common agent of food poisoning. It produces an illness that starts within a few hours of ingesting the food and lasts about 24 hours.

3. ____________________ is a cellular enzyme whose activity is commonly affected by bacterial enterotoxins, resulting in the overproduction of cAMP.

4. ____________________ is a food intoxication caused by an obligately anaerobic gram-positive bacillus which grows in improperly sterilized canned foods (mostly home-canned low-acid foods).

5. ____________________ is the most common of the mycotoxins in the developed countries; it produces liver damage and may be involved in the development of cancer of the liver. A common source is peanuts.

6. ____________________ are mechanisms used by noninvasive bacteria to attach to the inner surface of the intestine. Toxin production in the intestine itself produces the disease symptoms.

7. The ____________________ and the Vibrionaceae are the two families of bacteria that contribute to the production of noninvasive gastroenteritis.

8. ____________________ of an enterotoxigenic type produces traveler's diarrhea (also known as Montezuma's revenge).

9. ____________________ is a severe gastroenteritis caused by a small, curved, gram-negative organism which produces an enterotoxin that increases the activity of cellular adenylate cyclase.

10 ____________________ is a genus of bacterium capable of invading the epithelial layer of cells in the intestine and producing an acute bacillary dysentery as a primary effect of their toxin (Shiga toxin).

11. ____________________ is another gram-negative bacterium capable of invading the epithelial layer of cells and producing gastroenteritis; it is a common contaminant of eggs and poultry products.

12. ____________________ produces undulant fever, a disease typically transmitted to humans through consumption of the milk of infected animals (goats, cows).

13. ____________________, also called amebic dysentery, is caused by *Entamoeba histolytica*.

14. ____________________ is a protozoan disease which is trivial in adults but can cause severe damage to the human embryo; it is most frequently acquired by contact with cat feces.

15. ____________________, the flatworms, are involved in a variety of human infestations involving the subgroups Cestoda and Trematoda.

16. ____________________ are the definitive host of the beef tapeworm (*Taenia saginata*) and the pork tapeworm (*Taenia solium*).

17. The ____________________, *Clonorchis sinensis*, causes a potentially severe liver infestation most commonly acquired from eating raw fish infected with the metacercariae.

18. ____________________ is a disseminated nematode infestation of humans acquired from eating improperly cooked pork or bear meat.

19. ____________________ and the rotaviruses are the most common causes of viral gastroenteritis.

20. ____________________, once called serum hepatitis, commonly causes chronic liver disease and has been implicated in liver carcinoma.

<u>MASTERY TEST</u>

1-25: Circle the choice that best answers the questions.

1. Which of the following does not produce its main effects by means of a preformed toxin?
   a. *Clostridium botulinum*
   b. *Staphylococcus aureus*
   c. *Bacillus cereus*
   d. *Vibrio cholerae*

2. One of the most important characteristics of the enterotoxin produced by *Staphylococcus aureus* is its:
   a. extreme toxicity
   b. cytotoxic effects
   c. heat lability
   d. heat stability
   e. solubility

3. Which of the following is most likely to cause the death of the human that is victimized by its food intoxication?
   a. *Clostridium botulinum*
   b. *Staphylococcus aureus*
   c. *Bacillus cereus*
   d. *Clostridium perfringes*
   e. *Escherichia coli* (EPEC)

4. The ability or inability to ferment the sugar ____________ is of taxonomic value in the Enterobacteriaceae.
   a. glucose
   b. sucrose
   c. lactose
   d. mannitol
   e. xylitol

5. Which of the following is NOT an acronym for one of the pathogenic strains of *E. coli*?
   a. ETEC
   b. NANB
   c. EHEC
   d. EPEC
   e. EIEC

6. Which of the following is an *E. coli* toxin which closely resembles the cholera toxin, choleragen?
   a. ST
   b. STP
   c. ET
   d. LT
   e. ATP

7. The main effect of the toxin discussed in the previous question is an activation of adenylate cyclase which results in the overproduction of _________ by intestinal cells.
   a. mucous
   b. cGTP
   c. cATP
   d. cGMP
   e. cAMP

8. Shiga toxin and the Shigalike toxins I and II produced by EHEC strains of *E. coli* kill intestinal cells by:
   a. causing them to leak ions and fluid
   b. rupturing their cell membranes
   c. blocking protein synthesis
   d. blocking DNA replication
   e. interfering with cilia movement

9. Which of the following has been implicated in the production of chronic gastritis and duodenal ulcers in humans?
   a. *Helicobacter pylori*
   b. *Campylobacter jejuni*
   c. *Vibrio parahaemolyticus*
   d. *Salmonella typhi*
   e. all of the above

10. Which of the following is NOT a possible source of *Salmonella sp.* infection of humans?
   a. drinking contaminated water
   b. handling infected turtles
   c. eating raw, contaminated eggs
   d. eating uncooked or undercooked chicken
   e. all are potential sources

11. Chronic carriers of *Salmonella typhi* often harbor the bacterium in their:
   a. nasal sinuses
   b. liver bile ducts
   c. esophagus
   d. bronchial tubes
   e. lymphatic system

12. Which of the following is a small gram-positive bacillus that causes an intracellular meningitis infection with high mortality and is acquired by eating contaminated milk products such as cheese?
   a. *Listeria monocytogenes*
   b. *Campylobacter jejuni*
   c. *Yersinia enterocolitica*
   d. *Brucella abortus*

13. Both *Bacteroides* and *Fusobacterium* are capable of behaving as extremely virulent opportunistic pathogens if they leave their normal habitat, the human:
   a. nose
   b. skin
   c. pharynx
   d. intestine
   e. urinary tract

14. Which of the following causes a primary amebic meningoencephalitis which is invariably fatal within 3 to 6 days following initial symptoms?
   a. *Amoeba histolytica*
   b. *Acanthamoeba*
   c. *Naegleria fowleri*
   d. *Giardia lamblia*
   e. *Toxoplasma gondii*

15. Which of the following is a flagellated protozoan which is the most frequent cause of waterborne diarrhea in the U.S.?
   a. *Amoeba histolytica*
   b. *Acanthamoeba*
   c. *Naegleria fowleri*
   d. *Giardia lamblia*
   e. *Toxoplasma gondii*

16. Which of the following causes hydatid disease in humans?
   a. *Taenia saginata*
   b. *Taenia solium*
   c. *Hymenolepis nana*
   d. *Echinococcus granulosus*
   e. *Fasciolopsis buski*

17. Which of the following is an exclusively human parasite, with no intermediate host at all?
   a. *Taenia saginata*
   b. *Taenia solium*
   c. *Hymenolepis nana*
   d. *Echinococcus granulosus*
   e. *Fasciolopsis buski*

18. Which of the following is commonly known as the pinworm?
   a. *Ascaris lumbricoides*
   b. *Enterobius vermicularis*
   c. *Hymenolepis nana*
   d. *Echinococcus granulosus*
   e. *Fasciolopsis buski*

19. Which of the following does not produce a gastrointestinal infection?
  a. Coxsackievirus
  b. herpesviruses
  c. poliovirus
  d. echovirus
  e. rotavirus

20. Which of the following is highly contagious, commonly produces a mild illness which may not even be diagnosed, and never produces a chronic infection?
  a. Hepatitis A
  b. Hepatitis B
  c. Hepatitis C
  d. Delta ($\delta$) virus (HDV)
  e. Hepatitis E

21. Which of the following is a defective virus that is unable to produce its own capsid; it must invade a cell that is already infected by another member of this list?
  a. Hepatitis A
  b. Hepatitis B
  c. Hepatitis C
  d. Delta ($\delta$) virus (HDV)
  e. Hepatitis E

22. Thrush, an oral infection common in the newborn but also occurring in adults with diabetes or endocrine disorder, is caused by which of the following?
  a. *Treponema vincenti*
  b. *Candida albicans*
  c. *Bacteroides melaninogenicus*
  d. *Actinomyces israelii*
  e. Herpes simplex Type I

23. All members of the herpesvirus group have a genome composed of:
  a. segmented double-stranded RNA
  b. nonsegmented double-stranded RNA
  c. double-stranded DNA
  d. single-stranded DNA
  e. single-stranded RNA

24. Which of the following is a member of the herpesvirus group which causes pronounced cytopathic effects on human cells, may persist as a latent infection, and can cause severe congenital defects in the unborn fetus?
  a. Delta virus
  b. Cytomegalovirus
  c. Rotaviruses
  d. Epstein-Barr virus
  e. Herpes Simplex Type I

25. Infectious mononucleosis is one disease known to be caused by ______________, although it has been implicated in Burkitt's lymphoma and a chronic fatigue syndrome.
   a. Delta virus
   b. Cytomegalovirus
   c. Rotaviruses
   d. Epstein-Barr virus
   e. Herpes Simplex Type I

ANSWERS TO LEARNING ACTIVITIES

Fill-in-the-blank questions:

1. Food intoxications; 2. *Staphylococcus aureus*; 3. Adenylate cyclase; 4. Botulism; 5. Aflatoxin; 6. Colonization factors; 7. Enterobacteriaceae; 8. *E. coli*; 9. Cholera; 10. *Shigella*; 11. *Salmonella*; 12. *Brucella* sp.; 13. Amebiasis; 14. Toxoplasmosis; 15. Platyhelminthes; 16. Humans; 17. Chinese liver fluke; 18. Trichinosis; 19. Norwalk-like agents; 20. Hepatitis B.

**MASTERY TEST ANSWERS**

| | | | | | | | | | | | | |
|---|---|---|---|---|---|---|---|---|---|---|---|---|
| 1 d | 2 d | 3 a | 4 c | 5 b | 6 d | | 7 e | 8 c | 9 a | 10 e | 11 b | 12 a |
| 13 d | 14 c | 15 d | 16 d | 17 c | 18 b | 19 b | 20 a | 21 d | 22 b | 23 c | 24 b | 25 d |

## CHAPTER 27

## PATHOGENS THAT ENTER THE BODY VIA THE GENITOURINARY TRACT

### CHAPTER SUMMARY

**Urinary tract infections** may involve the urethra (**urethritis**), the bladder (**cystitis**) or the kidneys (**pyelonephritis**). The urethra is frequently contaminated with opportunistic organisms such as *Escherichia coli*, *Klebsiella pneumoniae*, *Proteus mirabilis*, etc. If they ascend into the normally sterile bladder they can cause cystitis. A common cause of such spread is catheterization. Pyelonephritis (infection of the kidneys) is generally due to an **ascending infection** from the bladder *via* the ureter. The same organisms involved in cystitis are generally involved in kidney infections, although bloodborne invasion by *Staphylococcus aureus*, group A streptococci and *Mycobacterium tuberculosis* is not uncommon.

**Vaginitis** (inflammation of the vagina) is often due to endogenous opportunistic infections. Prolonged antibiotic therapy or endocrine disorders (e.g. diabetes) can result in an overgrowth by *Candida albicans*; the use of superabsorbent tampons is associated with **toxic shock syndrome** vaginitis. Sexual transmission seems to be involved in infections caused by the gram-negative bacterium *Gardnerella vaginalis* and by the protozoan *Trichomonas vaginalis*.

**Sexually-transmitted diseases** (**STDs**) have undergone a dramatic increase in incidence in the past thirty years, aided in part by the "sexual revolution" of the 1960s. First described in Europe in the late 15th Century, **syphilis** continues to be a leading member of the STD cast. *Treponema pallidum*, a spirochete, is the causative agent. Initial infection results in a localized lesion called a **chancre** which usually heals spontaneously. **Secondary syphilis** involves the spread of the agent via the bloodstream to diverse locations where secondary lesions form on the skin and in mucous membranes, eyes, bones, and the central nervous system. Spontaneous recovery occurs in one fourth of all patients, another quarter apparently retain a latent infection for life. Approximately one half of all secondary syphilis infections progress to **tertiary syphilis** years after the initial infection. Lesions called **gummata** form in the central nervous system causing paresis (insanity) or in the cardiovascular system causing aortic aneurysm;

eyes, skin, bones or viscera may also be involved. **Congenital syphilis** occurs when *T. pallidum* crosses the placenta into the fetus; it can kill the fetus or be expressed in a lethal infection in the newborn.

Due to the extreme difficulty of growing *T. pallidum* in the laboratory, diagnosis of the disease depended for years on the crossreaction that occurs between anti-syphilis antibodies and a beef heart antigen called **cardiolipin.** This antigen is the basis for the **Wassermann** test, as well as more modern tests such as the **VDRL** (**V**enereal **D**isease **R**esearch **L**aboratory) test, and the **RPR** card test. Specific tests (which are more expensive to perform) use antigen derived from live *T. pallidum* (virulent forms grown in rabbit testes or an avirulent form - the **Reiter strain** - grown in culture). Examples of such tests are the **FTA-ABS**, **DFATP** and **MHA-TP**.

**Treatment** of syphilis depended for many years on the compound developed by Paul Ehrlich called **arsphenamine** (an organic arsenic compound). Penicillin continues to be the treatment of choice, as the agent is quite sensitive to it.

*Neisseria gonorrhoea*, the **gonococcus** that causes **gonorrhea**, is currently infecting Americans in epidemic numbers. This delicate, **gram-negative diplococcus** is spread by sexual contact. It causes a generally **asymptomatic** infection in females, even though it is a major cause of **sterility** in chronic cases. In males the disease is characterized by **urethral inflammation** and painful voiding; spread to the prostate and epididymis is not uncommon. **Bacteremia** with spread to skin, heart, eyes , meninges, or joints (where it can cause **gonococcal arthritis**) occurs most commonly in pregnant women. Recovery does not confer immunity to reinfection. Active infections have been treated with **sulfonamides**, until resistant strains developed. Penicillin was effective for many years, until **penicillinase** activity was acquired by the gonococcus. Spectinomycin was the replacement drug of choice until resistant strains developed.

**Gonorrheal ophthalmia neonatorum** is an infection of the eyes of newborns which can result in blindness. It is acquired by passage through the birth canal of infected mothers and was prevented for many years by the instillation of **silver nitrate** in the eyes of newborns. Vaccines to this pathogen do not appear likely, as it has a genetic capacity to change its surface antigens (fimbriae and a surface protein called protein II) to new forms.

**Chancroid** is an STD caused by *Haemophilus ducreyi*. The disease is common in the tropics and results in small ragged ulcers on genitalia, regional lymph node enlargement, marked swelling, and pain. Recovery produces no permanent immunity.

*Chlamydia trachomatis* can be divided into 15 different serotypes which cause a diverse collection of ailments. **Trachoma** is an ancient infection of the conjunctival cells of the eyes which, untreated, eventually results in blindness; it is caused by serotypes A, B, Ba, and C. It is spread by direct contact with fingers or contaminated towels or clothing. **Latent infections** are common with this and other chlamydial infections.

**Serotypes D through K** cause **inclusion conjunctivitis** in infants (and rarely in adults). The agent is spread by sexual contact and is associated with cells of the cervix and the lining of the urethra in both sexes. **Nongonococcal urethritis** is the **most common STD** occurring in the United States; the symptoms of this infection are mild, or it may even be asymptomatic (especially in women). **Sterility** due to scarring of the **fallopian tubes** is not uncommon. Infants can develop infections of the conjunctiva while passing through the birth canal and develop an acute purulent inflammation (although blindness is not a complication). **Infant pneumonitis** is also associated these same serotypes, again acquired by passage through the birth canal of an infected mother. Prior to the use of chlorine in pools, adult conjunctivitis from this agent was common.

**Lymphogranuloma venereum** is caused by serotypes L-1, L-2 and L-3 of *Chlamydia trachomatis*. Common in the tropics and spread exclusively *via* sexual contact, this disease is occasionally seen in the U.S. The most pronounced symptoms are due to lymph node involvement; some enlarge dramatically to form **buboes** which may eventually obstruct the lymphatic drainage of the area and produce engorgement of the genitalia and rectal stricture.

**Herpes simplex type 2** (**HSV-2**) is transmitted during sexual intercourse and appears to produce a life-long infection with periodic recurrences of overt disease. Primary infections may involve **painful lesions** on the **vulva**, **vagina**, **cervix,** or **perineum** of the female or similar lesions on the **glans**, **prepuce** or **shaft** of the male **penis**. Transmission even in the absence of overt symptoms is apparently possible. **Neonatal herpesvirus** infections are frequently fatal or, if not, commonly result in permanent damage to the eye or central nervous system. Delivery by **cesarean section** is recommended if the mother has active symptoms of herpes infection. Some epidemiological evidence suggests a connection between HSV-2 and **cervical cancer**.

**HIV** (**h**uman **i**mmunodeficiency **v**irus) is the etiological agent of **AIDS** (**a**cquired **i**mmune **d**eficiency **s**yndrome). This disorder is characterized by a **total loss of immune function** and the subsequent development of a wide spectrum of **opportunistic infections** (including those caused by *Pneumocystis carinii*, cytomegalovirus, atypical mycobacteria, etc.). A high incidence of an unusual malignancy called **Kaposi's sarcoma** is also characteristic. The **retrovirus** that causes the disease infects a number of different body cells, including those of the central nervous system, but its main effects develop from its destruction of **T-helper** (**Th**) cells. Transmission can apparently occur through blood, semen, vaginal fluids, or breast milk and may involve an **extremely long asymptomatic period** in which transmission is possible even though overt symptoms are absent. Blood tests such as **ELISA** (**e**nzyme-**l**inked **i**mmuno**s**orbent **a**ssay) and the **Western blot** analysis can detect antibodies to the agent and are being used both to screen blood donors and to assist diagnosis. Therapy by means of the drug **AZT** (**az**ido**t**hymidine) has prolonged life but offers no hope of a cure.

**Human papillomaviruses** (**HPV**) include those that cause **warts** on the hands and feet as well as several that are sexually transmitted and are associated with **anogenital** and **cervical** warts. A strong association between infection from HPV 16, 18, 11, 31, 33 and 35 and the development of **cervical and penile cancer** is being suggested by Harold zur Hausen and other workers; integrated HPV genomes have been isolated from cervical, penile, and vulval cancers.

OBJECTIVES A study of this chapter will inform you of:

1. The types of organisms frequently involved in urinary tract infections.
2. Techniques used for laboratory diagnosis of a urinary tract infection.
3. Organisms causing vaginitis.
4. The epidemiology, pathogenesis, and laboratory diagnosis of syphilis.
5. The types of infection that may be caused by the gonococcus.
6. The problems involved in making a gonococcal vaccine.
7. The disease chancroid.
8. The range of infections caused by *Chlamydia trachomatis* and its role as the cause of nongonococcal urethritis.
9. Genital herpesvirus infection and the potential role of HSV 2 as a cause of cervical cancer.
10. The epidemiology of human immunodeficiency virus and the mechanism by which it causes AIDS.
11. The problems involved in making a vaccine for AIDS.
12. The types of infections caused by human papillomaviruses and their role as causative agents of genital cancer.

## LEARNING ACTIVITIES

### Vocabulary

Having read the chapter, you should be able to define or cite the significance of the following terms. If you cannot, look them up in the text. Terms are presented in the order you will encounter them in the book.

kidney
ureter
bladder
urethra
cystitis
pyelonephritis
catheterization
opportunistic
ascending infection
enumeration
pour plate
dilution loop
vaginitis
endogenous

paresis
aortic aneurysm
congenital syphilis
Wassermann test
VDRL test
RPR card test
FTA-ABS test
DFATP test
arsphenamine
*Neisseria gonorrhoea*
gonorrhea
gonococcus
penicillinase

infant pneumonitis
nongonococcal urethritis
lymphogranuloma venereum
buboes
T strain mycoplasma
*Ureaplasma urealyticum*
Herpes Simplex Type 2 (HSV-2)
latent infection
neonatal herpes
cervical cancer

| | | |
|---|---|---|
| *Gardnerella vaginalis* | gonococcal arthritis | human immunodeficiency virus |
| *Trichomonas vaginalis* | probenecid | HIV |
| STD | fimbriae | acquired immune deficiency syndrome |
| *Treponema pallidum* | protein II | AIDS |
| syphilis | *Haemophilus ducreyi* | Kaposi's sarcoma |
| chancre | chancroid | retrovirus |
| secondary syphilis | *Chlamydia trachomatis* | T-helper cells |
| tertiary syphilis | trachoma | AZT |
| gummata | inclusion conjunctivitis | ELISA test |
| | TRIC | Western blot test |
| | | human papillomavirus (HPV) |

Complete each of the following statements by supplying the missing word or words.

1. ____________________ is a term used to describe an infection of the urinary bladder.

2. ____________________ is a term used to describe an infection of the kidneys.

3. ____________________ is by far the most common cause of non-sexually transmitted diseases of the urinary tract.

4. ____________________ is a medical procedure which often results in cystitis.

5. ____________________ vaginitis has been associated with the use of superabsorbent tampons during menstruation.

6. ____________________, a protozoan, is a common cause of sexually-transmitted vaginitis.

7. ____________________ is the causative agent of syphilis.

8. ____________________ results from the spread of the syphilis agent from the initial chancre to other parts of the body *via* the bloodstream.

9. ____________________ (insanity) and aortic aneurysm are common results of tertiary syphilis, due to the formation of gummata in the central nervous system and in the circulatory system.

10. ____________________ is a lipid antigen derived from beef heart tissue which coincidentally reacts with antibodies directed against *Treponema pallidum*. It forms the basis for such laboratory procedures as the Wassermann test, the VDRL test, and the RPR card test.

11. ____________________ was the first successful treatment for syphilis; it was developed by Paul Ehrlich.

12. ____________________, the gonococcus, is the causative agent of gonorrhea; it is a close relative to the diplococcus that causes meningitis (meningococcus).

13. ____________________ was used historically to combat gonorrheal ophthalmia neonatorum; its use has been supplanted by erythromycin and tetracycline.

14. ____________________-producing gonococci were first discovered in 1976 and now account for over 40 percent of clinical isolates. This has required the pursuit of other therapeutic agents.

15. ____________________ is a relatively common STD in the tropics which is caused by *Haemophilus ducreyi*; it is characterized by ragged ulcers on genitalia, marked swelling, and pain.

16. ____________________ is a disease of the eyes often resulting in blindness; it is spread by contact with the fingers of infected individuals or contact with contaminated towels or clothing.

17. ____________________ is an STD which is common in the tropics but also occurs in the southern U.S. It involves enormous swelling of lymph nodes (buboes) and sometimes produces blockage of lymph ducts. It is caused by the L-1, L-2, and L-3 serotypes of *Chlamydia trachomatis*.

18. ____________________ can produce a fatal infection in newborns who acquire the virus while passing through the birth canal of a woman with an active infection. Delivery by cesarean section can avoid exposure.

19. ____________________ is the causative agent of AIDS.

20. ____________________ cells are the critical target of the virus that causes AIDS; once they are destroyed the immune system collapses.

## MASTERY TEST

1-25: Circle the choice that best answers the questions.

1. Which of the following is NOT considered to be part of the urinary tract?
   a. bladder
   b. kidney
   c. ureter
   d. urethra
   e. vagina

2. Which of the following is NOT a common agent of cystitis?
   a. *Escherichia coli*
   b. *Streptococcus pyogenes*
   c. *Klebsiella pneumoniae*
   d. *Proteus mirabilis*
   e. *Pseudomonas aeruginosa*

3. The most common agents of pyelonephritis are derived from ascending infections but several bloodborne agents are also capable of causing this disease, including:
   a. *Escherichia coli*
   b. *Staphylococcus aureus*
   c. *Streptococcus pneumoniae*
   d. *Proteus vulgaris*
   e. *Serratia marcescens*

4. Which of the following is NOT a rule involving the evaluation of voided urine specimens?
   a. $10^5$ or more bacteria per ml indicate a urinary infection
   b. $10^3$ to $10^4$ bacteria per ml requires a retest
   c. $10^3$ per ml indicates urethritis, not cystitis
   d. $10^3$ or less per ml is not considered significant

5. Vaginitis caused by *Candida albicans* is not a common condition in normal females but is relatively common in:
   a. anorexics
   b. depressed patients
   c. diabetics
   d. menstruating females
   e. catheterized females

6. Which of the following is thought to have been the most common agent of STD in 1950 but was unrecognized at the time?
   a. *Chlamydia trachomatis*
   b. *Treponema pallidum*
   c. *Neisseria gonorrhoea*
   d. *Haemophilus ducreyi*

7. Which of the following may have been brought to Europe by Columbus' crew, or may have entered Europe from Africa in about 1500?
   a. *Chlamydia trachomatis*
   b. *Treponema pallidum*
   c. *Neisseria gonorrhoea*
   d. *Haemophilus ducreyi*

8. Which of the following is the first symptom of infection by the agent of syphilis?
   a. congenital syphilis
   b. gummata
   c. secondary syphilis
   d. tertiary syphilis
   e. chancre

9. Which of the following results in spontaneous recovery in one fourth of patients, a latent infection in another one fourth, and develops into another stage of the disease in one half of patients?
   a. congenital syphilis
   b. latent syphilis
   c. secondary syphilis
   d. tertiary syphilis
   e. primary syphilis

10. Which of the following can directly produce insanity or potentially fatal lesions in the circulatory system?
   a. congenital syphilis
   b. latent syphilis
   c. secondary syphilis
   d. tertiary syphilis
   e. primary syphilis

11. Which of the following syphilis tests does NOT depend upon antigen derived from *Treponema pallidum* cells?
   a. FTA-ABS
   b. DFATP
   c. MHA-TP
   d. TPI
   e. RPR

12. Infection with *Neisseria gonorrhoea* is commonly asymptomatic in:
   a. males
   b. newborns
   c. females
   d. tropical peoples

13. *Neisseria* bacteremia with spread to skin, heart, eyes, meninges or joints (with consequent development of gonococcal arthritis) is most common in:
   a. immunosuppressed AIDS patients
   b. pregnant females
   c. neonatal victims
   d. asymptomatic males

14. Which of the following is a good description of the causative agent of gonorrhea?
   a. gram-positive streptococcus
   b. gram-negative streptococcus
   c. gram-positive motile bacillus
   d. gram-negative diplococcus

15. A vaccine to protect against gonorrhea infection is:
   a. already available
   b. in clinical testing stages
   c. being developed in Japan
   d. highly unlikely to be achieved

16. The A, B, Ba and C strains of *Chlamydia trachomatis* are the ones most commonly involved in producing:
    a. trachoma
    b. nongonococcal urethritis
    c. lymphogranuloma venereum
    d. infant pneumonitis
    e. inclusion conjunctivitis

17. Strains D through K of *Chlamydia trachomatis* are implicated in all of the following EXCEPT:
    a. inclusion conjunctivitis
    b. infant pneumonitis
    c. nongonococcal urethritis
    d. trachoma

18. *Ureaplasma urealyticum* has been implicated in which of the following infections?
    a. cystitis
    b. pyelonephritis
    c. nongonococcal urethritis
    d. lymphogranuloma venereum
    e. inclusion conjunctivitis

19. Infections caused by herpes simplex type 2 virus can be treated by which of the following drugs?
    a. penicillin
    b. acyclovir
    c. AZT
    d. erythromycin
    e. probenicid

20. Infections of the newborn caused by herpes simplex type 2 are frequently:
    a. asymptomatic
    b. mild conjunctivitis
    c. latent infections
    d. fatal

21. Herpes simplex type 2 infections have been associated with which of the following cancers?
    a. cervical
    b. breast
    c. penile
    d. ovarian
    e. testicular

22. The HIV (human immunodeficiency virus) is a(n):
    a. double-stranded DNA virus
    b. retrovirus
    c. single-stranded defective RNA virus
    d. oncogenic virus

23. Which of the following is NOT one of the common agents of opportunistic infections occurring in AIDS patients?
   a. *Pneumocystis carinii*
   b. cytomegalovirus
   c. atypical mycobacteria
   d. *Giardia lamblia*
   e. *Toxoplasma gondii*

24. The most common overt symptom of human papillomavirus infection is the production of:
   a. buboes
   b. warts
   c. lesions
   d. chancres
   e. blisters

25. According to Harold zur Hausen, HPV DNA is found in ___________ of cervical, penile, and vulval cancers.
   a. about 25 percent
   b. about 50 percent
   c. about 75 percent
   d. virtually all

## ANSWERS TO LEARNING ACTIVITIES

Fill-in-the-blank questions:

1. Cystitis; 2. Pyelonephritis; 3. *Escherichia coli*; 4. Catheterization; 5. Toxic shock syndrome; 6. *Trichomonas vaginalis*; 7. *Treponema pallidum*; 8. Secondary syphilis; 9. Paresis; 10. Cardiolipin; 11. Arsphenamine; 12. *Neisseria gonorrhoea*; 13. Silver nitrate; 14. Penicillinase; 15. Chancroid; 16. Trachoma; 17. Lymphogranuloma venereum; 18. Herpes simplex type 2; 19. HIV; 20. T-helper (Th).

**MASTERY TEST ANSWERS**

| | | | | | | | | | | | | |
|---|---|---|---|---|---|---|---|---|---|---|---|---|
| 1<br>e | 2<br>b | 3<br>b | 4<br>c | 5<br>c | 6<br>a | | 7<br>b | 8<br>e | 9<br>c | 10<br>d | 11<br>e | 12<br>c |
| 13<br>b | 14<br>d | 15<br>d | 16<br>a | 17<br>d | 18<br>c | 19<br>b | 20<br>d | 21<br>a | 22<br>b | 23<br>d | 24<br>b | 25<br>d |

## CHAPTER 28

## PATHOGENS THAT ENTER THE BODY VIA THE SKIN OR BY ANIMAL BITES

### CHAPTER SUMMARY

Intact skin is an excellent barrier to invasion by microorganisms, but any break in this barrier can allow the skin to become a portal of entry. One of the most important pathogens that enters the body through the skin is ***Staphylococcus aureus***, one of three species of *Staphylococcus* (the other two are *S. epidermidis* and *S. saprophyticus*). *S. aureus* is the only species capable of producing **coagulase**, an enzyme which activates a **coagulase reacting factor (CRF)**, which in turn causes **plasma to clot** by conversion of fibrinogen to fibrin. *S. aureus* is also **ß-hemolytic**, producing four different hemolysins ($\alpha$, ß, $\gamma$, and $\delta$). Other toxins produced by *S. aureus* include a **leukocidin** (kills white blood cells), an **exfoliatin** (an exotoxin that causes sloughing of the epidermis), **penicillinase**, **hyaluronidase** (spreading factor), **staphylokinase** (lyses blood cots), and **protein A** (inhibits phagocytosis by binding to Fc portion of IgG, destroying its opsonin activity). The exfoliatin is involved in a disease called **SSSS** (**s**taphylococcal **s**calded-**s**kin **s**yndrome) which occurs in infants and immunosuppressed individuals.

**Staphylococcal pyrogenic toxins** (A, B, and C) are similar to streptococcal erythrogenic toxins and can cause a scarlet-fever-like rash. Their general effect is to cause **fever** and to greatly enhance the susceptibility to lethal **shock** caused by endotoxins. Toxin C may prove to be identical to **TSST-1**, the toxin involved in **toxic shock syndrome (TSS)**. This disorder is typically associated with the use of **superabsorbent tampons** during menstruation; *S. aureus* resident in the vagina or introduced by contamination of the tampon by the fingers grows vigorously in the highly aerobic, low $Mg^{2+}$ environment of the tampon. Toxin production results in **increased interleukin-1** and **cachectin (tumor necrosis factor)** production; interaction with endotoxins produces **fever** and **irreversible shock**.

Other *S. aureus* maladies include: **abscesses**, **boils (furuncles)**, **carbuncles**, staphylococcal **osteomyelitis**, wound infections, **enteritis**, and **pneumonia**. People with the most susceptibility to infections of these types include the newborn, surgical or burn patients, people receiving immunosuppressive drugs, and those with immunodeficiency diseases. Influenza or measles infections predisposes one to staphylococcal pneumonia. An additional problem associated with *S. aureus* infections is the organism's increasing **resistance** to a variety of antibiotics.

*S. epidermidis* is a member of the **normal flora** of the skin and was formerly thought to be innocuous; recent involvement of this species in **nosocomial infections** of **joint** and **vascular prostheses**, and **urinary infections** is changing this perception. *S. saprophyticus* is a common cause of urinary tract infections in women.

***Streptococcus pyogenes*** normally enters the body through the mouth or respiratory system, but can also cause infections by invading through the skin. **Cellulitis** is an infection involving the skin, subcutaneous tissues and the lymphatics; **erysipelas** is an acute infection of the skin characterized by red, edematous lesions; **puerperal fever** is an acute infection of the uterus typically occurring after childbirth.

***Pseudomonas aeruginosa*** is a gram-negative strict aerobe which is a normal resident of the human intestine and skin. It is an **opportunistic pathogen** capable of causing (1) **urinary tract infections** when introduced by catheter, (2) **meningitis** when introduced by lumbar puncture, (3) **respiratory infections** when introduced *via* respiratory ventilators, (4) fatal **sepsis** in people with leukemia or immunosuppression, and (5) severe infections in burn and wound patients. The organism is resistant to many antibiotics and is thus hard to control if it does get a foothold. It secretes a variety of toxins and enzymes, including a **leukocidin**, the enzyme **elastase** (which digests elastin, a component of arterial walls), the enzyme **collagenase** (digests collagen), and a potent material called **exotoxin A**. Exotoxin A has an effect identical to **diphtheria toxin** (hydrolyzes NAD, binds the ADP-ribose moiety to elongation factor 2, freezes ribosome, prevents protein synthesis, kills cells).

**Leptospirosis** is a disease which is contracted by the absorption of ***Leptospira interrogans*** through skin abrasions or through intact mucous membranes. The most common source of the infection is **animal urine**, particularly that of **dogs**. The infection is spread by the bloodstream to various parts of the body including the **liver**, **kidney**, **meninges**, and **conjunctiva**. **Weil's disease**, one variation of the infection, has a fatality rate of 25 percent.

**Bejel** (Arabia), **yaws** (tropics), and **pinta** (Mexico, Central and South America) are diseases caused by members of the genus *Treponema*. All three involve skin lesions with extensive tissue destruction which may involve disfigurement. Bejel and yaws are typically diseases of children, pinta can affect any age group. Direct contact or fly bites can transmit the agent from person to person.

**Tetanus** (lockjaw) is a potentially fatal disease caused by *Clostridium tetani*. The organism is an **obligate anaerobe** with very poorly developed invasion capacity; its spores must be introduced into **necrotic wounds** for it to be successful. It secretes a potent **neurotoxin** which diffuses from the localized site of infection and binds to receptors on spinal nerves, interfering with the regulation of neurotransmitters that control the **relaxation of muscles**. The effect is **convulsive contraction** of voluntary muscles, often resulting in death. **Immunization with toxoid** is quite effective; antitoxin treatment is also useful.

**Gas gangrene** is a deadly infection caused by a number of species of bacteria but especially by *Clostridium perfringens*. The organism is an obligate anaerobe and, like *C. tetani*, can only survive in deep, necrotic wounds. The effects of the infection are largely due to enzyme and **lethal toxin** secretion by the agent (accompanied by massive amounts of gases produced by fermentation). **Lecithinase** is an enzyme which is sometimes called the **alpha toxin**; its action is to hydrolyze the cell membrane component lecithin, causing **cell membranes** to leak and resulting in cell death. θ **(theta) toxin** is a **hemolytic** substance with **cardiotoxic** properties. **Collagenase** (digests collagen) and **hyaluronidase** (digests hyaluronic acid), and **fibrinolysin** (breaks down blood clots) all allow the spread of the organism through tissues. The most common source of infection is soil contamination of wounds.

**Dermatophytoses** are infections of the skin involving fungi that utilize keratin for growth. The infection does not extend into subcutaneous areas of the body. Three genera of fungi are involved, *Trichophyton*, *Microsporum*, and *Epidermophyton*. **Tinea pedis (athlete's foot)** is typically produced by *Trichophyton* or *Epidermophyton*. **Tinea corporis (ringworm** of skin) is typically caused by *Trichophyton*. **Tinea capitis (ringworm of scalp)** is most often caused by *Microsporum* or *Trichophyton*. **Tinea unguium (ringworm of the nails)** may be caused by any of the genera mentioned above, but most commonly by *Trichophyton*.

**Subcutaneous mycoses** penetrate below the skin, can spread systemically *via* the lymphatic system, but tend to remain localized. All causative agents are normal soil inhabitants. **Sporotrichosis** is caused by *Sporothrix schenckii* which is commonly found in soil but also on wood and moss; infections frequently result from inoculation by **splinters**, **thorn pricks**, and handling of **sphagnum moss**. Subcutaneous nodules appear and develop into a **necrotic ulcer**. The primary ulcer heals but new ones appear in adjacent areas and often migrate into **lymph channels** where infection can persist for years. **Primary pulmonary sporotrichosis** can occur if fungi enter *via* the respiratory tract.

**Chromomycosis** (also called chromoblastomycosis or verrucous dermatitis) is caused by a variety of fungi including members of the *Fonsecaea*, *Phialopora*, and *Cladosporium* genera. Commonly found in rotting wood and decaying vegetation (especially in the tropics), the agents typically enter the body *via* a **puncture wound**. Feet and legs are the most common sites of infection which begin as **violet papules** which may last for months to years and spread to adjacent areas. Very rarely the infection spreads *via* the bloodstream to involve other parts of the body, including the lungs and the brain.

**Anthrax** is caused by *Bacillus anthracis*, the first pathogen isolated in pure culture (by **Robert Koch**). The first systematic vaccination was also accomplished with this organism (by **Pasteur**). Virulent forms have a **capsule** solely composed of **D-glutamic acid** (a plasmid contains the gene) and produce potent **exotoxins** (the genes for these proteins are on a second plasmid). The primary effect of the toxins is to produce increased intracellular **cAMP** (especially in polymorphonuclear leukocytes). This effect results ultimately in reduced capacity for phagocytosis (also influenced by the **antiphagocytic** capsule). **Endospores** produced by these organisms can remain viable in soil for many years. Primarily a disease of sheep and cattle, humans are generally infected from handling contaminated hides or fleece. **Pulmonary anthrax** was common among wool-sorters; **cutaneous anthrax** can be acquired from handling hides or by contact with infected livestock. Cuts in the skin or abrasions are required by the organism. Untreated, both forms are generally fatal (as is **gastric anthrax** which is acquired by eating contaminated meat). Animal **vaccines** based on live, attenuated bacteria are effective (although toxic); human vaccination is currently limited to **toxoid** injection which has a short effectiveness.

The disease **rat-bite fever** is actually two diseases with similar symptoms. One version, known as **Sodoku**, is common in Asia and is caused by the gram-negative organism *Spirillum minor*. A local lesion at the site of entrance gives rise to fever, swelling of regional lymph nodes, and a skin rash. The other version, called **Haverhill fever**, is common in the United States; it is caused by the gram-negative organism *Streptobacillus moniliformis*. Large epidemics have occasionally occurred *via* the consumption of **contaminated milk** from infected cows (the first was in Haverhill, MA).

**Rabies** (**hydrophobia**) is a **fatal viral disease** which enters the body *via* the **bite** of infected animals. Bats, dogs, raccoons, fox, wolves, skunks, coyotes, and cats are common reservoirs and generally must bite the victim to spread the disease. Some cases are acquired by contact with contaminated saliva or urine. **Incubation period** is long (1 to 3 months) unless the bite is on the face, in which case incubation periods as short as 10 days are known. Once symptoms start (headache, nervousness, fever, paralysis) the disease is 100 percent fatal. Pasteur developed the **Pasteur treatment** in 1885 (injection of **dried central nervous system tissue** over the course of many days). **Allergic responses** have been dramatically reduced (as has the number of injections required) by the use of virus grown in human diploid cell cultures. Dogs can be vaccinated with a **live, attenuated virus**, and a **recombinant vaccinia virus** which produces rabies virus glycoprotein is being tested for use in wild animal populations.

**Schistosomiasis** is an extremely common **blood fluke** infestation which causes much misery around the world. Unlike other flukes which must be eaten as metacercaria, the blood fluke **cercaria** larvae directly enter the body by **boring through the skin** (the **invasion stage** of the disease). A specific snail is always the intermediate host (none live in the U.S. thus the infection cannot be acquired here). Adult worms exist as mated pairs in mesenteric blood vessels (the **acute stage** of the disease begins with egg laying); most of the symptoms are due to allergic responses to their eggs (characteristic of the final, **chronic stage** of the disease). *Schistosoma mansoni* is found in Africa, South America, the West Indies and Puerto Rico. Eggs are deposited in the wall of the **intestine** and eventually leave the body with **feces**. *S. japonicum* occurs exclusively in the Far East and, like *S. mansoni*, is spread *via* eggs deposited in human feces. The eggs of this species, however, are sometimes carried to the liver and central nervous system where **cirrhosis** and **brain lesions** result. *S. haematobium* is found in the Nile River Valley and in the Near East. Unlike the other two, its eggs enter the **bladder** and leave the body in the **urine**. Proper sanitation would go far toward eliminating this disease, as would elimination of the snail intermediate hosts. Treatment involves agents that are quite toxic.

OBJECTIVES Study of this chapter will acquaint you with:

1. The role of the staphylococci as etiologic agents of human infections.
2. The proposed mechanism of action of staphylococcal toxic shock syndrome toxin.
3. The problem of *Pseudomonas* infections in burn victims.
4. The epidemiology of leptospirosis.
5. The pathogenesis of tetanus and gas gangrene.
6. The types of infections caused by the dermatophytes.
7. The organisms causing subcutaneous mycoses.
8. The virulence determinants of *B. anthracis*.
9. The etiological agents of rat-bite fever.
10. The epidemiology of rabies and the type of vaccine being used in humans.
11. The epidemiology of the blood flukes.

LEARNING ACTIVITIES

Vocabulary

Having read the chapter, you should be able to define or cite the significance of the following terms. If you cannot, look them up in the text. Terms are presented in the order you will encounter them in the book.

*Staphylococcus aureus*
*S. epidermidis*
*S. saprophyticus*
coagulase
CRF
ß-hemolysis
$\alpha, \beta, \gamma, \delta$ toxins
leukocidin
exfoliatin
SSSS

*Pseudomonas aeruginosa*
exotoxin A
diphtheria toxin
elastase
collagenase
*Leptospira interrogans*
Weil's disease
bejel
yaws

dermatid
subcutaneous mycoses
sporotrichosis
chromomycosis
anthrax
*Bacillus anthracis*
Robert Koch
wool-sorter's disease
malignant pustule

penicillinase
hyaluronidase
staphylokinase
protein A
pyrogenic toxins
abscess
boil
furuncle
carbuncle
staphylococcal osteomyelitis
enteritis
toxic shock syndrome
TSST-1
interleukin-1
cachectin
*Streptococcus pyogenes*
cellulitis
erysipelas
puerperal fever
pinta
*Clostridium tetani*
tetanus
neurotoxin
*Clostridium perfringens*
gas gangrene
toxemia
lethal toxins
lecithinase
θ-toxin
fibrinolysin
DNase
dermatophytoses
dermatophytes
keratin
ringworm
*tinea*
Tinea pedis
Tinea corporis
Tinea capitis
Tinea unguium
cutaneous anthrax
*Spirillum minor*
rat-bite fever
Sodoku
*Streptobacillus moniliformis*
Haverhill fever
*Schistosoma*
schistosomiasis
blood flukes
invasion stage
acute stage
final stage
cercaria
*S. mansoni*
*S. japonicum*
*S. haematobium*
rabies
hydrophobia
Negri bodies
Pasteur treatment

Complete each of the following statements by supplying the missing word or words.

1. ____________________ production sets *Staphylococcus aureus* apart from all other species of *Staphylococcus*.

2. Staphylococcal ____________________ are responsible for fever and a greatly enhanced susceptibility to endotoxic shock.

3. ____________________ is a disorder related to TSST-1, which is probably identical to pyrogenic toxin C.

4. ____________________ is an especially serious opportunist in burn and immunosuppressed patients.

5. ____________________ is a disease whose symptoms are entirely due to a neurotoxic exotoxin.

6. ____________________ is caused by *Clostridium perfringens* and several other species of the genus.

7-20: The names of the causative organisms have been scrambled in the following table; unscramble them.

| CAUSATIVE ORGANISM | DISEASE(S) |
|---|---|
| *Bacillus anthracis* | Gas gangrene |
| *Clostridium perfringens* | Tetanus |
| *Clostridium tetani* | Leptospirosis |
| *Epidermophyton sp.* | Wound, burn infections |
| *Leptospira interrogans* | Boils, furuncles, carbuncles, impetigo |
| *Microsporum sp.* | Cellulitis, erysipelas, puerperal fever |
| *Pseudomonas aeruginosa* | Bejel, yaws, and pinta |
| *Schistosoma sp.* | Schistosomiasis |
| *Spirillum minor* | Anthrax |
| *Sporothrix schenckii* | Rat-bite fever (Sodoku) |
| *Staphylococcus aureus* | Tinea pedis and Tinea corporis |
| *Streptococcus pyogenes* | Tinea capitis and Tinea pedis |
| *Treponema sp.* | Tinea corporis, Tinea capitis, and Tinea pedis |
| *Trichophyton sp.* | Sporotrichosis |

## MASTERY TEST

1-25: Circle the choice that best answers the questions.

1. Which of the following is NOT one of the features of *Staphylococcus aureus* which contributes to its pathogenicity?
   a. leukocidin
   b. $\alpha$ toxin
   c. hyaluronidase
   d. streptokinase
   e. protein A

2. The symptoms of SSSS (staphylococcal scalded-skin syndrome) are mostly due to which of the following staphylococcal products?
   a. coagulase
   b. $\alpha$ toxin
   c. exfoliatin
   d. pyrogenic toxin A
   e. hyaluronidase

3. Protein A is an unusual product of *S. aureus* which binds to the Fc portion of IgG and thus prevents opsonization. The effect of this is to reduce:
   a. antibody binding efficiency
   b. phagocytosis
   c. lysosomal breakdown (degranulation)
   d. blood clotting

4. Staphylococcal pyrogenic toxins (A, B, and C) are most similar to:
   a. streptococcal erythrogenic toxins
   b. diphtheria toxin
   c. $\alpha$-enterotoxin of *Shigella sp.*
   d. neurotoxic exotoxin of *C. tetani*

5. *S. aureus* is associated with all of the following EXCEPT:
   a. boils (furuncle)
   b. osteomyelitis
   c. pneumonia
   d. toxic shock syndrome
   e. pyelonephritis

6. *Streptococcus pyogenes* is associated with all of the following EXCEPT:
   a. cellulitis
   b. erysipelas
   c. scalded skin syndrome
   d. puerperal fever
   e. impetigo (secondarily)

7. *Pseudomonas aeruginosa* is associated with all of the following EXCEPT:
   a. gastroenteritis
   b. urinary tract infections
   c. meningitis
   d. respiratory infections
   e. burn infections

8. Exotoxin A of *Ps. aeruginosa* is identical in action with:
   a. pertussis toxin
   b. cholera toxin
   c. botulinin
   d. Shiga Toxin I
   e. diphtheria toxin

9. Leptospirosis is generally acquired by contact with:
   a. cat feces
   b. cattle hides
   c. dog urine
   d. swine saliva
   e. rat bites

10. Bejel, yaws, and pinta are all caused by an organism which is indistinguishable from the causative agent of:
   a. syphilis
   b. gonorrhoea
   c. herpes
   d. toxoplasmosis
   e. schistosomiasis

11. The causative agent of tetanus is:
   a. an obligate aerobe
   b. a facultative anaerobe
   c. a facultative aerobe
   d. an obligate anaerobe

12. The symptoms of tetanus are entirely due to:
   a. an endotoxin
   b. an enterotoxin
   c. a pyrogenic toxin
   d. a neurotoxin
   e. a leukocidin

13. Gas gangrene is known to be caused by all of the following EXCEPT:
   a. *Clostridium perfringens*
   b. *Clostridium botulinum*
   c. *Clostridium novyi*
   d. *Clostridium tridium septicum*
   e. *Clostridium histolyticum*

14. All of the agents of gas gangrene are common residents of:
   a. skin
   b. respiratory system
   c. soil
   d. clothing
   e. urinary tract

15. Death from gas gangrene is generally due to:
   a. toxemia
   b. shock
   c. bacteremia
   d. septicemia
   e. meningitis

16. Which of the following is NOT involved in the progress of gas gangrene?
    a. fermentation gases
    b. lecithinase
    c. collagenase
    d. hyaluronidase
    e. exotoxin A

17. Athlete's foot (tinea pedis) is generally caused by which of the following?
    a. *Microsporum canis*
    b. *Microsporum audouinii*
    c. *Epidermophyton floccosum*
    d. *Sporothrix schenckii*

18. Chromomycosis, a relatively common tropical subcutaneous mycosis, is caused by:
    a. *Cladosporium sp.*
    b. *Trichophyton sp.*
    c. *Epidermophyton floccosum*
    d. *Sporothrix schenckii*

19. The unusual capsule of *Bacillus anthracis* which aids it in avoiding phagocytosis, is composed of:
    a. peptidoglycan
    b. dextran
    c. polysorbate
    d. D-glutamic acid
    e. lecithin

20. Wool-sorter's disease is a human variety of anthrax which involves a ________________ infection.
    a. pulmonary
    b. cutaneous
    c. gastric
    d. renal

21. The variety of rat-bite fever also called Haverhill fever is caused by:
    a. *Leptospira interrogans*
    b. *Spirillum minor*
    c. *Treponema sp.*
    d. *Streptobacillus moniliformis*

22. Members of the genus *Schistosoma* differ from all other flukes discussed in the stage of development that enters the human host; the ________________ stage.
    a. proglottid
    b. cercaria
    c. metacercaria
    d. scolex
    e. hydatid

23. Which of the following is the variety of blood fluke common in the Nile River Valley?
    a. *S. mansoni*
    b. *S. japonicum*
    c. *S. haematobium*
    d. *S. aegyptius*

24. The intermediate host of all members of the genus *Schistosoma* is:
    a. domestic swine
    b. fresh-water snails
    c. fresh-water fish
    d. fresh-water crustaceans

25. Which of the following is NEVER a reservoir of the rabies virus?
    a. rat snake
    b. raccoon
    c. fox
    d. vampire bat
    e. domestic cat

ANSWERS TO LEARNING ACTIVITIES

Fill-in-the-blank questions:

1. Coagulase; 2. pyrogenic toxins; 3. Toxic shock syndrome;
4. *Pseudomonas aeruginosa*; 5. Tetanus; 6. Gas gangrene; 7-20: below.

| CAUSATIVE ORGANISM | DISEASE(S) |
|---|---|
| ~~*Bacillus anthracis*~~<br>*Clostridium perfringens* | Gas gangrene |
| ~~*Clostridium perfringens*~~<br>*Clostridium tetani* | Tetanus |
| ~~*Clostridium tetani*~~<br>*Leptospira interrogans* | Leptospirosis |
| ~~*Epidermophyton sp.*~~<br>*Pseudomonas aeruginosa* | Wound, burn infections |
| ~~*Leptospira interrogans*~~<br>*Staphylococcus aureus* | Boils, furuncles, carbuncles, impetigo |
| ~~*Microsporum sp.*~~<br>*Streptococcus pyogenes* | Cellulitis, erysipelas, puerperal fever |
| ~~*Pseudomonas aeruginosa*~~<br>*Treponema sp.* | Bejel, yaws, and pinta |
| *Schistosoma sp.* | Schistosomiasis |

| CAUSATIVE ORGANISM | DISEASES |
|---|---|
| ~~*Spirillum minor*~~<br>*Bacillus anthracis* | Anthrax |
| ~~*Sporothrix schenckii*~~<br>*Spirillum minor* | Rat-bite fever (Sodoku) |
| ~~*Staphylococcus aureus*~~<br>*Trichophyton sp.* | Tinea pedis and Tinea corporis |
| ~~*Streptococcus pyogenes*~~<br>*Epidermophyton sp.* | Tinea capitis and Tinea pedis |
| ~~*Treponema sp.*~~<br>*Microsporum sp.* | Tinea corporis, Tinea capitis, and Tinea pedis |
| ~~*Trichophyton sp.*~~<br>*Sporothrix schenckii* | Sporotrichosis |

**MASTERY TEST ANSWERS**

| | | | | | | | | | | | | |
|---|---|---|---|---|---|---|---|---|---|---|---|---|
| 1<br>d | 2<br>c | 3<br>b | 4<br>a | 5<br>e | 6<br>c | | 7<br>a | 8<br>e | 9<br>c | 10<br>a | 11<br>d | 12<br>d |
| 13<br>b | 14<br>c | 15<br>a | 16<br>e | 17<br>c | 18<br>a | 19<br>d | 20<br>a | 21<br>d | 22<br>b | 23<br>c | 24<br>b | 25<br>a |

# CHAPTER 29

## PATHOGENS THAT ENTER THE BODY VIA ARTHROPOD BITES

### CHAPTER SUMMARY

The effective barrier of the skin is easily breached by the mouthparts of **arthropods** such as ticks, fleas, mosquitos, mites, sandflies, and lice. If these organisms are harboring pathogens and successfully transmit them, the are referred to as **vectors**. What may be the most infamous epidemic disease, **bubonic plague** (the "Black Death"), is spread by the bites of arthropods. The agent of this disease is the gram-negative rod *Yersinia pestis* (formerly *Pasteurella pestis*); it's virulence factors include (1) **Fraction 1** (F1), an antiphagocytic capsular antigen, (2) the **V/W antigen**, also antiphagocytic, and (3) an **intracellular toxin** which acts on the vascular system and induces irreversible shock and death.

The normal **reservoir** of the plague bacillus is **wild rodents**, especially rats, but also including ground squirrels, prairie dogs, wood rats, and mice. Infection of these animals is referred to as **sylvatic plague**. When domestic rats meet wild, infected rodents, the **domestic rat** becomes infected. As they die, the **rat fleas** move to humans and spread the disease *via* regurgitation into the wounds they cause. Once past the barrier of the skin, the bacillus moves into regional lymph nodes, causing them to swell (forming **buboes** - hence the name **bubo**nic plague); from the lymph system the organism spreads into the blood. Subcutaneous hemorrhages give the skin a black appearance (the Black Death). In some cases spread to the lungs results in **pneumonic plague** which can be spread from person to person without vector involvement. Pneumonic plague is invariably fatal (untreated), bubonic plague has a **mortality rate** of 60 to 90 percent (again, untreated).

*Francisella tularensis*, a gram-negative pleomorphic rod, causes **tularemia** (also known as deer fly fever and market fever). This disease is normally spread among the wild animal reservoirs (especially rabbits) *via* a variety of arthropods, including flies, fleas, lice, and ticks. Humans contract the disease from **handling the infected animals** (especially rabbits but including domestic dogs and cats) or by (1) being bitten by infected **deer flies** (in the Southwestern U.S.), (2) being bitten by infected **wood tick** (in the Midwest and Northwest). Drinking contaminated water is another source of infection. A **necrotic ulcer** develops at the site of the bite, but the organism rapidly enters the **lymphatic system** where it **grows intracellularly** in monocytes and polymorphonuclear leukocytes. The organism then moves into the bloodstream from whence it can spread everywhere. **Septicemia, meningitis**, and **eye infections** are common consequences of the infestation. Antibiotic therapy is disappointing, and relapses are common; in both cases probably due to the intracellular location of the pathogen.

**Relapsing fever** is caused by several species of the spirochete genus *Borrelia*. *B. recurrentis* is spread human-to-human by the **body louse**, all other species are spread by the tick *Ornithodoros* (which can also serve as a reservoir, since it can pass the agent to its offspring transovarially). The primary mammalian reservoirs are rodents, ground squirrels, monkeys, and armadillos. The organism enters the bloodstream directly from the wound and causes **multiple lesions** in the spleen, liver, kidneys and gastrointestinal tract. The fever lasts 4 to 5 days, then ceases; a **relapse** occurs in a week to 10 days. This pattern repeats itself 3 to 10 more times before recovery. The key to relapses is a spontaneous change in the organism's **surface antigens**, specifically the "**variable major protein**" (**VMP**). Different versions of this protein are linearly coded on a **plasmid**, only one gene is active at a time. **Transposition** results in a silent gene moving to the expression site.

**Lyme disease** is caused by another tick-spread member of the genus *Borrelia*, *B. burgdorferi*. The reservoir of this disease is white-tailed deer, mice, voles, raccoons, dogs, chipmunks and birds; it is spread by the deer tick, *Ixodes dammini* (in the east) and by *Ixodes pacificus* (in the west). It has also been isolated from deer flies, horse flies, and mosquitos. The infection begins with a skin lesion at the site of the bite, progresses to headache, fever, stiff neck, malaise, and swollen lymph glands. **Weeks or months later** encephalitis, myocarditis, and musculoskeletal pain may develop. Still later **arthritis** may develop and sometimes becomes chronic. **Latent infections** seem to develop in about 50 percent of treated patients.

All **rickettsial diseases**, except Q fever, are spread *via* the bites or arthropods. Most of these diseases are normally found in wild animals, with humans being accidental hosts. An important exception is **epidemic typhus**, which is an exclusively human disease and is spread by the human body louse or head louse. Since rickettsiae are so difficult to grow in the laboratory, a test involving the bacterium *Proteus* has been developed. The **Weil-Felix test** depends upon the coincidental presence of identical antigens on the surfaces of rickettsiae and *Proteus*; the pattern of serum reaction with *Proteus* antigens helps to identify the nature of the infectious agent.

*Rickettsia rickettsii* is the causative agent of **Rocky Mountain spotted fever (RMSF)**, a disease which is actually more common in Virginia, Maryland, North Carolina and Georgia. The infection is spread by the wood tick, *Dermacentor andersoni* (in the west) and by the dog tick, *Dermacentor variabilis* (in the east). The tick may be the **reservoir** as well, as offspring are infected by transovarian means. Dogs may be another important reservoir. The agent reproduces in the nucleus and cytoplasm of the infected cell, characteristic of all "spotted fevers" and of **rickettsialpox**. The disease is severe and potentially lethal, if untreated. The best defense is regular surveillance of the body for ticks; they cannot pass on the infection for approximately 4 hours (the **rejuvenation period**). Chloramphenicol or tetracyclines are effective treatments.

**Rickettsialpox**, caused by *Rickettsia akari*, was first described in New York City in 1946; it is now known to exist worldwide. The house mouse is the reservoir, the vector is the house mouse mite. The disease is relatively mild, consisting of a primary lesion, fever and chills, and a rash. **Epidemic typhus**, caused by *Rickettsia prowazekii*, is a much more serious disease. Spread from human to human by lice (although it also infects the flying squirrel), it is a disease associated with poor sanitary conditions. It is particularly common during warfare. The disease is characterized by an overwhelming **bacteremia**, growth of rickettsia in endothelial cells of the blood vessels, neurological changes, and a macular rash. Sanitation is the best control. Apparent recovery may actually mask a **latent infection**, as is shown by **Brill's disease** (also called Brill-Zinsser disease). This mild form of typhus occurs in people who apparently harbor live rickettsiae from previous attacks.

**Endemic flea-borne typhus** (also called **murine typhus**) is caused by *R. typhi*. The agent is similar enough to *R. prowazekii* that immunity to one disease confers immunity to the other. The disease is less severe than epidemic typhus. The major reservoir is the rat, the vector is the rat flea. **Scrub typhus**, an Asian disease also called **tsutsugamushi fever**, is caused by *R. tsutsugamushi*. The normal reservoir is rodents, the vector is the larva of mites (chiggers). Severe headache, chills, and fever constitute the main symptoms; recovery may take several months. Miticides are an effective control.

*Rochalimea quintana* is the causative agent of **trench fever**, an exclusively human disease spread from person to person *via* lice. The disease is characterized by fever, headache, exhaustion and a roseolar rash. Good sanitation is the most effective control method. **Ehrlichiosis** is a disease characterized by intracellular rickettsial growth within leukocytes. **Potomac horse fever** (equine ehrlichial colitis) is caused by *E. risticii*, a **canine ehrlichiosis** is caused by *E. canis*, and humans contract a mononucleosislike infection from *E. sennetsu* (common in Japan and Malaysia). The brown dog tick, *Rhipicephalus sanguineus* can apparently transmit *E. canis* to humans, producing a disease hard to distinguish clinically from Rocky Mountain spotted fever.

**Hemoflagellates** are flagellated protozoans transmitted to humans by insects; two genera are important, *Trypanosoma* and *Leishmania*. Hemoflagellates exhibit a change in body plan from an immotile **amastigote** to a **promastigote** with a free flagellum, to **epimastigote** and **trypomastigote** stages with progressively more internalization of their flagellum. All four stages are rarely found in the same host. **Gambian trypanosomiasis (West African sleeping sickness)** is caused by *Trypanosoma gambiense* and is transmitted by the **tsetse fly**. Intermittent bouts of fever are interspersed with asymptomatic spells until the organism invades the CNS where it causes **meningoencephalitis** which is ultimately fatal. The intermittent nature of the symptoms are caused by a **change in surface antigens**; a single trypanosome has several thousand different genes that encode for a surface **glycoprotein**; only one gene is active at a time. By the time an immune response is being mounted, the organism has changed, successfully evading the defense system. A similar disease called **Rhodesian trypanosomiasis** (or **East African sleeping sickness**) is caused by *Trypanosoma rhodesiense*; it is also spread by the tsetse fly, but the reservoir is wild animals, instead of other humans. The disease is often fatal *before* the development of meningoencephalitis.

*Trypanosoma cruzi* causes **Chagas' disease (American trypanosomiasis)**. The reservoir is wild animals (including rodents, opossums, and armadillos); the vector is the **reduviid bug** (also called triatomid bugs). The vectors commonly inhabit houses and bite victims as they sleep; they always defecate when they bite, and their **feces** are loaded with the **trypomastigote stage** of the pathogen. The parasite moves through **regional lymph nodes** to the bloodstream. The liver and spleen are typically infected, but infection of the **heart** by the amastigote forms leads to inflammatory responses and enlargement of the heart. The disease is often fatal in young children; it may be chronic in older victims.

*Leishmania tropica* causes **cutaneous leishmaniasis** (also called **Oriental sore**). The vector is the sandfly, *Phlebotomus*, in which the parasite is found in promastigote form (it reproduces in vertebrates as the amastigote form). The region about the bite develops into an ulcer which heals as a disfiguring depigmented scar. **Mucocutaneous leishmaniasis**, caused by *L. braziliensis*, typically affects the nasal septum, lips and soft palate; if untreated, death from secondary bacterial infection is common. The reservoir for this agent is the dog in India, rodents elsewhere. **Visceral leishmaniasis**, also called **kala-azar**, is seen in the Near and Far East, southern Russia, the Mediterranean area, parts of Africa, and in Central and South America. The causative agent is *L. donovani*, the normal reservoir is other humans and dogs (rodents and other wild animals as well). Gross enlargement of the **liver** and the **spleen** results in **90 percent fatality rate** in untreated cases (arsenicals or amphotericin B yield good results).

The **sporozoa** are a group of obligately parasitic protozoans that have very complicated life cycles. *Plasmodium sp.*, the causative agent of **malaria**, for example, reproduces sexually in the gut of the *Anopheles* mosquito (**microgametes** fusing with **macrogametes** to form an **ookinete**); the **oocyst** forms outside the stomach wall. Within the oocyst hundreds of **sporozoites** are produced which migrate to the mosquito's **salivary gland**; they are introduced into the blood of their new host when the mosquito bites. Within humans the **preerythrocytic cycle** begins when sporozoites invade liver cells where they change into **trophozoites**. The trophozoites enlarge greatly, their nuclei divide into hundreds of nuclear masses producing the **schizont** stage; when cytoplasm and a membrane surrounds each nucleus, the resultant cell is called a **merozoite**. Merozoites may reinfect a liver cell, or they may begin the **erythrocytic cycle** by invading a red blood cell (erythrocyte). Within the erythrocyte each merozoite changes again into a **trophozoite** (called a **ring stage**). The trophozoite's nucleus divides, producing the **schizont** stage which once again becomes 12 to 28 merozoites. The release of the merozoites results in chills and fever, the main symptoms of the disease. These cycles may repeat for 3 to 6 weeks. **Relapses** are common thereafter, indicating that the parasite persists in a **latent form** in some exoerythrocytic state. Control *via* elimination of mosquitos has been attempted; quinine derivatives are useful for treatment of the disease. A vaccine may prove possible, utilizing the **circumsporozoite protein** as the immunizing antigen (effectively blocking the initial stages of the invasion). **Babesiosis** is a malaria-like disease caused by the sporozoan *Babesia microti* (reservoirs in rodents, dogs, cats, and cattle). Humans are infected from the bite of an infected *Ixodes* tick (the same species that transmits Lyme disease).

**Filariasis** is a generic term applied to an infestation by members of the roundworm (nematode) superfamily **Filarioidea**. Females do not lay eggs but rather give birth to larvae called **microfilariae**. *Wuchereria bancrofti* is a primary cause of an **obstructive filariasis** generally called **elephantiasis**. Humans are the reservoir of the parasite which is spread from host to host by mosquitos of the genera *Culex*, *Aedes*, or *Anopheles*. Adult worms reside in **lymphatic ducts** (especially in the groin and genital areas) where a **hypersensitivity** reaction to them sometimes results in the production of fibrous tissue. This causes obstruction of lymphatic flow and ultimately leads to extensive edema in the legs, scrotum, female genitalia, or breasts. Diagnosis is by identifying microfilariae in blood which is complicated by the **nocturnal periodicity** of this stage (few or none are produced during the day, most are released between 10 P.M. and 2 A.M.) Hypersensitivity reactions are best treated with antihistamines and steroids; lymphatic obstructions must be corrected surgically. The drug diethylcarbamazine (Hetrazan) kills the microfilariae and the mass administration of this drug to all infested individuals could **eliminate the disease**.

**Malayan filariasis** is caused by *Brugia malayi*, which is quite similar in its effects to the infestations caused by *W. bancrofti*. The mosquito *Mansonia* spreads the infestation from animals reservoirs including monkeys, dogs, cats and other humans. Mosquito control is practiced by using herbicides to destroy the water plant *Pistia stratiotes*, an essential component of the life cycle of the mosquito.

*Loa loa* is often called "the African eye worm" and produces the disease **loiasis**; it is spread by mango or deer flies from a reservoir in wild monkeys or infected humans. The adult worms migrate through subcutaneous tissues, occasionally causing localized **hypersensitivity** inflammations called **Calabar swellings**. Migration of the adult worms over the facial area, across the nose, or through the conjunctival tissues of the eye is painful and conspicuous. **Diethylcarbamazine** kills both adults and microfilariae and mass treatment of carriers could dramatically reduce the spread to uninfected individuals.

African **river blindness** is caused by infestations by the worm *Onchocerca volvulus*; it is spread *via* bites of the black fly. Adult worms live in subcutaneous nodules but the microfilariae migrate to other parts of the body, including the eyes. Toxins or an allergic reaction to their presence results in **ocular lesions** which produces blindness in 500,000 new victims a year. A skin inflammation called **onchodermatitis** results in thick, wrinkled, hyperpigmented skin. Mectizan, a new drug, promises to eliminate this disease by killing the microfilariae and preventing the production of offspring by the adult worms. Merck and Company has offered to give the drug to the World Health Organization (WHO) for administration to victims and susceptible individuals.

Arthropod vectors also spread viruses, especially those in the **arbovirus** group (**ar**thropod-**bo**rne viruses): the families **Togaviridae** and **Bunyaviridae**. The most common vector is the **mosquito**. The Togaviruses are all enveloped RNA viruses and are divided into two genera: ***Alphavirus*** and ***Flavivirus*** (they differ mainly in hemagglutination capacity). **Yellow fever** is caused by a member of the genus *Flavivirus*; reservoirs include humans in urban areas, monkeys, marmosets and marsupials in the jungle. The virus is spread by *Aedes aegyptius* mosquitos in urban areas (jungle yellow fever is spread by *Haemogogus*). The connection between the disease and the bites of mosquitos was established by **Walter Reed**. The disease symptoms include headache, backache, fever, prostration, nausea and vomiting. Severe **liver damage** is common, leading to **jaundice** on the fourth or fifth day of the illness. Control in urban areas is achieved by eliminating the mosquitos.

**Dengue fever** (**break-bone fever**) is caused by another flavivirus transmitted by *Aedes* mosquitos. It is occasionally epidemic in southeast Asia, sporadic in Central America and the Caribbean Islands. Symptoms include headache, backache, fatigue, muscle and joint pains, as well as fever. Control *via* elimination of the *Aedes* mosquitos is most effective.

The **epidemic encephalitis viruses** are mosquito-borne arboviruses found worldwide. Western equine encephalitis (**WEE**), eastern equine encephalitis (**EEE**), and St. Louis encephalitis (**SLE**) are found in the U.S., while Japanese B encephalitis (**JBE**) is found in Asia. EEE is a severe disease with a **high mortality rate**; even those who recover often are left with a severe neurologic disorder. JBE is also a severe disease, but WEE and SLE are both relatively mild. All viruses are introduced into the victim by the bite of a mosquito, spread to lymphatic tissue and internal organs, then eventually reach the central nervous system. The primary **reservoir is birds**, although horses frequently become infected. The viruses are considered to be so dangerous that diagnostic laboratories will not attempt to grow them to confirm the cause of illness. As usual, the best control is to eliminate the mosquito vectors.

**Bunyaviridae** are another group of mostly mosquito-borne viruses. The **California encephalitis group** is found in rabbits and rodents and is spread by the *Aedes* and *Culex* mosquitos; they cause a moderately severe disease with low mortality. **Sandfly fever virus** is spread by the sandfly *Phlebotomus papatasii*; it is common in the Mediterranean region. The **Colorado tick fever virus** was once included in this group but has recently been reclassified as an Orbivirus. It causes a relatively mild disease that is spread by the wood tick.

<u>OBJECTIVES</u> This chapter should familiarize you with:

1. The epidemiology of bubonic plague.
2. The spread and management of tularemia.

3. The role of ticks and lice in relapsing fever.
4. The characteristics and epidemiology of Lyme disease.
5. The role of arthropod vectors in the spread of rickettsial diseases such as typhus, Rocky Mountain spotted fever, rickettsialpox, scrub typhus, and Q fever.
6. The mechanisms whereby protozoa such as *Trypanosoma, Leishmania, Plasmodium* and *Babesia* are acquired by humans.
7. The epidemiology of the blood and tissue nematode infections.
8. The characteristics and epidemiology of the arthropod-borne virus diseases, including yellow fever, dengue fever, and the viral encephalitides.

## LEARNING ACTIVITIES

### Vocabulary

Having read the chapter, you should be able to define or cite the significance of the following terms. If you cannot, look them up in the text. Terms are presented in the order you will encounter them in the book.

*Yersinia pestis*
bubonic plague
Fraction 1 (F1)
V/W antigens
sylvatic plague
buboes
Black Death
pneumonic plague
*Francisella tularensis*
deer fly fever
market fever
*Borrelia recurrentis*
variable major protein (VMP)
*Borrelia burgdorferi*
Lyme disease
Weil-Felix test
*Rickettsia rickettsii*
rejuvenation period
tsetse fly
*Trypanosoma gambiense*
Gambian trypanosomiasis
West African sleeping sickness
meningo-encephalitis
*Trypanosoma rhodesiense*
trypomastigote
epimastigote
promastigote
amastigote
Rhodesian trypanosomiasis
*Trypanosoma cruzi*
American trypanosomiasis
Chagas' disease
reduviid bug
*Leishmania tropica*
ring stage
microgamete
macrogamete
ookinete
oocyst
exoerythrocytic state
circumsporozoite protein
*Babesia microti*
babesiosis
Filarioidea
filariasis
microfilariae
*Wuchereria bancrofti*
Bancroftian filariasis
elephantiasis
lymphangitis
lymphadenitis
nocturnal periodicity

Rocky Mountain spotted fever
*Rickettsia akari*
rickettsialpox
*Rickettsia prowazekii*
epidemic typhus
Brill's disease
*Rickettsia typhi*
endemic typhus
murine typhus
*Rickettsia tsutsugamushi*
scrub typhus
tsutsugamushi fever
*Rochalimea quintana*
trench fever
*Ehrlichia canis*
ehrlichiosis
Potomac horse fever
hemoflagellates
cutaneous leishmaniasis
Oriental sore
mucocutaneous leishmaniasis
*Leishmania braziliensis*
sandflies
*Leishmania donovani*
visceral leishmaniasis
kala-azar
*Plasmodium sp.*
malaria
*Anopheles*
sporozoite
trophozoite
schizont
merozoite
erythrocytic cycle
preerythrocytic cycle
*Brugia malayi*
Malayan filariasis
*Loa loa*
African eye worm
loiasis
Calabar swellings
*Onchocerca volvulus*
river blindness
onchodermatitis
Togaviridae
Bunyaviridae
arboviruses
*Alphavirus*
*Flavivirus*
yellow fever
*Aedes aegyptius*
dengue fever
break-bone fever
epidemic encephalitis viruses
WEE
EEE
SLE
JBE

Complete each of the following statements by supplying the missing word or words.

1. ____________________ is the causative agent of bubonic plague.

2. Subcutaneous ____________________ gave rise to the common name of bubonic plague, the Black Death.

3. ____________________ are the natural reservoir of the plague bacillus, their disease is called sylvatic plague.

4. ____________________ are the most common source of direct tularemia infections in humans, usually derived from butchering dead, infected animals.

5. Antigenic changes in the ____________________ (VMP) of *Borrelia recurrentis* is responsible for the recurrent nature of relapsing fever.

6. ____________________ is caused by another member of the genus *Borrelia, B. burgdorferi*.

7. ____________________ is a late-developing complication in some patients who acquire the disease discussed in question #6.

8. ____________________ is the only rickettsial disease which is NOT spread by means of arthropod vectors.

9. ____________________ is distinct from the other rickettsial diseases in being almost totally spread from human to human by means of the human louse (although the American flying squirrel also harbors the pathogen).

10. ____________________, also called tsutsugamushi fever, is spread *via* chiggers, the larvae of mites; it is common in Asia.

11. ____________________ is a general term used to describe parasites like *Trypanosoma* and *Leishmania*.

12. ____________________, also called West African sleeping sickness, is caused by *Trypanosoma gambiense*.

13. The ____________________ is the vector of both West African and East African varieties of sleeping sickness.

14. ____________________, also called Oriental sore, is spread through the bite of infected sandflies (*Phlebotomus sp.*).

15. The ____________________ form of the *Plasmodium* parasite is the one that moves from infected cell to infected cell in humans.

16. The ____________________ form of the *Plasmodium* parasite is the one that enters the bloodstream *via* the bite of an infected mosquito.

17. ____________________ is a complication of long-term infection by *Wuchereria bancrofti*; it is the consequence of a hypersensitivity reaction to the adult worms and results in severe edema.

18. ____________________ is a disorder caused by *Onchocerca volvulus*, one which might be eliminated through the use of a drug called mectizan.

19. ____________________ is a general term for the main groups of viruses that are spread by means of arthropod bites.

20. ____________________, also called EEE, is a severe viral disease spread by mosquitos from the main reservoir, birds.

## MASTERY TEST

1-25: Circle the choice that best answers the questions.

1. Which of the following is NOT one of the virulence factors used by *Yersinia pestis* in causing disease?
   a. Fraction 1 (F1)
   b. V/W antigens
   c. D-glutamic acid capsule
   d. intracellular toxin

2. A bubo is:
   a. an enlarged subcutaneous blood vessel
   b. a subcutaneous nodule containing adult worms
   c. a subcutaneous hemorrhage
   d. a swollen lymph node

3. Which of the following is NOT a potential source of infection by *Francisella tularensis*?
   a. the bite of an infected *Anopheles* mosquito
   b. drinking water contaminated by dead infected animals
   c. handling the bodies of infected animals
   d. the bite of infected deer flies
   e. the bite of infected ticks

4. Ticks can be both vectors and reservoirs of some diseases due to the possibility of ____________________ infection of tick offspring.
   a. subcutaneous
   b. transurethral
   c. transovarian
   d. reduviid bug
   e. retroperitoneal

5. Lyme disease is spread through the bites of all of the following EXCEPT:
   a. *Ixodes dammini* ticks
   b. *Ixodes pacificus* ticks
   c. deer flies
   d. mosquitos
   e. sandflies

6. The Weil-Felix test depends upon the coincidental possession of identical antigens on the surfaces of rickettsiae and the bacterium ________________.
   a. *Staphylococcus*
   b. *Streptococcus*
   c. *Escherichia*
   d. *Proteus*
   e. *Borrelia*

7. Rocky Mountain spotted fever is caused by:
   a. *Rickettsia rickettsii*
   b. *Rickettsia akari*
   c. *Borrelia recurrentis*
   d. *Rickettsia prowazekii*
   e. *Rickettsia tsutsugamushi*

8. Which of the following is the causative agent of rickettsialpox?
   a. *Rickettsia rickettsii*
   b. *Rickettsia akari*
   c. *Borrelia recurrentis*
   d. *Rickettsia prowazekii*
   e. *Rickettsia tsutsugamushi*

9. The discovery of a typhus-like infection in recent immigrants by ____________ led to the discovery that the agent of epidemic typhus can be carried in a latent state.
   a. Reed
   b. Koch
   c. Ricketts
   d. Weil
   e. Brill

10. Endemic flea-borne typhus is also known as:
   a. sylvatic plague
   b. tsutsugamushi fever
   c. rickettsialpox
   d. murine typhus
   e. typhoid fever

11. Ehrlichiosis is a disease that mimics Rocky Mountain spotted fever and is spread to humans by the bite of ticks that have fed on infected:
   a. dogs
   b. cats
   c. rats
   d. horses
   e. armadillos

12. Which of the following is NOT one of the morphological stages of the hemoflagellates?
   a. amastigote
   b. promastigote
   c. epimastigote
   d. trophozoite
   e. trypomastigote

13. The intermittent attacks characteristic of Gambian trypanosomiasis are believed to be due to changes in:
   a. cells being attacked by the parasite
   b. a surface glycoprotein of the parasite
   c. the circumsporozoite protein
   d. the variable major protein

14. The normal reservoir of *Trypanosoma gambiense* is:
   a. domestic cattle
   b. ticks
   c. wild herbivores
   d. monkeys
   e. humans

15. Chagas' disease is caused by *Trypanosoma cruzi*; the vector of this disease is:
   a. mosquito
   b. tick
   c. sandfly
   d. reduviid bug
   e. deer fly

16. Which of the following is NOT one of the species of Plasmodium that is known to cause malaria?
   a. *Plasmodium vivax*
   b. *Plasmodium ovale*
   c. *Plasmodium nova-belgiae*
   d. *Plasmodium malariae*
   e. *Plasmodium falciparum*

17. Which of the following is the vector of the malarial parasites?
   a. Tsetse fly
   b. *Rhipicephalus sanguineus*
   c. *Anopheles* mosquito
   d. *Aedes* mosquito
   e. *Culex* mosquito

18. Sexual reproduction of the malarial parasite takes place:
   a. in human liver cells
   b. in mosquito stomach
   c. in human blood cells
   d. in mosquito salivary gland

19. The multinucleate stage of the malarial parasite which can develop in liver cells or in erythrocytes is called:
   a. sporozoite
   b. merozoite
   c. microgamete
   d. trophozoite
   e. schizont

20. Which of the following is commonly called the "African eye worm"?
   a. *Wuchereria bancrofti*
   b. *Brugia malayi*
   c. *Loa loa*
   d. *Onchocerca volvulus*
   e. *Ascaris lumbricoides*

21. Yellow fever is caused by a member of the genus:
   a. *Alphavirus*
   b. *Betavirus*
   c. *Gammavirus*
   d. *Flavivirus*

22. The most severe effect of yellow fever is on the:
  a. central nervous system
  b. liver
  c. spleen
  d. lungs
  e. eyes

23. Which of the following is the primary vector of yellow fever?
  a. *Aedes aegyptius* mosquitos
  b. *Anopheles sp.* mosquitos
  c. *Culex sp.* mosquitos
  d. *Aedes reedii* mosquito

24. Which of the following is a severe disease with a high mortality rate?
  a. WEE
  b. EEE
  c. SLE
  d. ABE

25. Sandfly fever virus is spread by which of the following vectors?
  a. *Ixodes sp.*
  b. *Phlebotomus sp.*
  c. *Anopheles sp.*
  d. *Rochalimea sp.*
  e. *Tsetse sp.*

ANSWERS TO LEARNING ACTIVITIES

Fill-in-the-blank questions:

1. *Yersinia pestis*; 2. hemorrhages; 3. Rodents; 4. Rabbits; 5. variable major protein; 6. Lyme disease; 7. Arthritis; 8. Q fever; 9. Epidemic typhus; 10. Scrub typhus; 11. Hemoflagellates; 12. Gambian trypanosomiasis; 13. tsetse fly; 14. Cutaneous leishmaniasis; 15. merozoite; 16. sporozoite; 17. Elephantiasis; 18. River blindness; 19. Arboviruses; 20. Eastern equine encephalitis.

**MASTERY TEST ANSWERS**

| | | | | | | | | | | | | |
|---|---|---|---|---|---|---|---|---|---|---|---|---|
| 1 c | 2 d | 3 a | 4 c | 5 e | 6 d | | 7 a | 8 b | 9 e | 10 d | 11 a | 12 d |
| 13 b | 14 e | 15 d | 16 c | 17 c | 18 b | 19 e | 20 c | 21 d | 22 b | 23 a | 24 b | 25 b |

# CHAPTER 30

# MICROBIOLOGY OF WATER AND SEWAGE

## CHAPTER SUMMARY

One of the most important medical advances in history was the recognition of the need for pure drinking water; water that is safe to drink is said to be **potable**. Water which contains poisonous chemicals or pathogenic organisms, no matter what its appearance, is referred to as **contaminated water**. Water that has an undesirable appearance or taste (contaminated or not) is said to be **polluted water**. Water which is not safe to drink is **unpotable**.

Water will always contain microorganisms, but pathogenic microbes do not usually make up part of the natural flora. Microbial population density can be measured by the **standard plate count**. **Diluted samples** of water are mixed with liquified nutrient medium in a petri dish, allowed to solidify and grow, then **colonies are counted**. Multiplying the number of colonies by the dilution factor gives one the number of organisms per milliliter in the original sample. Anaerobes, autotrophs and other species will not grow under these conditions, thus the number produced by this test may greatly underestimate the total number.

More important than the number of microbes present is the **kind** of microbes present. **Contamination with feces** is the single most common cause of unpotability, thus even very small numbers of an organism like *Escherichia coli* are more important than much higher populations of normal water residents. Detection of fecal contamination often begins with **lactose fermentation** tests; absence of fermentation in the **presumptive test** rules out contamination by *E. coli*. Production of **acid and gas** in lactose broth tubes is **presumptive evidence** of *E. coli* presence. A **semiquantitative** measure of the number of lactose-fermenting organisms involves preparing 5 tubes of lactose broth each with, respectively, 0.1 ml, 1.0 ml, and 10.0 ml of water added. Consultation of a standard table allows the determination of the **most probable number** (**MPN**) of coliforms present in 100 ml of original sample.

A lack of fermentation may rule out the presence of *E. coli*, but fermentation could still be due to nonenteric organisms. A **confirmed test** involves transferring a loopful of medium from positive fermentation tubes to a medium containing

**brilliant green lactose bile broth**; formation of gas in these tubes confirms the presence of **coliforms**. A **completed test** involves streaking a positive brilliant green lactose broth tubes on **Endo** or **eosin methylene blue (EMB)** plates. The development of colonies with a **green, metallic sheen** is positive; atypical mucoid colonies that appear pink should also be examined. Either colony type is then repeat tested for lactose fermentation and for the presence of gram-negative rods; a **positive completed test** is scored if both are valid.

Not all coliforms are indicative of contaminated water, however. *Enterobacter aerogenes*, for example, will test out with a positive completed test yet is NOT a fecal form. Transferring positive organisms to sterile lactose broth and demonstrating growth at **42.5°C** eliminates all but coliforms from the intestines of warm-blooded animals. Further, biochemical proof is derived from the **IMViC** tests: *E. coli* is **positive** for **indole** production, **positive** for the **methyl red** test, **negative** for the **Voges-Proskauer** test, and **negative** for the **citrate** test (+ + - - ); *Enterobacter aerogenes* is - - + +. Yet another test, the benefits of which are speed and the ability to sample large volumes of water, is the **membrane filter technique**. Water is passed through a membrane filter, then the filter is placed on a special pad saturated with **Endo broth**; the production of metallic green colonies is positive; a count of their number gives one an idea of degree of contamination.

**Natural water self-purification** of streams and rivers used to be sufficient; the actions of aerobic bacteria converted organic wastes to inorganic form (**mineralization**). This process becomes impossible if the organic content is so high that microbial action totally depletes the **oxygen supply** (anaerobic activity is simply too inefficient). High concentrations of **inorganic nutrients**, particularly **phosphate**, produces another problem - the **overgrowth of algae**. When the algae die and decompose, further depletion of oxygen supplies occurs, fish die, and the organic load fails to be reduced. Petroleum pollution and the accumulation of **nonbiodegradable synthetics** further complicates the situation.

Water that is contaminated with enteric disease organisms has the capacity to transmit typhoid fever, paratyphoid fever, bacillary and amebic dysentery, giardiasis, cholera, poliomyelitis, hepatitis, and *Leptospira*. Such water must be **purified** before it can be consumed. The first step in water purification is generally the removal of suspended materials by means of **flocculation** (addition of aluminum potassium sulfate - **alum**). Many microorganisms settle out with the floc. The second step involves **filtration**, generally through sand and gravel. Such filtration removes more suspended materials and the cysts of *Giardia*. The final step in water purification involves **chemical treatment** with chlorine or ozone. Ozone has the advantage of improving the taste of water but its much higher cost makes it less practical.

The **primary goal of sewage disposal** is the reduction of the **biological oxygen demand (BOD)** of the material, thus reducing the likelihood that its release into rivers will result in serious depletion of oxygen. **Secondary goals** are to **inactivate pathogenic microorganisms** and to **remove excess** amounts of **phosphate** and **nitrate**. **Primary treatment** involves the removal of most of the solids in the waste flow by means of **flocculation** in large **sedimentation tanks**. The sedimented material, called **sludge**, is often further processed in other tanks by means of **anaerobic digestion**; anaerobic bacteria convert much of the organic matter to **methane** (which can be collected and burned for energy) and **carbon dioxide**. The final product may be incinerated, used as a fertilizer, or as a soil conditioner. It is important to realize, however, that sludge may still contain dangerous levels of **enteroviruses** (poliovirus, coxsackieviruses, hepatitis A virus, etc.).

**Secondary treatment** involves removal of the **soluble organic materials** and residual solids. The purpose is to reduce the **BOD** and is accomplished *via* **aerobic breakdown**. In the **activated sludge process** the effluent is aerated constantly and is heavily inoculated with bacteria by incorporating **activated sludge** (flocs that settled down in previous tanks). An alternative method, called the **trickle filter**, involves spraying the effluent on **gravel beds** 4 to 6 feet deep. **Mature beds** develop high levels of aerobic bacteria on the gravel surfaces and rapidly oxidize the organic materials.

**Tertiary treatment** is an expensive process that is not always practiced. Its purpose is to convert all **nitrogen** compounds to ammonia (which is volatile and can be removed in scrubbing towers) and to precipitate all **phosphates** as calcium phosphate. Sewage carried through tertiary treatment is considered to be environmentally benign.

OBJECTIVES The contents of this chapter are designed to acquaint you with:

1. The types of microorganisms one might find in water.
2. Methods for the enumeration of bacteria in water.
3. Tests for water potability.
4. The role of bacteria in the purification of streams.
5. Disease organisms spread via water and methods for their control.
6. Methods for sewage disposal designed to decrease the biological oxygen demand and to eliminate enteric pathogens.

## LEARNING ACTIVITIES

### Vocabulary

Having read the chapter, you should be able to define or cite the significance of the following terms. If you cannot, look them up in the text. Terms are presented in the order you will encounter them in the book.

| | | |
|---|---|---|
| water purification | coliforms | ozone |
| | fecal coliforms | BOD |

| | | |
|---|---|---|
| potable | IMViC tests | epidermo-phytosis |
| contaminated | indole | primary treatment |
| polluted | methyl red | sedimentation tanks |
| standard plate count | Voges-Proskauer | anaerobic digestion |
| unpotable | citrate | sludge treatment |
| enteric pathogens | membrane filter technique | secondary treatment |
| lactose fermentation | self-purification | aerobic breakdown |
| MPN | mineralization | activated sludge process |
| presumptive evidence | alum | trickle filter |
| | floc | tertiary treatment |
| | filtration | septic tanks |
| | chlorine | |

Complete each of the following statements by supplying the missing word or words.

1. ____________________ water is water that is safe to drink.

2. ____________________ water may look fine but contains poisonous chemicals or pathogenic organisms.

3. ____________________ water may not contain poisonous chemicals or pathogens but has an undesirable appearance or taste.

4. The ____________________ is a test used to determine the levels of microorganisms present in a water supply; it involves counting colonies that develop from diluted samples.

5. ____________________ contamination is established by the discovery of an organism that occurs only in feces, never free-living in nature.

6. ____________________ of lactose constitutes a presumptive test for presence of *E. coli.*

7. A ____________________ test involves transferring all positive presumptive test organisms to brilliant green lactose bile broth and observing the formation of gas in the tubes.

8. A ____________________ test involves the growth of all positive brilliant green lactose broth organisms on Endo or EMB, transferring all green or pink colonies to lactose broth and finding gas-producing gram-negative rods.

9. A ____________________ is a gram-negative, non-spore-forming, facultative organism that produce acid and gas from the fermentation of lactose.

10. ____________________ is an example of a nonfecal coliform whose presence does not indicate contamination of the water supply.

11. ____________________ is a set of biochemical tests used to distinguish fecal coliforms from nonfecal coliforms.

12. The ____________________ test detects the presence of acetoin, which is indicative of 2,3-butylene glycol fermentation.

13. ____________________ bacteria play a major role in the self-purification of streams and rivers.

14. ____________________ is the process of conversion of organic materials to inorganic matter.

15. ____________________ (aluminum potassium sulfate) is used to produce a gelatinous floc that aids in removing sediments from water.

16. ____________________ is the most commonly-used chemical treatment of drinking water largely because it is effective, relatively stable, and reasonably inexpensive.

17. ____________________ treatment of sewage has the primary intent of reducing the BOD in the effluent.

18. ____________________ is the product of primary treatment of sewage; it may contain hazardous levels of enteroviruses.

19. The ____________________ method of secondary sewage treatment involves spraying the effluent on beds of gravel that are heavily colonized by aerobic bacteria.

20. ____________________ treatment of sewage involves the removal of excess quantities of nitrogen and phosphorus.

## MASTERY TEST

1-25: Circle the choice that best answers the questions.

1. Which of the following is NOT considered to be a natural resident of water?
   a. sulfur bacteria
   b. pathogenic forms
   c. free-living spiral forms
   d. spore formers
   e. pigmented forms

2. Numbers obtained from the standard plate count represent _______ percent of the total number of bacteria detected with acridine orange staining.
   a. 1
   b. 5
   c. 25
   d. 50
   e. 75

3. Any water contaminated with feces contains enteric pathogens and is, therefore, ______.
   a. potable
   b. safe to use in ice machines
   c. safe for agricultural use
   d. unpotable

4. Fermentation of _________ is presumptive evidence of the presence of *Escherichia coli*.
   a. glucose
   b. glycogen
   c. fructose
   d. eosin
   e. lactose

5. The semiquantitative method of enumerating coliforms which involves inoculating 5 broth tubes each with 0.1 ml, 1.0 ml, and 10 ml of water sample then comparing results to a table gives one the ________ of organisms per 100 ml of water.
   a. MTV
   b. MHC
   c. MPN
   d. MVD
   e. MUC

6. The presence of brilliant green and/or bile in media prevents the growth of:
   a. gram-negative organisms
   b. gram-positive organisms
   c. nonenteric coliforms
   d. enteric coliforms

7. *E. coli* forms colonies with a _______________ appearance when grown on an eosin-methylene blue lactose agar plate.
   a. pink, mucoid
   b. pink, metallic
   c. green, mucoid
   d. green, metallic
   e. pink, green, mucoid and metallic

8. Growth of organisms at a temperature of _____ for 24 hours is only achieved by microbes from the intestines of warm-blooded animals.
   a. 25.3°C
   b. 37.5°C
   c. 20.5°C
   d. 42.5°C

9. The hydrolysis of tryptophan is the key to the ________ test.
   a. indole
   b. methyl red
   c. methylene blue
   d. Voges-Proskauer
   e. citrate

10. The production of large amounts of acids by means of the fermentation of glucose results in a positive ___________ test.
   a. indole
   b. methyl red
   c. methylene blue
   d. Voges-Proskauer
   e. citrate

11. The production of acetoin is an indicator of glucose fermentation to 2,3-butylene glycol; the __________ test looks for its production.
   a. indole
   b. methyl red
   c. methylene blue
   d. Voges-Proskauer
   e. citrate

12. The largest single advantage of the membrane filter technique of water quality assessment is:
   a. its extremely low cost
   b. its unparalleled accuracy
   c. its ability to test large volumes of water
   d. its usefulness in assessing sewage treatment success
   e. all of these are clear advantages

13. Which of the following is NOT a hindrance in the self-purification of streams and rivers?
   a. overloading of water with organic material
   b. excess quantities of inorganic phosphorus
   c. presence of petroleum products in water
   d. presence of nonbiodegradable detergents
   e. all of these are hindrances

14. Phosphate pollution has its effects indirectly *via* the stimulation of ____________ growth.
   a. bacterial
   b. protozoan
   c. algal
   d. fish
   e. pathogen

15. Which of the following is NOT a disease which can be acquired from contaminated water?
a. typhoid fever
b. cholera
c. bacillary dysentery
d. typhus
e. giardiasis

16. Which of the following is **the most common** waterborne disease in the United States (hint: the filtration step in water purification is critical in preventing it)?
a. typhoid fever
b. cholera
c. bacillary dysentery
d. typhus
e. giardiasis

17. Alum flocculation of water serves to:
a. remove protozoan cysts
b. kill pathogenic bacteria
c. inactivate enteric viruses
d. precipitate sediments

18. The single largest drawback to the use of ozone in purifying water is:
a. it is a greenhouse gas
b. it is expensive
c. it is explosively unstable
d. it is ineffective

19. The most common infection acquired at swimming pools is:
a. salmonellosis
b. conjunctivitis
c. trachoma
d. epidermophytosis
e. cholera

20. The primary goal in the disposal of sewage is:
a. reduction of biological oxygen demand
b. removal of pathogenic bacteria
c. reduction of phosphate concentration
d. precipitation of solids

21. Primary treatment of sewage produces a product called sludge which is often sent to a second tank to undergo:
a. aerobic digestion
b. activated sludge treatment
c. anaerobic digestion
d. flocculation

22. Secondary treatment of sewage is largely directed at:
  a. soluble organic materials
  b. sediments
  c. pathogenic bacteria and viruses
  d. phosphates and nitrates

23. Secondary treatment is an aerobic process which depends upon ample supplies of oxygen and:
  a. alum
  b. calcium precipitants
  c. aerobic bacteria
  d. scrubbing towers

24. Tertiary treatment is:
  a. required of all sewage treatment facilities
  b. practiced only if the efflux is to be drunk
  c. practiced only if ocean disposal is unavailable
  d. expensive, thus rarely performed

25. Sludge has often been used as a fertilizer or as a soil conditioner, but caution should be exercised due to the presence of ____________ in the sludge.
  a. viable pathogenic enteric bacteria
  b. high levels of *Giardia* cysts
  c. large quantities of pathogenic fungi
  d. viable pathogenic enteric viruses

ANSWERS TO LEARNING ACTIVITIES

Fill-in-the-blank questions:

1. Potable; 2. Contaminated; 3. Polluted; 4. standard plate count; 5. Fecal; 6. Fermentation; 7. confirmed; 8. completed; 9. coliform; 10. *Enterobacter aerogenes*; 11. IMViC; 12. Voges-Proskauer; 13. Aerobic; 14. Mineralization; 15. Alum; 16. Chlorine; 17. Secondary; 18. Sludge; 19. trickle filter; 20. Tertiary.

**MASTERY TEST ANSWERS**

| | | | | | | | | | | | | |
|---|---|---|---|---|---|---|---|---|---|---|---|---|
| 1<br>b | 2<br>a | 3<br>d | 4<br>e | 5<br>c | 6<br>b | | 7<br>d | 8<br>d | 9<br>a | 10<br>b | 11<br>d | 12<br>c |
| 13<br>e | 14<br>c | 15<br>d | 16<br>e | 17<br>d | 18<br>b | 19<br>d | 20<br>a | 21<br>c | 22<br>a | 23<br>c | 24<br>d | 25<br>d |

# CHAPTER 31

## MICROBIOLOGY OF FOOD AND MILK

### CHAPTER SUMMARY

**Food preservation** involves either **killing** the microorganisms present in food or **preventing their growth**. Common techniques for killing microorganisms include **heating** or **cooking** the food, adding high concentrations of **salt**, or using **radiation**. **Freezing** and **drying** do not kill microbes but do prevent their growth. **Lactic acid fermentation**, performed by members of the **Lactobacillaceae** and **Streptococcaceae** (the lactic acid bacteria), results in food preservation by lowering the pH of the food below that tolerated by most microorganisms.

**Sauerkraut**, for example, is cabbage that has been fermented by members of the genera *Leuconostoc* and *Lactobacillus*. Salt prevents the growth of competing species and also draws juices and sugars out of the cabbage. Anaerobic fermentation completes the transformation. **Pickles** involve a similar fermentation, although the salt content is generally much higher. Farmers preserve chopped plant materials called **ensilage** by allowing it to ferment in silos; the acids produced and the anaerobic conditions preserve the material for winter feeding to cattle. **Olives**, **summer sausages**, **soy sauce**, and **fish sauce** are other preserved, fermented products developed in various societies.

**Chemical preservatives** are widely used in the food industry. **Benzoic acid**, effective only at low pH, is used in high-acid products such as soft drinks, tomato products, and cider. **Sorbic acid**, also effective against yeasts and molds only at acid pH, is used mostly in cheeses, salad dressings, baked goods, beverages, and fruit juices. **Propionic acid** is also only effective at acid pH, and is used against molds in cheeses and baked goods. **Sodium nitrite** and **sodium nitrate** do inhibit the growth of microbes, but their main use is to produce the red color in preserved meats such as bacon, hot dogs, etc.

**Dried foods** cannot support the growth of bacteria if their **water activity** (**$a_w$**) is below 0.91 (0.80 for fungi). Water activity is the water vapor pressure of food (P) divided by the vapor pressure of pure water at the same temperature ($P_O$). An alternative to dehydrating food is the addition of **solutes** such as sucrose or sodium chloride; a 22 percent solution of NaCl, for example, has an $a_w$ of 0.86.

**Canned foods** are sterilized by heating, then sealed to prevent contamination. The food industry uses the **12-D concept** to gauge sufficient heating, the objective being to reduce the levels of *Clostridium botulinum* spores by 12 decimal places (essentially to zero).

**Low temperatures** do not kill microbes but do slow down or stop the growth of bacteria and fungi. Refrigeration extends the storage life of most foods, freezing is even more effective, as nothing can grow at the -18°C temperature of a freezer. **Radiation** (mostly **gamma rays** from $^{60}$Ca or $^{137}$Cs) is used in Europe and Japan for preserving foods; its use in the U.S. is currently restricted to killing insects in spices and fruits.

Microorganisms have been used to preserve food, and can also be used to **produce food**. **Single-cell protein** (**SCP**) refers to such products, mostly derived from **yeast** but also from algae, cyanobacteria and bacteria. Such foods contain up to 70 percent protein as well as large amounts of B vitamins. Carbohydrate sources for the microorganisms include low-value materials such as whey, sulfite waste, methane, potato starch, and molasses.

**Milk** is sterile until it reaches the milk ducts in the cow's udder. From there on it is subject to contamination from the tissues of the cow, the bodies of milk handlers, and from objects used to contain it. The most **common contaminants** are **lactic acid bacteria** such as *Streptococcus lactis* and *S. cremoris, Lactobacillus* species such as *L. casei, L. acidophilus, L. plantarum*, and *L. brevis*. Some of these organisms produce only lactic acid as a fermentation product (the **homofermentative lactic acid bacteria**), while others produce lactic acid, acetic acid, ethanol, and carbon dioxide (the **heterofermentative lactic acid bacteria**). None of these organisms is pathogenic, but they all can spoil the milk, causing its pH to fall and thereby curdling the milk protein, casein.

**Pathogenic organisms** can get into milk from infected cows or from infected milk handlers. **Bovine tuberculosis** (*Mycobacterium bovis*) and **brucellosis** (*Brucella abortus*) can both be controlled by inspection of cattle and elimination of infected individuals. Other contaminants (see below) are best handled by pasteurization or sterilization of the milk itself. Localized infections caused by *Streptococcus pyogenes* (streptococcal sore throat and scarlet fever) or by *Staphylococcus aureus* (food poisoning) are both possible sources of milk contamination. **Q fever** (caused by the rickettsia *Coxiella burnetii*) and **listeriosis** (caused by *Listeria monocytogenes*) are both dangerous diseases that can be spread by contaminated milk. Contamination by milk handlers can lead to **salmonellosis** (*Salmonella sp.*), **shigellosis** (*Shigella sp.*), **diphtheria** (*Corynebacterium diphtheriae*), **scarlet fever** or **septic sore throat** (*Strep. pyogenes*), and **gastroenteritis** (*Campylobacter jejuni*).

**Pasteurization** is the most wide-spread technique of ensuring the elimination of pathogens from milk; all techniques are gauged to destroy the hardiest agents likely to be in milk, the rickettsia *Coxiella burnetii* and the hepatitis A virus. Three techniques are practiced.

1. Heating the milk to 62.9°C for 30 minutes (**holding method**).
2. Heating to 71.6°C for not less than 15 seconds (**high-temperature method**).

3. Heating to 148.9°C for 1 to 2 seconds (**ultrahigh temperature method**). All three techniques are followed by rapid cooling.

**Milk testing** is a process that must be carried out on a regular basis. The **phosphatase test** is a simple enzyme assay that determines if the milk has, in fact, been pasteurized. The phosphatase enzyme is destroyed by heating, thus the test should be negative. The **standard plate count** is a method of determining the approximate number of live cells in a milk sample. Diluted milk is mixed with melted nutrient medium which is allowed to solidify and is then incubated. The colony count, multiplied by the dilution factor, gives one the number of cells per ml of the original sample. The **Breed count** is a direct microscopic count; cells stained by methylene blue are counted and a population density is calculated. The **reductase test** measures the loss of color of methylene blue dye when exposed to milk. Bacterial enzymes called **diaphorases** can donate electrons to methylene blue, reducing it and rendering it colorless. Specific tests for **coliform bacteria** are similar to those performed on water; tests for other kinds of organisms are only performed if a strong suspicion exists that they are present.

**Fermentation of milk** may be practiced for purposes of **preservation**, to enhance **taste**, or even to produce alcoholic beverages. Examples are: butter, yogurt, acidophilus milk, kumiss, kefir, and cheeses. All cheeses involved fermentation by bacteria or fungi but the exact species used, the conditions maintained during the fermentation, the type of milk used, etc. all result in important differences in the final product.

Milk is, finally, an important **immunological agent** in newborn mammals. Human infants are born with a good supply of **IgG** antibodies that entered their bodies across the placenta. These antibodies are joined by **IgA** molecules, which make up 97 percent of the total protein of the first milk (**colostrum**).

<u>OBJECTIVES</u> Study of this chapter will familiarize you with:

1. How foods can be preserved by a bacterial lactic acid fermentation.
2. The production and uses of single-cell protein.
3. The types of bacteria that are normally present in milk and their role in souring milk.
4. The source and types of diseases that may be transmitted in milk.
5. The techniques used for the control of milkborne diseases (including pasteurization).
6. Methods of testing milk for bacterial contamination.
7. The role of bacterial fermentations of milk to preserve and prepare milk products.
8. The immunological properties of milk.

## LEARNING ACTIVITIES

### Vocabulary

Having read the chapter, you should be able to define or cite the significance of the following terms. If you cannot, look them up in the text. Terms are presented in the order you will encounter them in the book.

food preservation
lactic acid bacteria
*Streptococcus*
*Lactobacillus*
*Leuconostoc*
*Pediococcus*
sauerkraut
pickles
ensilage
soy sauce
benzoic acid
sorbic acid
propionic acid
sodium nitrite
sodium nitrate
water activity ($a_w$)
12-D concept
single-cell protein (SCP)
milk ducts
Lactobacillaceae
Streptococcaceae
homofermentative
heterofermentative
bovine tuberculosis
*Mycobacterium bovis*
brucellosis
*Brucella abortis*
*S. pyogenes*
*S. aureus*
Q fever
*Coxiella burnetii*
salmonellosis
*Listeria monocytogenes*
shigellosis
diphtheria
pasteurization
holding method
high-temperature method
ultrahigh temperature method
phosphatase test
standard plate count
Breed count
reductase test
fermented milk products
colostrum

Complete each of the following statements by supplying the missing word or words.

1. ____________________ and drying are probably the two oldest known forms of food preservation.

2. ____________________ of microorganisms in food can be achieved by heating, cooking, or irradiating the food.

3. ____________________ and drying don't kill microbes, but only prevent their growth.

4. ____________________ bacteria are the most important group used in food preservation techniques.

5. ____________________ is added to shredded or sliced vegetables destined to be fermented in order to draw out the juices and sugars.

6. ____________________ is a term applied to the finely chopped green corn plants which farmers pack into their silos for winter cattle feed.

7. ____________________ olives are lightly treated with lye, then fermented for 6 to 10 months.

8. ____________________ is a fungus which begins the fermentation process of soy beans that eventually results in the formation of soy sauce.

9. ____________________, sorbic acid, and propionic acid are all chemical food preservatives which are most effective in acid pH foods.

10. ____________________ ($a_w$) is defined as $P/P_O$; levels below .91 are hostile to bacteria.

11. The ____________________ is used by the food industry when determining the amount of heat needed to sterilize canned foods.

12. ____________________ is the term applied to the food product derived from yeast, cyanobacteria, or bacteria.

13. ____________________ and Streptococcaceae constitute the most common contaminants of milk.

14. ____________________ lactic acid bacteria produce only one product - lactic acid - during their fermentations.

15. ____________________ is the causative agent of bovine tuberculosis; it can contaminate the milk of infected cows and cause disease in humans.

16. ____________________, which causes Q fever, is the organism of greatest concern to those calibrating their pasteurization techniques.

17. ____________________ added to milk which contains large numbers of leukocytes will cause the milk to clump or gel.

18. The ____________________ method of pasteurization produces a product that can be stored for several months without refrigeration.

19. The ____________________ is a direct, microscopic technique for determining the number of bacteria in a milk sample.

20. ____________________ (first milk) is extremely high in antibody content.

## MASTERY TEST

1-25: Circle the choice that best answers the questions.

1. The most important preservative effect of the activities of lactic acid bacteria is:
   a. lowering the pH of the fermented food
   b. production of toxic lactic acid compounds
   c. production of lactic, acetic, and propionic acids
   d. raising the pH of the fermented food

2. Which of the following does NOT kill microbes, but rather preserves food by preventing their growth?
   a. radiation
   b. heating
   c. freezing
   d. cooking
   e. salting

3. Which of the following is NOT involved in the fermentative preservation of foods?
   a. *Streptococcus*
   b. *Lactobacillus*
   c. *Leuconostoc*
   d. *Staphylococcus*
   e. *Pediococcus*

4. Sauerkraut, pickles, and other "fermented" vegetables reach a final pH of about:
   a. 1.5
   b. 3.5
   c. 5.5
   d. 7.5
   e. 9.5

5. Which of the following is NOT fermented?
   a. liverwurst
   b. summer sausage
   c. Hungarian salami
   d. Genoa salami
   e. Lebanon bologna

6. Which of the following is NOT restricted to acid foods for full preservative effect?
   a. benzoic acid
   b. sorbic acid
   c. propionic acid
   d. sodium nitrate

7. Which of the following correctly represents the value of "water activity"?
   a. $a_w = P_o/P$
   b. $a_w = P_o * P$
   c. $a_w = P/P_o$
   d. $a_w = P * (P_o/P)$

8. Dehydration of food, or the incorporation of a ____________ can change the $a_w$ to an inhospitable degree.
   a. solvent
   b. desiccant
   c. emollient
   d. adsorbent
   e. solute

9. Fungi can grow at $a_w$ levels ____________ that tolerated by bacteria.
   a. lower than
   b. greater than
   c. about the same as
   d. much greater than

10. Typical home freezers can preserve food for long periods of time because nothing can grow at the __________ temperature maintained by these devices.
    a. 0 to +6°C
    b. 0 to -6°C
    c. -12°C
    d. -18°C
    e. -12 to -24°C

11. One organism which is actually killed by freezer temperatures is the causative agent of:
    a. botulism
    b. gastroenteritis
    c. malaria
    d. pneumonia
    e. trichinosis

12. Bacteria which ferment carbohydrates to a variety of end products including lactic acid, acetic acid, ethanol and carbon dioxide are referred to as:
    a. homofermentative
    b. pleomorphic
    c. heterofermentative
    d. polymorphofermentative

13. Which of the following is NOT a member of the normal flora of milk?
    a. *Streptococcus lactis*
    b. *Streptococcus cremoris*
    c. *Streptococcus pyogenes*
    d. *Lactobacillus acidophilus*
    e. *Lactobacillus plantarum*

14. Which of the following is NOT a relatively common contaminant of milk introduced by dairy personnel?
    a. *Salmonella sp.*
    b. *Shigella sp.*
    c. *Streptococcus pyogenes*
    d. *Corynebacterium diphtheriae*
    e. *Mycobacterium sp.*

15. The addition of detergent to a milk sample containing many thousands of leukocytes per milliliter causes the milk to clump and gel. The molecule released by the detergent responsible for this behavior is:
a. DNA
b. protein
c. lipids
d. carbohydrates
e. RNA

16. If a filter paper disk is soaked with a milk sample then placed in a petri dish inoculated with *Bacillus subtilis* and the growth pattern shows a clear zone around the filter paper disk, the milk is contaminated with:
a. *Listeria monocytogenes*
b. botulinin toxin
c. antibiotics
d. *Mycobacterium bovis*
e. leukocytes

17. From among those listed below, select the one that the pasteurization process has the hardest time killing.
a. tuberculosis
b. Q fever
c. typhoid fever
d. diphtheria
e. foot-and-mouth disease

18. Which of the following is NOT one of the methods of pasteurization commonly used?
a. heating the milk to 62.9°C for 30 minutes
b. heating the milk to 121.4°C for 15 minutes
c. heating the milk to 71.6°C for 15 seconds
d. heating the milk to 148.9°C for 1 to 2 seconds

19. Which of the following is NOT one of the routinely used tests of milk?
a. phosphatase test
b. reductase test
c. Breed test
d. standard plate count
e. brucellosis test

20. Which of the following is the agent used in the reductase test?
a. malachite green
b. organic phosphate compounds
c. methylene blue
d. crystal violet

21. The production of yogurt differs from the production of acidophilus milk largely by means of the species of ______________ used in the fermentation.
a. *Streptococcus*
b. *Lactobacillus*
c. *Listeria*
d. *Staphylococcus*
e. *Leuconostoc*

22. A key ingredient in the making of many cheeses is the enzyme ______________ which curdles the milk.
a. rennet
b. phosphatase
c. curdlase
d. lactoferrinase
e. acidophilase

23. Roquefort cheese differs from a cheese like cheddar mainly in the secondary fermentation performed by:
a. lactic acid bacteria
b. propionic acid bacteria
c. fungi
d. nematode worms

24. The newborn human infant possesses some immunity to diseases by means of the passage of __________ across the placenta.
a. IgA
b. IgD
c. IgE
d. IgG
e. IgM

25. The "first milk" (colostrum) contains large quantities of:
a. IgA
b. IgD
c. IgE
d. IgG
e. IgM

ANSWERS TO LEARNING ACTIVITIES

Fill-in-the-blank questions:

1. Salting; 2. Killing; 3. Freezing; 4. Lactic acid; 5. Salt; 6. Ensilage; 7. Green; 8. *Aspergillus*; 9. Benzoic acid; 10. Water activity; 11. 12-D concept; 12. Single-cell protein; 13. Lactobacillaceae; 14. Homofermentative; 15. *Mycobacterium bovis*; 16. *Coxiella burnetii*; 17. Detergent; 18. ultrahigh temperature; 19. Breed count; 20. Colostrum.

**MASTERY TEST ANSWERS**

| | | | | | | | | | | | | |
|---|---|---|---|---|---|---|---|---|---|---|---|---|
| 1 | 2 | 3 | 4 | 5 | 6 | | 7 | 8 | 9 | 10 | 11 | 12 |
| a | c | d | b | a | d | | c | e | a | d | e | c |
| 13 | 14 | 15 | 16 | 17 | 18 | 19 | 20 | 21 | 22 | 23 | 24 | 25 |
| c | e | a | c | b | b | e | c | b | a | c | d | a |

# CHAPTER 32

## AGRICULTURAL AND INDUSTRIAL MICROBIOLOGY

### CHAPTER SUMMARY

The most important elements used to make up organic molecules are constantly being recycled; microorganisms play the dominant role in this recycling. The first step in this process involves the breakdown of macromolecules in dead plant and animal bodies. **Putrefaction** is the **anaerobic** decomposition of **proteins** by bacterial enzymes. Bacterial **proteolytic extracellular enzymes** hydrolyze the protein into free amino acids which are absorbed by the microbes. Within the cell amino acids are **deaminated** (with the release of **ammonia**) or **decarboxylated** (with the release of **foul-smelling basic amines**). **Decay** is the **aerobic** breakdown of complex materials; it, too, is carried out by means of extracellular enzymes secreted by **bacteria** and by **fungi**. **Fermentation** is the **anaerobic** breakdown of **carbohydrates** and results in the production of **stable fermentation products** (e.g. ethyl alcohol, lactic acid, acetone). It is carried out by bacteria and fungi (especially yeasts).

Further processing of organic materials by microbes results in their conversion to **inorganic form**. This is the key to the "organic cycles" such as the **carbon cycle**. Inorganic carbon, in the form of **$CO_2$**, is **reduced** to organic form largely by the process of **photosynthesis**. Plants, algae, photosynthetic bacteria and cyanobacteria are the main players in this phase of the carbon cycle. The **oxidation** of organic compounds back to carbon dioxide (with the liberation of energy and heat) occurs when **heterotrophic organisms** metabolize their food or when humans burn **fossil fuels**. Bacteria and fungi are critical in converting the carbon in the bodies of dead plants and animals to carbon dioxide. Some think that our burning of fossil fuels and cutting down the rainforests is setting the stage for a radical change in the carbon cycle resulting in a dramatic increase in atmospheric carbon dioxide levels. Because of its capacity to retain heat near the Earth's surface, $CO_2$ is the main player in the **greenhouse effect** and **global warming**.

The **nitrogen cycle** begins with the microbial decomposition of proteins; the **deamination** of amino acids produces ammonia (the process of **ammonification**).

Plants can use ammonia directly as a nutrient, or it may be taken up by chemosynthetic autotrophic bacteria which oxidize it to **nitrites** (*Nitrosomonas*) and **nitrates** (*Nitrobacter*). This process is called **nitrification** and again results in a form of nitrogen that plants can use as a nutrient. Other soil-dwelling bacteria, however, practice the detrimental process of **denitrification**; in a four-step process they convert nitrate ($NO_3$) back to nitrite ($NO_2$), nitrite to nitric oxide (NO), nitric oxide to nitrous oxide ($N_2O$), and nitrous oxide to molecular nitrogen ($N_2$). Major players in this process are soil bacteria that are using the nitrogen oxides as alternate electron acceptors (**anaerobic respiration**).

**Nitrogen fixation** is a microbial process that converts atmospheric nitrogen gas to ammonia. **Free-living nitrogen fixers** live in soil or in water and convert $N_2$ to $NH_3$ on their own; most of them are **cyanobacteria** or members of the bacterial genus *Azotobacter*. **Symbiotic nitrogen fixers** live in root nodules of plants (*Rhizobium* in the roots of legumes, the actinomycete *Frankia* in the roots of alder trees). The process involves an enzyme called **nitrogenase** which captures nitrogen gas and reduces it with the aid of an unknown reductant. Much ATP is utilized in the process.

The **sulfur cycle** begins with the decomposition of proteins; two sulfur-containing amino acids found in proteins are **methionine** and **cysteine**. The sulfur atoms are broken off as part of hydrogen sulfide ($H_2S$) which is an essential nutrient for both the **green sulfur** and **purple sulfur bacteria**. They use $H_2S$ as a **reductant in photosynthesis**, producing elemental sulfur as a waste product. Sulfur (S) is further oxidized by chemoautotrophic soil bacteria to the sulfate ion and sulfuric acid ($H_2SO_4$).

Industrial production of leather, linen, coffee, cocoa, vanilla, tobacco, and cheeses all depend upon the activities of bacteria for the **curing process**. Wine and beer are produced with the aid of yeast, *Saccharomyces cerevisiae* and *S. carlsbergensis* respectively. **Wine production** involves the crushing of sugar-rich grapes, the addition of **sulfur dioxide** to kill undesirable microorganisms, and the inoculation of the juice with selected strains of yeast. Fermentation produces an alcohol content of 12 to 14 percent.

Beer production is more complicated, since no free sugar is found in the grains it is made from. The barley must be **sprouted** first; the embryonic plant produces enzymes that break down much of the starch to sugar. This produces **malt** which is then dried, dissolved in water and mixed with other grains for further starch hydrolysis. Filtration follows, then the addition of hops; this produces the **wort**. The wort is then boiled, filtered, and inoculated with yeast. **Cold fermentation** for 8 to 14 days results in the production of beer. Normal beer contains up to 22 percent of the original starch calories in the form of **limit dextrans** - short chains of glucose which were joined to the starch molecule by an **$\alpha$1-6 glycosidic bond**. Barley enzymes cannot break these bonds. **Light beer** uses a fungal enzyme to hydrolyze the limit dextrans, which are then fermented more completely by yeast; this reduces the caloric content of the product. **Vinegar** can be produced from wine or beer (in which case it is called malt vinegar). The agent of this process is *Acetobacter* which oxidizes ethyl alcohol to acetic acid. This aerobic process may be carried out in barrels **(batch method)** or in columns filled with wood shavings and inoculated with *Acetobacter* (the **continuous generator** method).

Microbes are also used in the production of **solvents** and, recently, **alcohol fuels**. Ethanol, acetone, and butanol have historically been made by microbes; in Brazil large-scale ethanol production from sugar cane is being used as an alternative for expensive imported oil. **Enzymes** from microbial sources have uses in the food industry; starch may be hydrolyzed to glucose by **glucoamylase** or **α-amylase** then the glucose converted to super-sweet fructose by **glucose isomerase**. Bacterial **proteases** have been used in detergents and as meat tenderizers. Microbial production of specific amino acids is also an important industrial process. **Lysine** and **glutamic acid**, in particular, are produced by mutant bacteria that have lost the ability to regulate the synthesis of these amino acids.

**Pharmaceutical** production by microbes is big business; **antibiotics** alone constitute a multi-billion dollar industry. Materials such as antibiotics that have no role in the growth and reproduction of the organism are called **secondary metabolites**. Microbes are also used by the pharmaceutical industry in a process called **bioconversion**. The synthesis of some complex compounds may include several steps that are most efficiently done by microbes, with the rest being done chemically. An example is the conversion of the alcohol sorbitol to the sugar sorbose by *Gluconobacter*. Sorbose is then easily converted to vitamin C synthetically.

**Recombinant DNA technology** (genetic engineering) is attempting to alter the genetic nature of crop plants by means of the bacterium ***Agrobacterium tumefaciens.*** This organism causes a cancer-like growth in infected plants that persists even after no bacterial cells are present. Tumor production is accomplished by incorporation of the **Ti plasmid** into the plant cell's chromosomes. **Eucaryotic-type recognition signals** in the plasmid permit its transcription by plant enzymes. Attempts to introduce the genes for nitrogen fixation into plant cells *via* this plasmid have been made.

**Bacterial hybrids** created by recombinant DNA technology include a modified *Pseudomonas fluorescens* that produces a toxin that kills cutworms and a modified *Pseudomonas syringae* which does not synthesize a protein the serves as a nucleus for ice crystal formation on plant leaves. **Recombinant vaccines** have been produced that either (1) consist of a virus or microorganism that has been altered so it no longer produces disease, or (2) result from the insertion of a gene into *E. coli* or *S. cerevisiae* which then produces the antigen desired (with no pathogenic potential). Human genes cloned into these same organisms has resulted in the production of large quantities of **human insulin**, **human growth hormone**, and **human interferons**. Yet another aspect of this technology is the production of **DNA probes** that provide an extremely sensitive way to detect the presence of infective organisms in patients. Probes for a variety of bacterial and viral diseases have been produced and many more are to follow. One of the ultimate goals of recombinant DNA technology is to supply functional DNA to individuals suffering from a deficiency of a particular gene.

OBJECTIVES After study of this chapter, you should comprehend:

1. The recycling of elements through putrefaction, decay, and fermentation.
2. The steps involved in the carbon cycle, nitrogen cycle, and sulfur cycle.
3. Production of wine, beer, and vinegar.
4. Production of industrial chemicals, enzymes, amino acids, and pharmaceuticals.
5. The role of recombinant DNA techniques in plant engineering, vaccines, human products, probes for diagnostic procedures, and gene therapy.

## LEARNING ACTIVITIES

### Vocabulary

Having read the chapter, you should be able to define or cite the significance of the following terms. If you cannot, look them up in the text. Terms are presented in the order you will encounter them in the book.

organic cycles
putrefaction
basic amines
decay
fermentation
topsoil
carbon cycle
oxidized carbon
reduced carbon
greenhouse effect
nitrogen cycle
ammonification
deaminase
*Nitrosomonas*
*Nitrobacter*
nitrification
denitrification
*Thiobacillus denitrificans*
nitrogen fixation
free-living nitrogen fixers
*Azotobacter*
symbiotic nitrogen fixers
*Rhizobium*
legumes
nitrogenase
sulfur cycle
hydrogen sulfide
green sulfur bacteria
purple sulfur bacteria
*Thiobacillus ferrooxidans*
sulfur dioxide
*Saccharomyces cerevisiae*
dessert wines
malt
wort
*Saccharomyces carlsbergensis*
$\alpha$1-4 linkages
$\alpha$1-6 linkages
limit dextrans
*Acetobacter*
vinegar
batch method
continuous generator
organic solvents
enzymes
fructose
glucose isomerase
proteases
antibiotics
secondary metabolites
bioconversion
*Agrobacterium tumefaciens*
Ti plasmid
bacterial hybrids
recombinant vaccines
virulent agent
DNA probes

Complete each of the following statements by supplying the missing word or words.

1. ____________________ is the anaerobic decomposition of proteins by bacterial enzymes. It typically produces foul-smelling byproducts.

2. ____________________ is defined as the anaerobic breakdown of carbohydrates resulting in the formation of stable products.

3. ____________________ is the final oxidation product of all carbon-containing compounds.

4. ____________________ is the most important metabolic process that results in the production of reduced carbon compounds.

5. ____________________ is the term applied to the action of deaminase enzymes which remove the amine groups from amino acids and release them as ammonia.

6. ____________________ is a genus of bacteria known for its capacity to oxidize ammonia to nitrites; *Nitrobacter* carries the process on, converting nitrites to nitrates.

7. ____________________ is the name of the process which converts nitrates to nitrogen gas. This microbial activity dramatically reduces the fertility of soils.

8. ____________________ are the most important members of a group called free-living nitrogen fixers; a bacterial genus which is also a member of this group is *Azotobacter*.

9. ____________________ is the genus of bacteria that lives in root nodules of legumes and fixes atmospheric nitrogen.

10. ____________________ is added to crushed grapes to inhibit less desirable species of organisms so that *Saccharomyces cerevisiae* can carry out its fermentation.

11. ____________________ is the term applied to barley which has been allowed to germinated and has then been dried.

12. ____________________ are short glucose polymers that remain in normal beers due to the inability of barley enzymes to cleave $\alpha$1-6 linkages; they are eliminated in light beer *via* the action of a mold enzyme.

13. ____________________ is the genus of bacterium used to produce vinegar.

14. ____________________ is produced from glucose through the action of glucose isomerase, a bacterial enzyme. It is much sweeter than glucose or sucrose.

15. ____________________ are compounds produced by organisms that are not directly involved in the growth and reproduction of the organisms; antibiotics are an example.

16. ____________________ is the name of a process in which a microbe is used to perform a step or two in a complex chemical synthesis, the balance of the process being conducted synthetically.

17. ____________________ is the causative agent of crown gall disease, a cancer-like condition in plants.

18. ____________________ vaccines are produced by (1) altering viruses or bacteria so that they are no longer infective or (2) producing the antigen in *E. coli* or *S. cerevisiae* by gene splicing.

19. ____________________ are cloned pieces of DNA from various bacteria or viruses that are capable of detecting extremely small quantities of DNA or ribosomal RNA in the target organism (including humans).

20. ____________________ is a primary goal of recombinant DNA technology and involves the introduction of functional genes into patients suffering from genetic deficiency disorders.

MASTERY TEST

1-25: Circle the choice that best answers the questions.

1. The very foul-smelling (putrid) compounds produced during the process of putrefaction are chemically:
   a. sulfhydryls
   b. carboxylic acids
   c. basic amines
   d. acid decarboxylates

2. The process of decay, which is practiced by bacteria and fungi, is a(n) ______________ one.
   a. anaerobic
   b. facultative
   c. aerobic
   d. aerotolerant

3. Which of the following is NOT an example of a stable fermentative product?
a. ethyl alcohol
b. lactic acid
c. acetic acid
d. carbon dioxide
e. butyric acid

4. Human interference in the __________ cycle is resulting in changes in the Earth's atmosphere which may result in global warming (Greenhouse Effect).
a. carbon
b. nitrogen
c. oxygen
d. sulfur

5. The process called ammonification involves the removal of ____________ groups from ____________.
a. carboxyl ... amino acids
b. amino ... nucleotides
c. carboxyl ... secondary metabolites
d. carboxyl ... $\alpha$-keto acids
e. amino ... amino acids

6. The oxidation of ammonia to nitrite and then to nitrate is a result of the process called:
a. ammonification
b. denitrification
c. carbon reduction
d. nitrification

7. Which of the following is a prime mover in the process of denitrification?
a. *Nitrosomonas*
b. *Nitrobacter*
c. *Thiobacillus*
d. *Azotobacter*

8. Which of the following is a free-living nitrogen fixer?
a. *Nitrosomonas*
b. *Nitrobacter*
c. *Thiobacillus*
d. *Azotobacter*

9. Plants in the ____________ group have root nodules filled with symbiotic nitrogen fixers and significantly improve soil fertility when planted.
a. rose
b. legume
c. pine
d. grain
e. aspen

10. Hydrogen sulfide released during the process of putrefaction and decay is converted to ________ by the purple and green photosynthetic bacteria.
a. sulfur
b. sulfides
c. sulfites
d. sulfates
e. nitrates

11. In the process of denitrification an enzyme called ____________ catalyzes the conversion of nitric oxide to nitrous oxide.
a. nitrate reductase
b. nitrite reductase
c. nitric oxide reductase
d. nitrous oxide reductase
e. nitrogenase

12. The end product of denitrification is:
a. $NO_3$
b. $NO_2$
c. NO
d. $N_2O$
e. $N_2$

13. *Rhizobium* is the best-known symbiotic nitrogen fixer, but the Actinomycete genus __________ is also important.
a. *Azotobacter*
b. *Streptomyces*
c. *Mycobacterium*
d. *Frankia*
e. *Nocardia*

14. The fermentation period for a dessert wine (e.g. sherry, port, muscatel) is ___________ that for a typical red or white dinner wine.
a. longer than
b. about the same as
c. shorter than
d. much longer than

15. The source of enzymes used to hydrolyze starch to sugar during beer production is:
a. germinating barley grains
b. mold enzymes
c. yeast enzymes
d. synthetic in America, natural in Europe

16. Limit dextrans exist in normal beers because the starch hydrolyzing enzymes cannot break the __________ bonds.
a. $\alpha$1-4
b. $\beta$1-4
c. $\alpha$1-6
d. $\beta$1-6

17. A system for producing vinegar that consists of a column filled with wood shavings that have been inoculated with *Acetobacter* is called:
a. fractional distiller
b. batch method
c. oak clarifier
d. continuous generator

18. The industrial production of ethanol, acetone, and butanol, once produced through microbial fermentation, now comes from:
a. genetically engineered plants
b. petroleum
c. distillation of land-fill exudates
d. direct chemical synthesis

19. Which of the following would be classed as a secondary metabolite?
a. antibiotics
b. ethanol
c. lactic acid
d. carbon dioxide
e. ribosomal RNA

20. The process in which microorganisms are used to catalyze certain steps of a synthesis, the balance being carried out by chemical synthesis, is called:
a. recombinant DNA technology
b. bioconversion
c. fermentation
d. microbe-assisted direct synthesis

21. An example of the process discussed above is:
a. the production of vinegar from wine
b. the conversion of acetic acid to propionic acid
c. the conversion of sorbitol to sorbose
d. the conversion of malt to wort

22. The key asset possessed by the Ti plasmid of *Agrobacterium tumefaciens* is:
a. directly useful genes
b. built-in herbicide resistance
c. capacity to spread throughout the plant
d. eucaryotic-type regulation signals

23. DNA probes are useful for:
a. carrying desired genes into target cells
b. detecting minuscule amounts of DNA in organisms
c. producing virus-free vaccines
d. all of the above

24. Which of the following is a human genetic deficiency disorder that has been experimentally treated with recombinant DNA techniques?
a. Tay-Sachs disease
b. Hemophilia
c. SCID (severe combined immunodeficiency)
d. Lesch-Nyhan syndrome

25. One way to introduce a functional gene into human cells is by means of:
a. a retrovirus
b. a DNA probe
c. a recombinant vaccine
d. enterotoxigenic *E. coli*

## ANSWERS TO LEARNING ACTIVITIES

Fill-in-the-blank questions:

1. Putrefaction; 2. Fermentation; 3. Carbon dioxide; 4. Photosynthesis; 5. Ammonification; 6. *Nitrosomonas*; 7. Denitrification; 8. Cyanobacteria; 9. *Rhizobium*; 10. Sulfur dioxide; 11. Malt; 12. Limit dextrans; 13. *Acetobacter*; 14. Fructose; 15. Secondary metabolites; 16. Bioconversion; 17. *Agrobacterium tumefaciens*; 18. Recombinant; 19. DNA probes; 20. Gene therapy.

**MASTERY TEST ANSWERS**

| | | | | | | | | | | | | |
|---|---|---|---|---|---|---|---|---|---|---|---|---|
| 1 | 2 | 3 | 4 | 5 | 6 | | 7 | 8 | 9 | 10 | 11 | 12 |
| c | c | d | a | e | d | | c | d | b | a | c | e |
| 13 | 14 | 15 | 16 | 17 | 18 | 19 | 20 | 21 | 22 | 23 | 24 | 25 |
| d | c | a | c | d | b | a | b | c | d | b | c | a |